The Successful Relationships Guide:
Volume 1:

Top secrets for

Building a Successful Relationship:

Volume 1 – A blueprint and toolbox for couples and counsellors: C101

By Dr Jim Byrne

With Renata Taylor-Byrne BSc (Hons) Psychol

The Institute for Emotive-Cognitive Embodied Narrative Therapy (E-CENT), in cooperation with KDP-Amazon. 2018

Published by: The Institute for Emotive-Cognitive Embodied-Narrative Therapy, 27 Wood End, Keighley Road, Hebden Bridge, West Yorkshire, HX7 8HJ, UK

Telephone: 01422 843 629

Distributed by KDP-Amazon.

~~~

Website: https://ecent-institute.org/

~~~

Cover design: Charles Saul. Website: http://www.charles-saul.co.uk/

~~~

ISBN: 9781790244775

~~~

Contents

Appendices

Preface

By Jim Byrne, DCoun

What is this book about?

This book is an introductory guide to the following subject:

How to have a happy and successful couple relationship (which could be a marriage, *pair bond*, civil partnership, or *sex-love relationship*).

It's designed to be helpful for:

- Committed, long-term couples; or young people starting out on the journey of building a loving relationship;

And for:

- Counsellors and therapists (who want to learn from the author's experience of providing couples therapy for twenty years);

And for:

- Self-help enthusiasts, and students of human relations.

It deals with a broad range of knowledge and skills, spread across three volumes, and is based on the author's thirty-four years of study of couple relationships; and his twenty years' experience of helping couples to improve, revive, restore (or dissolve) their relationships with their long-term, committed, sex-love partners.

This first volume is an *essential foundation* for what comes later.

The fundamental need for this book

Why is this book so important? What makes it different from other forms of marriage guidance and relationship advice which are available today?

Firstly, most modern resources for couples – including books, articles and blogs – are designed to *inform* the reader of certain *facts* about love and relationship, without teaching *how to* **change** habitual ways of being. Some may want to help couples to change their habits, but they do not go far enough in this direction. They do not provide *tools for habit change*.

But this book, in addition to *informing* the reader, also sets out to *help individuals to change themselves*, at *deep, non-conscious, emotional levels*, so that they become better lovers, and more successful relationship partners.

Secondly, many books about couple relationships focus upon a single source of research, or a restricted area of investigation, while this book is as broad-based as any book on couples could be – with the exception that we do not go into any significant detail about homosexual relationships, though we do touch upon them.

So we deal with sex, and love, and the meaning of relationship; and how to build a relationship; and how to communicate within couple relationships; how to manage conflict constructively; how to avoid the common myths about relationships; how to establish healthy boundaries in relationships; how to manage your body-brain-mind for optimum functioning in your intimate relationships; how to manage your emotions; the importance of avoiding the 'orgasm gap' (by understanding the importance of the clitoris); how to change your habitual ways of behaving; how you were shaped for relationship in your family of origin, and how you can reshape yourself for more effective, more enjoyable relationships; and much more besides.

We also look at why *a* **happy** *marriage* is such an important goal to pursue:

> According to Professor Jonathan Haidt (2006)[1]:
>
> "A good marriage is one of the life-factors most strongly and consistently associated with happiness[2]. Part of this apparent benefit comes from 'reverse correlation'. Happiness causes marriage. Happy people marry sooner and stay married longer than people with a lower happiness set point, both because they are more appealing as dating partners and because they are easier to live with, as spouses[3]. But much of the apparent benefit is a real and lasting benefit of dependable companionship, which is a basic need; we never fully adapt either to it or to its absence[4]". (Page 88).

Notice that he says "A good marriage", and not just "a marriage"! A bad marriage is a curse!

~~~

Why we choose the partners we do!

There is research to support the idea that people choose their love partners *non-consciously*[5], on the basis of *habit*. (Teachworth, 1999). And, also that we tend to have conscious goals for the type of mate we would like, but that *we then choose our mate on the basis of a non-conscious goal* about which we know nothing. (Gladwell, 2006; and Lewis, Amini and Lannon, 2001). Therefore, it is clearly pointless producing a list of 'rules of love' (Templar, 2016) and assuming people will be able to read them and then follow them. If is clearly pointless to offer such lists, if we do not at the same time show them *how to get those rules into their non-conscious brain-mind*, from where the lists can inform their non-conscious goals for partner selection. And that is why we have structured this book so that the reader can reprogram themselves; change their non-conscious goals; and change their 'radar device' for finding a partner. This 'radar device' is their *inner model of an ideal couple* (called, by us, 'The Inner Couple'. [Teachworth, 1999]).

Anybody who studies this book, in the ways we recommend, will find that:

- their relationship behaviours change for the better (because their non-conscious goals have changed!);

- their emotional intelligence will increase; and

- they will find themselves either choosing a *better* partner, or working successfully with *their current partner* to produce an amazingly satisfying relationship together.

See Appendix 'K' for guidance on how to study this book in order to produce behaviour change and improved emotional intelligence. In addition, we have also included Appendix 'M', on general *habit-change processes*; and Chapter 11 on how to change your 'Inner Couple' blueprint or 'relationship guidance system': from *dysfunctional* to *emotionally healthy!*

Why relationships fail

About fifty percent of all marital relationships end in divorce. The most obvious reasons for this include:

- lack of commitment to keeping the relationship alive;

- lack of care and attention by one partner to the other;

- infidelity; or sexual jealousy (justified or unjustified);

- lack of sexual satisfaction in the relationship,

> - partly because of the 'orgasm gap', whereby 75% of women are not treated to an orgasm by their partner

> – and partly because, when women become unhappy with their partner, sexual contact declines.

- and partly because of communication breakdown.

This subject has recently be revisited by a group of researchers. According to a study by Shackleton, Barlow and colleagues (2018), at the University of Exeter, UK, there are four common reasons for relationships to break down:

"The first two (are) incompatibility and unrealistic expectations..."

But why would anybody choose an incompatible partner? The viewpoint expressed in our book is that we choose incompatible partners because our parents were actually incompatible, and we simply copy what we experienced by observing their relationship – outside of our conscious awareness. And our expectations of relationships also come primarily from what we saw our parents do, compounded by

> (i) poor models we have seen in films; and

> (ii) the lyrics of love songs we have heard, often subliminally

hypnotizing us into unhelpful beliefs about love.

It is the contention of this book that we will go on choosing incompatible partners until such time as we work at reforming our model of relationships – otherwise called our 'Inner Couple'. We teach our readers how to do that in Chapter 11 below.

Shackleton et al., (2018) continue:

"The second two" (reasons for relationship breakdowns, were) "...failure to deal with issues, and failure to nurture the relationship..."

Again, these patterns of poor relating are most likely copied from the couples' parents. Indeed, the authors of the University of Exeter research report know this to be true, since they write:

"...Couples in thriving relationships in both samples had realistic expectations of marriage and relationships, *shaped by examples they had seen through the marriages of their parents or other family members*". (Shackleton et al., 2018).

On the other hand, Richard Nelson-Jones, in his 1986 book on human relationship skills, suggests that, in addition to our parents, we are also influenced in the development of our relationship skills by brothers and sisters; grandparents; aunts and uncles; older friends; community leaders; peer groups; teachers; famous people; fictional people; and advertising. (Pages 14-15).

While Nelson-Jones may have a point, it has often been found that it is primarily the modelling provided by parents that most strongly affects a person's approach to relationships, both in terms of skills, and in terms of partnership choice(s). (Teachworth, 1999).

And, as mentioned already, we address the question of how to *change* those early parental influences in Chapter 11, below.

~~~

Human nature and love

Love is central to what it means to be human – and the other side of the coin is, of course, hatred! We often seem to have a greater capacity to access our feelings of anger and hate than our feelings of love and affection. But it is precisely by getting in touch with our feelings of love, and spending our life loving a significant other person, that we experience a sweet, warm 'feeling of completeness' in our hearts.

To do that well – to get in touch with our feelings of love in a helpful way - we have to understand the nature of love and relationship, at least as well as we understand how to do our work; how to drive; or how to practice our hobbies or recreational activities. And this requires effort and practice; training and learning. It has to become *habitual*, and that means *driven from non-conscious levels of mind*.

~~~

According to a well-known *Rolling Stones* song: "We all need someone to lean on..." However, if you *over-rely* upon your partner, and lean on them too much, you will become vulnerable to falling over if they step back. So you need to have some degree of *autonomy* from your partner, as well as feeling you can rely upon them when you need their support.

We are essentially *social, connected* and *related* beings, and not completely *separate* individuals. We attach to our mothers in the first six months of life – securely or insecurely. Later we separate from mother (if development is normal), and, in adulthood, we (normally) attach to a sex-love partner; often in marriage or cohabitation.

No man or woman is an island, complete unto themselves, according to the poem by John Donne. We are *interdependent* beings. We rely upon each other, but we must also be capable of acting independently, when that is the emotionally healthy option. (But not *too independently* – and especially not *avoidantly!*)

Love is the glue that holds us all together, and binds us to our nearest and dearest. And love, paradoxically, is also the energy that fuels our sense of autonomy; our capacity to be ourselves, and to stand on our own two feet.

Love of others in the present moment binds us together, and *internalized love,* from our childhood socialization, fuels our sense of autonomy and self-regard.

Love can be the source of enormous joy, comfort, fun and satisfaction in life. But the unsuccessful quest for love can be the greatest source of misery.

Love - like charity - begins at home

The experience of love begins in our mother's arms, in the earliest days of life; but more especially from the age of six months to three years. Our experiences of mother-love (and father-love), in this stage of our development, shapes us for life – making us 'securely attached' or 'insecurely attached' in relationships - though we can change our 'attachment style' (to some degree) later in life, through some forms of *attachment therapy* and/or a *curative relationship* with a secure partner. (See section 1.2.3(c); section 3.8; and sections 6.10 to 6.12(b) below).

Furthermore, the first ten years of our life is a kind of 'apprenticeship' for our own adult life.

We observe our mother and father (or main carers) relating to each other; and we decide which one we like most as a role model for our own adult life. This one is called our 'Adult role model', or 'model for our adult role in relationships'. (This is a more specific application of the principle, advanced by Claude Steiner [1990], to the effect that, *when we are very young, we choose a character to identify with, and create a script based on that characters words and actions*).

We then store a memory of the *other parent* as a template for our future life partner. This one is called our 'Mate model, or 'model for our future partner'.

And then puberty hits us with a hugely disorienting and stressful wave of disturbing and disorganizing hormones! And we struggle through our teenage years hoping (consciously) to find a stable resting point up ahead, while (non-consciously) following a life script we co-authored with our parents when we were too young to have any sense!

Another way of saying all that is this: We are mesmerized by our parents' relationship and lifestyle, and this becomes the *hypnotic trance* that guides our future life! (Wolinsky, 1991).

However, this could suggest 'mysterious forces', which has nothing to do with the processes involved. The two processes that underlie our *life and relationship scripts* are:

> - *Experiences* (of relationships); and:

> - *Stored memories* of those experiences.

All of our actions in the present moment are guided by *stored experiences* from the past; and our relationship actions in the present are guided by stored experiences of relationships in the past – how mother, and father related to us; and how we related to them.

~~~

Love and the human brain-mind

To have any hope of reaching mature adulthood, every single human being, male and female alike, has to traverse the vast emotional minefield of *adolescence*. And, according to Carl Gustav Jung, adolescence lasts from puberty (around the age of twelve or thirteen years) until the age of forty or forty-five years of age!

Many of us seem to feel we have 'arrived', fully grown up, at the age of sixteen or eighteen years of age. But at those ages, we are constantly at the mercy of powerful surges of strong feelings from the emotional centres of our brain-mind, because the 'reasoning centres' - based in, or managed from, the frontal lobes of our brain – do not become fully operational until the age of twenty-five or twenty-six years of age.

Juvenile passion

This is an important fact, because it tells us something about the unreliability of juvenile love – or 'puppy love'.

As an illustration of this fact, in 1774, in Germany, a twenty-four year old Johann Wolfgang von Goethe published a novel - *(The Sorrows of Young Werther)* - which told of the unrequited love of Werther for Charlotte. It is a story of impossible longing for a young woman who is already engaged to another man. It is an obsession. It is characterized - as John Armstrong (2003)[6] writes - by four forms of intense emotional states: "...longing, rapture, doubt and the sense that one is in touch with the source of all value". This story by Goethe formed the cornerstone of a new Romantic movement in Western Europe, which was a form of madness, often ending in the suicide of the lovesick young men who pursued this cult.

Today, we are all affected by the love songs that permeate our daily cultural experience. And many of the most influential and most disturbing love songs are written by individuals who were below the age of twenty-five years when they wrote them, and thus in thrall to their uncontrollable passions.

Shakespeare's story of Romeo and Juliet was also formative of our culture's attitudes towards Romantic love; and Juliet was just thirteen years of age in that story. How old was Romeo? This question is explored by Durbanville (2015) like this:

> "The ages of Romeo and Juliet are significant in understanding how they come to such a tragic end because it is their youth and inexperience and their inability to see beyond their immediate circumstances that causes them, Romeo in particular, to act so irrationally. Romeo is so overwhelmed by his circumstances and so immature in his actions that he is apparently just a teenager of perhaps sixteen years old, definitely younger than eighteen because by eighteen a young man of his standing would be expected to be able to lead men into battle and so he would not act so impulsively".[7]

~~~

Beyond juvenile passion

Much of the popular culture of love, which assails us from love songs and stories of love, is about *frustrated* or *unrequited* love, engaged in by immature individuals.

These are not good models for our own love lives. If we want to be happy in love, we have to look beyond these juvenile forms of obsessive and doomed love.

Or as John Armstrong (2003) writes:

> "Real love is love that lasts and withstands the difficulties which a prolonged relationship inevitably brings. The problems of love occur not when passion is rejected or when fate intervenes to cut off a relationship at the earliest stage. It is ironically when we are loved back, when a relationship develops, that love is put to the test. It is the long term that we want to understand; we are in search of a mature conception of love". (Pages 6-7).

And that is what we address in this book: a mature conception of love; and the knowledge and skills – and habits - required to build a real, lasting, committed loving relationship.

~~~

Our target audiences

We have written this book for anybody who wants to understand mature love, and to build a mature sex-love relationship.

But we also intend it to be a resource for those professionals who guide and counsel couples regarding how to resolve the problems they find themselves confronting in relationships which have run into difficulties.

This group includes: couple counsellors; psychologists; psychotherapists; psychiatrists; social workers; priests and vicars; and senior members of extended families, who may sometimes be called upon to advise more junior members of their families.

It should also be of interest to students from a broad range disciplines.

All of these target groups of readers need to understand the following ideas and practices:

(a) Principles of happy relationships;

(b) Problems of couple conflict;

(c) Communication styles, strategies, and breakdowns; and:

(d) The basics of sexual satisfaction and sexual difficulties.

The final two chapters summarize the main learning points for two main audiences:

- Chapter 12 is for individuals and couples; and:

- Chapter 13 for counselling and therapy professionals, and students of those professions.

I hope you find this book very helpful for your purposes.

~~~

Jim Byrne, Doctor of Counselling, Hebden Bridge, November 2018

~~~

Chapter 1: Understanding love and relationship

1.1 Introduction

"For one human being to love another, that is perhaps the most difficult of all our tasks... the work for which all other work is but preparation."

Rilke (2011)

~~~

Only about two percent of couples, who find themselves in an unhappy marriage, will ever consult a marriage guidance counsellor or couple's therapist: (Agnew, 1996)[8].

And most of them leave it till the eleventh hour before they seek help.

This makes it very difficult for the profession of couple's therapy to get a fighting chance of succeeding in saving very many marriages.

I have been more fortunate than most couple therapists, in that I get a good ratio of salvageable marriages to 'lost causes'. And I have had a high rate of success, and lots of feedback from satisfied clients, who managed, with my help, to turn their relationships around – from *terminal* to *thriving*.

I have been helping couples – and individuals within couples – for about twenty years. Mostly they consult me after their relationship has been declining in happiness and satisfaction *for a number of **years***. And mostly they have *very little idea **why*** their relationship has gone wrong, or what they could possibly do about it.

I have learned how to be a successful couple's therapist as a result of reading lots of books on love, relationship, communication and sex. I have also been through a successful course of couple's therapy with my wife - and I have been through relationships skills courses - to improve my own marriage. And I have applied my learning - from books and courses and personal experience – to the challenges of helping hundreds of couples to improve their relationships.

Over the years, I have identified eighteen important principles of happy relationships, which I teach to all of my couple's therapy clients. And I will present the first six of those principles in this volume.

I have also identified a range of communication skills which you need to master if you want to have a happy couple relationship; and I teach those skills in this book.

~~~

In this chapter, I want to talk about love and relationships, in ways which are not common in our western (or eastern) cultures.

Love, and relationship, like charity, begin at home. If you had a loving mother, to whom you felt securely attached, then you will most likely feel securely attached to your adult love-partner. If your mother and father related to each other in loving ways, you are likely to automatically relate to your adult love-partner in loving ways. (See Lewis, Amini and Lannon, 2001).

Love (when it's good) is a wonderful state of being. But when it goes wrong, in a sex-love relationship, it can be a living hell. This book is designed to help those people for whom love has gone wrong – or at least somewhat wrong – and also to help those who want to build a happy relationship in the future; and those (like counsellors) who want to help couples to build better relationships.

1.1.1 Steinbeck on love

This wonderful state of being (in a happy state of love) is expressed well by John Steinbeck, the author of *The Grapes of Wrath*, in a letter to his son, Thom:

"New York, November 10, 1958 - Dear Thom: We had your letter this morning. I will answer it from my point of view ...

"First — if you are in love — that's a good thing — that's about the best thing that can happen to anyone. Don't let anyone make it small or light to you.

"Second — There are several kinds of love. One is a selfish, mean, grasping, egotistical thing which uses love for self-importance. This is the ugly and crippling kind. The other is an outpouring of everything good in you — of kindness and consideration and respect — not only the social respect of manners but the greater respect which is recognition of another person as unique and valuable. The first kind can make you sick and small and weak but the second can release inside you strength, and courage and goodness and even wisdom you didn't know you had". (From Steinbeck and Wallsten, 1989)[9].

So there is the point. Love can be good, or bad. When it's good, it's truly magnificent, uplifting. A taste of the divine.

But when it's bad, it's horrid. An example would be the existence of *domestic violence, emotional abuse, or cold neglect* in your relationship.

Or *inequality* (meaning the relationship is 'designed' to benefit one partner more than the other!) As Mary Beard (2017) writes:

"When it comes to silencing women, Western culture has had thousands of years of practice". (Page xi).

No self-respecting male lover should do anything to continue this despicable tradition. And no self-respecting female lover of a male partner should place *personal responsibility* on her male partner for those thousands of years of oppression. He is only responsible for *how he conducts himself today!* You will *both* have to work hard, using the strategies outlined in this book, to learn *how to communicate with each other as respectful equals!*

Humans have a capacity to be both good and evil. (See Appendix F, below, for a description of our tendencies towards acting like a 'Good Wolf' or a 'Bad Wolf'). If we want to be good, moral people, we have to work hard to grow our 'Good Wolf' side, and to shrink our 'Bad Wolf' tendencies. This book aims to teach you how to love, based on growing your Good Wolf.

But to begin, we have to explore what we *mean* by love, when we speak of *good love!*

In modern Britain, as in the USA, there are probably several generations of married individuals who have had some kind of basic (technical) sex education in school. However, that sex education was probably a tiny portion of their learning about sexual relationships; most of which probably came from:

(1) Conversations with (ill-informed) peers;

(2) Reading misleading books (for men) about male sexual prowess (like the myth of the 'Big Steel Cock')[10];

(3) And books and magazines (for women) which overly-romanticized the process of engaging in a lifelong sex-love relationship;

(4) And watching soap operas on TV, and listening to love songs, both of which model totally unrealistic, and mainly undesirable, neurotic relationships.

But perhaps *the main vehicle* for learning about sex-love relationships, in the round, is observing what went on between your parents when you were very young – and normally *too young to remember*[11]. For it was at that time that you most likely chose one of your parents to be your *role model* – or *exemplar* - for how you would live when you were fully grown up. (This is your 'Adult role model').

And you would have chosen the other parent to be a *template*, or *pattern* for the marriage partner you would choose. (This is your 'Mate model').

And then you would have taken that 'Inner Couple' *script* into your adult life, below the level of conscious awareness, and acted it out since that time. We will return to this subject later, in Chapter 11.

~~~

For now, to set the scene, let us look at one of the main *reinforcers* of our couple-script from childhood: the *lyrics* and *emotional tones* of popular love songs.

Popular music has both positive and negative aspects and effects.

1. Some of it proves very helpful for young people to process their difficult emotions about love and relationships. (For example, when my first marriage broke down, when I was just thirty years old, I found myself often listening to, and revelling in, the lyrics of *10cc's* song, 'I'm Not in Love!' The emotional tone of that song put me in touch with my feelings of grief about my ex-wife, and allowed me to process, digest [and 'complete'] those very difficult emotions).

2. Some songs put us in touch with our positive emotions of love for our current partner. One of my female friends recently told me that the song that most aptly expressed her love for her partner was Millie Small's song, from 1964, titled 'My Boy Lollipop'.

3. But some pop songs undoubtedly teach unrealistic expectations of love and relationships; and help people to crank their emotions up too high, into anxious or angry jealousy; or down too low, into a sense of depressed abandonment. ("You are the wind beneath my wings!" - "Like a bridge over troubled water, I will lay me down!" – "Every road that takes me, takes me down. I'm playing solitaire!")

1.1.2 Some unrealistic love songs

Let us take a look at the top three wedding songs, as at 6th December 2017, which we can assume to be widely influential.

The titles and artists' names (according to 'Spotify') were:

1. *All of Me*, by John Legend;

2. *Marry You*, by Bruno Mars; and:

3. *Thinking Out Loud*, Ed Sheeran.

So what are the *key sentiments* of these songs, and some of the *problems* with the ideas they promote?

Let us begin with John Legend:

1.1.2(a) All of Me, by John Legend

"Give your all to me; I give my all to you. ... Cos I give you all of me..."

This is a completely unrealistic lyric.

Why: Well, what exactly is this "all"? The emotional tone of the song is somewhat *neurotic*: like a *crying baby*, asking mommy for 'everything'.

He will give her (the *promise* of) 'everything', as long as he can have her totally to himself! (But once he's got her, isn't it true – in your experience, dear reader - that he will then want to go to the pub; to the football game; to play card games with his buddies? To spend long hours on his career? And so on. So then, how will she have his 'all' when he spreads it around so thinly?!)

In reality, no such 'total possession' of another person is possible. We have to 'stand' in love, not 'fall' into this kind of *pit of symbiosis*, which is about *melting together* with a *symbolic* mother (or father) – until that wears out, or falls apart because it is so oppressive of one or both partners!

~~~

Then we move on to:

1.1.2(b) Bruno Mars' Marry You

It begins like this: "Hey baby, I *think* I want to marry you!"

That *could be* a positive message. Do you (the listening young person) now begin to think you would *like* to marry your partner? If 'yes', or you are thinking about it, then this lyric could (at least theoretically) be a good message to hear at this time.

Then, 'why' does he think he wants to marry her? "Is it this look in your eyes?" he asks himself. "Or is it just these dancing tunes? I don't care baby! I think I want to marry you!"

This sounds a little reckless. He has a strong 'feeling' he wants to marry his 'baby'. He doesn't know why. It just 'feels right'. And that could also be good. Love is primarily a feeling state (isn't it? Or is it? More on this later, below).

Next line: "Just say 'I do'...."

So, now it's revealed as a *disguised* proposal of marriage. What Mars is saying to 'his baby' is this: "I think (perhaps) I want to marry you. But before I make a real proposal, just you go ahead and say you actually *do* want to marry me!" Then what?

Then he feels *confident enough* to ask properly?

Or: Then he is free to *not* ask?

Or: Then he is free to *misrepresent* the facts of who proposed to whom?

This is not good guidance for the teenaged or twenty-something listener. Don't you think we should give young people some kind of practical guidelines for choosing a romantic mate? Some way to determine if they are compatible? Some tools for communicating about what they are getting into?

~~~

And then we move on to Ed Sheeran's *Thinking Out Loud*:

1.1.2(c) Thinking Out Loud, Ed Sheeran.

This is the piece that jumped out at me: "I keep making the same mistakes, hoping that you'll understand". And then "...Baby now. Take me into your loving arms. Kiss me under the light of a thousand stars".

The first bit, "I keep making the same mistakes", suggests two possibilities. Firstly, that Sheeran *doesn't learn well from his mistakes*, in which case, his baby should run a mile!

Secondly, it could be a way to legitimate sexual infidelity, or verbal abuse, or gambling away the grocery money: "I just *made that mistake* again, baby!" But it's not clear from the song what he means at all about 'mistakes'.

However, if it is to do with abuse or infidelity then, his baby should just end it!

He's hoping she will understand - but her understanding is not obligatory, and often not appropriate; and what is required instead is that he *learn from his mistakes,* and not expect her to keep forgiving him his errors or transgressions!

But then he goes into total Baby Mode: "Take me in your loving arms"...

This line sounds like a request from a little boy to his mother. A mature man, in a loving relationship, is capable of *reaching out his own arms,* and *embracing* his wife or partner.

But horror of horrors is yet to come: "Kiss me under the light of a thousand stars".

How *realistic* is that? (Bear in mind, Sheeran is 26 years old; and thus the frontal lobes of his brain, or the reasoning centres of his brain, are not yet fully online, and normally not strong enough to damp down his emotional responses to the world until around this age. [And he could have written this song when he was twenty-five or younger!] But he has a long history of cranking up his manic love sickness, and so his ability to damp down his emotional surges may come later in life, if at all! [Some people never seem to 'grow up' and get control over their overly-aroused emotions. {And, of course, we always need some *external assistance* with this task!}]).

My two main observations are these:

Firstly, if he *wants* a kiss, he should *initiate it,* (and check for *an agreement* that his partner is open to this!), and not *ask* for it, like a *child.* Or like a passive, insecure partner.

And secondly: the kiss should just be enough, without the *impossible* embellishment of "the light of a thousand stars" - which is just pure *schmaltz.*

~~~

All three of these songs (and many of the others in the top fifty, no doubt) are based on *unrealistic expectations* and *childlike sentiments*. But mature, adult love is not like this at all – and has to be managed from a more conscious, reasoning part of the brain, in addition to the heart.

Let us then begin to look at defining a more adult approach to love and relationship.

1.2 Defining love and relationship

1.2.1. What is love?

To begin with, let me point out that there are two *domains* in which the concept of 'love' is operable and important.

The first domain is 'life in general'; and the second domain is 'pair bonding', or *couple relationships*. This book is primarily about pair bonding, or couple relationships, so our emphasis is going to be primarily on this second domain. But we must not forget the first domain. As Lewis, Amini and Lannon (2001) write, in the preface of their wonderful book on love:

"From birth to death, love is not just the focus of human experience, but also the life force of the mind, determining our moods, stabilizing our bodily rhythms, and changing the structure of our brains. The body's physiology ensures that relationships determine and fix our identities. Love makes us who we are, and who we can become" (Page viii).

However, our theory in emotive-cognitive therapy suggests that the line between good and evil, love and hate, runs right down the middle of the human heart. Some of us learn to be mainly loving, and a little hating; while others of us learn to be mainly hateful, and a little loving. (A *quantitative, or positivist, psychologist* would anticipate that most of us will be found to be clustered in the middle ground between love and hate!)

We learn *how to love* (and hate) in our mother's arms. And we learn *who to love* (and hate); and how much to love (and hate); and how widely to love (and hate) other people; from observing the loving (and hating) habits of our parents.

~~~

One way to begin to define 'love' is to look up the word in an English dictionary. According to my dictionary[12], love means:

"n. 1. A strong feeling of affection.

2. A strong feeling of affection linked with sexual attraction.

3. A great interest and pleasure in. ..."

For the purposes of this book, on couple relationships, it seems to me that definition 2 above is a good, basic, overall definition of what we are talking about. At least as a starting point; a core definition.

But then we have to define 'affection', which my dictionary renders as:

"n. A feeling of fondness or liking".

So that gives us a definition of love as "A strong feeling of affection (or fondness and liking) linked with sexual attraction".

So, if you feel a strong sexual attraction towards somebody, but no feeling of affection, or fondness and liking, then that is, by definition, *not love!*

But *affection* is not the only emotional component with love. There are also the "natural limbic inclinations" – or inclinations of the emotional centres of our brains – of *loyalty* and *concern*. And the desire to serve and give to the loved one. (Lewis, Amini and Lannon [2001], page 215).

This sounds a lot more sober and realistic than the sentiments expressed in the love songs explored in the introduction, above; which are all about something called 'falling in love', or 'being in love'; which must now be distinguished from 'loving'.

But first, let us take a look at a juvenile definition of love, from a recent novel by Julian Barnes (2018), writing about the main character, Paul, when he was nineteen to twenty-one years old:

"He remembered his own early attempts to define love, back in the Village, alone in his bed. Love, he had ventured, was like the vast and sudden uncreasing of a lifelong frown. Hmm: love as the end of a migraine. No, worse: love as Botox. His other comparison: love feeling as if the lungs of the soul had suddenly been inflated with pure oxygen..." (Pages 204-205).

Such juvenile definitions of love cannot help us to know how to love. So let us continue with our quest to produce a better definition.

1.2.2 Distinguishing 'loving' from 'being in love'

Anglo-American culture, as well as much European culture, seems to be more excited about the fleeting quality of 'being in love' than the more mundane processes of 'loving' another human being. (Lewis, Amini and Lannon, 2001; page 206)[13].

The process of 'falling in love' and 'being in love' are habit-based responses to re-stimulation of patterns of relating that we witnessed in our parents, when we were too young to evaluate the goodness or rightness of those patterns. So we 'fall in love' when we encounter, in our adult lives, an individual who matches us in much the way our mother and father 'matched' each other – whether that match was happy or unhappy, healthy or dysfunctional! (Lewis, Amini and Lannon, 2001; and Teachworth, 1999).

'Being in love' is a form of blind passion, driven from early childhood memories of the bond between mother and father. *Loving*, on the other hand operates from a different part of the emotional wiring of the individual. *Adult love* depends upon 'knowing' the other person.

Or, as expressed by Lewis, Amini and Lannon (2001): "*Loving* derives from *intimacy*, the prolonged and detailed surveillance of a foreign soul". (Page 207). (See the discussion of 'intimacy' below).

Love requires us to be able to see, and admire, the 'otherness' of the love object.

'Being in love' is like a return to the mother's arms; but it only lasts for a short time.

'Loving' is a more *mature* process whereby one partner *gives* love – or *attention, affection, service, or regard* - to the other, and finds that it is returned; with no expectation or demand that it be returned.

In *loving*, there is *mutual regulation* of affective (or feeling) states. Each partner *meets the needs* of the other, because we humans cannot regulate our own affects (or feeling states) in the absence of some external assistance. Or as Lewis, Amini and Lannon express it: "Each *takes perpetual care* of the other, and, within concurrent reciprocity, both thrive". (Page 208). This approach requires a good deal of shared *time* and *attention*.

By loving our partner, we *regulate* their emotional states, and this makes them resilient in the face of life's stressors, and helps them to feel whole. (Whereas, in the 'in love' process, there is often a sense of *incompleteness*, and a sense of *insecurity*, and a desire to *suck the blood of love* out of our partner, with no sense of the need to reciprocate! [After all, we did not have to reciprocate our mother's love of us; and we may also have seen a lack of reciprocation between our parents when we were growing up!])

~~~

1.2.3 Theories of love

Let us now take a look at a couple of theories of love.

1.2.3(a) A psychological theory of love

To begin with, let us now take a look at a definition of love – as a noun - from my dictionary of psychology: (Coleman, 2002)[14]:

"An intense feeling of fondness or attraction, deeper and stronger than liking, especially when associated with a romantic or sexual attachment to someone".

This is very similar to the dictionary definition explored above.

Coleman (2002) then continues:

"According to a popular taxonomy proposed by the Canadian sociologist John Alan Lee in *The Colours of Love: An exploration of the ways of loving* (1973), there are three primary and three secondary types of love that blend into different shades like colours, the three primary types being *Eros* (erotic or passionate love), *ludus* (ludic or playful love), and *storge* (storgic or friendly/ affectionate love)..."

And I would maintain that all three of those three primary types of love – the passionate, playful and affectionate - are essential for a happy couple relationships. But the songs above seem to largely emphasize Eros, or passionate love – and often in the form of the passionate love of a *virtual baby* for its mother figure (or mother substitute!)

Coleman (2002) then described the three secondary types of love, the most important, for our purposes, being this:

"...*mania* (manic or obsessive/possessive love, a combination of Eros and ludus)".

And, certainly, it seems to me, much of the content of the love songs that are popular with wedding parties today contain a good deal of *mania*, but in a rather *desperate, childlike* form. What is missing is a degree of *Adult*[1] *realism!*

We clearly need a more *balanced* model of love than that which we have explored so far. And that is where Coleman (2002) takes us next:

"According to the *triangular theory* of love proposed in 1986 by the US psychologist Robert Jeffrey Sternberg..., there are three basic components of love, namely *passion* (sexual desire), *intimacy* (confiding and sharing feelings), and *commitment* (intention to maintain the relationship), different combinations of the three components yielding eight basic types..."

---

[1] When I use the word *Adult*, *Parent* or *Child*, with an initial capital letter, I am referring to the 'Adult, Parent and/or Child *ego states*' (or states of the personality) as described in Transactional Analysis. See Appendix B.

It seems to me that this combination of three components yields an Adult form of love – to which we must then add a reasonable (but not excessive) component of the playfulness of the Child ego state, plus the caring attitudes of the Nurturing Parent ego state. (See Appendix B for an introduction to Transactional Analysis and the concept of 'ego states'). This gives us the formula, that:

Love is a combination of passion, intimacy and commitment (plus playfulness and nurturance) – with the Adult ego state (rather than the Needy Child) in the executive position (or in charge of) the total personality!

The problem with many relationships today is that they are built almost exclusively on *Needy Child passion* – with little or no intimacy or commitment or healthy playfulness! And when one partner *repeatedly* operates from *Needy Child passion*, the other is likely to become *resentful* and *zap* them from Critical or Controlling Parent ego state.

And when those relationships eventually die, as die they must, when the embers of passion die down, from eighteen months to 30-36 months into the (marital form of the) relationship, all that keeps them together then is *habit*, and *minimal commitment* to keep on keeping on, through misery and disappointment.

~~~

1.2.3(b) Love as 'passion, intimacy and commitment'

Let us now take a look at those three elements of love: passion, intimacy and commitment:

1.2.3(b)(i) Passion

Passion is not listed in my dictionary of psychology, nor in my dictionary of philosophy. But in my Oxford English dictionary (Waite, 2012) there is a definition of passion, as a noun (or thing), as follows:

"1. Very strong emotion. 2. Intense sexual love. 3. An intense enthusiasm for something..."

And when a lover is said to be *passionate*, this involves "intense emotion, enthusiasm, or sexual love".

So it's a strong emotion. But remember – not all emotions are *positive*, even if they are *strong*. There is obviously intense liking; intense love; intense curiosity or interest. But there is also *intense anger*; intense *jealousy*; intense *hatred*.

But when we talk of passion as a component of love, we obviously mean intense feelings of liking, caring, respecting, and curiosity and interest in the loved one. However, when things go wrong in intensely passionate relationships, the result is often a flipping over into intense negative emotionality, including hatred, anger and often violence or emotional abuse.

And those intense, negative emotions tend to kill sex-love relationships dead!

1.2.3(b)(ii) Measuring passionate love

It is highly unlikely that anybody ever experiences pure passionate love. (Whitbourne, 2012)[15]. After all, we are socialized to be responsible, cautious, and balanced in our actions. It must be rare indeed to see anybody give themselves totally to the urgings of passion, except for a passing brain-storm!

Indeed, Whitbourne (2012) has presented the components of the Passionate Love Scale, developed by Hatfield and Sprecher (1986)[16], and it clearly is a set of balanced emotive, cognitive and behavioural components, as follows:

"*Cognitive components*

1. Thinking about or being preoccupied with your partner

2. Idealizing your partner or the relationship

3. Wanting to know your partner and wanting your partner to know you"

"Emotional components

1. Being sexually attracted to and aroused by your partner

2. Feeling good when things go well

3. Feeling bad when things go badly

4. Loving and wanting to be loved in return

5. Wanting complete and permanent union"

"Behavioural components:

1. Trying to find out how your partner feels

2. Providing service to your partner

3. Being physically close to your partner".

And as Whitbourne (2012) writes: "Passionate love clearly involves more than sexual attraction. The cognitive, other emotional and behavioural components balance out the urge to get physical with your loved one".

Indeed, it does seem to me that this classification of 'passion' includes many elements that would also appear under the headings of *intimacy* and *commitment*.

1.2.3(b)(iii) Sexual Passion

And it also seems that, although the sense of physical *urgency* for sexual union is likely to decline significantly after the first two to three years of your relationship, many of the cognitive and behavioural components can be kept alive through a *commitment* made by your Adult ego state! A commitment to keep your relationship alive; vibrant; and to continue to pleasure your partner, *because you want to,* rather than because you are *driven* in that direction by your nature! And with regard to the elements that decline, it seems to mainly be the *sense of urgency*; and the sense of strong *attentional focus.*

Some of the things we need to do to keep sexual passion alive beyond the honeymoon period include the following:

(a) Make *a commitment* to be a source of (mutual) pleasure for your partner;

(b) Express love for each other, verbally; and remember to kiss and cuddle! (Gottman, 2017).

(c) Create the time for weekly dates for romantic, quality time together. (Northrup, Schwartz and Witte, 2014).

(d) Agree on a *mutually workable frequency* of sexual encounters – they don't always have to include full intercourse, or even orgasm. But regular physical contact of a sexual nature, at an *agreed* frequency, will keep the passion alive in your relationship. Frequency can vary significantly from one couple to another, and there is no universal standard. According to the International Society for Sexual Medicine: "The 'right' frequency is one that satisfies both partners. It may take time to figure this out, but putting the focus on intimacy, communication, and bonding with a partner is more important than worrying about numbers, targets, or the sexual frequency of other couples". (ISSM, 2018)[17].

(e) Find out what your partner *likes* in the way of sexual stimulation, and within reason, try to facilitate that. Read a good book on the subject, such as *The Joy of Sex*, by Alex Comfort (updated by Susan Quilliam, 2008/ 2011). (See Appendix G, on 'The Importance of the Clitoris'. Plus Appendix H, on Daniel O'Beeve's Piecemeal Sex Education).

(f) Eat the kinds of foods that promote sexual potency and vitality, such as vitamins A, E and C (and/or get these vitamins from supplements). Plus selenium and zinc; and a broad spectrum multivitamin and mineral supplement. Add B vitamins to keep your stress level low, as stress interferes with the sex urge. Onions, garlic and ginger, and chilies, are a helpful extra. And Gingko Biloba may help with blood flow to the genitals.

(g) Exercise regularly to keep your body-mind in a fit condition.

(h) And get sufficient sleep on a nightly basis.

(i) Treat sex with respect, and the seriousness it deserves, (but without losing a sense of playfulness!) Avoid internet pornography and other forms of overstimulation. *Simple sex, combined with love and tenderness, is wonderful in its own way.* It does not need additional 'whistles and bells'. Or as Susan Quilliam, the now famous British sexologist, said, in a *New York Times* interview, in 2008: "Have fun, have love, have sex. But don't give yourself a hard time if you're not doing it 24-7". (Lyall, 2008)[18]. Frequency is a *personal matter* for the couple!

(j) And don't trivialize or downgrade or belittle sex; or reduce it to a smutty form of recreation. It is a serious matter, if only because it *bonds us* to the person with whom we have sexual relations. (Don't get bonded to the *wrong person*, because you thought 'sex is just recreation'. Make sure you choose *a suitable partner*, and work at continually breathing life into *both* your *love and affection*, on the one hand, and your *sexual interaction*, on the other hand!)

~~~

1.2.3(c) Intimacy

The second component of our definition of love is this: *intimacy*.

But what does 'intimacy' mean?

According to my English dictionary (edited by Waite, 2012):

Intimacy, as a noun (or thing) means:

"1. Close familiarity or friendship.

"2. A familiar or private act or remark".

My dictionary of psychology (Colman, 2002) cites the distinction created by Erik Erikson between 'intimacy', on the one hand, and 'isolation', on the other. This suggests that intimacy is primarily a form of *connection* to another human being – and combining that with Waite (2002), we can conclude that *'intimacy is a close, warm connection to another human being'*. (It's about *attachment!*)

Then, Robert Bolton (1979/1986) gives us this definition: "Intimacy has been defined as 'the ability to express my deepest aspirations, hopes, fears, anxieties, and guilts to another significant person repeatedly'." (Page 135).

So, intimacy may be *a close, warm connection to another human being, in which open communication - of who I am, what I want and don't want - and what I think, feel and do - can be conducted in the confident expectation of respectful acceptance by the other person.*

In his book on *attachment* in psychotherapy, David Wallin (2007)[19] has this to say about 'intimate attachments':

"Throughout our lives we are prone to monitor the physical and emotional whereabouts – the accessibility and responsiveness – of those to whom we are most attached. Thus, especially once *felt security* is added to *proximity* as the set goal (of secure attachment), attachment must be seen as an ongoing human need rather than a childlike dependency that we outgrow as we grow up. As Bowlby (1980) put it:

> 'Intimate attachments to other human beings are the hub around which a person's life revolves, not only when s/he is an infant or a toddler, but throughout his/her adolescence and his/her years of maturity as well, and on into old age'. (Page 442 of Bowlby, 1980).

This description indicates that the desire for, and urge towards, intimacy, is not just some kind of *individual, infantile, overreliance on another* – as was often suggested by rational therapists – but is actually part of our innate, survival-oriented attachment mechanism. (See the description of *Attachment styles*, below [in Chapter 6, sections 6.10 – 6.12(b)]).

So, clearly, *intimacy is a basic human need*, which includes the need for both *emotional* and *physical* closeness. But many of us (and perhaps mainly emotionally rigid males, but also some females) tend to reduce intimacy to sexual contact, and those individuals then feel upset when they don't achieve the sexual closeness they desire. On the other hand, with a more *balanced* approach to emotional and physical intimacy, there is not the same weight of expectations placed on 'mind-blowing' sex! (Gordon, 1969/2016)[20].

One of the requirements of intimacy is *equality* between the individuals involved. Hence, there has been a huge *limitation of intimacy* in the past, as men have often assumed superiority over their female partners. Since the earliest recorded stories of the lives of men and women, there has been a strong tendency by dominant males to silence the female voice: (Beard,

2017).

And, since we all come from families, in the past, with dated approaches to equality, it is difficult for us, today, to achieve intimacy. Clearly, to achieve intimacy, you must begin to dismantle any tendency towards inequality in your relationship; to abandon any ideas of male dominance (or female dominance!); and also to substitute *assertive communication* for dysfunctional ways of relating. Specifically:

- some women need to give up nagging; while some need to give up passive, 'door-mat' behaviour. And:

- some men need to give up aggressive dominance; while others need to give up passive withdrawal in the face of nagging.

(See Chapters 4, 6, 7, 8, 9, 11 and 12; plus Appendices B, D, E, F, J and M.)

Then, to continue to build intimacy, you need to learn to build trust. And one way to do that is to share with your partner some little secret from your past. This will normally elicit a similar kind and level of sharing from them. And, if and when it does, you can reciprocate with a slightly more risky revelation; and your partner is (most often) likely to response in kind. To the degree that they respond in kind, you can continue to reveal more and more of 'who you are'; 'where' you have come from; 'where' you have been on your journey through life; and your hopes and dreams, and so on. (If they do not respond positively to this kind of trust-building exercise, then you have to wonder if you are in a viable relationship; and take action accordingly! [Like getting out!])

In this way, over time, you become more and more emotionally intimate. This is an expression of the fourth element of Erich Fromm's definition of love: *Knowledge*. Getting to know your partner, at a deeper level than anybody else knows them; and letting them get to know you. (See the Attachment sections, 6.10-6.12(b), in Chapter 6, below).

~~~

Most of the definitions looked at so far have emphasized the 'need for intimacy'. But what about the *capacity to be available – intimately –* for your partner? Fortunately, Gordon (1969/2016) has dealt with this side of intimacy like this:

"At the heart of intimacy ... is empathy, understanding, and compassion; these are the humanizing feelings".

So, perhaps our final attempt to define intimacy should look like this:

Intimacy is characterized by two elements:

(1) A *close, warm connection to another human being, in which open and honest communication of who I am, what I want and don't want, and what I think, feel, and do, can be conducted in the confident expectation of respectful acceptance by the other person;* and:

(2) *Reciprocation*: To reciprocate intimacy – or to return it to our lover, by treating them as they treat us - *we must show our partner empathy, understanding, and compassion,* as these are the humanizing feelings.

Two aspects of this 'close, warm connection' which have not been brought out so far are as follows: With our Adult ego state – or our 'reasoning ability' - in the executive position in our personality, we must deploy, as appropriate;

> (a) Nurturing Parent *care* of our partner; plus:

> (b) Playful Child *engagement in light-heartedness* and *fun* activities.

We need to move, as appropriate from Adult functioning, to *Nurturing Parent* functioning, to *Playful Child* functioning, in order to avoid the machine-like, Mr Spock qualities of *Exclusive Adult* functioning!

And we need to avoid criticizing our partner from Critical or Controlling Parent ego state. (See Appendix B).

~~~

1.2.3(d) Commitment

Commitment is the third element of our definition of love.

But what do we mean when we say we are making a commitment to our partner; or to our marriage? According to one relationship expert online, you should:

"Define (commitment) for yourself to the point that it's crystal clear in your mind what your vision of commitment is, and exactly what it will look and feel like through each of the stages (of your relationship). Knowing what it is for you makes all the difference in the world." Jane Garapick, (2014)[21].

But let me help you to do that defining task. According to my English dictionary (Waite, 2012), commitment (as a noun) means:

"1. Dedication to a cause or policy.

"2. A promise.

"3. An engagement or duty that restricts freedom of action..."

This is clear and helpful. If I make a *commitment* to my partner, then I am *promising* something. Such as, to be *faithful* to her. To *love* her. To *be there* for her. To put her *before* all others. To *work* at making the relationship *happy* and *secure* for her. This is a dedication to the cause of 'forsaking all others', which restricts my freedom of action in many ways, but which gives me a home-base and a happy relationship with the one I love.

So what about you?

Q1: What does commitment mean to you?

Answer:

Q2: And to your partner?

Answer:

Write down the answers to those two questions, and make sure you both agree what you are committed to; and then keep your promises to each other, as if your partner had constant CCTV of your actions in the world. If you think you can cheat on your commitments, you must either be very young, very stupid or immoral, or very inexperienced! You cannot successfully cheat on your commitments, because *the Law of Karma* will always catch you out, if not today, or this week, then a little further down the line!

Be good! Make a clear commitment; and then stick to it, no matter what the temptations might be to break it! Lying and cheating are no basis for a high level of self-esteem! If you want to be *happy* and *healthy*, keep your promises, no matter what temptations come your way!

~~~

1.2.3(e) Summing up about love

We have now explored the three components of our definition of love: passion, intimacy and commitment. For comparison purposes, let us look at three other definitions of love. This should help us to ground our definition; to broaden and enrich it.

Firstly, let's look at John Armstrong's (2002)[22] perspective on love:

1.2.3(f) Mad, passionate love

Armstrong (2003) writes about Goethe's first novel ('The Sorrows of Young Werther'), published in 1774, which introduced a new, romantic vision of love. "This short book", says Armstrong, "presented a simple, and seductive, vision of the nature of love: *Love is a feeling*. It is still, in its basic elements, the dominant vision of love today".

But if you read Armstrong's summation of Goethe's description of the feelings of young Werther, then you will be forced to conclude that this is actually an *infantile* kind of love; and an *insecurely attached infant* at that. And, of course, as Armstrong admits, this kind of love only lasts a few days, or weeks or months. It cannot be sustained. Reality eventually intrudes, and at that point, what we need is *a more Adult approach* to love. One, as we have indicated, that is based upon commitment to our beloved; and a desire to work at deepening our intimacy, by sharing our secrets with each other; and by working to maintain physical passion, empathy, equality and acceptance.

If you are prone to be *overly-romantic*, and to feel *horribly tortured by your love feelings,* then you should read Armstrong's (2002) book as an antidote.

~~~

1.2.3(g) Erich Fromm's definition of love

In his book, *The Art of Loving*[23], Erich Fromm defines love as comprising *care, respect, responsibility* and *knowledge* of your partner. How do these qualities fit with our definition of love as passion, intimacy and commitment? They certainly are not equivalent definitions. And, in my work with couples, I have often found it helpful to emphasize care, respect and responsibility, as those qualities were often missing from one or both sides of the relationship. Therefore, I think our earlier definition cannot stand alone. It has to have Erich Fromm's definition added in. Like this:

Love is defined by the following qualities: Passion (automatic and willed); Intimacy (including care, respect, and sharing personal knowledge with each other); and commitment (including taking responsibility for our own side of the relationship). And let us not forget *nurturance* and *playfulness*!

~~~

1.2.3(h) M. Scott Peck´s definition of Love

In *The Road Less Travelled*[24], M. Scott Peck defined love like this: "Love is a process of extending yourself in the service of another".

Where does that fit into our definition of love? It seems to fit quite well under 'commitment'. So our expanded definition of love now becomes this:

Love is defined by the following qualities: Passion (automatic and willed); Intimacy (including care and respect and sharing personal knowledge with each other, to achieve emotional and physical closeness); and commitment (including taking responsibility for our own side of the relationship; and extending ourselves in the service of our beloved [in adult; nurturing; and playful ways]).

Not wanting to continue this conversation endlessly, I will bring it to a close with two points made by John Armstrong (2003), near the end of his book.

Firstly, love is *a basic human need.*

And secondly, and finally, love is "an *achievement!*" It does not fall from the skies. It is not an *automatic adult entitlement!* It is not *issued* by the state. It cannot be *bought*. It has to be *built*, with your own fair hands, on a *daily* basis, over and over and over again!

~~~

1.2.4 What is a relationship?

This seems like a simplistic sentence. Surely everybody knows what a relationship is: right? Wrong!

In some ways, the concept of relationship is very simple. It is what happens when a baby is born, and is handed to its mother. She forms a relationship with the baby. She spends enormous amounts of time with the baby, attending to its needs; focusing on trying to read what is going on inside of the baby. When the baby gets to about five or six months of age, it takes up the same focus. Trying to stay attached to mother through time; focusing upon what she might be thinking or feeling. This relationship has two main components: time, and physiological connection; connection of the emotional centres of two brains.

When the baby grows up, and becomes an adult, sexual/cultural being, it seeks a mate. And an analogous process to the original mother-baby relationship begins: a bond is formed, based on *time* and the *connection and mutual regulation* of two emotional centres of human brains.

But there is a further complication.

1.2.4(a) Learning by watching and listening

We know (non-consciously) 'what' a relationship is as a result of watching our parents relate when we are too young to know we are 'making a video' of their relationship, as a (non-conscious) guide to our adult life. And, since not all relationships between mothers and fathers, in family homes, are happy, we have different definitions (or 'models') of relationship (in our heads), depending on how our specific parents related to each other.

One classification of these different kinds of relationships is found in Attachment Theory, developed by John Bowlby, Mary Ainsworth and Mary Main. (See Wallin, 2007). This is one of the most researched and confirmed theories of human development, and shows that, as a result of how we are parented in the first few years of life, we tend to develop one of three kinds of 'attachment styles': (a) secure; (b) anxious-ambivalent; and (c) anxious-avoidant. (See Chapter 6, sections 6.10 to 6.12(b)).

Because of these *different* attachment styles, and our experiences of observing how our parents related to each other, we have *particular expectations* – negative and/or positive - of our own adult relationship(s).

We also get definitions of relationships, or clues as to what they are, or what they should be, from love songs on the radio or TV; and from soap operas on TV; or from love stories we read as teenagers. Or Shakespeare, studied in school (e.g. *Romeo and Juliet*; or *Othello*).

~~~

But what about formal definitions of relationship? Well, I got the following definition of relationship from my English dictionary (Waite, 2002):

"Relationship", as a noun (or thing):

"1. The way in which two or more people or things are related.

"2. The way in which two or more people or groups behave towards each other.

"3. A loving and sexual association between two people". (Page 610).

The third of those definitions comes closest to defining the kind of relationship we want to explore. It includes love *and* sex.

But none of those definitions, or maps of relationships, really help us to know how to build a successful relationship for ourselves.

So, let us, instead, begin by taking a look inside the marital relationship of a man who studied human communication skills at doctoral level; and then wrote a great book on *People Skills*: Robert Bolton (1979/1986).

1.2.4(b) Insights into Robert Bolton´s marital relationship

In the frontispiece to his *People Skills* book, Robert Bolton posted a tribute to his wife, Dot, which I will present in snippets:

"TO DOT
"My best friend,
closest companion, fun playmate".

This could be a description of my relationship with Renata (who has been my wife since 1986; and my life partner since 1980). And I have tried to persuade my couple's therapy clients, over the years, to aim for this kind of relationship.

I do realize that many man are 'men's men', and that they enjoy playing or watching sports events with their 'mates' during their leisure hours; rather than walking in the countryside with their wife or partner. But this kind of *distant, remote relationship* cannot compare (for either partner, male or female) with the kind of relationship Bolton is describing above. (And Lewis, Amini and Lannon, 2001, argue that shared time is an important building block of couple relationships; and they argue that modern American culture is ripping relationships apart by promoting so many distractions from spending time with one's marriage partner!)

Note also Bolton's reference to his 'fun playmate'. This is the aspect referred to earlier as *Playful Child involvement* in relating.

Bolton continues his tribute to Dot:

"Enabler of my various selves,
nurturer of my dreams".

I take those two lines to mean: "Because of the flexible way you relate to me, I am able to move around flexibly between my personality elements – or sub-personalities – and/or my ego states (Nurturing Parent, Adult, and Playful Child ways of being. [See Appendix B]) And this helps me to keep growing".

Again this links back to our earlier definition of love, which includes the involvement of the *Nurturing Parent* ego state.

He continues:

"Marvellous wife –
sensitive, loving, and genuine
with me, our children, parents, and friends".

This is self-explanatory. Bolton admires his marvellous wife. Furthermore, Dot is sensitive and loving, and that is part of the "care and respect" element of love.

Next:

"Effective in tasks that sustain our common life –
colleague, teacher, partner".

This is a very interesting clause in his tribute, because it contrasts so greatly against the idea that *relationships are all about getting into bed* with somebody. Relationships involve a hell of a lot of work, especially if you have children, which most married couples do. As Werner Erhard once said: "Relationships require the kind of commitment that mountain climbing requires. No point getting up on the side of a mountain, with a family in tow, and then quitting!"

So relationships are practical, and involve hard work; but they are also profoundly sustaining, psychologically; and they involve various shared roles. So Dot is not 'just a wife'; but also a colleague, a teacher; and a partner. Both partners should be able to learn from each other, and to take turns leading and following.

Bolton continues:

"I love it that when I am with you
I most often discover, choose, disclose
the selves I really am".

This means there is lots of mileage in close relationships for all kinds of *personal development* and *psychological growth* to take place. Or, as Shakti Gawain says: "Relationships are *the **best** seminar* in town!" And what she meant by that was this: *If you want to grow yourself, get into a relationship. That will greatly stretch your head (and your heart)!*

Robert Bolton then continues:

"I love my experience of you as
a life-full, love-full,
value-full person".

So, Dot is full of life – vibrant and exciting. Full of love – which means care, respect, tenderness, and so on. And full of value for Robert. He values her, and indeed they are equals in every sense! They value each other equally. This is most important, as *inequality of treatment* or *expectations,* in a sex-love relationship, is likely to destroy the relationship in record time!

Finally, he writes:

"Imperfect, changing, growing, becoming,
yet rooted, consistent –
a friend for all seasons.
You are 'something else'."

Our partners are always *imperfect* human beings (just like ourselves!), and we have to accept them the way they are (so long as they are not violent, abusive, or acting illegally or immorally!) Or we should *ask them* (politely and respectfully) to change some *particular aspect* of their behaviour, so long as we are *willing* to allow them to influence us to change some aspects of our own behaviour, to an *equal* degree.

And Bolton returns to the question of 'friendship'. Dot is his *best friend*. And *two* other things are worth noting:

1. He does not mention *sex* once; and that is because in polite society, men do not draw attention to the sexuality of their partner. They celebrate it *privately*, and *respect* their partners as sexual beings, with *sexual needs* which the man has to find out, and to satisfy, and not just to impose his appetites and tastes upon her. And:

2. He resorts to *euphemism* in the end: *You are 'something else'*, he writes. This is unavoidable, I think, because the *beauty* and *glory* of our sex-love partners are *beyond words*; utterly beyond being described. What he is saying, in that final line, is this: "You, for me, are *unutterably* magnificent and wonderful".

His *gratitude* for her love is palpable!

~~~

That then is an insight into what I would see as a healthy, *positive* relationship between life partners; pair-bonded partners; or sex-love partners. Let us now home in on *the beginnings of a **definition** of a positive, sex-love relationship.

1.2.4(c) Werner Erhard's definition of relationship

Back in the 1970's, Werner Erhard (1981) - (in his audio program, 'Relationships: Making them work') - came up with a three part definition of relationship, which is a good starting point, and which went like this:

1. "A relationship is an understanding and being aware of another person's way of being. That is to say, a relationship is the condition of

understanding and being aware of another person".

(Notice there is no "entitlement" to anything in this statement! That it allows the other person *to be*, exactly the way they are!)

~~~

2. "Successful relationships are based on agreed on goals".

That does not mean that my partner must agree to my goals, or vice versa. Instead it means, I support my partner in pursuing her goals; and she supports me in pursuing mine.

(Notice there are no "sergeant majors" in this statement; no "directors"; no "leaders" and "led"! And no "right goals" and "wrong goals" – though there has to be *a sense of morality* about goals!)

~~~

3. "If you want to have a really powerful relationship with anybody, you have got to stop *making them wrong*".

And making them wrong means describing them as being bad/wrong when their ideas/ values/ goals or behaviours deviate from your idea of what they *should* be!

(Instead of making them wrong, as a whole person, you should try this: Separate the person from the problem; talk about the problem in terms of your interests, not your positions[25]; and aim for compromises and trade-offs, not victories and win-lose outcomes. Let your partner influence you, if you want them to let you influence them[26]).

1.2.4(d) Developing a revised definition of positive relationships

Let us now revisit part one of the definition:

> 1. A relationship is an understanding and being aware of another person's way of being. That is to say, a relationship is the condition of understanding and being aware of another person.

Originally, I thought this definition was *fixed* and *final,* and that it was wholly positive. One of the great advantages of this definition is this: It eliminates all sense of entitlement to 'getting something out of' a relationship. And it provides a kind of neutrality to the relationship, which strips the concept of any baggage you might be carrying from your childhood.

I worked with this definition for years, and this work changed (improved) the way I performed in my relationship with Renata, because of the nature of this definition. That is to say, I reviewed this definition over and over again, day after day, week after week, and month after month, *until it ran my life.* Or, until it *'overwrote'* whatever definition of relationship I had made up - (or 'co-created', with my mother and father) - during my early childhood, and which had tended to run my relationship with Renata, from non-conscious levels of mind, up to discovering Werner's definition of relationship.

However, now, thirty-four years after learning and utilizing this definition, I beg to differ with Werner Erhard.

I think I can now offer a better version of part one of his definition, like this:

> 1. *A positive sex-love relationship is a voluntary, bonded attachment to an emotionally significant other, who is equal, respected and cared for; and who reciprocates my egalitarianism, respect and care. It is also a mutually regulating (physiological) system of attuned emotionality.*

~~~

I still like part two of Werner's definition, as follows:

> 2. "Successful relationships are based on agreed on goals". That does not mean that my partner must agree to my goals, or vice versa. Instead it means, I support my partner in pursuing her goals; and she supports me in pursuing mine. (Notice there are no "sergeant majors" in this statement; no "directors"; no "leaders" and "led"!)

And perhaps this should be updated like this:

> 2. *Successful relationships are based on mutually agreed goals between equal individuals; and mutually satisfying shared activities; in substantial periods of time spent together; resulting in a 5:1 ratio of positive to negative moments.*

Agreed on goals, however, are subject to the principle of an equal right to influence each other. So, if my partner wants to influence me to go for the kind of home and garden that she wants, then I have the right to an equal degree of influence, such as, where we take our annual holiday for the next few years.

To sustain this kind of give-and-take approach to negotiating goals, it is important to be able to distinguish between things that matter a lot to you, and things which are less important to you. Then you can more easily trade away those things which matter least to you, in exchange for those things that matter most to you; provided this also works for your partner.

When you hit an issue which is crucially important to each of you, then you have now hit a 'mutual problem'; and I will write about mutual problems in volume three of this series.

~~~

I still broadly accept part three of Werner Erhard's definition of relationship, as follows:

> 3. "If you want to have *a really **powerful** relationship* with your partner, you have got to stop *making them wrong*".
>
> And making them wrong means describing them as being bad or wrong – or becoming angry and shouting at them, or using verbal putdowns with them - when their ideas/ values/ goals or behaviours deviate from your idea of what they *should* be!

Instead of *making them wrong*, it would be advisable to:

- Separate the person from the problem; talk about the problem in terms of your interests (meaning yours *and theirs*), not your *positions*; and aim for compromises and trade-offs, not victories and win-lose outcomes. And:

- Let your partner influence you, if you want them to let you influence them.

But perhaps this third part of the definition of relationship should be rewritten like this:

> 3. If you want to have a really powerful relationship with your partner, you must *give up criticizing them* or *putting them down*. Instead, aim to use *assertive complaining*, or *conditional appreciation messages*, to get them to change problematical behaviours (provided you will allow them to influence you to change some of your behaviours).

~~~

1.2.5 Practical Exercise:

Please write each of the three elements of the definition of relationship, (which are reproduced below), on a separate 3" x 5" file card; or on separate sheets in a pocket notebook.

> 1. A positive sex-love relationship is *a voluntary, bonded attachment to an emotionally significant other, who is equal, respected and cared for; and who reciprocates my egalitarianism, respect and care.*

> 2. Successful relationships are based on *mutually agreed goals between equal individuals (including goals for sex, recreation, reproduction and lifestyle); and mutually satisfying shared activities; in substantial periods of time spent together; resulting in a 5:1 ratio of positive to negative moments.*

> 3. If you want to have a really powerful relationship with your partner, you must *give up criticizing them* or *putting them down*. Instead, aim to use *assertive complaining*, or *conditional appreciation messages*, to get them to change problematical behaviours

(provided you will allow them to influence you to change an equal amount of your behaviours).

Carry these definitions around with you for the next 90 days. (You might then need to extend that to 180 days, depending on the progress you make!)

Read each of them every day; and try to think about the implications of each of those three definitions:

- for your current relationship;

- for past relationships; and

- for your need to change some aspects of your approach to relationship.

~~~

If you review those three elements of definition, over and over and over again, day after day, week after week, and month after month, you will eventually develop a capacity for relationship which is extraordinary – and most likely in the top five percent of the population of the world!

But more importantly, you will be in a *durable, positive, mainly happy* sex-love relationship; and you and your partner will both be happy, *more often than not!*

How do I know that this is the case? Because that is what I did, back in 1984-86, and that is the kind of relationship I – in cooperation with my wife (Renata) - was able to build as a result!

In the process you will have moved into that area of human functioning which was defined by Dr Erich Fromm as:

Respect for your partner;

Taking responsibility for your side of the relationship; and:

Showing care for your partner.

~~~

Focus upon learning this new material by reviewing it at least three times:

Tick that you've read this chapter once: ☐

Before you more on to Chapter 2, please read this chapter a second time: ☐

And a third time: ☐

~~~

When reading and re-reading this chapter, please underline those points that seem most important to you.

Make notes in the margins, as necessary, as quick reminders of the content of a paragraph or a page.

And turn down the corner of the page, when the content is so important you want to find it again, quickly and easily.

Also, add important points, with their page numbers, in your own index to this book, in Appendix 'L', below. (Turn down the top corner of the first page of Appendix 'L', or put a paperclip on it, so you can easily find it every time you need to make an entry, or to find a reference).

~~~

Chapter 2: Some common myths about relationships

2.1 Background

Over a period of more than twenty years, I have observed the behaviours of many couples, and asked myself this question:

*"What must this person believe – what must be their **attitude** – in order to account for their spectacularly unworkable behaviour in relation to their marriage partner?"*

What I discovered, from asking myself that question, is that most people behave as if they are driven – compulsively and persistently – by one or more of the fourteen myths about relationships which are described in the next section.

2.2 Common myths about relationships

Of course, it is not the case that everybody carries the *same* myths about relationships. Some have extremely passive attitudes, encapsulated within a myth; while others have extremely aggressive attitudes. Some have fairy tale myths, while others have disaster myths.

Where do these myths come from?

They seem to mainly link back to the early childhood experiences of the individual, who often copied them from their parents. And/or they get instilled into the child and adult person via the mass media; especially films/movies, love stories, love songs, novels, women's magazines, macho male comic books, and so on.

Under normal circumstances, we would expect that an individual, from an emotionally healthy and emotionally intelligent family background, would have a set of *reasonable expectations* of romantic relationships. And, conversely, individuals who come from emotionally unhealthy or emotionally unintelligent families will normally be found to have *unreasonable* and *unrealistic expectations* of, and unhelpful myths about, couple relationships.

So let us take a look at the fourteen most common myths about romantic relationships that I have encountered in my work with couples:

Myth No.1: Getting married is the solution to all my personal, emotional and practical problems.

This myth leads to the individual 'going to sleep' in their relationship, as if they were a baby in their mother's arms. We could call this the *Sleeping Baby syndrome.*

Why is that a problem? Because, in order to build a successful relationship, both partners have to be wide awake, and alert to what is happening.

When something begins to feel 'wrong', it is important to start talking to your partner, and asking relevant questions:

> *'Are you unhappy about something?'*

> *'Have I done something to upset you?'*

> *'I have a feeling something is bugging you. Can we talk about it?'*

> *'Is there something you are not telling me?'*

Those kinds of questions can be thought of as 'negative enquiry' (which is a good thing!), and reflect an active, assertive approach to relationships, and a 'levelling' or honest approach to direct communication.

Getting married – or entering into a committed couple relationship – is the solution to *one problem*, and *one* problem alone. And that is the problem of not being in a committed relationship. Apart from that, it is important to realize that a marriage will throw up all kinds of *new problems*, such as:

How to *adjust* to your partner.

How to *share* a common living space.

How to *communicate* about desires and preferences.

How to *stay awake* in the new situation.

How to *balance* your *own* needs and the *needs* of your partner.

How to show *care* and *respect* for your partner.

How to decide on the *frequency* of love-making.

How to *discuss, plan and manage* the household budget.

How to manage the *boundaries* between you.

How to *decide* whether or not to have a baby; and how to *incorporate* a new baby into your lives as a couple, if and when you do proceed. (This is often like dropping a hand grenade into the relationship!)

And it would not be too difficult to add more and more items to this list of problems that often arise out of getting involved in a committed *pair bond* or *couple relationship*.

Of course, getting involved in *a **happy** couple relationship* will provide benefits as well as problems.

The most important benefits include:

- the fact that both partners can help to regulate their mate's emotional states;

- helping them to feel well-regulated and whole;

- strengthening them in the face of life's stressors; and:

- sharing time-structuring, enjoyable leisure activities together; as well as:

- sex, conversation and shared interests.

~~~

Myth No.2: The best relationships involve no conflict whatsoever.

This myth is often held by people who are *fearful of conflict*; and who therefore want to make sure they can *avoid* conflict. We could think of this as the *Scaredy Cat syndrome*. (This does not just apply to women. Many physically big men are terrified of interpersonal conflict with a woman! According to Gottman [1997]: 70% of his research participants who *flooded with stress hormones*, when their partner was volatile, were men!)

Scaredy Cat types try to avoid asking for anything, or communicating any form of discontent. Then, when their partner asks for something, in an assertive manner, or expresses discontent, the 'extreme peace-lover' Scaredy Cat tends to go to pieces; because they cannot abide conflict. (It may be that **most humans** have a fear of conflict – though some more than others!)

So these individuals often give in to unreasonable requests or demands from their partner; over and over again; until a point is reached where they cannot give in anymore; and then they explode in their poor, unsuspecting partner's face; causing lots of damage to the relationship. And thus their unrealistic passivity leads, eventually, to equally unrealistic, and unreasonable, explosive anger, and verbal and/or non-verbal aggression.

However, there is an alternative to this unworkable approach. If you read *People Skills*, by Dr Robert Bolton (1979/1986), you will find this statement: "The best relationships exist on *the **other side** of conflict!"*[27]

That is to say, to get to the *greener fields of happy relationship*, you have to pass through some conflict. And the best way to pass through that conflict is to learn how to 'assert your reasonable rights', as described in Chapter 7, below.

You have to be willing to fight for your rights; but you also have to make sure that you 'fight fairly'.

And self-assertion skills are the best way to ask for what you want; to say no to what you do not want; to find out how your partner feels; and to communicate your preferences and wishes.

~~~

Myth No.3: Happiness in my relationships is just a matter of 'the luck of the draw'.

Individuals who carry this myth tend to say, 'Just my luck', when things go wrong. This is a total *refusal* to take any responsibility for what happens in the world, as it they were completely passive pawns in a universal game of chess.

However, the truth is that there are certain things we all can control, and certain things we cannot control. It's not always easy to identify which is which, but one way to proceed is to draw two columns on a pad of paper, like this:

A. What I <u>can</u> control ☑	B. What I <u>cannot</u> control ☒
1a. Writing my problems down in this pad or journal. 2a. Trying to analyze, in writing, what happened? What might have caused it? And how might I influence what happens next? 3a. Discussing my couple-problems with a good couple's therapist. 4a. Reading a good book on how to manage a happy relationship.	1b. Who my parents were, and what they taught me about relationships and communication when I was a child. 2b. How my partner will respond when I raise an issue with him/her. 3b. And so on...

Another version of Myth No.3 says that 'relationships are determined by the stars, and they do not need to be managed by us!'

This is a completely false idea. Your capacity to have a relationship was determined in your family of origin. But anything you learned at your mother's (and father's) knee, can be unlearned; and some better relationship skills can be learned and applied instead. (For example, if you were raised in a broadly Christian family, you would have learned from your parents that Santa Claus would come on Christmas Eve, climb down the chimney – even if you didn't have a chimney! – and leave you a present under the Christmas tree. But you no longer believe that. And you no longer believe that the greatest pleasure in life is to be allowed to play out late on a summer's evening! So, if you can change those values and attitudes, you can also change the values and attitudes that you learned about love and marriage from your family of origin.

I have personally learned to become more self-assertive, more skilfully communicative, more loving, more playful, more fun to be with; and much more besides. I learned that I am not a fixed entity. I can change and grow – *and so can you!* But to begin the process, you have to start by taking *some responsibility* for what happens in your relationships! If there's a problem in your life, then you are responsible. Not necessarily in the sense of having 'caused it'. But, if it is ever going to be solved, then you must step up to the wicket and start swinging your cricket bat! Start playing the game as if the outcome mattered! Which it does!

Of course, it takes two to tango, and your partner also bears some (50%!) of the responsibility (on average, over the long haul!) for whatever happens within your relationship. But it is important to step forward and take your side of the responsibility for solving the problem. That tends to work much better than stepping forward to point an accusatory finger at your partner! That will just cause *more problems*. (If you want to have a really powerful relationship with your partner, you have got to stop 'making them wrong'! (Blaming them; criticizing them; and damning them!]).

~~~

Myth No.4: Once my relationship becomes unhappy, I cannot improve it!

This is a very widespread myth. It is a form of fatalism. Or 'fixed mind set'. An 'open mind set' accepts that we can reflect, learn and grow. A fixed mind set believes that things are set in concrete. If things begin to fall apart, there is nothing anybody can do about them, according to this myth.

Sometimes people may invoke God at this point. Or they might think it is their 'karma'. Of course, in a sense it is their karma, if that is what is happening to them. But karma means 'the law of cause and effect'. So all you have to do is to investigate the *causes* of the unhappiness in your relationship, and work at *fixing* the causes, and then you get *new* 'effects'; *new* outcomes; new *karma*; and a *new* life.

So, don't make the mistake of allowing an unhappy relationship to run on and on. (Most couples who seek counselling help do so *about seven years after* the problem first arose!) Stop and ask yourself, perhaps in writing, in a journal, notebook or diary:

"What has gone wrong with my relationship?"

"When did this unhappiness begin?"

"What was happening immediately before I noticed the unhappiness? Did I do something to bring this unhappiness into being? Or did I forget to do something - or fail to do something - which caused this unhappiness to emerge?"

Try to create answers to these questions; arrive at some kind of understanding of what has gone wrong; and then approach your partner to share you understand and/ or concerns with them. (According to Shackleton *et al.* 2018, "...thriving couples carved out time to talk about the minutiae of the day or deeper level issues as needed and this open communication fuelled intimacy").

You should write out how you are going to raise the issue, so it doesn't cause *additional* problems:

Do not imply that your partner is *solely responsible* for the unhappiness. Take your share of responsibility (50% normally); and do that up front! Begin by focusing on what you could have done differently or better. (Their contribution can wait; unless they were primarily responsible for initiating the problem, in which case you need to use the assertiveness skills in Chapter 7, below).

Ask for quiet time in which to discuss your concerns.

Explain your understanding of the problem of unhappiness; and ask your partner to share their perceptions with you. (They may be very different from your perceptions!)

And, if all else fails, consult a good couple's counsellor who has been recommended to you.

~~~

Myth No.5: If my relationship goes wrong, it must be my partner's fault!

This is the common tendency of **blaming others**; and refusing to take any responsibility for what happens in life. This can happen because you were harshly shamed by your mother and/or father when you did anything wrong as a child. As a consequence, you feel intense feelings of shame when your behaviour falls short of some very high standard of expectation which you have internalized. Thus the necessity to *project the 'badness' outside of yourself*, on to the nearest 'scapegoat'.

But if you blame your partner, then you are making your relationship essentially unworkable in the longer term. Elsewhere in this book – see Chapter 1, section 1.2.4(d) - I have described a three-part definition of relationship, the third part of which was this:

> 3. If you want to have a really powerful relationship with your partner, you must *give up criticizing them* or *putting them down*. Instead, aim to use *assertive complaining*, or *conditional appreciation messages*, to get them to change problematical behaviours (provided you will allow them to influence you to change some of your behaviours).

Now think about this. If your partner went around blaming you a lot; insisting that the fault was *always* and *only* on your side: how long do you think your love for them could survive? ("Not long!" I hear you admit!)

And how long before the relationship breaks down under the sheer weight of negativity, and unhappiness? (Again, "Not long!" Just a couple of years of misery, and then divorce. Or worse: Just *ten or fifteen years of intense misery*, and then a miserable divorce!)

So, remind yourself of this: "It takes two to tango!"

"There is normally some fault on both sides, when things go wrong!"

And, even when the problem was wholly initiated by your partner, loving-kindness dictates that you should find a kind and caring way to communicate your desire for change to your partner.

Apply the Golden Rule to this situation.

The Golden Rule dictates that we should not treat another person less well than we would wish to be treated if our roles were reversed! So, if the fault for a problem was wholly on your side, how would you like your partner to raise that issue with you?

"Quietly, kindly, gently, and constructive!" I hear you say.

So, apply the Golden Rule, and treat your partner at least as well as you would wish to be treated if your roles were reversed!

~~~

Myth No.6: I have the right to say and do whatever I like, and my partner should just accept me the way I am!

Before an individual gets involved in a couple relationship, they have a lot of freedom of movement; and freedom of action. They go where we want, within the bounds of possibility, taste and imagination. They have nobody to 'answer to'.

Once we get involved in a relationship, however, we move from independence to *interdependence*. We still retain some of our former freedoms, but we give up some of those freedoms for the benefits of stable, supportive, loving relationship. We expect to be able to depend upon our partner, and they expect to be able to depend upon us, some but not all of the time, for the meeting of some of our needs, including time-based attention, and emotional support.

It is not at all realistic to adopt this position:

> "I want the **benefits** of relationship, but I also want the **freedom** to come and go as I please, regardless of the needs and desires of my partner!"

A relationship is a compromise. If we choose our partner well, we may *often* be able to express our wishes, and not cause any offence to, or conflict with, our partner. But just as a Person X may have expectations of how their partner (Person Y) *should behave* whenever they (Person X) visit their own family of origin (accompanied by Person Y) – so also do they (Person Y) have *the right to ask* Person X to accommodate their needs for particular kinds of behaviour on certain comparable occasions.

If we choose our partner badly, we may find that they are too often – or too negatively – inclined to operate from that part of their personality called 'the *Controlling Parent* ego state'. (The Controlling Parent ego state is copied from the Controlling function in our own parents, back in childhood; including declarations about what the other person 'should' and 'should not' do! [The Controlling Parent ego state has a good and bad side. The good side relates to health and safety issues; while the bad side is about restricting the freedom of others to make their own choices and decisions].)

And if our partner is strongly into operating from the Bad side of their Controlling Parent ego state, then they will go to unreasonable lengths to stop us doing what we wish to do; to make us do what they want us to do; and so on.

In this situation, it is important to know that it is not okay for them to operate from their (bad) Controlling Parent side to your (malleable) Adapted Child side, except in *emergency situations*. For most normal purposes, you and your partner need to be able to relate to each other on the basis of Adult-to-Adult relationship patterns (with some elements of Playful Child and Nurturing Parent ego states added in).

See Appendix B, for a brief introduction to the theory of Transactional Analysis (TA).

When marriage partners operate from 'I have a right to do whatever I like', they are often operating from 'Rebellious Child ego state'; often in response to a partner who is high on Bad Controlling Parent ego state. (See Appendix B and Chapter 7, below).

~~~

Myth No.7: I do not have the right to influence my partner or to ask them to change any aspect of their behaviour.

This myth causes individuals to be very passive in relation to their partner. They ask for nothing; and feel weak and inclined to comply when asked to do something by their partner.

The problem with this approach is that it cannot lead to an equal relationship; and most unequal relationships are either doomed to fail and fall apart; or doomed to fail and stay together in misery.

If you had a choice of one of three kinds of relationships, as follows, which would you choose?

1. A relationship which is doomed to fail and fall apart?

2. A relationship which is doomed to fail and stay together in misery?

3. Or an equal relationship in which you have to fight (fairly, and assertively) – from time to time – to keep the relationship equal; but which is happy and at peace more than 80-85% of the time?

It's no contest, right? You should go for option 3, if you are at all logical and reasonable; and emotionally healthy.

But, in order to do that, you would have to move to a new position. One which asserts that "I have a right to influence my partner, up to, but not more than 50% of the time (on average); and my partner has an equal right to influence me, up to, but not more than 50% of the time (on average)".

If you would both adopt that position, then you would eventually achieve a great relationship of equality, dignity, peace, love and (a little, occasional) conflict (which has to involve 'fair fighting' in *non-aggressive* forms! [See Chapter 7 below].)

~~~

Myth No.8: To be acceptable at all, a relationship has to <u>serve me</u> like a dutiful mother serves her child.

This is the *Omnipotent Baby syndrome,* and some spoiled children take this myth into their marriages, and make a total mess of it. They often seem to be succeeding when they find a partner who operates from attitudes described under Myth No.7 or Myth No.9.

Most often, couples get together because their learning from their families of origin fit each other perfectly. A person who grows up with parents who meshed, because they have this combination of Myth No.7 and Myth No.8, will tend to model themselves on one of those 'myths in action' and seek out a partner who lives from the other, complementary 'myth in action'.

The problem, however, is that the 'needs' of the *Omnipotent Baby partner* are limitless; and the subservience of the *Servant partner* eventually will run out, dry up, and become jaundiced and jaded and rebellious.

The *Servant partner* often exacts a charge for their services which is not expected by the *Omnipotent Baby,* who in time may come to regret ever trying to exploit the *Servant partner.*

Our recommendation is to *Grow Up,* and act from *Egalitarian Adult.* Accept that you "cannot make a *profit* from a relationship".

You must aim to break even. To give as much as you get. To love your partner from a sense of plenitude, and not to try to suck love out of them, like a needy baby.

~~~

Myth No.9: I have to be a perfect partner; to love and serve my partner; and if they become unhappy, then I have failed. So then, I must try harder!

This myth makes the true believer into an anxious wreck, because it is impossible to be a 'perfect partner', and that is what they are trying to be. They are bound to fail, over and over again, because humans can *never* achieve perfection!

When this kind of *Perfectionist Love Servant* chooses an *Omnipotent Baby* type, then the stage is set for a horrible life of demands, followed by failures to fulfil them; anger and retributions from the *Omnipotent Baby*; guilt and shame on the part of the *Perfectionist Love Servant*, followed by more anxiety; more demands; more failures; more guilt and shame; and so on; until they reach the unhappy end to their relationship.

You do not have to be a perfect partner. You can't do it anyway. If you were a *god* or a *goddess*, then you'd be perfect. But remember, you are just a human being.

If it is true that you 'have to serve your partner', then, the Golden Rule would insist, they also 'have to serve you'. And what is the logical balance point? Fifty-fifty! If you have to serve them (fifty percent of the time), then they also have to serve you (the remaining fifty percent of the time!). If you had to be perfect (which you cannot ever be) then your partner would also have to be perfect (which they also cannot ever be!)

If *you* are willing to accept *their* imperfections, then (the Golden Rule would insist) they *must* also accept your imperfections.

If your partner becomes unhappy, you should enquire into the source of their unhappiness, and if it is something you can help to reduce (without undermining your own equality) then you might very well want to help them to overcome their problem of unhappiness.

But if their need is for you to act against the Golden Rule - to allow them to **Win** while you **Lose** – or to allow them to be 'Top Dog', while you serve as the 'Under Dog' - then you should **deny** that you are making them unhappy; and **insist** that *they are making themselves unhappy*, by having *unrealistic expectations* that you will serve them more than they are willing to serve you!

If your partner is unhappy, that does not *necessarily* mean you have failed.

If they are unhappy because you are standing on their foot - or seeing somebody else behind their back; or failing to care for and respect them as much as they care for and respect you - then you are culpable (or blameworthy), and you should stop that.

But if they are unhappy because they want to get more 'juice' out of you than they contribute to you, then *that is **their** problem*; and you certainly have not failed.

To 'succeed' in giving your partner more than they give you, on average, over the medium to long-haul, is actually to 'fail' as a human being.

To succeed as a human being, you have to stand tall, side by side with your partner, in *total equality*! If you give in to their *Omnipotent Baby demands for **unequal** treatment*, then you have failed to be a full human being!)

~~~

Myth No. 10: I can drink as much alcohol as I like and it will not interfere with my capacity to communicate effectively with my partner.

A small amount of alcohol, drunk socially, may have some benefits; though it's a good idea to stick to the healthy limits set by the health authorities in your society. In the UK, the limit is currently 'two units' of alcohol per day. (The new [2016] guideline says: "... men and women who drink regularly should consume no more than 14 units a week - equivalent to six pints of beer or seven glasses of wine" per week. And: "Tough new guidelines issued on alcohol have cut recommended drinking limits and say *there is no such thing as a safe level of drinking*". BBC News)[28].

Many of my most troubled couple-clients have had alcohol problems, either through over-use by one partner or by both. The level of conflict was seen, even by them, to be at its worst when they were drunk; but this did not lead them, automatically, to recognize that they should learn to control their drinking in the interest of the relationship, and/or their own happiness.

Part of the reason why alcohol is a problem, as explained by Transactional Analysis (TA) theory, is this: You effectively knock out the part of you that contains your conscience! And when you knock out your conscience, you tend to behave immorally!

To clarify that theory: Your personality is made up of three parts, as described in Appendix B, below. Those three parts are labelled as distinct 'ego states', or states of the personality. The labels are: Parent ego state; Adult ego state; and Child ego state.

The Parent ego state is copied from our own mother and father, and contains *codes of conduct, rules and conscience.*

When we begin to drink alcohol, after a couple of drinks, the Parent ego state – which is brain-based – is knocked out, or deactivated. Thus our conscience is lost. We are then dependent upon the reasoning capacity of our Adult ego state to keep our behaviour within the normal social range for our society, community and family. After a couple more drinks, the Adult ego state is knocked out, or deactivated. Our life is now being directed by our Child ego state, which is *at best* an emotional seven-year-old, who can be good or evil: and we can even regress further, to age three or four.

Now, our partner steps forward and says something that is frustrating or thwarting or challenging. And we have nothing to guide us but our seven-year-old self, at best! And *a bad-tempered seven year* old is not a good judge of how to respond to frustrations and difficulties!

Thus you can see, drinking alcohol is *disastrous* for romantic relationships, and for much else besides!

If you want to have a happy relationship, you must discipline yourself to stick to the official drinking limits, as an absolute maximum.

~~~

Myth No.11: I can live a sedentary lifestyle; eat as much junk-food as I like; use strong medications; and it will not interfere with my capacity to have a happy relationship.

Sedentary lifestyles – or living like a couch potato, and driving instead of walking or cycling; and avoiding physical activity as a primary goal – has the effect of reducing your physical fitness, as well as your thinking/ feeling capabilities. This is highly likely to impact your sexual vitality adversely. What does the research say?

"A study conducted at the University of California-San Diego tracked 78 middle-aged men on an aerobic exercise program. The subjects exercised at moderate intensity for 60 minutes a day, three or four days a week. After nine months of continuous exercise, these subjects reported that their sex life was more satisfying as far as stamina and orgasms. In comparison, 17 male subjects that performed light workout routines such as walking at a comparatively slower pace stated that they had no substantial improvement in their sex lives".[29]

~~~

With regard to food, we have found that it is important to distinguish between those foods that you need to eliminate, and those you need to include in your diet.

Eating junk food tends to cause, or exacerbate, emotional disturbances, like anxiety, depression and anger. All of these negative emotional states can be tolerated by your partner *when they are **clearly** beyond your control*, and you are **clearly** *trying to do something to improve them*. But if you are angry because you insist upon eating junk food, including trans-fats, then you will damage your relationship with your partner, because there are no mitigating circumstances: meaning no good reasons for your partner to tolerate your anger.

If you make yourself anxious, by over-consuming gluten, caffeine, and sugary foods, this may quickly attach itself to insecurities, and make you unreasonably jealous about your partner's movements; thus precipitating angry conflict, and a sense, in your partner's mind, of being 'made wrong' unjustifiably.

And if you become depressed, through alcohol use or over-consumption of sugary foods, social pressures may dictate that you take antidepressants. But antidepressants commonly cause sexual dysfunction in a high proportion of users; so it is better to manage depression without these drugs; and there are very good alternatives to taking drugs for depression. If you insist upon taking antidepressants, and you suffer from sexual dysfunction, you may seriously undermine the quality of your relationship. But this is not the only way to damage your sexual performance:

"Many other factors seem to affect sexual desire and performance. Alcohol, nicotine, coffee, marijuana, and sugar are some of the pleasure drugs that may reduce sexual vitality, as can many pharmaceuticals, such as tranquilizers, anti-hypertensives, particularly beta-blockers, and birth control pills or hormones...".[30]

~~~

And now for the good foods:

If you want to have a happy sex-love relationship with your partner, then you both need to pay attention to your physical and mental health. There are many foods that enhance sexual health and vitality, such as:

Maca root powder; tarragon; cloves, whole or ground; fresh basil; watermelon, including the skin; truffles; cinnamon; vanilla; natural source vitamin E; and many more besides[31].

Some of the most important foods you can eat for sexual health and vitality include the following:

Avocados; whole almonds and/or flaked almonds; onions, including red onions; garlic, raw on salad vegetables; wild Alaskan salmon; sardines; mackerel; and some white fish; carrots and leafy greens, like cabbage and lettuce, bok choi; blueberries and black raspberries; tomatoes, and red-centred watermelon; figs; cayenne pepper. Also take a vitamin 'C' supplement; plus a good, strong multivitamin; and natural source vitamin E, 400iu in strength; eat foods that provide about 20 mgs of iron per day, or take a supplement; avoid trans-fats, found in processed foods; and keep saturated fats low; eat zinc containing foods, like lamb, sesame seeds, pumpkin seeds, and green peas.

~~~

You should also avoid putting on excess weight, as obesity is known to cause erectile dysfunction in men. Obesity can also lead to negative emotional states, which can reduce sexual health and sexual satisfaction.

You should aim to eat unprocessed foods. Mainly eat salads, or lightly cooked vegetables; with a small amount of meat, perhaps once weekly; and oily fish (like salmon, sardines, mackerel) twice or three times per week. Eat wholegrains (if you can tolerate them; many people cannot eat grains without developing health problems). Eat beans and brown rice (which is the safest grain to eat, if you have problems with other grains). Avoid added sugars; eat fruit sugars in moderation[32]. (See our book on How to Control your Anger, Anxiety and Depression, using nutrition and physical exercise - Taylor-Byrne and Byrne, 2017)[33].

~~~

Myth No.12: I can sleep when I like, and as little as I like, and this will not impair my capacity to have a happy relationship.

This myth ignores the fact that insufficient sleep makes you irritable, and being irritable is not a good way to establish a loving, sexual connection with your partner. Sleep disruption or sleep deprivation also reduces your energy, which makes it less appealing to engage in sexual activity. Sleep apnoea is linked to lower testosterone, which reduces sexual activity directly[34].

Sleep insufficiency interferes with your emotional functioning, and lowers your emotional intelligence, and your reasoning ability. All of these effects of sleep insufficiency will make it more difficult to maintain a happy sex-love relationship, both inside and outside the bedroom.

To be precise, the reduction in emotional intelligence, caused by inadequate sleep, will make it difficult for you to read your partners non-verbal communications, including facial expressions, which will render you unfit to engage in effective communication.

You must arrange to get 7.5 to 9 hours of restful sleep, in a cool, darkened room, each and every night, if you are to be healthy enough to be able to function well sexually, emotionally and otherwise in your relationship. It is also advisable to go to bed at the same time each night, to establish a set sleep pattern; and to always go to bed at the same time as your partner.

Do not take mobile phones or computer screens or TV screens into the bedroom, as they tend to disrupt your sleep, by reducing the production of melatonin, which is the hormone that triggers the onset of sleep.

You should also make dates for love-making, at a frequency that is agreeable to both of you; and do not rely upon *spontaneous* love-making, as this will tend to happen less and less frequently, especially after the honeymoon period (of about two to three years) is over.

~~~

Myth No.13: I do not have to do anything to keep my marriage alive and vibrant. It should just take care of itself.

This is the *Lazy Baby syndrome*. Lazy Baby is passive and unrealistic. People who are controlled by this myth tend to be indifferent to the needs of their partner, and also to be disappointed by the quality of their relationship.

They do not recognize that a relationship is an exchange of equal values. I give to my partner and s/he give back to me.

They have a sense of entitlement. Their basic stance in life is this: "The world should give me what I want and need, without my having to ask for it, and I certainly do not need to *earn* it!"

When the world fails to give them what they desire, they sulk, which is a form of passive, or repressed, anger.

Their partner feels neglected by them, and shuts down communication from their side. This makes Lazy Baby even sulkier, and the relationship spirals downhill pretty fast.

The antidote to the Lazy Baby syndrome is to recognize that love is an exchange of equal values. That, in order to get love, we need to be willing to **create** *loving experiences* for our partner.

In relationships, over the medium to long haul, there's no such thing as a 'free lunch'. In the very short-term, partners may put out more than they get back, but once they notice that the relationship is *fundamentally unequal*, the relationship is heading for termination, or ongoing volatile conflict!

~~~

Myth No.14: Men and women differ significantly in the area of sexuality; and men do not have sexual problems or concerns

While it is true that women and men have different types of sexual organs, which work in different ways; and that many women are more focussed on the love element of sex-love, and many men are more focussed on the sex element of sex-love, there is still a great deal of exaggeration about the fundamental differences.

According to Zilbergeld (1995): "A common myth in our culture deals with the supposed sexual differences between men and women. According to this bit of fantasy, female sexuality is complex, mysterious, and full of problems, while male sexuality is simple, straightforward, and problem-free". (Page 9)[35].

This author goes on to argue that "...men really do have concerns about sex, even though they may try to pretend that this isn't so". (Page 13). Some of these concerns related to premature ejaculation, erectile dysfunction, and inability to achieve orgasm. Others arise out of the fact that they have no idea how to pleasure a woman, and they often realize that their ill-informed approaches to sexual intimacy are not having the desired effect upon their female partner.

There are, of course, some things that men need to learn about the location of the female centre of sexual excitation, which is the *clitoris*, at the top of the vagina, hiding under a little hood. (See Appendix G; and ask your *established, intimate*, female partner to introduce you to her clitoris!). And there really are things that individual women need to learn about what interests and satisfies their male partner. (So ask him!)

Women have often been short-changed in the bedroom, because their male partners have not learned the seat of the female orgasm (the clitoris), and men have been similarly victimized by the same mythology of penis-centred sex that they learned from unreliable sources.

As Zilbergeld writes: "...men have been duped about sex. They have accepted unrealistic and, in fact, super-human standards by which to measure their equipment (penis), performance, and satisfaction, thus ensuring a perpetual no-win situation. Whatever men do, it's somehow not enough, not when compared to the standards they learned". (Page 16).

The final point here, of course, has to be that the so-called 'sex education' that men acquire from their peers, and various myth-making authors, is grossly misleading. (Especially the 'Big Steel Cock' myth!). The myth-makers who misled the author of this book, by promoting a delusional model of human sexuality, included: Henry Miller, D.H. Lawrence, Harrold Robbins, Ian Fleming, and others. (See Appendix H on one man's inadequate sex education).

2.3 Comments on myths

There are probably many more unrealistic myths that affect how individuals see their relationships, and their roles within those relationships. But this brief review of the most common fourteen should help you to know some of the main pitfalls to avoid in creating or working on your own relationship.

Based on our observations of individuals outside of couple's therapy contexts, we think there is a fifteenth myth which goes like this:

"Since I have failed to make a success of two (or three, or more) marriages, or couple relationships, therefore I have to now *give up completely!*"

This myth, which does not show up in couple's therapy, because the individual has quit the 'arena' completely, is probably based on a combination of shame, fear of failure, and perfectionism.

Individuals who suffer from Myth No. 15 should be told the story of *Robert the Bruce*, the king of Scotland, who was initially defeated by the English army in battle, and ended up hiding in a cave. In that cave he saw a spider swinging on a thin strand of web. The spider was trying to swing itself from one wall of the cave to another, in order to build a web; and it failed over and over and over again. But it refused to give up. It kept on trying; and trying; and trying; until it finally succeeded.

Robert the Bruce was inspired by this tenacity and persistence, and he went back to wage many battles which resulted in the independence of Scotland from England in 1314.

From this lesson we gained the injunction: "Try, try and try again!"

And that is what people should do who have been unsuccessful in love in the past. Try, try and try again; preferably after having some psycho-therapy or counselling to unearth the sources of their problems with relationships.

Or, as Winston Churchill famously said: "Never, ever, ever, ever, ever give up!"

~~~

Study guidelines: Tick that you've read this chapter once: ☐ - Before you more on to Chapter 3, please read this chapter a second time: ☐ - And a third time: ☐

~~~

When reading and re-reading this chapter, please underline those points that seem most important to you.

Make notes in the margins, as necessary, as quick reminders of the content of a paragraph or a page.

And turn down the corner of the page, when the content is so important you want to find it again, quickly and easily. Also, add important points, with their page numbers, in your own index to this book, in Appendix 'L', below.

~~~

Chapter 3: The case of Ken Clark and his family of origin

3.1 Preamble

In this chapter we outline a case study of a man who, because of his family of origin, had a disastrous approach to relationships. He spent many years in total unhappiness. But he persisted in trying to find a way forward, and at last he did succeed.

3.2 Family of origin

Ken Clark had the great misfortune of being born to a couple who had an arranged marriage. They had not loved each other. They had not been friends. They were brought together by a 'match maker'. They had a marriage of convenience. His mother wanted a home and a breadwinner, and his father had a small farm. His father wanted sex, and the comforts of home, and his mother had been a domestic servant and knew how to keep a home.

When Ken was growing up, he was unaware of the nature of his home life. It was just 'home life'; just the way it was; just the norm. He did not know that there were families where mother and father *liked each other*; *loved* each other; *kissed* each other; held hands; cuddled; and *enjoyed* each other's company.

He did not know that there were families where the parents took *a delight* in their children's individuality; their vitality; their sense of fun.

He thought misery and coldness were the *norm*.

But, at some level, he *knew he was unhappy*. He knew he did not enjoy being at home. So, from his early teens, he arranged to be out of the house all day, and most of the evening, most days of the week.

Then, at the age of eighteen years, he left home, and moved to a city about two hundred miles from his parents' home town. He was determined never to go back again.

3.3 'Escaping' from home

Ken got himself a job, and a place to live. Then he found places to dance at the weekend, where he hoped to find a girl who would like him. He had been attending dance halls in his town of origin, since the age of sixteen or seventeen, without much luck with the girls. He had had a few dates, but they tended to peter out after the first or second date.

Now he was trying again, in a new city. And again, he had a few, occasional dates, but nothing came of them. He did not seem to be able to attract a steady date.

He joined the army, and met lots of girls through his work. But nobody seemed to be keen on him. He was not a bad looking young man. He looked a bit shy and he had no small talk. But he always dressed in a fashionable way, and tried to be friendly.

He did manage to establish a steady dating arrangement with one of his fellow soldiers; a girl about two years younger than himself; and she took him home for Christmas. But during that holiday, something went wrong, which resulted from his inability to be genuine, honest, consistent in the self-story that he told her. He did not have a solid sense of self; and he was not self-accepting. He 'put on a show'; or had a 'false self'.

He came out of the army prematurely, because he hit a major social-emotional crisis; a serious rejection by his male peers. He licked his wounds, and moved on to a new town. There he met a woman six years older than himself, and they established a sexual relationship. She told him up front that she tended to fall in love with a man, to love him exclusively for about six or eight weeks, and then to fall in love with somebody else. Ken assured her that this would not happen in his case. (This is an indication of *the power of self-delusion*).

About eight weeks after their relationship began, she was, as predicted, unfaithful to him.

This was a strong echo of how his mother had been with his father. But he did not pause long enough to enquire into the possible connection between those two facts.

But if Werner Erhard had been present, he would have told Ken that we tend to marry somebody who is a lot like our parent of the opposite sex. So, in a sense, Ken had "married his mother". Of course, if Werner had told him this, Ken would have insisted that he had left his mother behind when he was fourteen years old – by spending very little time at home. That he had severed his connection completely, at the age of eighteen years, by leaving her in their city of origin, and moved hundreds of miles from her.

Werner would have countered that: "You are still carrying her in your head and your heart"; but Ken would have been unable to comprehend or digest that information, at this stage.

3.4 'Escaping' from the original escape

When Ken realized that his girlfriend had betrayed him, he moved on again, to a new city, leaving her behind. But in that town he failed to find a girlfriend, so he moved again, this time, back to his city of origin – four years after leaving. He touched base with his family, and found his mother had left his father, and gone off with a new lover. So Ken was spared the difficulty of seeing her – if difficulty it would be. (What did he know about such things?)

Now Ken got a job, and returned to dancing at the weekends, in the same dance halls he had frequented four to six years earlier. And in one of those dancehalls he re-met a girl he had danced with when he was eighteen years old, in the city to which he had originally escaped. They began dating once or twice each week. But it did not go very well. For some reason, he would not hold her hand when they were walking in the street; even though he gave her sexual satisfaction in the evenings, in her apartment, through digital stimulation. (She was not willing to have intercourse with him).

If David Wallin (2007) had been there, he would have said that Ken had an obviously 'avoidant attachment style'. He did not want anybody to get too close to him. And the most likely explanation was that his mother had overly controlled him, for which purpose she had to 'get hold of him' – to get in close. And she used this closeness to hurt him, punish him and control him, and to verbally and emotionally abuse him, and to threaten him with further punishment.

This new relationship (with his former girlfriend, Jill) was not very satisfying to Ken, and after a few months he decided to leave. It was obvious to any Martian watching their parting that she did not love him. She did not care for him. She was attached to him for some *unhealthy* reason.

3.5 Moving on again...

Ken left; and once again went hundreds of miles away, to a new city; a different one from the previous 'escape'. There he got a job – or rather, a series of jobs – and began looking for a girlfriend. But this time he was not able to use dancehalls, because this city had a very different cultural matrix from the ones he already knew. He did not feel able to dance or socialize in this new way. So he spent all his time in political activity: all day, every day.

Some psychodynamic psychotherapists would say that this was just a 'displacement activity' – an ersatz substitute for dating and mating. Politics would not betray him. Politics would not try to control him. And politics could not reject him, or refuse to allow him to *perform, act,* and 'be there'.

Then a very strange thing happened. He was invited to a 'dinner party' by some of his senior colleagues from his political party. He went along, at seven o'clock on the appointed Saturday night, and found that, not only were his hosts present, but they had also invited a young woman –

somebody he knew from his political activities. Let's call her Loren!

Anyway, the meal was very luxurious and enjoyable, and there was plenty of wine – (which would have knocked out his 'Parent ego state'. See Appendix B). After the party, he and Loren left together, and ended up in bed together. Ken 'failed to get out of the bed again'. He was smitten; and in a sense he had 'nowhere else to go'. Of course, he had his own shared flat; but it was cold and empty. He was now 'glued to Loren'. And their marriage followed soon afterwards. (It was not a romantic marriage. There were no protestations of love. She demanded to know if he thought there was any difference between 'marriage' and 'living together', and if there was, then she wanted to be married. She said this with an angry face, and with tears running down her cheeks. He did not ask: "What the f*** is happening here?" He simply replied: "Okay. Let's get married". Nobody proposed. There were no love songs. (Indeed, he refused to go to see the movie, 'Love Story', with her! [Because it was 'too soppy'? Who knows? Ken was not conscious of his motivations, in this, or any other respect]!)

The average Martian observer would, at this stage, have scratched their head and said: "Hang on! How is this possible? He has just been fitted up with an 'arranged marriage', just like his mother and father. But in this culture, arranged marriages are as rare as hen's teeth! How come he hasn't noticed that he is repeating a pattern from his parent's lives?"

And if Sigmund Freud had been there, he would have answered his Martian interlocutor like this: "That's how it goes. We humans engage in *repetitive compulsions* all our lives. We are *compelled* to *repeat* patterns from the past, because we are *creatures of habit*, wired up by our experience!"

3.6 The nature of Ken and Loren's marriage...

The marriage between Ken and Loren was unhappy from the start – unhappy even before the marriage was formalized. They had frequent upsets. She would become angry at him for some neglect; some omission; some absence; some incompetence; some disappointment. He would feel hurt; he would sulk. Near the beginning of the relationship, long before the formal marriage, he would leave their apartment early in the morning with this song going around and around in his sore, unhappy, depressed mind: "And it's too late baby now; it's too late. Though we really did try to make it. Something inside *has died*, and I have tried but *I just can't fake it!*"

"But hang on a minute", our Martian wants to say. "If he knows something has died; and he thinks he just can't fake it; why does he go ahead and marry her?"

Freud and Erhard step forward and chorus in perfect harmony: "Because that was what Ken saw his parents do to and with each other! They were *miserable*, and they *stayed with each other*. And that is all he knows, when it comes to 'models' of relationship!"

3.7 The horrible, slow end of the relationship...

So they got married, and Ken turned out to be just like his dad, in one obvious respect: He had no idea how to make money! He was stony broke all of the time!

And Loren was just like his mother in at least one obvious respect. She berated him for his lack of enterprise; his lack of earning power; his passivity and poverty.

Ken did not spot these parallels. And they soldiered on. He took some technical training to try to increase his earning power, and did for a while; but he was obsessed by his political activities, and he recognized that he was not sufficiently well educated to be good enough at politics. So he enrolled in a college course – full time – to study politics and economics – and thus lost him his income from work.

Loren's respect for Ken – if ever there had been any – was now at rock bottom. And after four years of marriage, he suspected she was having an affair. And indeed he caught her kissing a political colleague, and she admitted they were having an affair.

But still he could not leave her. (If Werner Erhard heard this story, wh would comment: "Just as Ken's father could not leave Ken's mother when he discovered she was having [yet another] affair! Whatever they did before, you can bet they'll do it again!" And if Freud were here, he might say: "And this is another example of the 'repetition compulsion' [or tendency to repeat past behaviours]!").

And so they soldiered on. Ken felt miserable. He could no longer have sex with Loren, because she continued to have an affair with her lover. But he could not leave her; until, two years later, he began to break down. He was going out of his mind.

And when they finally split, Loren was pregnant – and nobody knew who the father was. ("See", says the Martian. "Another repetition compulsion". "Tell me more", says Freud. "Well", says the Martian: "Ken's father used to ask his neighbours if they'd seen a red-haired milkman hanging around his house, when two of his youngest children were born. And he [Ken's father] eventually proved that his youngest daughter could not have been his, because she was born twelve months after he and his wife had stopped sleeping together!")

So Ken walked away in a very bad psychological state. And he spent eighteen months licking his wounds before he could date another woman.

3.8 The post-split reckoning...

Years later, Ken reflected up what had happened between him and Loren, and came up with the following conclusions:

1. We are shaped by our family of origin.

2. Our patterns of relationship are dictated by the patterns of relating that we witnessed between our mother and father in the first five to seven years of life. (We copy and record these patterns in images and feelings, and store them non-consciously in long-term memory for later use).

3. We develop an "attachment style" to our mother, and later to our father.

The three attachment styles are these: *Avoidant* (which Ken was); *Anxious-ambivalent* (which Loren was); and *Secure* (which Ken eventually learned to be, after much therapy!) (These attachment styles are stored non-consciously as *Internal Working Models* of relationship, which we use later in life, in our adult relationships).

4. Our attachment style asserts itself – from non-conscious levels of mind - in our romantic relationships, when we have grown up. (The idea that we can simply decide, as follows - "I will never relate to my partner like my father related to my mother" - is pure fantasy. The conscious functions of the brain-mind are much weaker than the non-conscious, habit-based, emotive functions of the brain-mind).

5. Our psychological wiring for relationship exerts control over us through the 'compulsion to repeat old patterns' – which is commonly called 'the repetition compulsion', or 'patterns of learned behaviour'; or 'habitual ways of relating'!

6. Once we are wired up (non-consciously) by our childhood experience, only an intensive therapeutic intervention can change the wiring.

7. Some, but not all, of the therapeutic work can be based on self-help; but the idea that "whatever is *created in relationship* can only be *reformed in relationship*" has a great deal of validity. Therefore, at least some of this therapeutic reformation of the personality has to be done in a relationship with a caring other, who has to have a secure attachment style, and who must also 'know' (consciously or non-consciously) *how to re-parent an adult person.*

8. The final resolution of our childhood shaping for particular relationship patterns involves reformulation and revision of our 'Inner Couple'. We have to move beyond the 'movie in our heads' of mother and father relating to each other in negative ways, to a revised movie (which is a fantasy!), created in psychotherapy, in which mother and father *change the way they relate to each other, from a negative pattern to an actively loving and caring, positive pattern.* (See Chapter 11).

9. The result of the work described in item 8 above is this: We still engage in *repetition compulsions*, but now they are repetitions of the *revised (fantasy)*

relationship in our heads, instead of the original relationship which we actually witnessed as a young child.

3.9 Postscript on Ken's new relationship pattern

If Ken Clark had not done the hard labour of analysing his childhood, and relating it to his adult relationship patterns, he would still be living in misery – leaving for work every morning in a state of raw, emotional misery – listening to the voice in his head singing the mournful song: "And it's too late baby now; it's too late; Though we really did try to make it...".

Instead, because he did *the hard work of going through the necessary psychotherapy,* he has now been happily married to his best friend for thirty-two years, and happily related to her for thirty-eight years.

You too can do the work needed to change your non-conscious patterns which guide your relationship feelings and behaviours.

The resulting happiness and joy, and peace of mind, is a reward well worth working for!

~~~

Study guidelines

Tick that you've read this chapter once: ❑

Before you more on to Chapter 4, please read this chapter a second time: ❑

And a third time: ❑

~~~

When reading and re-reading this chapter, please underline those points that seem most important to you.

Make notes in the margins, as necessary, as quick reminders of the content of a paragraph or a page.

And turn down the corner of the page, when the content is so important you want to find it again, quickly and easily.

Also, add important points, with their page numbers, in your own index to this book, in Appendix 'L', below.

~~~

Chapter 4: Communication skills for couples

4.1 Introduction

> "Professor Howard Markman, director of the Centre for Marital and Family Studies at the University of Denver, Colorado, says he can predict which relationships will fail. The biggest sign is poor communication and inability to handle conflict". (Agnew, 1996).

One of the main things that we (Jim and Renata) agree upon, as a couple, is this: *Human communication is very difficult; and most people are not particularly good at doing it.*

One of the main reasons that couples do not communicate well is that they do not realize how difficult it is to get your message across to another person. Most people assume that what they say will be understood by their partner in exactly the way they intended it to be understood – instead of being distorted by interpretations based on the hearer's background.

Communication is not at all what most couples think it is.

In the next section, below, we will begin to define communication; and then move on to describe forms of listening.

After that we will look at some of the things that people say and do that block the communication between one person and their partner.

We will then look at 'active listening', as opposed to merely 'hearing' your partner's words.

Then we will introduce a helpful process for facilitating communication between couples, called 'formal listening time'.

And finally, we will take a look at 'barriers' and 'boundaries' in couple relationships.

4.2 What is communication?

Communication is about 'creating experiences for others'. If I smile at you and say, "I'd really appreciate it if you would pass the salt", I am creating an experience for you. Most people receiving that communication will tend to respond positively: happy to cooperate. They will experience my communication as respectful, kind, and cooperative. The salt will be passed to me, with pleasure; perhaps eight or nine times out of ten!

But not everyone will be happy with this kind of request, and not everyone will respond so cooperatively – because this communication – this *created experience* – does not go **directly** to the listener's 'receiver of information'. In fact, it has to pass through two or three barriers. The first is ambient noise. The second is internal distractions. And the third is the listener's own *interpretation filters*.

(1) *Ambient noise.* All communication messages are affected by some degree of noise. Anything that distracts the listener from hearing the message, or hearing it clearly, or hearing it fully – counts as 'noise' or interference. If loud rock music is playing in the background, the person to whom I spoke might not hear the word 'salt'; or might not realize I am speaking to **them**; or might be so irritated by the rock music that they cannot pay attention to anything else.

(2) *Internal distractions.* Also, if they are emotionally preoccupied by some negative experience in their own life, then that may block their ability to *hear* me; to *attend* to what I am trying to communicate; or to *understand* 'where I am coming from'.

(3) *Interpretation.* Every attempt to communicate anything to anybody must pass through their 'interpretation filters', which are shaped by that person's social experience, from childhood onwards. If the person to whom I am addressing my communication shares a common background with me, and we have had a lengthy relationship, there is a very good chance that they will most often understand what I am saying in pretty much the way I intended it to be understood. However, if we have *divergent* backgrounds; or the person is under a lot of *stress*; they are much more likely to *misunderstand* what I'm trying to communicate.

What kind of experiences should we try to create for our sex-love partner?

Some theorists, especially within Attachment theory and Affect regulation theory would argue that you should try to help your partner to "feel felt".

That means that *you create for them the experience that you have a good idea what they are feeling,* and you *validate those feelings;* often by 'feeling along with them', which is one definition of empathy.

Somewhere, Oprah Winfrey has argued that there are three questions your partner will normally have in mind when evaluating how you are relating to them, and those questions seem to be:

1. Did you *hear* me?

2. Did you *see* me?

3. And did my statement *mean anything* to you?

And I would add these questions:

1. Do you *love* me?

2. Do you *care* for me?

3. Do you *respect* me?

4. Are you on *my side*?

5. And, are you *safe* to relate to? Can I *risk* saying what is in my heart? Or will you *step on my feelings* without knowing the pain you can cause me to feel?

4.3 Forms of listening

There is also the problem that *listening takes different forms.* The three most obvious forms are these:

1. *Passive listening*, or merely hearing, with no real engagement with the content of the speech.

2. *'Leading responses'*, which occur when the listener insists upon imposing their own agenda upon the speaker's life. These responses are often referred to as 'roadblocks to communication', because they effectively prevent an ongoing stream of communication. But worse than that, they normally result in a breakdown of communication, attended by negative feelings.

And:

3. *'Active listening'*, in which the listener responds to the speaker by 'reflecting' back the *meaning* of what the speaker said, or the *emotional content* of what the speaker said.

Passive listening is destructive of relationships, because it shows a lack of regard for the speaker. Indeed, it can signal *contempt* or *indifference*. The person who nods and says, 'Yeah!', while operating on automatic, with little real conscious awareness of what the speaker is saying, is the archetypal passive listener. ('Yeah, yeah, yeah', while look away, is even more offensive and hurtful!)

Leading responses often involve ignoring the other person's concerns, or insulting their intelligence by implying that the listener knows better how to solve the speaker's problem than the speaker ever could!

Let us now take a look in detail at

- the major 'roadblocks to communication';

- some guidelines for active listening; And also:

- some guidelines for an exercise called 'listening time', (which is an opportunity for one person to talk through their concerns, with active listening from the other person, but not in the context of informal conversation. This exercise can be used to help your partner to resolve their own concerns and difficulties, without sending 'roadblocks'.)

4.4 Roadblocks to communication

According to the creator of the 'EST Communications Workshop', Werner Erhard, most people cannot communicate because what they call communication is actually *not communication*. Most people confuse 'communication' and 'speaking'. But 'speaking' is not 'communication' for the following very simple reason:

Firstly, in my effort to 'communicate with you', I create an experience for you. I might, for example, try to create a 'word picture' for you. But then:

Secondly, you 'recreate', or 'interpret' my word picture. You 'make it mean something'. And that is what Werner Erhard called 'your listening'. Your 'listening' is your already-always pattern of interpretation of what it means to be spoken to by somebody who looks like me; sounds like me; and who uses the kinds of words I just used. You are already wired up by your experience to *pre-determine what it means* that I said what I said.

Your idea of what 'communication is' comes from *your experience* in your family of origin. And just as your model of relationship comes from your 'Inner Couple' (of mum and dad), so also does your communication style – your 'listening' - come from them – and in particular from the one which is your "Adult Role Model". (When you were very young, you will have 'decided' [non-consciously] to model yourself on one of your parents. Possibly the parent of the same sex, but not necessarily. This is normally the parent you admired the most; and they became your model for 'how to be an Adult'; which we call "your Adult role model". The other parent, then, becomes your 'Mate Model', or your image of how your future 'love mate', or marriage partner, will relate to you).

Of course, when you went to school, your communication style may have changed somewhat, to fit into that environment. Your 'listening' went through some kinds of *subtle* or *not-so-subtle* changes. However, later in life, when the 'chips are down' (or the stress level is up) in your adult sex-love relationship, you will tend to revert to communicating like your Adult Role Model (which is to say, mother or father).

No matter who your parents were, you are very likely to have learned some bad communication habits from them. (The less *emotionally intelligent* your parents were, the worse your communication style – or 'listening' - is likely to be – until you work on it!) The most ubiquitous of these bad habits is the use of 'roadblocks' in your communication.

Roadblocks to communication are the opposite of 'active listening'. Active listening involves attempting to faithfully follow what your partner is trying to communicate to you. But roadblocks to communication are attempts to take control of the communication, and to divert it into well-worn channels which suit the so-called 'listener', and not the speaker!

This is most often done by

- sending solutions,

- giving advice, or

- ignoring the other person's concerns.

Sometimes some of this may work okay, especially if your partner is relaxed and calm. But if your partner is under a lot of stress, then using those kinds of 'leading responses' will in fact block your communication; and cause it to break down, with the consequence that you may both end up feeling frustrated, angry and/or depressed.

The most common roadblocks, which we teach to our couple's therapy clients, are as follows:

Roadblock 1. Sending solutions: Here you assume that you know what the solution to your partner's problem happens to be, even before you have had time to hear the whole description of the problem. This can upset your partner, because they feel misunderstood, and also they may feel that their intelligence is being insulted. Your (unhelpful) 'solution' may be taken to imply that you know best what is good for your partner, and they are not as bright as you!

Antidote: The best antidote to falling into the roadblock of 'sending solutions' to your partner is this:

When you notice that you are about to *send a solution* to your partner, check to see if this is what they want.

You could say, "Are you *asking me* to help you to solve this problem?" If they say, "Yes, I am. Would you?", then it's safe to proceed to offer any solution that seems appropriate to you (especially if you preface your 'solution' with some version of this statement: "It seems to me that...").

But if your partner looks shocked, and says: "No! I'm *just telling you* how I feel!", then you should avoid sending solutions, and instead *use the skills of active listening*, which are described in section 4.5, below.

How would you *feel* if your partner quickly sent you a solution, every time you mentioned a problem to them? Probably not happy! So if you want to avoid making your partner unhappy, and road-blocking your communication with them, it is important to refrain from sending unrequested or uninvited solutions.

~~~

Roadblock 2. Giving advice: This is similar to sending solutions. But it can be even worse, in that, when you send a solution, there is not necessarily the implication that your partner 'should' implement it. But when you give advice, it is often difficult to avoid the implication that you think your partner 'should' proceed in the prescribed manner or direction. Your partner may feel they are being not only treated as an *ignorant fool*, but also that they are *under pressure* to implement your uninvited advice!

Antidote: Similar to the previous roadblock, the antidote here is to notice that you are about to dispense advice, and then tell yourself: "I'd better *check with my partner* to see if they want me to advise them; or if they are just letting off steam; or hoping that, by talking to me, they might be able to clarify their problem for themselves!" Then ask your partner: "Would you like me to *actively listen* to you, or are you *seeking advice*?"

Whatever your partner's response is, you should proceed accordingly. If they want you to *listen actively*, then use the skills described in section 4.5, below.

~~~

Roadblock 3. Ignoring your partner's concerns: Your partner may be very worried about something which *looks threatening to them*. (It might look *different* to you!) If you ignore their concern, and imply that it is not at all as fearful as they think, you are *impugning their judgement,* and 'making them wrong'. And you cannot have a powerful relationship with somebody if you insist upon *making them wrong; criticizing* them; or *patronizing* them.

Antidote: Remind yourself that it's okay for a person to have fears and anxieties. That you do not have to close them down. That you can handle having a partner who is *worried* about something. Remind yourself that you have not married a *nincompoop*; and that your partner is capable of *managing their own emotions*, with perhaps a *little* help from you, from time to time – *when they **ask** for it!*

Also, you can apply the **Golden Rule**. Treat your partner at least as well as you would wish to be treated by them, if your roles were reversed. If you were sharing a problem with your partner, would you want them to *ignore* your concerns? If the answer is 'No', then you should not, morally, ignore your partner's concerns.

~~~

Roadblock 4. Attempting to reassure your partner (when they have *not* sought reassurance): It might seem counterintuitive to say that reassurance has a *negative effect* upon relationships. Nevertheless, this is *true*, especially when your partner is feeling stressed. The negative effect comes from the gulf between your partner's *perception* (for example, that they are facing a threat or danger), and your attempt to *deny* that such a threat or danger exists. You are effectively *making them wrong*; or *discounting their feelings*; and that will cause them to feel upset, and alienated from you.

Antidote: When you notice that you are about to try to **reassure** your partner that their fears are unfounded, or something like that: stop! Ask yourself this question: "Has my partner **asked me** to reassure them? Have we talked about this to the point where I am **justified** in thinking that my partner is so *depowered* by their problem, and that they are so stuck in *Child ego state*, that they need me to help with some 'external affect regulation' – (which means *soothing their emotions*)? If yes, then you could say:

"I think you have reached the point where you need me to reassure you and comfort you. Am I right about that?"

And if they say, "Yes, you are right!", then your attempts to reassure them will not act as a roadblock, but rather as a relationship strengthener! (Because it shows sensitivity, care and respect!)

But if they say, 'No, I do not feel overly upset, and I am not asking you for reassurance', you should stick to active listening (as described in Part 2, below).

~~~

Roadblock 5. Blaming, criticizing and shaming: If your partner shares something with you, and you imply that they are to blame, they may feel that you have shamed them. This will not only cause them to feel bad (emotionally; which may feel just as bad as a physical injury to them), but they will almost always 'curdle' towards you. That is to say, the connection between you will become difficult, blocked and 'soured'.

If you criticize any aspect of your partner's behaviour, they may well feel shamed and put down (especially if they are under stress; but even if they are quite relaxed, they may be prone to 'crumple' under criticism!) So you must be very careful to *avoid **blaming** and **shaming** statements*.

(Some people are more prone to feeling shamed when anybody criticizes their behaviour: [See Joines and Stewart, 2002]).

Shame is the feeling that we get when we are *dramatically diminished* in the eyes of another. "From hero to zero", as the American vernacular puts it! (And even though Eleanor Roosevelt argued that 'Nobody can make you feel anything without your permission' – successfully ignoring criticisms and put-downs, or quickly discarding them, is *much easier **said** than **done**. **Why is this so?** Partly because we are socialized, by our family or origin, and our schooling, to feel certain ways when certain things are said or done to us. And partly because psychological pain and physical pain are mediated through overlapping areas of the brain)[36].

Antidote: Blaming, criticizing and shaming often are triggered by the emergence of a problem which affects both partners. Very often one partner will blame the other for having caused this problem, and the other partner will 'crumple' – or experience a huge drop in their sense of self-worth or self-esteem. This tendency is exacerbated by the *defensive habit* of trying to *deny responsibility* for any problems that emerge. The antidote to this problem has a number of elements:

(1) Try to convince yourself that, *if there's a problem in your life, then **you** are responsible* – not necessarily in the sense of having *caused* it, but certainly in the sense that, if you do not work at solving the problems in your life, you can be sure the Lone Ranger (or Batman, or Wonder Woman) is not going to ride up and sort it out for you! The problem will most likely get worse if you try to 'solve it' by blaming your partner; or by trying to ignore it. (If you try to ignore a problem, there is a good chance that your bad feelings about it will grow and grow, until you cannot suppress them any further; and you may then explode angrily! This also will not enhance your relationship; but will in fact make things worse!) The alternative is to work on the problem, collaboratively, with your partner, like this:

(a) Separate the people from the problem. Write the problem on a sheet of paper or card; place it on a table or similar surface; and stand side by side with your partner and ask them to help you to work at solving the problem. (The problem is the problem; your partner is *not* the problem!)

(b) Talk in terms of *interests* rather than *positions*. (See Chapter 6: Sub-section 6.9.3, on *Taking responsibility*).

(c) Or try a trade-off: "If I do X for you, will you do Y for me?" Trading off is based on the principle that you have the right to influence your partner, up to 50% of the time, or in 50% of conflict situations; while they have the right to influence you, up to, but not exceeding 50% of the time. This is the principle of *equality in relationships*.

(d) Or try a 'conditional appreciation message': "I'd really appreciate it if you would do X (instead of Y)". (See Chapter 7).

~~~

Roadblock 6. Excessive or inappropriate questioning: In E-CENT[37] counselling, we teach that questioning your partner can cause them to feel threatened. This is because questioning can "re-stimulate" old, childhood memories of being 'interrogated' by a punitive parent or teacher, who questioned your partner to collect evidence against them! The fact that this is *not* your motivation is irrelevant. You have to be sensitive to *how your partner is actually wired up*, by their experience, and not insist that "they *should not* be wired up in that way!" It will not help to insist that "they should know where I am coming from!"

Antidote: One cause of excessive and inappropriate questioning is this: We may often have a tendency to ask a question instead of making a statement. (There is a *statement* under the question, or behind the question, which remains *unstated*!) These kinds of indirect statements (masquerading as questions) are 'rhetorical devices' which are picked up by the listener as emotional manipulation, or indirect, negative messages. It would be much better - if you find you are asking a question that has a statement buried underneath it - to *just make the statement* instead of asking a question.

You could also be prone to ask questions in order to maintain control over your partner – which is an excessive and inappropriate use of your *Controlling Parent* ego state. The solution to this problem is to 'grow your Adult ego state'! (See Appendix B for more on these concepts).

Another cause of excessive and inappropriate questioning can be a feeling of *anxious insecurity*. This *anxious insecurity* may be an expression of an *insecure attachment style*. (See Chapter 6 [section 6.10 - 6.12(b)] for more on attachment styles). The excessive, inappropriate questions, in this case, are designed to collect *reassuring information*, so the questioner can 'go back to sleep'; or shut down their anxiety, and feel more secure. If this is the trigger for your excessive or inappropriate questions, then you should work on your problem of anxiety, perhaps with a counsellor, or a good book on the subject to how to reduce and control anxiety. Or work with *an attachment counsellor* on your *attachment style*.

On the other hand, your anxiety may be mainly caused by sedentary lifestyle, sugary diet, too much caffeine, and other lifestyle factors, such as inadequate or disrupted sleep. In which case you should work on your lifestyle, using the services of a lifestyle coach or counsellor, or read a good book on how to reduce your anxiety through lifestyle changes.

~~~

<u>Roadblock 7</u>. **Diagnosing**: This is a process whereby you can be seen to have assumed to Top Dog position, and also to be implying that you are 'the one who knows'. And, additionally, the one who knows that there is something wrong with your partner – and that the roots of their errors have to be *diagnosed* by you, and *made clear to them*. Well, you'd better have a suitcase packed if you want to do a lot of this kind of 'blemishing' of your partner.

Diagnosing is a form of relatively *negative labelling*; or 'putting your partner in a box'. And negative labelling is a form of *put-down*. *Diagnosing* shows up in encounters where one partner tries to figure out 'what's wrong' with their partner, with the implication that *they should change* in line with the diagnosis. This is called 'making your partner over', instead of *accepting them* the way they are. Or trying to change 'them', instead of trying to *influence, by fair means, a particular **behaviour** of theirs*.

Antidote: The main antidote to diagnosing what is 'wrong' with your partner, is this: Learn to accept that *your partner, as such, is OK exactly the way they are*. If there is a valid, tangible problem - (which is one that affects your personal domain: your time; your person; or your resources or possessions) – and it is clearly *caused* by your partner's *behaviour*, then you can use assertiveness skills instead of criticizing. (See Chapter 7). You should begin with a *conditional appreciation message* – like, "I'd really appreciate it if you'd do X instead of Y".

And if this doesn't work, then you move up to *Constructive Confrontation*: ("When you do X, I feel Y, because..."). This is an improvement because you have now substituted *assertive complaining* for *negative labelling and diagnosing*. It's okay to *assertively complain*, because assertive complaining is about *a behaviour*, and not about *your partner's essence*. (This skill, of *constructive confrontation*, will be explored fully in Volume 2).

Secondly, diagnosing is the stock-in-trade of the human tendency to operate from what is called 'the *Critical Parent* ego state'. (See Appendix B). The Critical Parent ego state can be recognized by the following features. Finger pointing. Scowling. Using words like "You should...".

"You must...". "Everybody knows...". "Don't...". And the ant
problem of over-use of Critical Parent ego state is this: *Grow you*
state. (See Appendix B).

Thirdly, diagnosing what is 'wrong' with your partner can also be driven
by a psychological problem which is called 'splitting'. Splitting is where –
classically – a baby comes to think of *caring mother* – who comes with food
when they are hungry – as 'Good Mother'; and *slow or absent mother* –
when they are hungry – as 'Bad Mother'. These are quick, emotive
evaluations of an experience, which is attributed incorrectly as belonging
to *Two Different Mothers. The Good One and the Bad One.*

As we grow up, we retain this primitive evaluation system, and –
especially when we are under a lot of stress, or are tired - we tend to split
significant others throughout our lives. If they behave well, from our point
of view, we put them on a pedestal, and see them as **Wholly Good**. But
when they behave badly, from our point of view, we push them head first
into the nearest rubbish bin! The antidote to **splitting** is this: Remind
yourself that **the Partner-that-I-love** is the *same person* as **the Partner-who-
frustrates-me.**

Teach yourself to distinguish between **your partner**, on the one hand, and
their behaviours, on the other. Then recognize that you have a right to
influence their behaviour, to exactly the same degree to which you are *willing*
to allow them *to influence yours* (but never try to use more than 50% of the
total 'influence for change' that is used *collectively* in your relationship).
Then learn the *assertiveness skills* from Chapter 7, and use them to influence
your partner's problematic behaviours. But always show care and respect
for them and their easily-bruised feelings!

4.5 Active Listening

Active listening is the opposite of *passive* listening.

The passive listener makes no attempt to *follow* what their partner is saying
to them. They hear what is said; and they most likely have emotional
feelings about those statements. But they do not try to pay conscious

attention to what is being said.

Active listening has, as its main aim, the desire to *follow* the **meaning** of what your partner is saying to you; and also to **understand the feelings** associated with the words.

The main components of active listening are these:

#1: *Adopting appropriate body language*, which involves facing your partner, observing their face; listening to their words; and interpreting their nonverbal communication, in terms of hand gestures, facial expressions, tone of voice, and so on.

#2: *Committing the time and attention* needed to hear and understand your partner. If you are tired, or preoccupied, it is better to level with your partner. Tell them you are tired, or preoccupied with a particular problem; that you want to listen and understand them; but that you will be better placed to do that at some agreed on time, perhaps later that day. (Don't put it off indefinitely, or too far into the future, or your partner will read this as indifference or neglect!)

#3: *Inviting* your partner to speak; and using *minimal verbal responses* – like 'Ah-ha', 'Yeah', 'I see', 'Anything else?' - to encourage them to keep speaking.

#4: *Reflecting* back what your partner says. And/or reflecting the emotion they seem to be communicating. You can reflect what your partner said, as if you were a mirror for their words. Examples could include:

"So you *think* that it would be easier to do X rather than Y...".

"You *don't agree* with the way the decision was made..."

"I hear you saying...(X)"

Do not add anything to what they have said.

On the other hand, you could reflect their emotional state to them:

"So you *feel* quite sad about that..."

"You seem to *be quite angry* towards (person's name)..." Etcetera. (See Volume 2 for detailed guidance on the skill of *reflective listening*).

"My guess is that this makes you quite anxious..."

Prompting your partner to continue speaking, when they seem to have dried up. "Please go on..." "Is there anything else?" Or make encouraging sounds, like *ah-ha; yeah:* (meaning 'got it'!)

This kind of active listening allows your partner to clarify their own thoughts and feelings, and to *feel felt (by you)!* To 'feel felt' is to feel *understood; empathized with;* and/or *cared about!*

4.6 Listening Time

One of the skills we teach in E-CENT couples therapy is planned, formal 'Listening Time' – where one partner can speak and be heard, without any interruption or roadblock from their partner. We begin by teaching our clients how normal communication should work, and when it might be necessary to set up formal Listening time:

4.6.1 Normal communication

Under normal circumstances, communication tends to be spontaneous, and free-flowing.

- It should involve a good balance of give and take: listening and speaking.

- It should involve a good balance of paying attention to the words and the non-verbal communication.

- It should involve a good balance between hearing the words spoken, and imagining (or 'getting') the emotional place from which those words are coming.

If all of those conditions are met – spontaneously and non-consciously – then the feeling, on both sides, of the quality of the communication, will be happy and contented.

However, if the quality of the communication does not feel good, not happy, and there is a lack of contentment on either or both sides, then it might be necessary to 'simulate' or 'create' the right kinds of qualities and conditions in the communication. This would be done by *conscious monitoring* of goal-driven communication.

Each partner would set out to make sure that their communication has, by design:

(1) A good balance of give and take: listening and speaking.

(2) A good balance of paying attention to the words and the non-verbal communication.

(3) A good balance between hearing the words spoken, and imagining (or 'getting') the emotional place from which those words are coming.

"Equality of treatment" has to be the watchword. Equal time shared; equal value attached to both party's communications; and equal effort paid to understanding and to being understood.

When this does not work, then it might be time to set up a system of 'Listening Time'.

4.6.2 Formal 'listening time'

'Listening time' is designed to ensure that each partner can get their concerns "off their chest" without tempting their partner to respond with a Roadblock (like *reassurance, advice,* or *ignoring the other person's concerns.* [These apparently helpful responses are actually serious 'roadblocks to communication', especially when the person trying to communicate the original message is under a lot of stress]. Roadblocks are described in section 4.4, above).

The 'listening time' procedure is this:

1. If you feel like communicating something which might be difficult to share, you ask your partner for 'listening time'. Or, if you want to get something off your chest, without attracting solutions and advice, you ask for 'listening time'. (You could ask your partner: "Could you please let me have 5 [or 10] minutes of listening time, during which you just listen, and do not offer any interventions?") Very often, the 'price' we pay for 'listening time' is the agreement to listen to our partner for a similar amount of time, on a subject that they want to talk about.

2. You both agree to set aside a little time (often 5 or 10 minutes each will be enough)!

3. You meet in a quiet place, where there are no distractions.

4. You decide who will 'go' first. (This person we will call the Speaker. The other person will serve as the Listener, for this first round).

5. The Speaker shares a concern, as briefly and succinctly as possible. (If it's a big concern, it should be broken down into several statements, and only the first statement is made, before pausing).

6. The Listener says: "I got that!" Or: "I hear what you're saying". (Meaning: "I heard and understood your words".)

7. The Speaker makes their next statement.

8. The Listener says: "I got that!" Or "I see!" Or "I hear you!"

9. The Speaker makes their next statement.

10. The Listener says: "I got that!" Or "I see!" Or "I hear you!"

11. The Speaker continues to make statements.

12. The Listener continues to "get it!!

13. If the Speaker seems to be drying up, the Listener asks: "Anything else?" Or: "Are you complete now?" Or: "Is that it?"

14. The Listener continues to 'get it' and to ask 'anything else' until the Speaker says, 'No, I'm complete now! Nothing left to say'.

15. The partners then switch over, and the Speaker becomes the Listener, and vice versa.

16. When it's all over, both partners thank the other for listening, and then they both *move on to something new*. They *do not* then use what they have heard, or learned, in order to start a 'post mortem' enquiry! Avoid post-mortems; and avoid sending solutions, later, about what came up during the listening time. *When it's over, it's **over**!*

~~~

I have taught this process to many couples, and they have reported great success as a result. It helps to clear up log-jammed communications, and to improve the felt sense of being close and intimate, while also avoiding those pesky *roadblocks* to communication!

4.7 'Barriers' and 'boundaries' in couple relationships

'Boundaries' in relationships are different from 'barriers' in relationships. **Boundaries** are **positive** *forms of self-protection* and self-definition. Boundaries delineate and surround our personal space.

'Barriers', on the other hand, are **impediments** to communication.

4.7.1 Defining barriers to communication

The most obvious barriers to communication are practical ones:

(1) The speaker does not speak clearly; or they use just enough words to 'express' their idea, as they understand it; but they fail to add *the **extra** words* or *elaborations* that would allow the listener to understand it.

(2) The speaker does not seek **feedback** *from the listener* to find out how the listener understood their communication. Thus, errors of interpretation in

the mind of the listener are left uncorrected.

(3) The speaker uses one or more of the 'roadblocks' described above.

On the other hand, one of the least obvious barriers to communication in relationships, which is related to item (2) above, was clarified and taught by Werner Erhard, on his *Relationships Course*. He argued that:

"The barriers in relationships are caused by the things that are **not** communicated".

What does this mean?

Let me try to illustrate it using an example of a communications breakdown between two people.

Firstly: If Suzie and Stan are in a relationship, and Suzie says something 'innocent' (in passing, non-blaming), but Stan *interprets it* as a criticism of him, he will 'crumple' – or experience a drop in his sense of self-esteem.

Secondly: According to Werner Erhard's proposition, if Stan *fails to communicate* his negative emotional experience to Suzie, then a 'barrier' is inserted between them, which makes it more difficult for them to communicate in a friendly and loving manner.

Thirdly: One such barrier block reduces loving communication a little; while several of them will reduce loving communication a lot!

Fourth: If you allow a lot of barrier blocks to build up in your relationship – by failing to communicate with your partner when they 'step on your psychological toes' – then eventually you will have 'a wall' between you!

This is a variation upon point (2) above. Point (2) puts the *responsibility* on the speaker to find out how the listener *understood* their communication. But Werner's refinement *puts the responsibility on the listener* to share with the speaker how the speaker's words have affected them.

If Stan knows how to process his emotions, and to avoid accumulating barriers in his communication, he will say something like this: "Ouch! I know you didn't *mean* to hurt me, Suzie. But that last comment of yours hit a 'crumple button'."

If Suzie is emotionally intelligent, and used to working for improved communication, she will spontaneously apologize. "Oh, I'm sorry Stan", she might say. "I certainly didn't **want** to have that negative effect on you!"

Stan should then *accept her apology*, and if he checks his feelings, he will most often find that the upset has cleared up, just because of his *sharing* it, and *Suzie's apology*.

If some elements of the upset are still there, then *it's Stan's responsibility* to continue to communicate with Suzie, *until the barrier has been dissolved*.

The worst thing Stan can do it to hide his negative feelings, about their communication, from Suzie. (If he tries to do that, he will most likely find that he has 'saved a brown stamp'. A brown stamp [in TA theory] is a token of *his anger towards her* – which can build up, over time, into a 'brown stamp collection'. If Stan accumulates 'brown stamps', instead of communicating about his upsets with Suzie, he will be inclined to 'cash them in', with a big, aggressive outburst, further down the line – thus damaging his relationship with Suzie).

The second worst thing Stan can do is to communicate his upset *aggressively*; by *criticizing* Suzie for upsetting him; or by *blaming* her for her words or actions. He needs, instead, to use an *assertive communication* style with Suzie. (See Chapter 7).

If Stan fails to communicate his upset with Suzie, he will tend to sulk, which will have a negative effect upon their relationship. He will find it difficult to get any positive communications out, in dealing with Suzie, as they become trapped under the negative communication that he is resisting sharing with her". If he learns to communicate assertively, he can get his negative communications off his chest, with minimal damage to the relationship, and with a resulting improvement in the quality of ongoing, happy and positive communications!

~~~

Then the question arises: *"Why would one partner be sensitive to having their behaviour criticized by the other, when they know, at some level, that their partner loves them?"*

We know from Professor John Gottman's work (1997) that criticism is corrosive of relationships, causing the criticized partner to *withdraw*!

We know from Robert Bolton (1979/1986) that labelling people and making negative judgements about them, causes *roadblocks* to the couple's communication. (This position is restated in Clinard, 1987).

And we know from the work of Joines and Stewart (2002) that some people are very sensitive to having their *behaviour* criticized. Joines and Stewart describe a system of 'personality adaptations', which has six personality types. Three of those types are particularly prone to feeling bad if you criticize (or appear to criticize!) their behaviour. Here are the reasons why:

#1: The first of these personality types is called 'Enthusiastic Over-reactors'. "...Since they were supposed to please others in order to be OK, Enthusiastic-Overreactors have (their) greatest defences in the area of their behaviour ... If one criticises their behaviour, they believe they are not-OK, since they see their duty as keeping everyone around them pleased". (Page 43). ...

#2: The second of these personality types is called 'Responsible Workaholics'. "Since (Responsible-Workaholics) were supposed to be perfect in order to be OK, (they) will have (their) greatest defences in the area of their behaviour. ... If one criticises their behaviour, they feel not-OK, since they are supposed to be doing everything right". (Pages 44-45) ...

#3: And the third of these personality types is called 'Brilliant Skeptics'. "Given how careful (a Brilliant-Skeptic) had to be as a child in order to survive, behaviour is the trap area for (them). Again they were supposed to be perfect and be strong. They certainly were not supposed to be childlike or playful. As a result, they equate criticism with shame and humiliation, since their behaviour is supposed to be above reproach". (Page 46).

So there are very good reasons to accept that your partner may be unavoidably sensitive to even the slightest implication that there may be something wrong with their behaviour. Try to be sensitive and caring in avoiding any implication that your partner is engaging in bad behaviour; or find ways to raise such issues sensitively and helpfully!

~~~

The next question has to be this: "Why does Partner Y fail to communicate back to Partner X that Partner Y is feeling hurt by something Partner X said or did?"

One way to try to answer this questions is as follows:

Irina Firstein, in an online blog, at *GoodTherapy.org*, set out to share with her readers: '... what I have learned from my (therapy) practice as well as from experts ...:

"One of the key elements in learning communication skills is to discover how to protect oneself adequately while reducing unnecessary defensiveness," writes communication expert Robert Bolton, PhD. This is a very important concept to understand when assessing (someone's) communication patterns. Why do we feel the need to protect ourselves when communicating? Psychologists and communication experts point out that we are riddled with fears, most of which are learned. We often fear:

- being judged negatively,

- failing to measure up to some imaginary standards,

- being laughed at,

- appearing stupid when we misunderstand someone,

- expressing emotion and losing control, and

- letting someone gain power over us and use it against us.

'When we feel fear, communication is impaired. To avoid being misunderstood, we say nothing; to keep from losing control of our emotions, we suppress them and don't communicate them; and in order to be liked, we say what we think others want to hear'. (Firstein, 2010)[38].

So, thinking back to the case of Stan and Suzie above, it is most likely that Stan would:

Firstly, feel bad because of some innocent thing that Suzie said, without her realizing it would negatively affect him.

Secondly, (Stan might) feel a resistance to sharing his upset feelings with Suzie, in case that makes matters worse. But how could it make matters worse?

(1) It could actually make matters worse if Stan communicates his upset unskilfully, and Suzie crumples, and becomes angry at him. Or if she becomes sad, and Stand then feels guilty!

(2) Stan could mistakenly assume that it will inevitably make matters worse, because:

  (a) Suzie might judge him negatively;

  (b) She might laugh at him;

  (c) She might think him stupid for misunderstanding her meaning; or for responding the way he does;

  (d) He might feel as if responding would result in his losing control of his emotions – sadness or anger – both of which he would find shameful.

  (e) Or he might think that letting Suzie know what he feels, and how vulnerable he can be, would allow her to control or dominate him.

However, Stan can get beyond those problems by studying this book, and learning to speak up; to refuse to collect 'brown stamps'; to ask for what he wants; to say no to what he does not want (see Chapter 7); to ask for listening time; to use reflective listening with Suzie; to be brave in his communication (without becoming insensitive or aggressive); and to keep working on his relationship, in partnership with Suzie, until they get *beyond frequent upsets*, and into the best that is possible, which is *infrequent upsets!* (Because they are human, Stan and Suzie will never reach a place where there are *no upsets* whatsoever!)

~~~

And now we move on, from barriers to boundaries.

4.7.2 Defining personal boundaries in relationship

Personal boundaries (unlike barriers!) are like doors on houses, gates on gardens, etc. They are designed to keep bad things out, and to let good things in. (Barriers in relationships, on the other hand, as shown above, are like roadblocks. They hold up all communication. But boundaries are different).

Boundaries are important parts of how we maintain our autonomy as individual human beings. Autonomy does not rule out intimacy. I can be autonomous from my wife, and also be intimate with her. I can accept those communications which do not step on my psychological toes; and on the other hand, if things go wrong, I can say "Just a moment darling! That particular action/statement hurt me, and I want to talk about that... (or negotiate a change in that), please, dear".

This involves conflict, but conflict that is *constructive* rather than *destructive*.

As Professor John Gottman says, in his 1997 book: "...a lasting marriage results from a couple's ability to resolve conflicts which are inevitable in any relationship. Many people tend to equate a low level of conflict with happiness and believe (that) the claim 'we never fight' is a sign of marital health. But I believe we grow in our relationships by reconciling our differences. That's how we become more loving people and truly experience the fruits of marriage". (Page 28).

Or as Dr Robert Bolton said: "The best relationships exist on the other side of conflict". (Bolton, 1979/1986).

Boundaries are healthy aspects of mature relationships, which begin when (and if) we are children in healthy relationships with our parents. (Barriers, on the contrary – as shown above - are unhealthy aspects of our adult relationships. Barriers arise out of unhealthy encounters with parents who either tried to control us inappropriately, or who were unresponsive, or unreliably responsive, and/or insensitive to our needs and our emotional states. And, of course, barriers can also arise out of our *innate* fear of conflict!)

Balancing autonomy and connection

One of the paradoxes of human need is this: We need *to be close* to significant others, to have love, affection, and connection; but we also need to be able *to act autonomously*, to be our own person – to be a self, separate and apart from our significant other(s).

That is a bit of a tightrope walk, knowing when to move towards our significant other, and knowing when to move apart. We need to know where our boundaries are, and to connect across that boundary in a way that works for both parties.

Now I want to clarify some more of what is within your boundaries and what is not.

What is a boundary?

A boundary is both a container and an excluder. Like your skin, (or the doors of your home), your interpersonal boundary keeps certain 'bad things' out while letting certain 'good things' in. You defend yourself against attack and harm, while opening yourself up to friendship and love. Additionally, your boundaries allow you to express certain positive states, while setting limits on your ability to inflict pain and suffering on your partner. Your boundaries also allow your partner to express love for you, while defending you against any form of verbal or physical abuse.

Your boundary with a love partner needs to allow love in, and even to allow healthy complaints about negative aspects of your behaviour to be received and considered. However, it needs to keep destructive feedback out – like aggressive put-downs, criticisms which imply that you are totally bad because you engaged in one, or a few, negative behaviours. (By contrast, *complaints* about **your behaviour** should be entertained, while **damnation of you as a person**, because of some behaviour you performed, should be defended against).

4.7.2(a) The feeling and attitude components of a boundary

Your feelings are part of your boundary. Your feeling, that you should not do a certain thing, or not allow a certain thing to be done to you, is an important guide to action.

If you are emotionally well, you will *feel it* when somebody is 'trying it on' with you, and you should trust that feeling and 'push back' to defend yourself.

If you are *not* emotionally 'well wired up', you may be susceptible to being 'guilt tripped' or frightened by another person, who wants to exploit you by controlling your decisions/actions. So it is important to work on your 'emotional wiring' – or your *emotional intelligence* - as part of the task of developing good relationship boundaries.

Your attitudes and beliefs are also implicated in your boundaries in relationships.

You learn your attitudes and beliefs in your birth family (or from your main carers), and these are either healthy or unhealthy attitudes/beliefs.

You may, for example, have learned to take *too much responsibility*, or *too little responsibility*, in your relationships. Your expectations of a relationship partner may be *realistic* or *unrealistic*. So, again, you need to examine and work on your attitudes and beliefs if you want to have healthy boundaries in your relationships. One way to do this is to start a daily journal, and write about your relationship every day.

Write about what you feel. (See Appendix E to deepen your understanding of your emotions).

Write about your implicit attitudes and beliefs about relationships. Do you find it easy to take on the definition of relationship contained in Chapter 1? If not, why not? What *are* your attitudes and beliefs about relationship?

4.7.2(b) The behavioural and values components of a boundary

Your habitual behaviours are also a component part of your boundaries. If you behave passively, you will be taken advantage of. If you behave aggressively, you will be feared and/ or resented. Both of these approaches are ineffective relational boundaries. The most effective relational boundary, in the realm of behaviour, is to be assertive – which means not too pushy, and not a push-over. To be assertive, you should *ask for what you want* (within reason) and *say 'no' to what you do not want* (within reason). You should communicate your wishes, wants, needs, thoughts and feelings to your partner, and attend to their wishes, wants, needs, thoughts and feelings.

Also, your values will play a part in your relationship boundaries. If you value honesty, integrity and love, you will be honest with your partner, both when they do something which pleases you, and when they do something that displeases you. You will be 'real' in the relationship, and you will not expect your partner to maintain a façade of false niceness. You will love your partner, and let their love into your life. You will show by your actions that you value care, respect and responsibility in your relationship.

Because there are only certain things you can control, and certain things which you cannot control, you will not be able to set guaranteed limits on the behaviour of your partner – except to ask them to change a behaviour you don't like, or to praise or thank them for a behaviour you do like. (However, you can withdraw physically if they act in ways that are unacceptable to you, such as being verbally or physically abusive). But most of your partner's behaviour will not be within your *control* – though it may be susceptible to your *influence*. However, you'd better be able to set limits on your own behaviour. If you feel angry towards your partner because of something they did (or failed to do) then you'd better not act that out *destructively* or *aggressively*. (Don't kick over the beehive if you want to collect honey!) You need to limit yourself to acting *assertively*, and not aggressively or passively. This is a form of self-control. (See Chapter 7).

4.7.2(c) The thought and desire components of a boundary

Your thoughts affect your boundaries, because your thoughts influence your feelings and behaviours. If you want to act appropriately, with healthy boundaries in your relationships, then you need to think straight – or perceive, feel and think straight - about your rights and responsibilities.

Crooked thinking begins with distorted perceptions, driven by false interpretations from the past. So you need to learn to subject your perceptions to the test of logic and reason, in so far as that is humanly possible. *Are your conclusions valid? Are you're arguments sound? In what way could you be jumping to the wrong conclusion about your partner's behaviour? How many different ways can you think of to interpret your partner's actions?* If your answer is 'one', then you have a problem with your thinking. There are normally several possible ways to interpret any event. The more potential interpretations you can think of, and the more you communicate about them, the more likely you are to develop and employ effective boundaries based on sound reasons.

You must also know how to manage your desires, if you are to have healthy boundaries. The *Buddhist psychology* view is that most human disturbance stems from *uncontrolled or inappropriate desires*. Unchecked or unregulated desire leads to alcoholism, drug addiction, gluttony, over-spending and debt, sexual infidelity, gambling addiction, verbal and physical abuse, sexual abuse; and conflict within relationships about thwarted desires. You must learn to keep you desires within reasonable bounds, so that you can behave well in your relationships; and also in order to identify unrealistic or inappropriate desires on the part of your partner, and to say 'no' to their lack of realism or their inappropriate requests.

4.7.2(d) The ability to give and receive love

The ability to give and receive love is the final component of your boundary in relationships. Some people give love, but are resistant to letting others love them. Some people *desire love* from their partner, but do nothing to *express love* for their partner. Some people try to manipulate or frighten others into giving them what they want, with no reciprocation. You can't have a successful sex-love relationship unless your boundaries are working well, and you can give and receive love, and say no to experiences of aggression, hatred, anger, abuse, hurt or exploitation.

4.8 The laws of boundary management

The three most important laws of boundaries in couple relationship are these:

1. The law of karma: "You tend to reap what you sow";

2. The law of responsibility: "You are responsible for your side of the relationship"; and:

3. The law of declared boundaries: "If you don't speak up, they won't know what you want and need".

The law of *karma* means that everything that happens within your marriage has been *caused*. It does not fall from the skies.

- Some of it is *earned* karma – which is *just (or fair) payback* for some good or bad action by you in the past.

- And some of it is *mere misfortune*. You were in the wrong place at the wrong time.

But *most* of the karma that occurs in a sex-love relationship is caused by *models of relationship* stored in the non-conscious minds of each partner (from their family of origin); and how those *non-conscious scripts* cause the partners to behave towards each other.

The law of *responsibility* says, if there's a problem in your marriage, then *you are responsible*; not necessarily in the sense of having caused it (though you may have contributed to it) – but certainly in the sense that, if it is ever going to be sorted out, then *you have to take responsibility for your side of sorting it out.*

And the law of *'declared boundaries'* states that you must tell your partner, directly or indirectly, what your boundaries are: meaning, what you want; what you would like; what you dislike; and what you will not put up with.

I will explore these three laws, in relation to a range of case studies from my clinical practice, in Chapter 8.

4.9 Conclusion

In this chapter, we have explored various aspects of communication skills, including active and passive listening; and roadblocks to communication; plus antidotes to those roadblocks; and formal *listening time*.

We also looked at *barriers* to communication; and the importance of having *boundaries* in your relationships.

If you put some effort into learning this knowledge and these skills, the quality of your relationship is highly likely to be greatly improved. For this reason, I recommend that you read this chapter three times, before proceeding to Chapter 5.

First reading ☐

Second reading ☐

Third reading ☐

~~~

Chapter 5: Kitty and Billy in search of love

5.1 Background

In this chapter we will take a close look at one dysfunctional relationship, to reveal some of the dynamics that go into the creating of a couple relationship.

But first, some psychological context:

Human beings have *some (small) degree* of conscious awareness; and we can consciously access *some* remembered images of relationships, marriages, couples, from our past.

However, we do not know what goes on the in the (non-conscious) *basement* of our minds. And that is where the bulk of our processing of information about interpersonal relationships is managed.

We do not know, for example, what our 'script for relationship' happens to be. We get that from our family of origin - (which is to say: we **co-construct it** in our family of origin) - and it builds up slowly, and subliminally, outside of our awareness; *and it runs our relationships in our adult lives.*

We drift through our teens, and, most often, into our twenties, until we meet the 'perfect match' to play out *the **script** of relationship* which we formed in the first few years of our life. (See Chapter 11 for more detail on this theory of the 'Inner Couple' template for adult relationships). In this new relationship, we either act as if we have 'modelled' ourselves upon our parent of the same sex, or the parent of the opposite sex. (Teachworth, 1999/2005).

And when I say we 'modelled ourselves' on somebody, I mean we 'copied their ways of being'; including their ways of relating to their partner: verbally and non-verbally.

And very often, this leads us into a great deal of misery (because many of us – perhaps 40% of us - had parents who were engaged in a miserable, insecure relationship; perhaps volatile, or silently anxious-hostile; or a mixture of the two).

Let us now take a look at one couple relationship, to see how some of these patterns take shape.

5.2 Kitty's story

Kitty was born into a family that was loveless. Her parents were dutiful but cold. She studied hard at school, and got a good job, which introduced her to travel, which got her away from her family.

She drifted for many years, got married at the age of twenty-four years, and then spent the next five years creating a sex-love relationship which had much in common with her parents' cold and unfulfilling, loveless marriage. Eventually she realized that her husband, Russ, (who was a *bossy blamer*: [See Appendix D}), was having an affair with their next-door neighbour. She tried to get Russ to put a stop to this, but he said he couldn't. Then he told her his 'mistress' was pregnant with his child, and he wanted to keep his marriage to Kitty, but to spend half his time with his mistress and his baby.

Kitty, (who was a *passive placator*: [See Appendix D]), tried to go along with this; and came close to having a nervous breakdown in the months that followed; and eventually the enmeshment with Russ came to a bitter end; and Kitty moved on. She travelled abroad for a couple of years, and then settled in a new city, far from Russ.

Her publicly declared stance on relationships now became this: that marriage was *hell*; that monogamous sex-love relationships were *impossible*; and that she was determined that she would remain *single*, forever.

On the other hand, her body craved the comfort of a close relationship.

5.3 Billy's story

Billy's early years were delightful. His mother was warm and loving, and she also loved Billy's father, Kirk. Kirk was reasonably close to Billy, but he preferred his two daughters, who were older than Billy. Kirk and his daughters had an entertainment group that did traditional folk dancing, and there was no role in the group for Billy.

Billy's mother and father both preferred girls to boys, and so Billy felt like a slight outsider. But he found that he could get the attention and affection of his family by being the 'cute kid' of the family. (He was a *passive placator*: [See Appendix D]).

Billy's father, Kirk, had served in the Second World War, and he was shot down over Italy, and detained in a prisoner of war camp for almost five years. This had a negative effect upon him, which somehow impacted his relationship with Billy. However, Kirk was a bit of a philosopher, and this rubbed off on Billy, who could not only play 'cute kid', to keep people on his side; but also he was able to intellectually rationalize his experiences, so that the negative ones didn't hurt so much. (In this sense, his secondary style of conflict management was as a '*Computer*': [See Appendix D]).

Billy did well in school, and then joined the Civil Service, where he worked hard, and got promoted. Then he met a girl and tried to settle down. But he found that his winning formula, of playing 'cute kid', could not placate his partner, Joyce (who was a bossy blamer: [See Appendix D]), who was very critical of the 'sloppy way' he dressed, and his 'unkempt hairstyle'.

After a couple of years, Billy got out of this relationship with Joyce, and fell for a new young woman, Wanda, who looked sad and forlorn, with big sleepy eyes. They got married and bought a flat. But this relationship did not bring satisfaction, because Wanda was not inclined to easily commit to monogamy. She said she wanted to be exclusively involved with Billy, but she had a wandering eye, and liked to flirt with the men who drank in their local pub. When Billy tried to raise any problems with Wanda, she would just ignore his concerns (which is a roadblock to communication [See section 4.4 of Chapter 4 above]; and also an expression of the *distractor* approach to conflict management: [See Appendix D, below]).

Wanda also thought Billy was 'a bit weird' because of his interest in philosophy, and his speculating about the nature of reality.

Billy's marriage was on the rocks almost from the beginning, and it was on its last legs, five years later, when Billy ran into Kitty, in the lounge bar of their local hotel.

5.4 Billy and Kitty get together...and fall apart

Billy and Kitty liked each other from the moment they met. There was no romantic element to it, but they became very good friends – best friends, almost from the beginning.

The weeks went by, and Kitty continued to crave a sense of physical intimacy, but she had no luck finding a suitable date. Meanwhile, she enjoyed her occasional friendly chats with Billy.

A few months down the line, Billy and Wanda split up.

Billy and Kitty had a couple of meals together each week, as friends, and sometimes they went for a walk at the weekend.

Kitty was very surprised, one day, when a spark of passion passed between them while they were out walking.

They began to date, and became lovers. But Kitty wanted to keep things informal. She was afraid to get too involved, because she was, at some level, convinced that relationships just don't work out; just can't work out! (In this sense, Kitty had 'an avoidant attachment style'. [See sections 6.10 to 6.12(b)]).

So they got close to each other; then Kitty would feel some dreadful negative emotion, and pull away. Billy was very understanding, and just went back to being friends, whenever Kitty got cold feet. This allowed Kitty to process her fears and anxieties about commitment, involvement, and the insecurity of romantic love as an "ember that often dies".

Months went by, then they grew closer. Then they decided to try living together. Kitty was very nervous about this, but bravely went ahead. Billy was now increasingly wary of Kitty's hot and cold pattern of 'coming and going', and he became a little standoffish. Eventually, Kitty had to go to America for a three month work assignment, and while there she realized that she wanted to make a commitment to Billy. So, when she got home, they discussed getting engaged, with a view to getting married the following year.

However, once they began to share a bedroom on a regular basis, a new pattern began to emerge. Every so often, Kitty would speak in an unkind, critical or judgemental way to Billy, which would hurt his feelings. Then they would become close again for a while; then Kitty would be critical and controlling again, and Billy would withdraw.

Eventually, they decided to take this problem to a marriage counsellor, or couple therapist.

5.5 Kitty and Billy go to marriage guidance counselling

This is what happened, and what they discovered:

1. They went to see a Transactional Analysis (TA) counsellor. (See the introduction to TA in Appendix B).

2. They both took a TA personality quiz, like the one you can find here: **https://tinyurl.com/he4f2sb**

3. It turned out that Kitty was too keen on operating from her 'Controlling Parent ego state'; while Billy was prone to slip into 'Adapted Child ego state' for a while; and then to flip into 'Rebellious Child ego state'. (See Appendix B for descriptions).

4. Their counsellor, Jemima, recommended that they both learn how to be more 'Adult' in their encounters, and to reduce their tendency to play Parent-Child games.

5. The way Kitty set about 'growing her Adult ego state' was as follows:

(a) She attended the Communications Workshop run by Werner Erhard and Associates, at the All Saints Building, at Manchester Polytechnic (now the Metropolitan University of Manchester). There she learned some of the communication skills which we have shared in this book, including the idea that *human communication is very difficult*, because of the fact that the hearer always has to *interpret* what the speaker *means* by their words and deeds! And, that the interpretations of the hearer are *coloured by their family of origin* and subsequent experiences. So if we do not check out the *intended meaning* of the speaker's communication, we may often be wide of the mark in our interpretations.

(b) She bought and studied extracts from Werner Erhard's audio program: *'Relationships – Making them work!'* From this program she learned the three-part definition of relationships taught in this book. (See Chapter 1). And, by reviewing those definitions over and over again, day after day, for months on end, she came to rewire her brain for a wholly new approach to relationship. (By reviewing those definitions yourself, you can repeat her success).

6. The way Billy set about 'growing his Adult ego state' was as follows:

(a) He read a range of books on assertive communication, to try to learn how to speak up; to ask for what he wanted; and to say 'no' to what he did not want. (One of those books was Robert Bolton's 'People Skills'; and the core skills from that book are taught in the present book).

(b) He then went to Coventry to participate in a weekend course on Assertiveness Skills, at Barry Hinksman and Associates, a Gestalt Therapy institute.

(c) And when he got home, he set about practicing what he had learned from Robert Bolton and Barry Hinksman. (According to Werner Erhard: "It does not matter what you *know*; it only matters what you **_do_** with what you know!" So we strongly advise you to practice the skills taught in this book, and to apply them in your relationships; otherwise nothing will change!)

7. Over a period of weeks, or perhaps a few months, Kitty learned how to reduce the intensity of her assertions (and demands!), which were mostly from Controlling Parent ego state; and to substitute more Adult requests and friendly communications. And Billy learned to be less passive, and more willing to say what he wanted, and what he would not agree to. These attempts on both sides to become more *Adult* resulted in a great improvement in the peace, harmony and love within their relationship.

8. A few years later, Billy discovered Rational Emotive Behaviour Therapy (REBT), which taught him (and later, Kitty) to distinguish between a person, on the one hand, and their behaviours, on the other. They both adopted this practice – by reminding themselves over and over again: "My *partner* is not their _behaviour_; and their *behaviour* is not _them_!" This had the desirable effect of helping them to give up 'splitting' their partner into 'Good Partner' and 'Bad Partner'.

From that point onwards, when one of them did something that frustrated the other, they now were able to remember that the 'Frustrating Partner' was the same person as the 'Non-frustrating Partner'. In other words, they gave up putting each other on a pedestal, when they had acted nicely; and then dumping them, head first, into the rubbish bin, when they had behaved in a difficult manner.

(However, a few years later again, they realized that you can go too far in distinguishing between *a person* and *their behaviour*. A good illustration of this fact is the case of domestic violence. It is not a good idea to accept domestic violence on the basis that your 'Violent Partner' is the same person as your 'Non-Violent Partner'. So there has to be a cut-off point for 'accepting' the difficult behaviours of your partner; and that cut-off point is the line which divides morality from immorality; and legality from illegality.

If you have difficulty finding that line, then use the Golden Rule. "How would I like my partner to respond to me, when I frustrate them?" The answer, from an emotionally healthy person *will **never** include statements like. "They can beat me, or verbally abuse me!"* So therefore, you should never beat (or strike, or slap, or push) your partner. Nor should you verbally abuse your partner; no matter how badly they behave; and no matter how much they might frustrate you.

Another moral guideline you can use comes from 'Rule Utilitarianism'. This guideline, which is designed to promote "the greatest good of the greatest number", asks: "What moral rule can I apply in my relationship when my partner frustrates me?" Note: There is no moral rule in any modern, major religion or spiritual tradition, or any legally constituted secular culture, which says, "You should beat those who frustrate you!" Nor that, "You should verbally abuse those who frustrate you!" My own answer to this question goes like this: "I should apply the Golden Rule. And, since I want my partner to treat me with *kindness* and *respect* when I frustrate them – intentionally or unintentionally – *I have to treat them with kindness* and *respect when they frustrate me*".

9. And a few years after finding REBT, (which Billy and Kitty have now both rejected, because of its extremism), they discovered the work of Professor John Gottman. In his book, 'Why Marriages Succeed or Fail'[39], John Gottman talks about the 'Four Horsemen of the Apocalypse', which spell doom for relationships.

The Four Horsemen are as follows: Criticism; withdrawal; contempt; and 'stonewalling'.

> (a). **Criticism**. This is like nitric acid in the heart of a relationship. It burns the love-ties and causes...

> (b). ...**Withdrawal**. This means the criticized partner withdraws from the criticizing partner. They may withdraw physically, by stepping back; or leaving the shared space; or they may just withdraw psychologically, emotionally – locking their tender feeling away in order to protect them! They most likely, as a minimum, will close down any conversational interchange; or become monosyllabic, and largely closed up.

> (c). **Contempt** is often the response (by the originator of the criticism) to the withdrawal. Contempt is essentially disrespectful, and it makes the recipient feel despised, inferior and worthless. This contemptuous response causes the criticized one to engage

in...:

(d). ...Stonewalling. This is a total refusal to communicate or cooperate. In effect, the criticized and disrespected one behaves like a stone wall. There is no getting through to them.

When a couple reaches stage four – stonewalling – they are very close indeed to the exit: the separation or divorce stage.

Reading Gottman's book, Kitty and Billy realized that these 'Horsemen' were precisely what had been affecting their relationship (before they went to marriage guidance). And they redoubled their commitment to avoid all forms of criticism in their relationships; plus sarcasm – which is also very corrosive! (This 'Four Horsemen' perspective is another way of understanding their earlier dynamic. It complements the TA perspective, since criticism and contempt come from the Bad side of the Controlling Parent ego state; and withdrawal and stonewalling fit in with the sulking tendencies of the Rebellious Child ego state).

~~~

As a result of the work they did, over the following months and years, to learn how to relate on an Adult-to-Adult basis, things became much better for Kitty and Billy. They were much happier in their relationship, for longer periods of time, and more consistently. And they grew increasingly close to each other. Twenty years later, they are still happily married, and they recommend marriage guidance or couple's therapy to anyone who will listen to their success story!

~~~

Study guidelines

Tick that you've read this chapter once: ❑

Before you more on to Chapter 6, please read this chapter a second time: ❑

And a third time: ❑

~~~

When reading and re-reading this chapter, please underline those points that seem most important to you.

Make notes in the margins, as necessary, as quick reminders of the content of a paragraph or a page.

And turn down the corner of the page, when the content is so important you want to find it again, quickly and easily.

Also, add important points, with their page numbers, in your own index to this book, in Appendix 'L', below.

~~~

Chapter 6: A marriage is not a possession

6.1 Prelude

One of the problems we all face in understanding, building, and adjusting to a marriage – or marriage-like, couple relationship (or civil partnership) - is that we are used to thinking of 'things', rather than 'processes'.

We are used to thinking about 'objects' rather than 'events'.

We are used to desiring *things*, and acquiring *things*. We are accustomed to being the 'owners' of 'things'.

But a marriage or couple relationship is *not* a **thing**, and a marriage cannot be a **possession**. Nobody can 'own' a relationship.

A marriage or couple relationship is a *process* - an *ongoing process* - that only exists when both partners *participate in its repeated construction*, and *reconstruction,* and *repair.*

As a metaphor, we could say (tentatively) that a marriage is a **house** that is built every day, and unless you commence building yours, every morning, when you wake up, it is likely to fall into ruinous decay!

But, again, we think of 'building' as a **process** of constructing a bigger *thing* (like a house) from smaller *things* (like bricks and mortar; wood, glass and slates; etc.

But a marriage, or couple relationship is not like that.

It is actually an **organic process**, constructed from *'events'*, rather than 'objects' – although some objects are required to make a relationship work. There is normally a marital home; furniture; food; flowers (sometimes!); and so on. But these objects are not central to the definition of, or the experience of, the relationship as such.

A *marital relationship* is made up of *a continuous sequence of events* which are either experienced as loving or non-loving; caring or non-caring; and respectful or disrespectful.

If you want to learn how to build a happy marriage, or a happy couple relationship, then this book will provide you with a roadmap and a set of building strategies, and a blueprint for happy relationship!

6.2 Unhappy couples

> "A strong relationship adheres to principles of social equality and respect for the individual in which everyone has an equal right to have their voice heard". Max Frost

On Tuesday 4th September 2018, Tom Whipple, the Science Editor of The Times (of London) reported on some new research by the University of Illinois which seems to show that even babies know the difference between fear-based and respect-based power, and the futility – in the long-term and overall, of trying to use bullying to lead or influence others. (Whipple, 2018).

I see a lot of couples in my counselling practice – sometimes both partners together; and sometimes one of the partners on their own. And they often have lots of pain in their lives. Pain which they could have avoided if they had studied the subject of 'how to love', and/or 'how to communicate'. But they were too busy running away from their lives; running away from the evidence that they hadn't a clue how to manage a relationship. Or too busy trying to make money, to make ends meet, or to try to solve their *relationship failings* with *business successes* (which, of course, cannot be done!)

They took driving lessons to master their motor car; they bought DIY magazines to learn how to use putty, and wallpaper paste, and paint. But they assumed that *everybody is born with a capacity to love and to be married* or *to cohabit.*

This is not true! Learning how to be a successful couple is a steep learning curve.

And about 50% of couples fail. They score an 'F' (for Fail) on their couples test; and another 'F' on their stress management test.

I want to spread happiness, to individuals and couples. And part of my belief system says that, if I want to spread happiness to individuals, I have, inevitably, to teach them how to become couples.

Why so?

Because being married, or enrolled in a stable couple relationship, seems to be important for reasonable levels of happiness. (Except when the marriage is bad, in which case it can seriously damage your health and happiness. [Liverpool, 2018])[40].

But let us check the positive effects of marriage with some researchers in the field of Happiness Research.

6.3 Looking at the research

According to Professor Jonathan Haidt (2006)[41]:

"A good marriage is one of the life-factors most strongly and consistently associated with happiness[42]. Part of this apparent benefit comes from 'reverse correlation'. Happiness causes marriage. Happy people marry sooner and stay married longer than people with a lower happiness set point, both because they are more appealing as dating partners and because they are easier to live with, as spouses[43]. But much of the apparent benefit is a real and lasting benefit of dependable companionship, which is a basic need; we never fully adapt either to it or to its absence[44]". (Page 88).

Notice that he says "A good marriage", and not just "a marriage"! A bad marriage is a curse!

In addition to these conclusions by Jonathan Haidt, more recent research shows that people who are well connected socially are also happier than isolated individuals[45].

In a later section of his book, Jon Haidt says that freedom can be bad for your health, and that a century of research supports Durkheim's conclusion that single people are most at risk of suicide. It seems there is lots of evidence that social connection is important for health and happiness. (See the previous Endnote, above). And there is emerging evidence that loneliness among modern Americans is being misread as depression.

On the other hand, there is research which suggests that men (in general) benefit more than women (in general) from getting married. It is not difficult to see how this could be. Perhaps women (in general) are more self-sufficient than men (in general) because women (in general) are often more emotionally intelligent (on average) than men (on average). And it may also be that women (in general) take on more responsibility for home building and tending to the relationship than their male partners (in general). If (most) women have too much responsibility for the home and family life, then they will tend to feel more ground down, and consequently less happy, than their male partners. This is an important issue for every male partner to address, and also a signal for women to stop putting up with inequality! Inequality destroys relationships! (And of course, inequality also crops up in [at least some] gay relationships between man and man, and woman and woman!)

~~~

In his book on why marriages succeed or fail, Dr John Gottman argued that it is not conflict in relationships that breaks them down.

What really matters, he argues, "…is how couples work out their differences. In fact, occasional discontent, especially during a marriage's early years, seems to be good for the union in the long run". (Page 24)[46].

(This echoes the point made by Robert Bolton, to the effect that the best relationships exist on the other side of conflict. You have to go through the conflict to get to the green fields of happy relationships. This often necessitates the learning of *assertiveness skills*, so you can ask for what you want, and say 'no' to what you do not want. [See Chapter 7, below]. If you try to work through your relationship-conflicts aggressively, your relationship will be damaged and ultimately destroyed).

Elsewhere, Gottman shared his discovery that men are very stressed by marital conflict; often much more than women are. And this may also feed into the negative effects of bad marriages.

And specifically with regard to sexual disagreements, Gottman's twenty years of research shows that "...what really matters is that you agree on what is acceptable (in the bedroom)". (Page 22).

Finally, with regard to the differential health benefits that men gain from marriage (on average) when compared with women (on average), it may be that most women need to be more assertive and self-caring in their relationships, and to learn to ask for (or fight for) equality, and to refuse to *serve* demanding husbands.

(And demanding or coercive, or unfair husbands [or wives; or gay partners] need to know: *You are digging a grave for your sex-love relationship!*)

6.4 Initial conclusion –   Marriage is good for you...

Overall, then, what is my conclusion?

1. You should aim to get married (or have a stable, equal, relationship [like a civil partnership]), to somebody you *like*, who is a *friend*; and who is as committed to having *an equal relationship* with you as you are with them.

2a. You shouldn't expect marriage, in and of itself, to *make* you happy.

2b. You should *expect* problems to arise, especially if you have (or had) an insecure attachment to your mother (and/or father). And you should expect some significant *adjustment problems* in the early years, and you must learn to work through them (including learning from books – like this one; and from counsellors and therapists, who can guide you into better ways of relating).

3. You should expect to have to *learn how to be a good marriage partner*;

otherwise you will end up as part of the statistic that says: *50% of marriages end in unhappy divorce*. (Learning to be a good marriage partner might involve reading up on the art of loving, and/or going into marriage guidance counselling).

4. You should aim to take *full responsibility* for your own side of the marriage (whether you are male or female!) This includes recognizing that 'a marriage is a *house* that is built every day'. If you do not take responsibility for building it every day, it may very well fall down!

5. You must learn *the art of loving*; which involves demonstrating:

(1) Care for your partner,

(2) Respect for your partner,

(3) Responsibility for your side of the relationship, and

(4) Knowledge of your partner, based on your *curiosity* about them.

And:

6. You must learn how *to be intimate* with your partner (which is primarily about communicating openly, sharing who you are, and being interested in finding out who your partner is; what they want; what they like; what they feel right now (and now, and now!); what turns them on; and so on); to show commitment to the relationship; and to create passion by acts of love.

6.5 Humans as interpreting machines (or organisms)

Humans are 'interpreting machines'; or, rather, organisms that *evaluate experiences subjectively*; on the basis of their early socialization and their subsequent experiences.

This has to be the case, because we do not (and cannot!) look out through our eyes and see 'the truth'.

We *interpret* everything that happens to us, in the light of our lifetime's experience, good and/or bad. Another way of saying this is that we always look at our present situation through a particular 'frame of reference', based on past experience. If you grew up in a dysfunctional family (like Ken Clark, described above; or even a significantly better family than Ken's, but still dysfunctional), then your interpretations will be relatively dysfunctional, or unhelpful, or disturbed.

If you grew up in an emotionally healthy family, your interpretations will be more self-helpful, more useful, and more viable as guides to action. (About fifty percent of us, apparently, are secure in our relationships – Levine and Heller [2011][47] – and that, coincidentally, is often given as the percentage of marriages that survive!)[48]

However, no matter where you grew up, you can re-learn how to relate well to other humans.

This book presents you with a basic curriculum for the learning of a secure attachment style, and a happy relationship.

6.6 Learning to relate more successfully

One of the ways I teach you some new interpretation patterns is through the use of Principle No.1 of my Principles of Happy Relationships.

This is how it works: Imagine you are looking out through a red window frame, around which the following slogan is written:

Red Window No.1: A marriage is a house that is *built* every day. It cannot be *owned* by anybody, and it cannot be expected to stand if it is not *constantly rebuilt*.

Outside of the window you visualize some kind of symbolic representation of your marriage or couple relationship, as it exists today. This might be a happy image; an unhappy image; a confused image; an uncertain image;

etc.

When you look at this symbolic representation of your marital relationship, through the frame of Red Window No.1, what do you learn?

If your image is an unhappy one, you helped to build that! You and your partner together build that. If it is not to your liking, how would you like to change it? What can you do to re-build your relationship so it is more in keeping with what you would like? How would it have to change in order for you to enjoy it and to feel happier? And how could you begin to do that building work? (It's okay to *ask your partner* to help you to rebuild your relationship; but do not make it *their job* to fix it, while you sit back and 'wait for improvements'! No improvements will ever happen if you are not fully involved in the rebuilding work!)

~~~

Write this slogan in a notebook. "**Red Window No.1**: A marriage is a house that is *built* every day. It cannot be *owned* by anybody, and it cannot be expected to stand if it is not *constantly rebuilt*."

(It might be a good idea to get a special notebook for use in connection with this work. Make some notes of a 'reflective writing' variety every day, to get these new ideas firmly into your long-term memory).

A marriage or couple relationship is not a *thing* that can be *owned* or *possessed*. It is, in fact, a *process of relating*, involving two socialized individuals, each of whom has a particular attachment style. Once you accept that your marriage is not a thing; and you cannot own or possess your partner, as if they were a thing to be possessed; you have a much better chance of relating to them successfully.

6.7 The mistake of claiming ownership of one's partner

Many individuals make the mistake of thinking a marriage or couple relationship is a **thing**; an **object**; which they have now "secured". They foolishly believe they now "own" a partner. But you can never *own* another human being. And you will know, if you have ever been through the breakdown of a marriage-like relationship, that *it disappears like fog* when the death-knell is sounded. *It no longer exists!*

The process of reframing your problems in your relationship begins by looking through one of the Red Windows, beginning with the first one:

Red Window No.1: A marriage is a house that is *built* every day. It cannot be *owned* by anybody, and it cannot be expected to stand if it is not *constantly rebuilt*.

I want you to assume that this slogan is true. If you look through this window frame, believing this slogan to be true, and you see a relationship (your relationship) that is filled with pain, then one of the implications is this:

You have <u>either</u>:

(1) **Built pain into your relationship**, by acts of omission or commission; or:

(2) You have **failed to identify and work at removing pain from your relationship**, by acts of omission or commission.

You might offer this objection: "This pain is *not being caused by me*. It's being *caused by my partner*. I play **no part** in it". But if you make that claim, then I will say: "But *you are responsible* for establishing *reasonable boundaries* in your relationship with your partner. If your partner is oppressing you, who is it who is *allowing them* to do that?" See sections 4.7 and 4.8 on *boundary management* in relationships.

6.8 A marriage is built by two people, and is ephemeral

Your marriage is a house that is *built by two people*, or *malformed by two people*, or *allowed to fall down by two people*.

One person cannot build a house *around another*, unless that other is *totally and irresponsibly passive*. One person cannot malform or distort a house which is *a joint project,* unless the other partner **goes along** *with the* *malformation.*

And one person cannot destroy the house of marriage and make the other person *a **victim** who **must** live in the rubble* of that destruction, unless the other party **agrees** to live in that rubble.

If you have difficulty grasping the concept of 'a process' as opposed to 'a thing', then you could try thinking of a relationship as *a thing-event.* One way to do that is to think of a marriage-like relationship, or co-habiting relationship, or civil partnership, as being like **a house that has to be built every day!** If you start each day by trying to build up a positive bond with another human being with whom you share living space, then by some point late in the day, it might feel as if you have some-*thing* established with them. But it can all unravel again, over a similar period of time, if you engage in either too much distance from them, or too much invasion of their personal space.

A marriage is a house that is built every day, by two people, so make sure you keep building, and don't go to sleep in your relationship. Also, do not use a wrecking ball when you want to communicate your frustrations or disappointments to your partner. That will only destroy that part of the house which is still standing.

6.8.1 The shape of the house of marriage

One way to begin to define some of the outlines of this 'house' of marriage - what is possible and what is impossible - would be to begin with two extreme definitions:

1. The first comes from Werner Erhard, (and was just one of his three interesting and helpful definitions). This is part one of his definition:

*"A relationship is an **understanding** and **being aware of** another person's way of being. That is to say, a relationship is the condition of understanding and being aware of another person".* (Notice there is no "entitlement" to anything in this statement!)

2. The second comes from 'exchange theory', which says: *'Love-Profit = (or*

is equal to) Rewards minus Costs. (Or we could say it like this: the profit of love is the surplus of rewards you receive over and above the costs you incur – JWB). The social exchange theory describes love as a "social exchange process, exchanging rewards and affording costs". In other words, if the interactions between lovers are reciprocal and mutually satisfying to both people, a relationship will continue. So in the equation written above, the rewards represent what one gets out of the relationship. This could be affection, recognition, intimacy, prestige, etc. Costs represent what one puts into the relationship. It may be similar to what you get like affection and so forth but this could also be time, money, care, sacrifice, etc. If the rewards are greater than the costs, one will experience love profits. For any person, receiving love profits is the best possible scenario.' (Coryro, 2007)[49].

What is wrong with these two perspectives? Or in what ways are they limited, or incomplete?

Firstly, Werner's statement is **too detached**. Humans enter into relationships as adults in ways that mimic their relationships of attachment from childhood – secure or insecure; and the insecure types are split between those who are **anxious** *and clingy*, on the one hand, and those who are **avoidant** *and withdrawing*, on the other. (As Werner himself recognized elsewhere, individuals tend to 'marry their parent of the opposite sex' by proxy, in order to try to complete some incomplete dynamic from the first few years of life. This perspective echoes some schools of psychodynamic psychotherapy).

Secondly, Coryro's statement is **too rational**. Humans are **emotional** *beings* who have some capacity to engage in reasoning and logic, but we do not run our lives from reason and logic. Our lives are run (in the main) from the non-conscious 'basement' of our minds by feeling-thinking patterns of stimulus and response pairings; and by our capacity to choose (non-consciously) between a range of thinking-feeling-behavioural options, which are normally quite limited.

And thirdly, Coryro's theory involves the concept of 'profit'. But if there is one thing I have learned from twenty years of couple's therapy it is this: **You can never make a profit out of a couple relationship; because it has to be completely equal; and you only get out what you put in!**

6.8.2 The dynamics of couple relationships

We have already indicated above that couple relationships are driven by a pattern laid down in the family of origin, by the relationship patterns engaged in by mother and father. This is Anne Teachworth's (1999/2005) model[50].

However, there is an earlier model which states that, more often than not, (or at least fifty percent of the time), a romantic relationship is a resumption, by proxy, of some family dynamic (between a mother or father and their child) which has lain unresolved in the basement of the minds of the two partners since early childhood. Now the 'battle is re-joined': Will 'baby' win? Or will 'big momma'/'big poppa' triumph?

One example of this kind of resumed dynamic that I commonly find with my couples in therapy is this:

A child has a distant mother and the child is distressed because he (or she) cannot get mother to respond with the kind of sensitive caring the child desires.

In time, the child grows up, and marries a *distant* partner, and tries to get that distant partner to respond in the sensitive, caring way that mother never did.

However, because the child-in-the-adult is so accurate in his (or her) choice of mate, there is actually *no hope* of ever getting a sensitive or caring response from their partner.

If this model is correct, and you have struggled in vain to establish a sensitive and caring relationship of mutual respect and a real sense of comforting intimacy with your partner(s), now you can begin to glimpse why your 'relationships' are so complex and troublesome! You have *'uncompleted relationship distress'* in the basement of your mind from the early years of your relationship with mother (and/or with father. [Mother is normally the most important parent, because her role comes first; and father joins in when baby is a few months old, or even later, sometimes]).

6.9 How to build the house of your relationship

The first thing you can do to build the house of your marital relationship is to show, daily and hourly, that you **care** *about* your partner, and care *for* them.

6.9.1 Showing that you care

Here are some ways to show that you care:

1. *Tell* your partner how much you love them; frequently; daily at least, or perhaps several times each day. *Show them* that you care how they feel, by checking on their feelings.

2. *Kiss and cuddle your partner* every day, at times and in ways that seem welcomed by them, indicating that this is comfortable and pleasurable for them.

3. If you are a man: buy flowers for your partner. If you are a woman: buy him a comparable gift. Do this from time to time – not once and for all!

4. Treat your partner kindly and gently. Do not use harsh language. Apologise when you get things wrong.

5. Share the burdens within the relationship in a way that is agreed to be equal. (That does not mean both partners have to contribute the same amount of money, or do the same amount of housework. But the balance should be a fair exchange, and agreed, mutually, to be equal. And show a willingness to change when your partner becomes upset about any imbalances within the relationship.

6. Listen to your partner's concerns, and their news from their daily activities. Show an active interest in them and their life.

7. Find out what they like – including their dreams – and try to support them in getting as much of that as they can.

~~~

6.9.2 Showing that you respect your partner

The second way you can build that house of your relationship is to show that you respect your partner. Some ways to do that include:

1. Avoid criticizing your partner;

2. Do not judge them harshly;

3. Do not blame them or put them down;

4. Avoid sarcasm; and use gentle language;

5. Do not use contemptuous words or non-verbal actions (like rolling your eyes);

6. Do not show impatience or irritability;

7. Support your partner's choices wherever you can;

8. Acknowledge whatever financial contributions your partner makes.

9. Announce your respect for your partner in the presence of others; and do not ever criticize them or put them down.

~~~

6.9.3 Taking responsibility

The third way you can build the house of your marriage is to take responsibility for your side of the relationship. This has three obvious aspects. The aspects that I am aware of are these:

1. I take responsibility for knowing what this relationship is about; what my partner wants from me; what my contribution is supposed to be; and how we plan and agree joint actions. After I ensure that I know what my responsibilities are, I make a commitment to (normally) always deliver what I am responsible for delivering (within the limits of my human fallibility!).

2. Then there is allocation of responsibility (rather than blame) for things that did not go according to plan. And in this area I operate according to the principle that I learned back in Bangladesh in 1977: "If there's a problem in my life, then I am responsible. Not necessarily in the sense of having caused it. But definitely in the sense that, if it is ever going to be sorted out, then I will have to play a decisive part in that resolution".

3. And finally, avoiding blame. Sometimes it may seem necessary to ask: "Who is responsible, in the sense of 'having caused this problem'?" However, that can be turned around, to become: "How are we going to resolve this problem?"

In this connection I follow Fisher and Ury (1997)[51], who teach these principles:

> (a) Separate the people from the problem. (The people are *not* the problem! The *problem* is the *problem*! Keep those two *separate*!)

> (b) Get the problem down on the table (figuratively), and stand shoulder to shoulder with your partner, addressing the problem, not the 'perpetrator'!

> (c) Talk in terms of 'interests' and not 'positions'. (A *position* is a kind of 'fixed value' or 'rigid requirement'. An *interest* is 'what I would like to be able to get out of this'. So there is what I would like to be able to get out of this problem (or the resolution of this problem); and there is what my partner would like to get out of this problem (or the resolution of this problem).

> (d) What is 'underneath' my first interest? And what is underneath your first interest? And what is underneath the thing that is underneath the first interest? All the way down until there is nothing left to explore. Then look at the things that are underneath your interest; and the things that are underneath your partner's interest; and compromise about how to move forward.

> (e) No blame! No judgements!

~~~

6.9.4 Knowledge: Build up your Love Maps

The fourth way to build the house of your relationships, I would suggest, is to build up a map of your partner's inner world. This is based on Professor John Gottman's Principle No.1[52], which is called "enhancing your **love maps**". What does that mean, in practical terms? Here are some ideas:

1. Ask your partner about their childhood experiences. What was their home life like? What about school experiences?

2. Ask them about their dreams. What would they like to achieve? Where are they hoping to get to in their career or in their personal life?

3. Ask them how they feel about the things that are happening in and around your families.

4. Ask them what they see as the future of your relationship and the family you are building.

5. Never lose *interest* in what goes on inside your partner.

~~~

6.9.5 Don't nag your partner.

The next 'house' building strategy is this: *Don't bicker and argue with your partner.* This principle is taken up by Dale Carnegie, in his famous book on winning friends and influencing people[53] (page 229), in which he shows that nagging is the quickest possible way to dig your marital grave – to kill your relationship. Who wants to be nagged? Who could enjoy, or even tolerate, being nagged? Nobody. The empress Eugenie destroyed Napoleon's love for her through her nagging, jealousy, and general tendency to harass her husband.

I will continue this subject in Chapter 7, when I come to look at how to communicate your grievances constructively.

6.10 Secure and insecure attachments in relationships

In my E-CENT paper on 'My Story of Relationship'[54], I describe how, at the age of 22 years, I had no idea what a relationship was; and how I was not in any significant way 'connected to' (or involved with) my mother (or my father).

Now, more than 45 years later, I understand some of the problems of that time and those dynamics:

Firstly, I had an **insecure attachment** to my mother, because she had not been sensitive and responsive to me when I was a child; and indeed, she had beaten me, and psychologically terrorized me.

Secondly, because of how she was, I had an '**avoidant** attachment style' towards her – that is to say: I kept her in view, and stayed (somewhat) physically proximate to her – with a good gap between us - but I *denied any need for her*, and did not communicate my feelings or thoughts to her. (To pull off this trick, I also probably learned how to prevent myself from communicating my feelings and/or thoughts *to myself!*)

Thirdly, this (avoidant style) became my style of relating to my father and my siblings, and later my school peers. I was avoidant and aloof, sombre and withdrawn.

When I reached puberty and longed for the company of girls (or at least one girl) I was unable to communicate that need. My winning formula was to *deny my need for love and affection*, for human warmth and connection.

Somewhere between 1984 and 1986, as a result of marriage guidance counselling (using Transactional Analysis) and the Erhard Seminars approach to relationship and communication skills, (and a whole lot of other therapeutic approaches), I learned to feel increasingly secure in my relationship with my then girlfriend (Renata), who I married in 1986.

When I came across Dr Albert Ellis and his Rational Therapy (REBT), in 1992, his philosophy linked up with my old attachment style.

His idea that *we do not need to be loved or approved by anybody* echoed my original avoidant attachment style, and I began to re-state that idea as my own belief, while at the same time (paradoxically, and thankfully!) managing to love and be loved by Renata.

It was not until after the disintegration of the REBT monolith, when Al was removed from office in 2005, and I began to try to understand what had happened to cause the Albert Ellis Institute to implode, that I realized that Albert Ellis had had *an avoidant attachment style*, until he got together with Debbie Joffe (when he was in his mid-eighties), at which point she helped to shift him to a more secure mode of operation. But he never recanted his *extreme rejection* of attachment needs in humans.

I, on the other hand, have moved on; and now recognize the supreme importance of our relationships with our parents when we are very young; which determines our attachment style and our capacity to love in adult life; and I teach this to my couple's therapy clients; and I teach those principles in this book.

There are *two insecure attachment styles*, according to attachment theory: the **avoidant** and the **anxious-ambivalent**. The avoidant style *denies a need for love*, and *the anxious style* **demands** and **craves** *total love and devotion*, like a needy baby. Or, to express it differently; when an anxious-ambivalent individual and an avoidant individual get together in a relationship, the anxious-ambivalent partner tries to *cling for dear life* to the other person, who, in response, tries to *run away* (or *keep a safe distance*) as quickly and as totally as possible.

6.10.1 The avoidant attachment style

Both of these styles, which are described below, can be represented as having musical anthems.

For example, the *avoidant attachment style* is well represented by the **10cc** song – *I'm Not in Love* – (which dates from 1976). It's about denying tender emotions, or the need for an intimate connection to another person – because of fear of the pain of rejection; or fear of being overly controlled.

Dr Albert Ellis had this 10cc-kind of *avoidance* of love-needs.

6.10.2 The anxious-ambivalent attachment style

This insecure attachment style is well summed up by Albert Ellis's own song:

"Love me love me, only me, or I'll die without you. Make your love a guarantee so I can never doubt you".

This is impossible to achieve, because nobody can love another person perfectly, or constantly. We love a number of people, to different degrees; and we tend to have a special loving relationship with one person. But that person also loves a number of other individuals to some degree. To demand absolute security in the mother's arms (or the wife's/husband's arms) is tantamount to *dying in their arms*, in order to avoid the pains and threats and dangers of life outside of mother's protection. And some marriage partners do indeed transfer this kind of demand to their partner, and are then doomed to the misery of dissatisfaction.

But there is also the 'secure attachment style'.

6.10.3 Secure attachment

The secure attachment style can *admit its need for love*, without making a big song and dance about it, or feeling the need to *deny* that it exists. And that is where I am today. I admit that I need to be loved, and that I enjoy being loved by my wife. I do not *deny* that I have emotional needs.

However, I am not a 'need machine'. I have both needs and a capacity to love; and I believe that if I love my partner there is a good chance that my own needs will be met in the process. (This is reminiscent of 'exchange theory' of relationship dynamics; without the hope of 'making a profit on the deal').

And again, there are healthy love songs which reflect the secure attachment approach to loving relationship - which is neither overly needy nor overly avoidant.

The examples that come to mind are Finbar Furey's 'Sweet Sixteen', and Al Green's 'Let's stay together'.

6.10.4 The need for love

In one of my E-CENT[55] papers I have argued that Ellis and I are **both** correct:

(1) *We do **not** need to be loved* (as he argued) – if all we want to do is to *survive*, after a fashion. (But it will not be much of a life).

(2) *We **do** need to be loved* (as the attachment theorists argue) – if we want to *thrive* and to feel *fulfilled* as fully functioning *human* beings.

You can find out your own attachment style at this website: **Attachment Styles and Close Relationships.** The web address is this: http://web-research-design.net/cgi-bin/crq/crq.pl.

If you find that you have an insecure attachment style, it is likely that you now know why you tend to experience (or have experienced) significant problems in your couple relationship(s).

6.11 Difficult relationship combinations

The most unstable kind of relationship is one between a partner who is avoidant and one is who anxious/ambivalent.

The reason this type is unstable is that – as mentioned above - the anxious/ambivalent partner tries to cling to the avoidant one. This sets off the avoidant partner's attachment system (alarm), which causes them to seek to avoid being controlled or contained (or becoming dependent!).

When the avoidant partner takes avoidance action, this sets off the attachment system (alarm) in the anxious/ambivalent partner, who consequently feels abandoned, or rejected, and who consequently tries even harder to get a grip on their avoidant partner; which causes their partner to withdraw even more. (Levine and Heller, 2011)[56]

If this sounds like your relationship, then it would be a good idea to see an attachment therapist.

If one of you can learn to develop a secure attachment style, that will help to stabilize the other partner. In time you can both begin to feel more secure.

Or you could study Levine and Heller's (2011) book, ('*Attached: Identify your attachment style and find your perfect match*').

6.12(a) Attachment theory and couples problems

Attachment theory was initiated or created by Dr John Bowlby, building upon some ideas that came from earlier theorists, and his experience of dealing with children who had been separated from their families for various reasons, and how emotionally distressed they found this separation.

But it was not just about children, as illustrated by a conversation with his son, Richard, in 1958:

"He said to me (wrote Richard, in the introduction to one of his father's books (1979/2005)[57], 'You know how distressed small children get if they're lost and can't find their mother and how they keep on searching? Well, I suspect it's the same feeling that adults have when a loved one dies, they keep on searching too. I think it's the same instinct that starts in infancy and evolves throughout life as people grow up, and becomes part of adult love'. I (Richard) remember thinking, well, if you're right, you're on to something really big!" (Pages vii-viii, Bowlby, 1979/2005).

And he was right!

Attachment theory is now the most respectable theory of human development, which includes emphases on:

(1) the way mother (and later father) helps to regulate the emotions of the new baby;

(2) how the child develops an internal Working Model of how they relate to mother and how they relate to father, and how mother and father relate

back to them;

(3) how this kind of interrelating produces either a sense of having 'a secure base', or an insecure attachment to mother (and/or father); and:

(4) how these secure and/or insecure attachment styles are carried forward into future, adult relationships.

The instinct to form a close bond with a significant adult other, at birth, seems to be genetically determined, and may have been an essential part of the survival mechanism of successful branches of human evolution. Those branches which did not generate such a strong sense of the need to attach to, and remain dependent upon, a helpful, protective, loving other, may have died out through neglect or by being preyed upon by other species. (See: Hart, 2011[58]; Wallin, 2007[59]; and Levine and Heller, 2011[60]).

The quality of the relationship formed at birth by mother and baby is clearly a result of the baby's genes and the mother's genes-and-culture. If the mother is *securely attached* to her own mother, there is a good chance that she will pass that on to her own child, by attending to that child in a sensitive and caring manner, reading the baby's mind, and soothing his or her emotions.

However, if the mother has *an insecure attachment* to her own mother, she is likely to pass that on, by being too distant, or too intrusive, in her handling of her baby; by not understanding him or her; and failing to soothe his or her emotions when they become distressed.

As mentioned earlier, the outcomes of the attachment experience of each baby leads on to an attachment style which is stable over time, but somewhat plastic, so it can be improved or worsened by later social experiences.

Based on the research work of Mary Ainsworth (1967; 1969), we can say that all babies tend to become distressed when their mother's become unavailable to them. But the *secure infants* are easily reassured and comforted when the mother returns. On the other hand, the *anxious infants* rush to the mother on her return, but are not easy to reassure – they want to punish mother, and have little trust in their connection to her.

They feel vulnerable.

Avoidant infants are even more disturbed. They pretend they are not distressed, and remain aloof from mother when she returns. But tests show that their hearts are racing just like the stressed, anxious infants, and their (swab tested) cortisol levels are just as high as the anxious infants, showing how stressed they are.

6.12(b) Levine and Heller on mismatched styles

Levine and Heller (2011) – mentioned earlier - took these attachment styles, and began to research how they play out in adult romantic relationships, using interviews and observations of couples in different contexts. (Page 16). They found that the couple who had sparked their interest originally (Tamara and Greg) revealed a troublesome pattern which is quite common. This pattern occurs when a person with an anxious attachment style gets involved romantically with a person with an avoidant attachment style. The avoidant person (in this case, Greg) behaves in such a cool and distant manner that they trigger the attachment system of their partner - (in this case, Tamara's anxious attachment style).

This causes Tamara's *attachment system* to go into overdrive, to try to get closer to Gregg. Tamara's attempting to get closer to Gregg activates his phobia of closeness and intimacy – which probably originally developed because his mother was outright rejecting of his bids for closeness, or she was punishing of him in some way. And so as Tamara approaches Gregg, Gregg withdraws; and as Gregg withdraws, Tamara becomes even more anxious.

Once Levine and Heller were able to clarify what was going on here, Tamara was able to unhook from Gregg, and to find a secure partner. Even though Tamara continued to have a basically anxious attachment style, her new secure partner would have been able to soothe her emotional state, and keep her calm.

This points to the second significant finding of Levine and Heller (2011), as follows:

Both the avoidant and anxious types fare better with a secure partner. The secure partner does not run away from the anxious type; and neither does the secure partner overly crowd the avoidant type. So one of the major findings of this research suggests that, if your experience tells you that you have an anxious or avoidant attachment style, then seek a partner who is secure. (About 50% of the population has a secure attachment style, so this should not be too difficult).

(Find out your attachment style, online at this website: **Attachment Styles and Close Relationships.** The web address is this: http://web-research-design.net/cgi-bin/crq/crq.pl.)

6.13 Back to principles of couple relationships

Over a period of almost twenty years, working with married and co-habiting couples, I have identified a number of key problems with the way individuals and couples understand (or, rather, misunderstand) what a relationship is. Because they define relationship inaccurately, they often have grossly unrealistic expectations of their partner and their relationship.

Back in the late 1970's, Werner Erhard came up with a three part definition of relationship, which went like this:

(a)   A relationship is an **understanding** and **being aware of** another person's way of being. That is to say, a relationship is the condition of understanding and being aware of another person. (Notice there is no "entitlement" to anything in this statement!)

(b)   Successful relationships are based on **agreed on goals**. That does not mean that my partner must agree to my goals, or vice versa. Instead it means, I support my partner in pursuing her goals; and she supports me in pursuing mine. (Notice there are no "sergeant majors" in this statement; no "directors"; no "leaders" and "led"!)

(c)   If you want to have **a really powerful relationship** with anybody, you have **got to stop making them wrong**. And making them wrong means describing them as being bad/wrong when their ideas/values/goals/behaviours deviate from our idea of what they **should** be! (Separate the person from the problem; talk about the problem in terms of your interests, not your positions; and aim for compromises and trade-offs, not victories and win-lose outcomes).

6.14 How to re-wire your brain for better relationships

If you were to review those three elements of definition, over and over and over again, day after day, week after week, and month after month, you would eventually develop a capacity for relationship which was extraordinary – perhaps in the top five percent of the population of the world! But more importantly, you would be in a durable relationship, and you and your partner would be happy![61] (How do I know that this is the case? Because that is what I did, back in 1984-86, and that is the kind of relationship I – in cooperation with my wife - was able to build as a result!)

In the process you would have moved into that area of human functioning which was defined by Dr Erich Fromm as: Respect for your partner; Taking responsibility for your side of the relationship; and: Showing care for your partner[62].

The principles outlined above are very important, but I also wanted to add some of the key gems of wisdom that I have discovered about how to develop successful relationship skills.

6.15 Introduction to my eighteen principles

Over the years I have tried to identify the most helpful insights on managing happy, loving relationships, and I have passed these on to my couple-clients. At the last count, I had collected, and/or developed, eighteen principles - or things you can do - which make the biggest and quickest contribution to improving your capacity to manage a happy couple relationship. (The number eighteen does not include Werner Erhard's three elements of relationship definition, above).

Here are a couple of my principles for you to consider. Four others will be outlined in the chapters which follow. (And the remaining twelve will be explored in Volumes 2 and 3 of this series).

The first one is the one we began this chapter with:

1. A marriage is a "house" that is built every day. What actions did you consciously take to build the "house" of your marriage today?

When you wake up in the morning, remind yourself that all you have is 'the foundations' of a relationship. You now have to build that relationship all over again; every single day. The house of your relationship is never complete. You can never 'clock off'.

A relationship is not something you HAVE, it is something you DO! It is a process rather than a thing.

If you go to sleep in your relationship, you will wake up to find it has collapsed from want of repair. Having destructive arguments with your partner about who is *right* and who is *wrong*, and especially who is 'top-dog' and who is 'under-dog', is equivalent to trying to polish the walls of your "house" with sledge hammers! You will wreck it in no time. So I ask again:

What actions did you consciously take today to build the "house" of your relationship?

What actions did you take to stop swinging the wrecking ball against the walls of your relationship?

Write your answers in your journal. If you have done nothing to build the house of your relationship, then apply the questions to the future:

What do you propose to do to build your relationship up? If you have no ideas, then you need to get some help to figure out what to do.

What do you propose to do to stop wrecking your relationship (if you are engaging in destructive behaviours, like angry or sulky communication, or avoiding your partner, or anxiously clinging to them and driving them away from you in the process)?

~~~

Principle No.4 leads on from this point, as follows:

Principle 4: Love is not a "nice feeling". Love is a process of "extending yourself in the service of another person". In what ways could you extend yourself in the service of your partner which would increase the flow of love from you to them? (And, later, back again! *Cast your bread upon the waters, for it shall return after many days!*)

Of course, we have expanded our definition of love, above, as follows:

Love is defined by the following qualities: Passion (automatic and willed); Intimacy (including care and respect and sharing personal knowledge with each other, to achieve emotional and physical closeness); and commitment (including taking responsibility for our own side of the relationship; and extending ourselves in the service of our beloved).

So, ask yourself:

1. How well do I demonstrate *passion* for my partner?

2. How well do I demonstrate and strive to achieve *intimacy* with my partner?

3. Do I take *full responsibility* for managing my side of the relationship?

And:

4. Do I take actions which could be seen as evidence that I 'extend myself' in the service of my partner'?

The content of this book should help you to improve your performance in each of those four areas of love. But if you feel you need further help with these areas of your life, then consult a good couple's therapist, preferably one who is recommended by somebody you know.

~~~

To be successful in love, you need to be able to **stand on your own two feet.** You need to be able to live on your own, and to learn to enjoy your own company. You should also avoid *'falling* in love' as that will only produce an unstable relationship. Instead, learn how to '**stand** in love'.

~~~

In Chapter 7 we will begin to look at how to clarify what is legitimate assertion of your wants and needs, and what is excessive aggression in pursuit of a win-lose strategy of relating. We will begin to look at legitimate boundaries and how to define and defend them.

~~~

Study guidelines

Tick that you've read this chapter once: ☐

Before you more on to Chapter 7, please read this chapter a second time: ☐

And a third time: ☐

~~~

When reading and re-reading this chapter, please underline those points that seem most important to you. Make notes in the margins, as necessary, as quick reminders of the content of a paragraph or a page.

And turn down the corner of the page, when the content is so important you want to find it again, quickly and easily. Also, add important points, with their page numbers, in your own index to this book, in Appendix 'L', below.

~~~

Chapter 7: How to act constructively, using loving-and-kind assertiveness

7.1 Introduction

Most people do not know how to communicate *assertively*. Communicating assertively means you asking for what you want, and saying 'no' to what you do not want, while at the same time showing respect for your own rights and the rights and sensibilities of the other person.

Some people are *too passive*, and behave like door-mats to their partners.

And some are *too aggressive*, and 'go to war' with their partner at the drop of a hat!

Here's a really surprising insight, from Professor Howard Markman, who is the Director of the Centre for Marital and Family Studies at the University of Denver, Colorado:

> "When women bring up issues, men tend to withdraw because *they are afraid of fighting*. We (at our centre) train men to *listen* to what their wife is saying, instead of closing down". (From Agnew, 1996).

(See Chapter 4, above, for our introduction to effective communication strategies – including active listening, and formal listening time).

A similar point was made by Professor John Gottman, at the Gottman Institute in Seattle, Washington. In his main book on marriage, Gottman (1997) writes that, in 70% of cases of volatile conflict between couples, it is the man (not the woman!) who fills up with stress hormones, and then closes down, because he cannot think while his brain is awash with adrenaline. (See also: Kiecolt-Glaser and colleagues., 1996)[63].

So more women than men are aggressive in their communication, and more men than women withdraw - (according to Kiecolt-Glaser, [1996];

Gottman [1997]; and Markman, in Agnew's [1996] newspaper article.).

Many women make the mistake of thinking men are so tough that they can be spoken to in any old rough manner at all, and they should be able to handle that kind of approach! But, in most cases (perhaps 70% of conflicts), *they can't!*

This is how Agnew (1996) expresses Professor Markman's view:

"Women ... (in Markman's relationship program) are encouraged to request a time to discuss a problem, rather than (a classic female error, apparently) demanding to have it out the moment the man walks through the door. ... What both sexes need ... is understanding rather than agreement".

~~~

However, there are many situations in which women feel *too vulnerable* to speak up, in case their partner becomes verbally or physically aggressive. This has been researched by a group of scientists in Maryland, US, and reported by Dr Elaine Eaker in 2007. It turns out that women who 'bite their tongues' during rows are four times more likely to die earlier than those who shout back. But this probably applies no matter what your gender happens to be, and the researchers conclude that "Both spouses really need to allow another person a safe environment to express feelings when they're in conflict".

~~~

Whether a couple have a relationship riven by conflict; or one in which they fail to communicate about their feelings; or one where one partner plays aggressive Top Dog while the other plays passive Under Dog – they are likely to be living in misery, and also making each other physically and mentally sick. (See Umberson, et al., 2006). Here is an extract from the abstract of Umberson's report:

"...marital strain accelerates the typical decline in self-rated health that occurs over time and ... this adverse effect is greater at older ages. These findings fit with recent theoretical work on cumulative adversity in that *marital strain seems to have a cumulative effect on health over time* — an effect that produces increasing vulnerability to marital strain with age. Contrary to expectations, *marital quality seems to affect the health of men and women in similar ways across the life course."*

New research at Ohio State University, in 2018, led by Dr Janice Kiecolt-Glaser, shows how conflicted marriages make people physically unwell. "We think that this everyday marital distress – for some people – is causing changes in the gut that lead to inflammation and, potentially, illness". (Kiecolt-Glaser, quoted in Knapton, 2018. See also, Kiecolt-Glaser, Wilson and Bailey, et al., (2018) and Ohio State University (2018))[64].

And we already know that leaky gut can trigger leaky blood-brain barrier, resulting in toxins getting into the brain, and affecting moods and emotions. (Enders, 2015: Pages 114-133).

So, nobody escapes. Marital strain and conflict affects men and women about equally; and this effect is likely to harm both *physical health* and *emotional wellbeing*.

And my proposed solution is that the partners in conflicted marriages - to avoid bad-tempered fights - should learn how to *communicate* more effectively; to have *personal boundaries*; and to know how to *assert their legitimate rights*.

~~~

In this chapter I have set out to introduce you to the most basic level of self-assertion skills.

This is because it can be profoundly demotivating to be introduced to skills which are just too difficult – or 'too scary'! – to be implemented.

So, instead, I am going to teach you a range of knowledge and skills which can fairly easily be implemented by almost any reader of this book.

Then, in Volume 2, I will present slightly more challenging skills, which you should by then be able to take in your stride.

If you have any difficulty implementing any of the ideas in this chapter, you could discuss how to proceed with a good coach, counsellor or psychotherapist, who can guide you through any difficulties that you experience.

However, my expectation is that, in most cases, you will find this material easy to work with, and experience no significant difficulty applying the knowledge and skills described below.

7.2 Passivity, assertion and aggression

If you want to be clear about the distinction between passivity, assertion and aggression, as forms of human behaviour, then the best model to use is this:

All human behaviour can be mapped on a continuum from passive to aggressive, via assertive; as shown in Table 7.1 below.

Passive	Assertive	Aggressive
Passive behaviour involves putting up with aggressive or bullying behaviour by others. Failing to ask for what you want. Giving in to others and being overly-compliant. Using flowery and diplomatic language to placate others. And being unwillingness to pursue your own needs and interests.	Asking for what you want. Saying no to what you do not want. Negotiating fairly about differences of opinion or clashes of interests. Owning your own viewpoint, by stating that "I wish..."; "I want.."; "I would like..."; etc. Rather than 'You-Statements' (like those in the *Aggressive* column). Expressing appreciation for what is given; expressing *conditional appreciation* for what is requested.	Aggressive behaviour involves treating others unfairly, by intimidating them, or demanding that they comply with your wishes. Aggressors offend against others in pursuit of their own interests. This often involves anger and verbal hostility. Can include physical violence. Blames others and fails to take any responsibility for their own actions. Points finger of blame, and over-uses You-Statements: "You should..."; "You must..."; "You have to..."; etc.

Table 7.1: Some indicators of passive, aggressive and assertive behaviour

Putting up with unfair treatment by one's partner is not a good way to build a happy sex-love relationship, since the conformity and compliance will build up into resentment of the dominator. It is much better for both parties to the relationship, and for the relationship as an institution, for both partners to behave in an assertive way with each other. This book will help you to learn how to do just that.

One of the problems that was identified by Gestalt Therapy theorists is that many couples tend to play an unhealthy psychological 'game', called Top-Dog/Under-Dog.

I have dealt with many couples where this game was played on a win-lose basis from week to week.

At the first session of couple's therapy, the couple would come in, and one of them would be 'inflated' (or 'puffed up') and the other would be 'deflated' (or depressed).

Before the second session, I would anticipate how that new session might go, but my guesses would be wrong, because this time the *previously deflated* partner would be *puffed up*, and the previous 'Top-dog' would now be the 'Under-dog'!

It was a *war* in the name of relationship! A sick game of "I'm the King (or Queen) of the castle. Get down you Dirty Rascal!"

If this is the kind of relationship (or, rather, 'involvement') that you have – or some variation on the gender war (or the partner war, in the case of gay relationships) – then the solution is to adopt the position, in principle, of Equal Dog – Equal Dog.

Refuse to entertain the idea that your partner could ever be *reduced in status or worth* in your relationship. *Insist* upon total equality for the two of you – no exception; no debate!

Make a commitment to end the war. *Commit* to total equality. *Commit* to fair (assertive) fighting about *interests*, and not *positions*. *Commit* to assertive communication; win-win encounters; and Equal Dog to Equal Dog relationship.

7.3 Realistic and reasonable assertion

> *"'It is very important for couples to be able to express negative feelings, and it's normal to disagree. It's how you handle the conflict that predicts your future', says Professor Markman".* (Agnew, 1996).

What is *legitimate assertion* of your wants and needs, and what is *excessive aggression* in pursuit of a win-lose strategy of relating?

Table 7.1 above contains the briefest of answers, which I will elaborate here:

7.3.1. Asking for what you want

Asking for what you want is legitimate self-assertion. But bear in mind that you will not always get what you ask for. Why not? Because if it is legitimate for you to influence your partner into giving you what you want, then, according to the Golden Rule, it is also legitimate for your partner to influence you into giving them what they want. How can this be resolved? Once you have committed to formal equality in your relationship, there is only one way to resolve this apparent tension, and that is to agree that each partner is entitled to influence their partner up to, but not beyond, *50% of the influencing* that is done over time.

Of course, it is not perfectly easy to measure how much your partner has influenced you, and how much they have reciprocated when you wanted to influence them. So some *goodwill* is needed. And a *cool* head. And a *warm* heart. And *an abandonment of petty squabbling* about crumbs that fall when the biscuit (or cookie) is broken in virtually equal halves!

When you want to ask your partner for something, make sure you have previously used 'appreciation messages' (or messages of thanks) – as described below, in section 7.3.5. Then use a '*conditional* appreciation message' – like "I would really appreciate it if you would agree to (X)". (See section 7.3.6 below).

7.3.2. Saying no to what you do not want

Saying 'No' is legitimate assertion. Unless, that is, your saying 'No' shows up for a jury of your peers as *an intransigent refusal* to allow your partner to influence you to the same degree (on average) to which you try to influence your partner.

Of course, we all have red lines. And our partners should not expect us to cross any of our own red lines. However, if you have so many red lines that it is virtually impossible for your partner to influence you anywhere near as much as you influence them, then they will almost certainly conclude that you are *not really committed to equality* in the relationship – and that will begin to pull the relationship apart! So, if you want to keep the relationship happy, durable, peaceful and secure, then you have to try to meet your partner halfway, as much as is humanly possible.

Opt for the middle way between saying 'No' too often, and saying 'No' too infrequently. When your partner asks you for something, and you feel a resistance, ask for time to think it over. Take the time, and check out your feelings. Is this a reasonable request? Is it unreasonable in any way? Do you 'owe it' to your partner to let them influence you this time, because they have let you influence them on sufficient occasions in the past? Does this request breach any of your 'red lines'? Is it immoral; or illegal; or would it cause you physical pain or emotional distress? If, on balance, you want to say no, then resolve to do so! And stick to your refusal, if it is a matter of principle!

Teach yourself that it's okay to say 'No'. If you do not have the right to say 'No', then you have no personal boundaries: no personal power. So own that power; and clarify those boundaries. You can practice saying 'No' in role plays, with a friend. Ask your friend to pretend they are having a party on Saturday night, and they want you to come. Their job is to think of at least seven sentences of invitation, including inducements. For examples:

Friend: "I'm having a party on Saturday night. Would you like to come?" (1).

You: "No!"

Friend: "I can lay on your favourite food. What is your favourite food?" (2a)

You: "Chinese" (for example).

Friend: "I'll lay on some wonderful Chinese food. Say you'll come to my party". (2b)

"No!"

Friend: "What's your favourite music?" (3a)

Etcetera, etcetera.

Your friend keeps trying to put pressure on you to attend the party, and you keep saying "No!"

And keep your face straight. Do not try to soft soap them with a smile. Do not let your posture droop. Stand up straight, and tell it how it is. "No! I don't want to come!"

After about six or seven attempts to persuade you, the most persistent person will normally give up and accept your refusal as being okay!

7.3.3. Negotiating fairly

Here is another example of reasonable assertion: Negotiating fairly about differences of opinion or about clashes of interests. And negotiating fairly means: (1) separate the people from the problem; (2) put the problem on the table and stand side by side to address it; (3) the problem is the problem – and your partner is not the problem; (4) talk in terms of your interests and not your positions; (5) seek to find out what is 'underneath' each of your interests; (6) seek to find some way of trade off on the basis of what is underneath your interests. (This system is derived from Fisher and Ury (1997) and Helen Hall Clinard (1985) and it will be expanded in Volume 2 of this series, in a section on 'mutual problem solving').

7.3.4. 'Owning your own viewpoint'

This is another expression of reasonable self-assertion. 'Owning your own viewpoint' involves admitting that "This is how it looks to me!"; rather than "This is how it IS!!!"

Instead of insisting that "It has to be like this...", consider using some preferential statements like these: "I wish..."; "I want..."; "I would like..."; etc.

This is much more democratic and fair than making absolutistic 'You-Statements', like these: "You should..."; "You must..."; "You are wrong, and I am right about...", etc.

Another important way of looking at this issue is to note that, in Transactional Analysis – which is explored in Appendix B – there is a distinction made between 'Parent language' and 'Adult language'.

Adult language involves the use of 'I-Statements': "I wish..."; "I want..."; "I would like..."; etc.

Parent language, (and especially Controlling Parent, and Critical Parent), is based on 'You-Statements'; for examples: "You should..."; "You must..."; "You have to..."; "You are wrong, and I am right about...", etc.

Another way of saying the same things is this:

Adult language normally consists of making *preferential* statements: "I would *prefer it* if you would... (do X instead of Y, [for example])". An exception would be when it comes to *defending your boundaries*, in which case you would use **a stronger I-statement**, like this: "I am *unhappy* about that behaviour, and I **will <u>not</u>** go along with...(X)".

7.3.5. Expressing appreciation

Thanking your partner for what is given to you by them, or done by them, for you, or for your joint home life, is another form of assertive behaviour. "Thanks for .... I really appreciate it that you ... (did X)" "I like the fact that you (did Y) which allowed me to (do Z)..." "Thanks for that nice cup of tea

(or walk in the country; or kiss on the cheek!)"

Thanking your partner for the things they do or say - which have a positive effect upon you - is important. The reason that it's so important is described by Helen Clinard (1987).

She calls this the skill of 'tracking positives'. She explains that it builds the self-esteem and the self-confidence of the person whose actions are appreciated. (And that's good for the health of the relationship!)

But she also points out that we each have a responsibility to teach our social environment - (which means the people around us, including our sex-love partner) - what we like and what we do not like.

The *appreciation message* helps us to teach them what we like.

7.3.6. Using conditional appreciation messages

These differ from *appreciation* messages, in that *appreciation messages* are about the **previous** actions or words of your partner, while *conditional appreciation* is about the preferred *future* actions or words of your partner.

Let's take a look at an example:

Let us assume I want to walk in the park, because it's a nice, sunny afternoon, and I'd like my partner to go with me. I could say:

"I'd *really appreciate it* if you would join me for a walk in the park".

My partner has three (main) options:

1. She could *agree* to go with me; on the basis that I have often done things that she requested of me;

2. She could point out that this is a *bad time* for her, and suggest an alternative time which would work for her. (This might reflect a boundary she has, like this: "I must get my daily quota of writing done before I go out to 'play'!" And if that is her boundary, I would want to honour it!)

3. She could attempt to negotiate a *different place* for our walk, and check to see if that would be *acceptable* to me as a compromise. (This might be based upon her *low threshold of boredom*; and the fact that I *often* want to walk around the park, while she likes more variety in her walking environments).

But the bottom line is this: I ask her *nicely*, in the context of *normally thanking her* when she does something nice for me; and this *combination* (of asking nicely, and thanking her as appropriate) enhances the chances of her agreeing to go with me. Or, to put it another way: Conditional appreciation messages tell your partner what you would like, and often what you would prefer them not to do, in the future (including the immediate future)! In this sense, conditional appreciation messages are a way to convey both my *desires* and my *boundaries* to my partner. And my boundaries are about "what I will allow in", and what I want to "keep out".

7.3.7. The power of operating from the 'I'm OK - You're OK' position

Some marriage partners assume that they are "OK", meaning *good*; but that their partner is "Not-OK", or *a bad person*. These kinds of partnerships are based on a Boss and a Follower; or the *Top Dog / Under Dog* model.

In other relationships, those roles flip around. Sometimes the man is The Boss (or Top Dog), and sometimes the woman is the Boss (or Top Dog).

Sometimes the flip-around process is driven by what we call 'splitting'; a process in which Partner 'A' thinks their Partner (B) is Okay, so long as Partner 'B's behaviour is generally perceived to be good. But if Partner 'B' engages in some bad behaviour, then Partner 'A' perceives them as 'All Bad'. (See my description of 'splitting' in section 4.4 of Chapter 4 above).

We teach our couple clients to reject both inequality in their relationships (and playing 'Top Dog/ Underdog' is one example of a strong commitment to inequality). And we also teach them to give up 'splitting' their partner into Good and Bad, and to relate to them as a Whole-Imperfect being who sometimes does well, and sometimes under-performs. (This does not, however, including any *excuses for immorality*: like domestic violence, sexual abuse or sexual infidelity, and so on!)

One of the ways we get them to give up these forms of splitting and inequality is by teaching them *the OK-Corral model* from Transactional Analysis, which is shown in Figure 7.2 below.

		Your Decision About Others	
		OK	Not-OK
Your Decision About Yourself	OK	1. I'm OK - You're OK	2. I'm OK - You're Not-OK
	Not-OK	3. I'm Not-OK - You're OK	4. I'm Not-OK - You're Not-OK

Figure 7.2: The OK Corral

This model helps people to understand that the healthy life-position to operate from is this: *"I'm OK and so are you (my partner)"* – just so long as we are both committed to acting as moral and socially-responsible individuals.

It also helps the individual to understand if they are operating from *negative attitudes* towards themselves or others. In TA, these could be classified as (conscious or non-conscious) *not-OK life-positions* (about self or others).

A *'not-OK' life position* could include either of the following attitudes:

(1) **"I'm not OK** because I cannot please my partner; (or I cannot get a job; or I cannot make a success of my career; or I cannot get along with others"; etc.) Or:

(2) **"You're not OK** because you frustrate me; (or threaten my self-concept; or because you challenge me in ways that make me feel uncomfortable)"; etc.

To have a happy couple relationship, you have to learn (or teach yourself) to always operate from the 'I'm OK – You're-OK' position, in your dealings with your partner. (The exception here is this: If your partner acts in a way which is clearly illegal or immoral – like using physical violence, or emotional bullying, or any form of coercion against you; or requiring you to do anything [for example, in the bedroom] which you really do not want to do, then they have crossed over into that territory which we call **'Bad Wolf' behaviour**, and you have to take action to stop them! [See Appendix F, below for more]).

~~~

7.3.8. Use of assertive body language

Body language is non-verbal communication; or leakage of bodily signals about emotional states. For example, if you saw two individuals across the street, and somebody told you one of them had just been fired from their job (sacked, or made redundant), and the other one had just been promoted, would you expect to be able to see the difference, without asking them any questions? Of course you would. Even if your ability to read body language is not particularly conscious, and you could not describe how you do it, I am convinced you would look for differences between:

1. The two faces: Which one looks happier, perhaps smiling broadly; and which one looks most dejected, or sad, or neutral, or worried?

2. The posture of the two bodies: Which one is looking downwards, head bowed? And which one is looking upwards, or straight ahead? Which one has the straightest, most erect spine?

3. Their pace of movement: Which one looks most vigorous? Which one looks slowed down, or lethargic?

4. Their use of eye contact: Which one is making *more open eye contact*? Which one looks down or away the most?

5. Body armouring: Does one of them have their arms folded across their chest, in a form of 'body armouring', or self-protection?

I am quite confident you would know in a glance which one had been promoted and which one was sacked or made redundant.

And now, suppose you cross the street, and can hear not only what they are saying to each other, but also:

5. Their tones of voice: Which one sounds surer of themselves? Which one sounds less sure of themselves? Which one sounds happier? Which one sounds least happy?

Since you can easily read the body language and non-verbal communication of these two described individuals, you must realize that other people read your body language all the time. If you are to communicate your boundaries assertively, you have to take a close look at what messages you are sending to your partner non-verbally.

If there are any weaknesses in your boundaries, your partner (and others) will be able to pick them up, non-consciously, through your body language; and may often violate your boundary at those points, without thinking about the implications of such violations.

I teach my clients the importance of this aspect of self-assertion with the following story:

Back in the 1980's, when assertiveness training was popular in the UK and the US, a woman (Janet) went on a weekend assertiveness training workshop. She was very upset by a male colleague of hers (Stephen) who constantly messed her around in their shared office by:

1. Borrowing her staple machine, and not returning it; often mislaying it so she had to waste time hunting for it.

2. Removing files from her desk, and hiding them in his desk drawers, until she was so stressed out about the missing information that he could return the files to her while laughing, and demanding to know: "Can't you take a joke?"

3. Making jokes at her expense ("ribbing her"), and frustrating her and putting her down.

So, she went to the weekend workshop; she studied all the sk
were teaching there; and spent her evenings planning how sl
those skills on Stephen to get him to stop giving her a hard time.

Then, on Monday morning she returned to work. In the foyer of her office
building, she ran through the skills she's learned; and thought about which
skill she's use when he did behaviour X, or Y, or Z. When she was
psychologically prepared for the worst, she got into the lift (elevator), took
three deep breaths; drew herself up to her full height and looked straight
ahead at her image in the mirror; put on her best "Don't f*** with me" face;
and pressed the button for the sixth floor.

The life whirred up to the sixth floor, Janet stepped out of the lift, crossed
the hallway, pushed open the door, expecting immediate trouble from
Stephen. Instead, what she saw was his jaw drop; his smile fade; and his
eyes go down to the paperwork on his desk. She said *nothing*, went to her
desk, and worked diligently all morning, until tea break, which she took
with a colleague on the fifth floor. She returned to her desk and checked
that her files and stationery items were all okay, and got on with her work.
She went out for lunch with a friend; and returned to a quiet afternoon at
her desk. At no point did she speak to Stephen. But he had got her
nonverbal message loud and clear. "Do not f*** with me!"

Body language! Body language! Body language! (But if you have to state
this boundary in language, remember to use *assertive* language, and not
aggressive language).

7.4 What's wrong with passivity and aggression

If you are too *passive* and *compliant* in your relationships, then you are not
going to get what you want from your relationships, and you may be
oppressed or exploited, or neglected and abused. The **sad truth** of human
relations is this; Bullies are **created** by victims at least as much as victims
are created by bullies! So don't behave like a *victim*, or you will very
likely become one!

On the other hand, if you are too aggressive and controlling in your relationships, you will alienate your partner, and destroy your relationships. If you are sceptical about this point, and think your partner should be able to handle your raising of your voice and expressing your frustrations in a volatile manner, then you need to know what the research by Dr John Gottman - one of the most respectable of marriage counselling researches – shows: One of Professor Gottman's most important research discoveries was this:

> When one partner behaves in a volatile (or angry) manner, the other partner fills up with the stress hormone, cortisol, which effectively prevents them from being able to reason about what is going on; therefore they tend to withdraw.

> This was true even in those cases where a small woman (wife) was volatile with a huge man (husband)!

For the two reasons stated above, what you need to be able to do is to find a 'middle way' between being *too passive* and *too aggressive*; and that pathway is called *'the assertive approach'*.

To find out just how assertive you are at the moment, please complete the Assertiveness Questionnaire shown in the next section.

7.5 An assertiveness questionnaire

The more appropriately assertive you are, the less stress will you experience in your relationships. So, how assertive are you?

Here's a little quiz designed to allow you to find out.

Please tick column 1, 2 or 3 against each statement below.

A tick in column 1 means "Almost always".

A tick in column 2 means "Sometimes"

A tick in column 3 means "Almost never".

Assertiveness Questionnaire

Statements of assertive rights	Col.1: Almost always	Col.2: Sometimes	Col.3: Almost never
1. I believe I have a right to be treated with respect as an equal human being.	✓		
2. I believe I have a right to ask for what I want, while recognizing that others have the right to refuse.	✓		
3. I ask for what I want.		✓	
4. I believe I have a right to make my own arrangements and agreements, without being controlled or bullied by others.			
5. I believe I have a right to change my mind, and to communicate that change.		✓	
6. I believe I have the right to change my beliefs and behaviours.			
7. I believe I have a right to say 'No' to requests from others.			
8. In practice, I can and do say 'No' to unreasonable requests, or requests that I want to decline.	✓		

...continued...

9. I believe I have the right to choose not to accept responsibility for others and their feelings and problems.			
10. I believe I have the right to say 'I don't know' or 'I don't understand'	✓		
11. I believe I have the right to ask for more time or more information	✓		
12. I believe I have the right to say 'yes' or 'no' and not feel guilty			
13. I believe I have the right to make mistakes and to take responsibility for them			
14. I believe I have the right to be independent of the goodwill of others (if I so choose) especially if the price of that goodwill is too high (as in unfair or unequal relationships).			
15. I believe I have the right to choose NOT to be assertive, when I want to choose that option			

7.6 The mark scheme and the definition of assertiveness

To mark this questionnaire, please award yourself three points for each tick in column 1; one points for each tick in column 2; and zero points for each tick in column 3.

You are perfectly assertive if you scored 45 points (the maximum). You are totally passive if you scored zero points. And your level of assertiveness is most likely to be somewhere between those two extremes.

If you scored less than 30 points, then you need to do quite a bit of work to become optimally assertive.

Study the fifteen beliefs in this questionnaire, above, and try to move yourself towards a more consistent set of assertive beliefs and actions. This should reduce your stress level. It should also get your more of what you are legitimately entitled to ask for, without damaging your relationship with your partner.

By contrast, being *aggressive* is stress-inducing, in that, by definition it is a strong expression of the "fight response", and could produce an equally aggressive response from the victim of your aggression. You are already overly-aroused when you are angry. But it is doubly stressful because, immediately after an individual becomes aggressive, they are liable to become *fearful* that their victim might retaliate, so they then may tend to feel anxious, which is the other form of over-arousal, also known as the "flight response".[65]

Reasonable assertiveness is characterized by the following types of behaviour:

(1) **Asking** for what you want, instead of expecting others to read your mind;

(2) Saying **'No'** to what you do not want, in a clear and reasonable manner; and:

(3) **Communicating** your appreciation for the things provided by others. (Helen Hall Clinard, [1985][66]).

(4) Saying 'I **would** appreciate it…' - when you make a request;

(5) Telling your partner how their behaviour affects you: (Saying, "When you do (X), I feel (Y), because (Z)"). (Robert Bolton, 1979/1986). (This skill will be fully developed in Volume Two of this book series).

If you want to see, and study, some role models of *assertive behaviour*, then you could go to YouTube, and search for videos on the following subjects: "Saying No assertively"; "Asking for what you want"; or "Assertive communication".

~~~

Study guidelines

Tick that you've read this chapter once: ☐

Before you more on to Chapter 8, please read this chapter a second time: ☐

And a third time: ☐

~~~

When reading and re-reading this chapter, please underline those points that seem most important to you.

Make notes in the margins, as necessary, as quick reminders of the content of a paragraph or a page.

And turn down the corner of the page, when the content is so important you want to find it again, quickly and easily.

Also, add important points, with their page numbers, in your own index to this book, in Appendix 'L', below.

~~~

Chapter 8: Boundary management issues - Including case studies

8.1 Introduction

Our personal boundaries are like the borders of a country. Country boundaries allow certain people in and keep certain people out. And personal boundaries allow good things in, and keep bad things out.

This chapter consists of two parts.

Part 1 deals with the origin and development of boundaries in relationships. It looks at the questions: *What are boundaries?* And *where do they come from?*

Part 2 deals with ways in which boundaries *malfunction* in relationships, causing emotional misery.

This is explored through the lens of a number of case studies of former couple-clients of mine.

In particular, I will look at ways in which those cases illustrate problems to do with maintaining reasonable, assertive, constructive, healthy, happy boundaries between the two members of the couple.

I will consider these illustrations under the following three headings:

1. Boundary violations that are related to the 'law of karma'; or the law of reaping and sowing. (The law that expresses the idea that *what you do* affects the *results* that you get.)

2. Boundary problems related to the 'law of responsibility'. (You have to *take responsibility* for yourself and your actions);

And:

3. Problems related to the law of 'declared boundaries'. (You have to *communicate your boundaries* to your partner).

8.2 Part 1: The origin of boundaries in childhood

Melanie Klein (1940)[67] was probably the first major theorist of childhood development to be able to empathically enter the mind of a child, in her imagination; and to infer what a typical child's early experiences probably feel like. And, in her view, young babies feel as if they are connected to everything; that they are part of everything; that everything is them. Gradually they became aware of 'things', or 'objects': a breast; a face; a hand. Also, an absent ('bad') breast. It probably feels as if 'mother' is an extension of themselves, which serves them ('good mother') and frustrates them ('bad mother'). These would be more *felt-evaluative labels*, and not linguistic word-labels.

For her own part, a good mother has *a weak boundary* with her baby, in the sense that she will often – or most often - put the baby's needs before her own needs; to a degree that she would never do with another adult, or somebody else's child. It feels, to the good mother, as if the baby is 'part of her', and that she herself is part of the baby's life.

8.2.1 The mother-baby relationship is where we all begin

It is now widely agreed among psychologist, psychiatrists and psycho-therapists that, in the first five to six months of life, every baby's perceptions and emotions are fragmented, and disconnected from each other. And the baby's mother (carer) is probably perceived by the baby as disconnected parts, or objects: face, breast, eyes, voice, arms, and so on.

However, we all know from our own experience that the mother and child will have to separate at some point, so the child can become autonomous, and live its own life, often far from the mother and father's home.

And this separation process begins – slowly, gradually – in the second six months of the baby's life. In this period of development, the baby learns to connect the various bits of mother together, to make a whole person. At the same time, in this period of development, every baby begins to perceive him-/her-self as a whole.

If the parents are reasonably emotionally healthy, then this process will continue at a rapid pace between six months of age and about three years of age. Of course, some parents are not able to handle this separation process, and so they find ways to thwart the baby's development, resulting in

- a sense of 'confluence', where parent and child feel as if they 'flow together'; or

- in the sense of a 'symbiosis', in which the mother and baby between them form one complete human! (More later on these two concepts).

8.2.2 Separation is the origin of boundaries

As the baby grows and develops, progressing from six months to twelve months of age, he/she begins to learn to *balance* negative and positive feelings about mother and about life as a baby. The extremes of love and hate (for the same person/object [meaning mother]) and joy and rage, begin to moderate each other, and the baby develops more self-control.

Babies also stop 'splitting' their mother into 'good mother' and 'bad mother', as they come to realize that the *good one* and the *bad one* are the same person. This process of giving up splitting the mother into good and bad probably results from the realization described by Dr Robin Skynner:

"It's very difficult to discover that you hate someone you love"[68].

So, at this stage, the baby is beginning to feel the first steps towards developing loving concern for its mother. And loving concern means that people look after each other, because they care about each other. (It is obvious that, if anything disrupts these developments, and the baby internalizes memories of a particularly negative or hateful mother, then there is not going to be much development of a sense of loving concern, and *this lack* of a sense of loving concern will negatively affect the individual baby's future prospects of having a loving relationship when they become an adult person!)

To sum up: During the period of six to twelve months of age, the baby is building a better map of the world; seeing self and mother as whole beings. Those two whole beings, on the baby's map of the world, have lines around them, which delineate where they begin and end. But this also implies *a line between them!* This growing awareness of a line (or 'boundary') between them, begins a process of separation. But this also brings up separation anxiety: a fear of losing mother as a lifeline.

This sense of separation does not happen all at once. It evolves during the period from six months of age and three years. In this time there is a growing awareness of separation, which activates the baby's 'attachment system'. (See Chapter 6; the sections [6.10 – 6.12(b)] on secure and insecure attachments in relationships).

But why bother with what happened when you were six months to three years of age? Because those early experiences (at a non-conscious level of your brain-mind) shape the very (psychological) foundations upon which you stand as an adult!

8.2.3 The 'Inner Couple', and their model of boundaries

When you were a young child, perhaps before the age of five years - and perhaps up to about the age of ten years - your mother and father *modelled* (or *demonstrated*) an approach to relationship for you. That is to say, they showed you *what a relationships* **is** – or what it was for them. In the process, they illustrated *their approach to* **boundaries**. (See Chapter 11). What does this mean? Well, a boundary is like a property line, which defines the limits of a particular piece of land, for example. In interpersonal boundary definition, we would say that a personal boundary defines your personal rules and values; and your feelings, attitudes and behaviours, and defines them as 'yours'. It also defines your personal space, and your right to have your body-mind, and your personal possessions, free from interference by others. (Most people in the rural areas of the world have a personal space around them of about two or three feet on all sides – forming a circle of space around them. [In urban areas this tends to decline to perhaps one foot all round: because of the need to travel in crowded public transport systems, queue in crowded shops, etc.] If anybody enters that space, the person feels a certain violation of their personal space!)

Your boundary line defines your 'personal domain', including the things which belong to you. And the things which are yours can legitimately be controlled by you. But your partner's boundary runs around them, their body, possessions, time, life, rules, values, thoughts, feelings and actions.

And you cannot directly control those things which belong to your partner. You can ask your partner to let you *influence them* in a particular respect - such as where to go for a holiday; but you cannot - or do not have the *right* to – *dictate* to them, or *control* them, in order to get them to go where you want to go. In such a situation, you have to 'trade off' what you want, for something your partner wants from you.

So, a boundary is a kind of self-defence system; but it also respects the other person's boundaries. It's a gateway that lets good things in, and keeps bad things out!

The problem in couple relationships, very often, is that people are not clear *what* their own boundaries are. (What they will *accept*; what they will *not* accept; what they *value*; and what their *limits* and *rules* are). And when they do know, they often *compromise* and let their partner *invade* their boundaries; or 'violate their personal space'; or abuse or exploit them! That kind of passivity – which is often engaged in to try to help keep the relationship alive - tends to *destroy* the relationship.

Trying to avoid conflict about boundaries in order to preserve a relationships is a big mistake. The *best relationships* exist on the other side of conflict (Bolton, 19719/1986); and it is important to engage in *healthy conflict – fair fighting* – to establish your boundaries, and to defend them. Negotiation, communication and trading-off become important ways of handling your boundaries between each other.

And it's important to give up...

... waiting for your partner to realize what you want and need, without you having to tell them;

... trying to manipulate your partner into giving you want you want and need, instead of asking for it;

...trying to control your partner, or...

...rescuing them inappropriately from the consequences of their own bad behaviour.

(When your partner behaves badly, and violates your *known boundary*, you have to *assertively* confront them. [See Volume 2; available in 2019. In the meantime: ask for what you want; say no to what you do not want; and communicate your feelings]).

8.3 Part 2: Case studies of troubled couples with poor boundaries

In this part, I want to present a range of case studies of couples I have helped over the past twenty years, who showed signs of having poor boundaries with each other.

I will examine those case studies under three headings, which relate to particular kinds of boundary issues.

8.3.1 The Law of Karma (or reaping and sowing)

In E-CENT[69] couple's therapy, we often borrow loan-words from other disciplines, and re-define them to make them fit for our own purposes. But we have a responsibility to make clear the sense in which we are using them. Therefore, please note, we do not use the concept of 'karma' in the original Hindu and/or Buddhist sense, in that we do not accept the idea that people are *reincarnated*. But we keep the sense of "the law of cause and effect" in this lifetime.

The simple version of the law of karma is normally presented like this: *"You reap what you sow!"*

But this is not quite correct. For a start: the major part of your karma is determined in your family of origin, and you do not 'sow' yourself into your family of origin. You are a product of your parents' genes and their culture(s), and that heritage determines most of what will happen to you in life. You are already almost fully shaped, as a person, before you have any chance to become conscious of being the 'driver' of your life. (This is just as well, because you – the conscious you – is not the driver of your life. Your life is determined, by and large, by the interaction of the non-conscious 'you' and its social environment!)

Werner Erhard used to quip that, "Your karma is what *happens* to you. You don't have to be very *wise* about that!"

But that definition seems to contradict the fact (which Werner recognized) that you **can** set goals; work **towards them** intelligently; work **against** bad habits; **strive** to establish good habits; and so on. And, in any case, legally, you are *assumed* to be the driver of your life, and you will be *held to account*, legally, if you break any significant legal rules of your society (and get caught!)

Properly speaking, the law of karma is the law of 'cause and effect'. But we need to distinguish between four sources of your karma, as follows:

(1) Some of it is about reaping what *you sow*;

(2) Some is about reaping what *your parents* sowed;

(3) Some is about reaping *what your community/society sowed*;

(4) And some is about being in the *wrong* (or right) place at the *wrong* (or right) time. These are called *'accidents* of history'.

But if you are ever going to get an improvement in your karma, you will have to *take responsibility* for driving your life, to the degree that you can!

Over the past twenty years, I have met many couples who have had inadequate boundaries in the area of karma (or cause and effect). Here are just three examples;

8.3.1(a) Couple 1: Debby and Tom

Debby D came to see me, in my office, on a cold, wet November morning. She looked undernourished, pale and sad. She told me that her partner, Tom, had refused to come with her. Indeed, he objected so much to the idea of couple's therapy, and verbally abused her to such a degree, that she had promised not to proceed. But she had come to see me anyway, because she was desperate. She and Tom had been together for ten years, and there had been trouble from the start. He treated her horribly; criticizing her approach to housekeeping, and her makeup. He frightened her so much that she had started biting her nails. Then she developed an obsessive-compulsive urge to scrub her hands until they bled.

I explored her history of relationships, working backwards from Tom, via two other serious relationships; and back to her relationship with her mother and father; and her parents' relationship with each other. Every single one of them had been abusive!

Debby wanted me to show her how to make Tom be more reasonable. It took a few sessions for me to get to the point of using the 'Best Friend Question' with her:

"Debby", I said. "Suppose your best friend had exactly the same problem. She came from a disturbed family background; she had three difficult relationships, in which her partner was verbally abusive with her; what would you advise your best friend to do?"

"Kick him out!" said Debby, without a moment's pause.

I then asked her: "If that seems to be the right solution for your best friend, is it also perhaps the solution for you and Tom?"

At this suggestion she shuddered: "But then I might lose him completely!" she protested.

"But what would be wrong with losing a partner who is abusive with you?" I asked.

"I don't want to lose him", protested Debby. "I love him. I just want him to change!"

I then tried to teach her the concept of 'logical consequences'.

"Suppose I decided to steal food items from shops", I began. "What do you think would be the logical consequence?"

"You'd most likely get caught, eventually", said Debby.

"And what is the logical consequence of getting caught?" I asked her.

"You would get a criminal record", she suggested.

"And what if I got a criminal record, but I persisted in stealing food from shops. What then would be the most likely logical consequence?" I asked her.

"You would most likely end up in prison", she told me.

"Okay", I said. "I agree with your understanding of logical consequences in this case. Now let us take another case".

"Okay", she agreed.

"Suppose a man got married to a woman, and then he began to be very critical of her housekeeping and her makeup. What do you think the logical consequence would be?" I asked her.

"He would destroy the relationship!" she responded.

"And suppose he destroys the relationship, and his wife sticks around, and he keeps on being verbally abusive with her. What then would be the most likely logical consequence?"

"She would have to leave him", suggested Debby.

"Okay", I said. "If that is the logical consequence in a *generic case* of 'a man and his wife', surely that must also be the logical consequence in the case of Debby and Tom?" I asked her.

She looked defeated. She looked down at her hands. "But I want to keep him!" she insisted.

"Well, let me sum up the situation then", I said. "You and Tom are in an abusive relationship, at least on his side. The logical consequence (or karmic debt) that Tom should earn is for you to leave him. But you protect him from this karmic debt, by sticking around and internalizing his abuse; and transforming his *karmic penalty* into your own obsessive-compulsive suffering. And not just obsessive-compulsive suffering, but also sadness and depression, and a sense of despair, and self-hatred".

Debby and I revisited this conversation several times, over a period of weeks, before she would accept that she was protecting Tom from receiving his own karmic debt (the end of the relationship), and that this was a form of masochism (or self-harm) on her part, which she learned in her family of origin.

Eventually, she had processed enough of the emotional heritage of her family of origin to be able to establish a firm boundary.

She came to see me one day and began: "I finished with Tom last Wednesday. I asked him to leave. He begged me to let him stay. He cried until I thought he would have a breakdown. But I stayed calm. I told him this was his karmic debt. That he was now reaping what he had sown. I packed his things in two bags and put them on the front doorstep. I closed the door behind him."

I stood up and applauded her heartily!

"I don't deserve to be treated with such sustained, sadistic abuse", she said.

"Absolutely true!" I told her. "Indeed, you do not deserve to be treated with *any degree* of abuse!"

The law of karma often operates slowly – but it is inexorable!

PS: Three years later, Debby came to see me with a problem of stress. I asked her about her relationship situation, and she told me she was happily married to a new man, called Stuart, who knew she would not take any kind of abuse from him. "When I first met him", she said, "I set out a clear boundary. I told him what you taught me: 'Don't mess with me!' And even though I am sometimes very tough with him, in setting out and defending a particular boundary, he respects me for it!" (Note: When setting boundaries – based on the injunction, 'Don't mess with me!' – you must do this *assertively* and not **aggressively**. See Chapter 7, above).

~~~

8.3.1(b) Couple 2: Una and Nigel

They sat opposite me, on the sofa, and I on an armchair. I explained that I would work with one of them at a time – they chose Una to go first – and that Nigel should not make any kind of verbal or nonverbal comment upon anything Una says. He should make a note, in the notebook provided, of anything he wished to correct, or comment upon, from Una's story about their relationship; and to wait until it was his turn in order to raise those issues with me. I then set my timer for ten minutes, and asked Una two questions, in sequence.

1. "How did you and Nigel meet, and what attracted you to him?" And then:

2. "What is the big problem in your relationship today?"

Una told a very positive story of how they met, and what attracted her to Nigel, which suggested to me that they had a lot going for them in their relationship.

She then told me that the big problem in their relationship was that she felt very insecure, and depressed, because, every couple of years, Nigel would leave her for another woman; live with that other woman for a few days, or weeks, or once for six months; and then he would come back to Una and move right back in with no real explanation or apology. And she would suffer his departures; and she would suffer on his return. But she still loved him, and wanted me to tell her how she could change him.

"You don't need to change him!" I told her. "You need to change yourself!"

Una looked bewildered. "But it's his fault", she protested. "He's the one who goes off and leaves me. And he's the one who comes back with no shred of guilt and no word of explanation!"

"But you are the one who *facilitates* that happening", I told her.

"How can you *blame* me?" she demanded, in a hurt tone of voice.

"I'm not *blaming* you", I told her. "I'm *explaining* the *karmic dynamics* of your relationship".

"What does that mean?" she asked.

"It means", I told her, "that it is *your responsibility* to teach Nigel what you like; what you dislike; what you want; and what you will not tolerate".

"But he knows I don't want him to go off and leave me. He knows I hate it when he comes back with no apology or explanation".

"But his ability to ignore what you say he 'knows' can only exist because *you are not teaching him the right lesson*". I told her. "What you are teaching him is this: When he leaves you, he gets the pleasure of a new body to sleep with for a while. And when he returns, he get the pleasure of 'being back home'. *Why* would he change?"

"So what do you think I'm doing wrong?" she asked me then, looking curious.

"You are not applying **the law of cause and effect**. You are not establishing any *boundary* over which Nigel *must not pass*. And you are *absorbing* the negative consequences of Nigel's bad behaviour!"

"What do you mean?" she asked, looking puzzled.

"Have you ever heard the adage, 'Every dog gets one bite!'?"

"Yes".

"And what do you think it means?"

"We tolerate our dog biting one person; which alerts us to a potential problem with the dog".

"And what do we do if the dog bites again?"

"We have it put to sleep!" she said.

"Now, I'm not advocating 'putting Nigel to sleep'", I said. "But if I was married to Nigel..."

At this point I paused, because of the incongruous image of me, a man of mature years, being married to this significantly younger man (who was already married). All three of us laughed, and then I turned my attention back to Una.

"If I was married to Nigel", I continued, "then, if he left me for somebody else, he *could not return* to me without *apologizing*; showing *remorse* – which Nigel seems not to have done with you – making *amends*; and *promising* never to do anything like that again. That would be my very strongly spelled out *boundary*. I would also spell out the logical consequences of his ever repeating that behaviour: *Instant* divorce; *selling* the house; *splitting* the assets 50:50; *no discussion*; *no debate*; *no road back!*"

When the buzzer went, I switched to working with Nigel. I asked him if he was aware of the *Golden Rule* – which requires us to always treat other people at least as well as we would wish to be treated by them, if our roles were reversed. He said he was. I asked him how he would feel if Una left him every so often; lived with, and slept with, another man for a while; and then 'returned home' as if nothing had happened. He said he would be very unhappy with such a situation. So I told him it was important to live from the Golden Rule, and that anything less was *immoral*, and bad for *his future happiness* in life (in accordance with the law of karma). "He who lives by the sword shall die by the sword!" I told him.

As they left the session, I handed them both a document which outlined the basics of self-assertion, as described in Chapter 7.

...

Two weeks later, Una and Nigel came back for another session. Una told me she had drawn up a written agreement, to the effect that, if Nigel ever repeated *his unfaithfulness habit* again, or anything *similar*, she would immediately pack a bag; move out; put the house on the market; and sue for divorce, with *compensation for emotional abuse*. She and Nigel had both signed it, and it was stored at her solicitor's office.

Thus Una had at last established a strong boundary, which spelled out the law of karma – of *cause and effect* – and of *logical consequences* - for Nigel. (Before this boundary had been established, Nigel had been functioning from *a self-indulgent Child ego state*. [See Appendix B on Transactional Analysis ego states]).

...

Two weeks later, Una and Nigel returned again. This time they both talked of the wonderful revitalization of their love for each other. They had re-found their *childhood sweetheart* states. They were making plans to travel to India for a one-month holiday. They were friends again. Una had forgiven Nigel; and Nigel, guided by a handout I had sent to him by email, was practicing developing *a sense of **remorse*** about all the pain he had caused to Una over a twenty year period; and attempting to communicate that remorse to Una. This is part of an inner boundary that Nigel needs to develop, based on *empathy* for those people with whom he interacts; plus the *Golden Rule*. He *should never* treat anybody in ways that he would not want them to treat him. But even if he forgets these teachings; he *knows* that Una will cut him out of her life – like a *cancer* – if he ever mistreats her emotionally again! Her boundary is far more important than Nigel's inner boundary (against his own bad behaviour), because it's Una's boundary that will keep Nigel in his responsible, 'Adult ego state', with one eye on his *moral behaviour*; and thus to help him to change for good!

~~~

8.3.1(c) Couple 3: Tanya and Tara

It was Tanya who phoned to make the appointment, and she told me she would be ***bringing*** her gay partner with her. That caused a mild alarm bell to go off, because, whereas you might 'bring' a child to the dentist, you should not 'bring' a *fellow adult* anywhere! When two people attend marriage guidance or couple's therapy, it should be *mutually agreed* that this will happen.

Anyway, when they turned up, there was no sign of resentment or resistance on the part of Tara.

I flipped a coin, and it was agreed that Tanya would work with me first, for ten minutes. She told me a very positive story about her first meeting with Tara, on one of the major marathon runs in the north of England. They had a long-distance relationship for a year, because of Tara's work, and then they managed to settle down in a house in Bradford, and they both worked from home. Then, a few months ago, Tara had accepted an international jet-setting consultancy, which took her away from home for days at a time. And Tanya felt very angry because she had a strong conviction that Tara was having an affair.

Then I worked with Tara, who told a relatively positive story about her first meeting with Tanya. She declared that she wanted to stay at home with Tanya, but she could not make enough money in the north of England to make ends meet. So she felt obliged to take her new consultancy job with a Danish company which required her to travel around Europe quite a lot.

I then applied the WDEP model with Tanya. I asked her:

"What do you want?"

She said, "I want to spend my evenings at home with my partner, and to have a quiet life".

"And what are you actually doing?" I asked next.

"I'm spending half my time at home on my own, and a good deal of my weekends travelling to different European cities to grab a few hours with Tara".

"And how well is your goal (what you want) lining up with what you are doing?" I asked next.

"It's not!" she told me. "I feel pulled apart".

Next I worked with Tara, and began by asking her:

"What is it that you want from this relationship?"

"I want to be able to see Tanya a lot, and have the kind of fun and loving sex that we had in the beginning".

"And what are you actually doing?" I asked her.

"I'm spending half the week travelling around Europe on my own", she told me; "and the other half fighting with Tanya about the fact that I won't give up my job and go home to be with her".

I then explained to both of them that they had entered a period of *incompatibility* in their relationship, because what they wanted from each other was not deliverable. Unless one of them changed what they wanted, no happy resolution was possible, short of separation.

...

One week later I saw Tara and Tanya as individual clients, because they each had non-couple issues they wanted to resolve with me. During my session with Tara, I learned that she resented the fact that Tanya was very over-controlling. Their original relationship contract included a quotation from Kahlil Gibran's book, 'The Prophet', which talks about how 'the tall tree shall not overshadow the smaller tree'. (Related to this symbolism, Tanya was a six-foot-two-inches tall, muscular blond, and Tara was a five-foot-two, wiry brunette!) I asked Tara if there was any substance to Tanya suspicion that she (Tara) was having an affair, and Tara told me *she had indiscriminate sex with predatory males* who she stumbled across in the hotels she stayed in when travelling around Europe. I replied, "So you're bisexual, and non-monogamous, while your partner thinks you are gay and monogamous! Is that right?"

Tara replied that she thought she was mainly gay, and that she only had sex with men, while on the road, because she was so angry at Tanya for trying to control her. (She was clearly operating from her 'Rebellious Child ego state'! [See Appendix B]).

Two days later, I saw Tanya on her own. I asked her if she felt she was controlling Tara in ways that might cause resentment, and she replied: "I don't want to control her. I really don't. But I can't trust that she will act in reasonable ways unless I keep a tight rein on her!" (She was clearly operating from an insecure form of 'Controlling Parent ego state.' [See Appendix B]).

One week later I saw them together in my office. Whilst working individually with each of them, for ten minute slots, I mainly tried to communicate these messages:

1. If one partner is too controlling, then the other one will predictably rebel; and if it is too difficult to rebel *immediately*, the pressure will build up into a *spectacular rebellion*.

2. If the controlling partner does not have the ability to figure out how to give up overusing their *Controlling Parent ego state*, and to move to mainly using their *Adult ego state*, then the control-rebellion dynamic will continue; the misery will continue; until such time as the degree of damage to the love-bond is greater than the strength of the 'glue' that holds the relationship together. And then separation will occur.

3. "Would you, Tanya, be willing to give up trying to control Tara; to learn to trust her? And would you, Tara, be willing to put up a strong boundary to being controlled by Tanya?"

4. In working with Tara, I tried to persuade her that the main problem in their relationship was that she had *weak boundaries*. "Why don't you accept that *you have to **stop Tanya** controlling you?*"

"Because....", she stumbled: "Because... that would cause conflict!" she told me.

"And your indirect aggression/rebellion does *not* cause conflict?" I asked her, rhetorically (for I knew that it did!)

"Well, yes... Eventually, it all comes to the same thing. We fight..."

"But this is because, along the way, *you are not 'fighting fair'*. You are *acting indirectly* to try to subvert Tanya's controlling tendencies. Why not just tell her outright: 'If you ***don't give up*** trying to control me, I will *leave* you!'?"

Tara looked puzzled! "But that would be so terminal!" she concluded.

"Well, it would only be terminal if Tanya *failed* to obey your boundary", I told her. "But what would happen if she *honoured* your boundary?" I asked.

She looked even more puzzled; and confused. Then her face cleared, and she smiled. "If she agreed to give up trying to control me, I would love her so much I would not want to be away from her for more than a few hours at a time!" She said this in a way that suggested a lot of emotional pain.

Tears came into her eyes, and she covered her mouth to silence a sob. Tanya reached out with her left hand and placed it on Tara's right hand, and they clasped hands tightly.

...

After the session, I emailed Tara and asked her if she would be willing to do an experiment: To give up traveling; to return home; to get a job near home; and to learn (from me) how to assertively maintain a boundary against being controlled by Tanya. She said she would.

"If you can maintain a strong boundary against being controlled, or abused, by your partner", I wrote in my next email, "then love has a chance to blossom. But if you do not maintain such a boundary, then you are teaching your partner that *it's okay to control and abuse you!* You reap what you sow".

~~~

8.3.2 The law of responsibility

Many people do not understand the concept of *responsibility*. I discovered the concept of responsibility from a book I read in Bangladesh, back in 1977. The book, which seems no longer to be in print, was titled, *If There's a Problem Here then I'm Responsible*. That seemed a perverse concept to me at the time (when I was just thirty years old!) Why would I be responsible, if there was a problem in my life? It seemed to me that throughout my life *I had needed to believe* that everything that had happened to me was the responsibility of somebody else. I was a *passive victim* of the actions of others. Of course, that was originally true. I was the passive victim of my parents' punishing tendencies; their controlling tendencies; their negative judgemental tendencies; and so on.

Originally, I had little or no freedom to speak of. So, *they were responsible* for everything that happened to me. But I got stuck with that attitude. When I reached my teens and left home, I simply transformed the idea that my mother and father were responsible for everything that was done to me, to the idea that 'other people' were responsible, for my happiness, my unhappiness, my opportunities, my goals, my outcomes, and so on. I was just a passive pawn in a world of active agents.

Of course, reading that book helped me to begin to take responsibility; and the first area in which I took responsibility was in my relationships. I thought back to my first marriage, which had ended the previous year. My ex-wife had had a prolonged affair which caused me a lot of emotional misery. But now I could see that I was at least partly responsible, in that, if I had loved her more actively, she would have been less vulnerable to being seduced by this other man. (And as the years went by, I became more and more convinced that, almost all of the responsibility was mine, in that I now believe that most normal women, who are actively loved by their partner, in a happy and calm life, with reasonable levels of passion, would never risk that – or throw it away - for a *fling* with somebody else! Therefore, almost all of the responsibility for maintaining a good relationship *for me*, rests *with me*! And almost all of the responsibility for maintaining a good relationship *for you*, rests *with you*! *You (largely) reap what you sow*, and thus you are (largely) *responsible* for what you reap, through the *mechanism* of sowing!)

~~~

Let us now take a look a three case studies of couples where responsibility was a problem:

8.3.2(a) Couple 4: Sheepish Shawn and Parental Patty

Shawn phoned me to say that he and his partner would like some couple's therapy, but that his partner had suggested that he have one or two sessions first, to work on his anger. Because he worked fixed hours every day, he had to have an evening appointment.

When he arrived, I noticed how muscular he was. He told me he did weight training and karate. But he told me in such a little voice; like a mouse; or a (very quiet) sheep! The contrast between his physical powerfulness and his 'ego weakness' was dramatic. He worked in a very physical job, lifting heavy weights all day. He came from a family of drunks, and had low emotional intelligence.

I asked him about his anger problem. He said it was all to do with his partner, Patty. They had been to school together, and they had been a couple since that time. Now they lived together. Patty had got him his job; found the house they lived in; and had them both saving to travel to South America for a one-year vacation.

"So, what is the anger about?" I asked him.

"Well, Patty doesn't like me drinking and snorting coke", he told me.

"And is this something you do a lot?" I asked him.

"No", he said. "In fact I don't really like drinking or snorting coke".

"So why do you do it?" I asked him.

"Well, all my mates do it; and they drag me into it!"

"Can't you resist them?" I asked.

"Well, we all live in a very tight community", he told me. "You can't escape!"

"So tell me about how the problem affects you and Patty", I told him.

"Well, she wants to stack up the savings for South America", he said. "And she gets mad when she realizes how much I've spent. And she picks on me. And blames me for not saving enough. And then I go to the pub and get drunk; end up snorting coke; go home, and we have a big fight".

"Do you love Patty?" I asked him.

"She's my best friend", he told me.

"But do you love her; and want to live with her".

"We've always been together", he told me. "She rescued me from my horrible family. I owe her everything".

"But do you love her, and want to live with her?" I repeated.

"I am doing"!" he said.

"I know you are", I said. "But do you really *want* to?"

"I wouldn't know what else to do", he said. "We've been together since we were sixteen. That's eight years! One third of my life. And she got me away from my family".

At this point I became acutely aware that the biggest problem faced by Shawn was that he had *no boundaries with anybody*. He was a passive pawn in a set of games he did not understand. So I resolved to teach him to take responsibility for defending his boundaries *by challenging him physically*, rather than by talking about them!

For a long time, I have been developing a technique of teaching boundaries physically, so that they go in at a deep, non-conscious level. The purpose of this teaching is to help the client to operate from a non-conscious attitude of 'Don't mess with me!' This is designed to be an *assertive* level of self-defence – which should be done using reasonable, assertive language - which protects the client from being controlled by others. But it has to be based on *an almost instinctive, non-conscious, physical reaction* against being invaded or violated.

So I asked Shawn to stand up. I placed a marker on the office carpet, which I described as 'the boundary between us'. I asked Shawn to stand on one side of this symbolic boundary line, and I stood on the other; each of us being about eighteen inches from the boundary line. I told Shawn that we each had a circle of space around us, called our 'personal space', which is about one meter in diameter.

Next I told Shawn that he is responsible for defending his personal space. He is responsible for making sure nobody crosses over his boundary line, without his explicit permission!

Then I asked him for his permission to put my hands on his shoulders; and I asked him to put his hands on mine. I told him this exercise was designed to test whether or not he was taking *sufficient responsibility* for defending his personal space. I announced that I was going to try my best to invade his space, and my success or failure would be a measure of his commitment to defending his personal space.

I then pushed him off his feet, and he landed on his back on the sofa behind him!

Despite the fact that he is more than six stone heavier than me, I pushed him off his feet. "This is how weak you are!" I told him. "Even though you lift weights; practice karate; and work at a manual job all day; this is how weak you are when faced with social pressure!"

He looked shocked!

So I told him not to feel defeated. We would rerun the exercise, and this time I wanted him to take full responsibility for keeping me out of his space; to try much harder.

Then we reran the exercise, twice, and he got better at keeping me out of his space each time. The third time, I could not budge him. He was like a brick wall!

Then I got really serious. I put a scarf around my head and took off my specs. "Now I'm your girlfriend, Patty", I told him, "and now I am going to force my way into your space, and insist that you must save a lot of cash for a holiday in South America".

We put our hands on each other's shoulders, and I began to push, while declaring, "You have got to go along with my plans! You cannot resist me!"

But he did. He held fast. He held the boundary. He took *responsibility* for managing his personal space, in the face of a *symbolic assault* by his domineering girlfriend.

...

A couple of weeks later, Shawn was back in my office. He had lots to report. He had stayed home for two Saturday nights, to save money. He had gone to the pub with his mates two or three times, but he set a limit on how much he would drink. And he absolutely refused to take any cocaine when it was pushed at him.

He also negotiated a new deal with his girlfriend regarding the holiday plans. He said he'd prefer to go to Spain for a week this year; and to France for a week next year. He told her that was more realistic for people who earned the kind of money they earned. She cried, and tried to resist his suggestion. But he stayed strong, and eventually she agreed. He told her, if they ever became rich, they could take a year out and go to South America. In the meantime, "we should be *more responsible*, and only make plans that work in terms of our earnings!" he told her.

He *took responsibility* for putting boundaries into his relationships. And he took responsibility for defending them.

...

Two weeks later, Shawn was back. His anger problem with Patty was largely a thing of the past. And now he wanted to know if he and Patty could come along next week to work on their communication skills. Of course, I was delighted to say 'yes'.

~~~

8.3.2(b) Couple 5: Kenny H and the 'irresistible sex offering'

Kenny H, and is wife, Vera, both phoned me, to see if I might be able to save their marriage. They did not want to book a joint appointment. They wanted to see me separately, because the level of hostility between them was very high. They both agreed that the problem was that Kenny had had an affair with the (female) lawyer who acted for their engineering company.

Kenny came to see me on Wednesday, and Vera was booked in for a session on Friday.

My first impression of Kenny was that he was youthful and athletic, but he walked with a surprising limp. Although he was fifty years old, he looked about thirty-five. He was very keen on 'fell running', (or hill running, which is mostly uphill, and difficult going); and he was out every morning running on the moors above their farmhouse, on the edge of Haworth.

He told me that his wife had found out that he had been having an affair with Suzie - their legal representative - because Suzie had been indiscrete, and told somebody who knew Vera. When Kenny got home from seeing Suzie, for a sexual liaison, last Wednesday, Vera had been waiting up for him, and she set about him with a big stick and bruised him badly around the torso and legs. He had not been able to run since then.

"Tell me about the affair", I prompted him.

"Nothing much to tell", he replied. "Suzie and I meet about monthly to review legal issues to do with contracts with customers and employees. About six months ago, Suzie came on to me. What could I do?" he asked me, with the innocent face of an altar boy. "It was an irresistible sex offering!"

"When you say it was irresistible", I said, "what do you mean?"

"You know how it is", he said. "Sex is sex. Never say 'no' to sex!"

"Was that in your marriage contract to Vera?" I asked.

Kenny looked bemused. "How do you mean?" he asked.

"Was this part of your agreement with Vera: 'We hereby agree that we – Kenny and Vera – will never say 'no' to sex!'?"

"Of course not", he said. "But we're both men. Yeah? We both know how it goes!"

"And how does it go?" I pushed him for further clarification.

"You can't say no to an irresistible sex offering, can you?"

"As a matter of fact, I can!" I told him. "And I have done. Famously once when I was miles from home, feeling lonely, and I was propositioned by a very nice American PhD student. In theory nobody would ever have known. It was – as you say – a 'sex offering'. But it was not 'irresistible'. If sex is irresistible to you, Kenny, then you should not have signed up to have *a monogamous relationship* with Vera".

"What do you mean?" he asked, looking decidedly unhappy with my line of argument.

"I mean this", I told him. "When you and Vera got married, you agreed to a *boundary* around your sex-love relationship. You and she were *inside that boundary*, and everybody else was outside of that boundary. And you *agreed* to that boundary. But in the back of your mind – it now seems - hidden from Vera and the congregation at your wedding, you had this *undeclared rule*, 'I do not recognize *any boundary* against having sex. I *refuse to accept responsibility* for managing my own sexuality in such a way as to keep my marriage vow to Vera. I am *not responsible* for my actions, because *sex offerings are totally irresistible!*"

"So you're siding with Vera against me? Is that it?"

"No", I said. "That is not it. I am siding with *justice*, and *fairness*, and standing for *the principle of responsibility* in maintaining our *agreed boundaries!*"

"This is bollocks", he blustered, standing up and lighting a cigarette. "I'm back on the fags because of all this ridiculous pressure!"

"In what way is it bollocks?" I asked him.

"No man can resist free sex", he declared, "unless there is something wrong with him!"

"I beg to differ with you", I told him. "I had a karate instructor some years ago who worked as a manager in a vocational college. One Christmas, there was a student party in the canteen, in the middle of the afternoon, on the last day of term before the Christmas holidays; and he was asked to attend to show *goodwill* towards the students. He turned up, was offered a drink, and then a 'hot, female student' (his words) asked him to dance to the rock music that was playing in the background. As a 'goodwill ambassador', he felt he had to play along with this invitation. During the dance, he realized that *this student wanted more than a dance*; it was what *you* might call 'an irresistible sex offering'. But this man, this hot-blooded married man, discretely left the canteen, went upstairs to his office; locked the office door; and took his phone off the hook. He then proceeded to sit there for about two or three hours, until the last person had left the building and one of the other managers had locked up. In this way he avoided creating precisely the kind of mess that you have created by giving in to your feelings of lust for Suzie!"

"Well thanks a bleeding lot!" he told me then, stubbing out his cigarette, and flopping back in his armchair. "So you're telling me it was all my fault; and I deserve to be in the mess I'm in!"

"No!" I corrected. "I'm telling you that each of us is *responsible* for managing our lives. We have to take *responsibility* for managing our boundaries with others. You failed to manage *your body boundary* with Suzie. And there are logical consequences that flow from that failure! You reap what you sow!"

"And that's it?" he wanted to know. "This is the kind of pointless prattle you get paid for?"

"My intervention here is **not** *pointless*, Kenny", I told him. "The point is very clear, and it is this: You have *broken* a serious boundary. Your wife is *very upset*. And you currently cannot begin to *fix* the problem with Vera because you do not *feel* for her! You do not *appreciate* the damage you've done, because *you do not take* **responsibility** for maintaining your 'agreed upon boundaries'; and you do *not* take responsibility for the *hurt* you cause to others; and you do *not* take responsibility for *cleaning up* the messes that you make!"

Kenny stared hard at me. Then he lowered his eyes, placed his hands over his face and sobbed.

~~~

I saw Vera on the Friday, and she was in a foul mood. She was hostile, and uncooperative. I asked her if she was here voluntarily, and she said she was. I would hate to see what she looks like when she is coerced to go somewhere against her will!

I asked her how she felt, and she said, "Awful!"

I asked her to tell me where she and Kenny were up to. She said, "Seeing you didn't help. He thinks he can just *apologize* and come waltzing back into my life, as if he had not slept with that slut!"

"Do you want to try to *rebuild* your relationship", I asked her, "or would you prefer to *separate*?"

"I'm not the problem", she told me. "He's the problem. He's moved out!"

"So, do you want to work towards a reconciliation, or does it feel more like a parting of the ways?" I tried again.

"He says we'd have to sell the house and factory if we split!"

"And how do you feel about that?" I asked.

"It's not up to me", she said.

Over a period of two full sessions, I worked hard to find a way forward for Vera and Kenny. But Vera would not take *any responsibility* – 50% would be enough - *for cleaning up the problem.* And Kenny had not taken any responsibility for having caused the problem. He blamed her, because she had created a system of separate lives for them. They had separate areas in the house where they spent most of their time. They slept together, and they had sex almost every day. She would call him, each evening, when she was ready for sex. (Was this the origin, or a part of the explanation, for the 'irresistible sex offering'). And he blamed her, because she left him too much on his own.

Then, about two weeks later, Kenny moved back in, and they resumed having sex. But it reminded Vera of Kenny's infidelity. And Kenny felt guilty but did not know how to show remorse.

Then they disappeared for a few weeks. And when Kenny came back, he had moved out.

When I asked him, "On what basis have you moved out?" he did not understand my question.

"Are you separating, divorcing, or what?" I asked.

"It's all up in the air!" he told me.

In other words, *neither of them had taken any responsibility for clarifying the new boundaries.*

Were they together?

Were the separated?

Were they in the process of separating?

Neither of them knew. Life was not something for which they took responsibility. Life was something which *happened* to them.

I assume that living separately eventually caused a legal separation and/or divorce. But since they were not responsible enough to see the process through to the end, I do not know the final outcome.

But one thing I do know. Unless they both learned to take *responsibility* for managing their lives in ways that are *egalitarian*, *principled*, *ethical* and *clearly boundaried*, they would never get beyond living in an unholy mess of anguished emotions.

~~~

8.3.2(c) Couple 6: Dotty and Ted, and the predatory Jezebel

Dotty came to see me because she was experiencing jealous rages against Ted, when he seemed to her to *allow himself* to be vulnerable to a predatory female neighbour (to the extent of *conversing* with her!), or to *appear* to encourage the 'Jezebel's' advances (by making himself *visible* to her, by standing in their garden, or in the open doorway).

Dotty's rageful responses had the effect of damaging her relationship with Ted, who broke off the relationship several times, because he found Dotty's 'irrational jealousy' unbearably stressful.

For her part, Dotty could not see what was wrong with her behaviour. She felt that anybody would respond like her, if their partner talked to an opposite sex neighbour who seemed predatory or overly-interested on one's partner.

One of the first principles that I taught Dotty, was that she needs to take **responsibility** *for her own feelings*. And to recognize that *she was* **responsible** *for any damage* she did to her relationship, by virtue of her uncontrolled angry outbursts.

I explained that reasonable levels of jealousy are normal, and the make us vulnerable. What we have to do with that vulnerability is to share it with our partner; to take responsibility for explaining clearly, and non-judgementally, how we would most likely feel if and when our partner engaged in a particular kind of action which triggered our jealousy. This is *a non-blaming approach* to dealing with jealousy. Jealousy is normal and natural, and we each owe it to our partner to refrain from engaging in actions which might trigger our partner's *reasonable jealousy*. But on the other hand, we need to address any tendency we find in ourselves towards *unreasonable jealousy*.

The next thing I taught her was to take responsibility for teaching Ted what she likes, and what she does not like, in a way which is non-demanding and non-manipulative.

For this purpose, I taught her to use both 'appreciation messages' and 'conditional appreciation messages'. (See Chapter 7, above). Every time Ted showed that he had taken her desires into account, especially in relation to how he interacted with neighbouring women, she was to tell him some version of, 'I appreciate it when you...'

And every time she wanted to avoid a particular outcome – (such as leaving home in the morning at a time which would cause them both to run into a neighbouring female who seemed 'overly-interested' Ted) – she was to use a *conditional appreciation message*, such as, 'I'd really appreciate it if we could leave home at (such-and-such a time) tomorrow, to avoid running into (person's name, or description)...'

The overall aim of this coaching was to teach Dotty that she was responsible for shaping her social world, to the degree that this was possible. And that she had to avoid "kicking over the bee hive" if she wanted to collect the "honey" (of happy, peaceful, loving relationship with Ted). She had to learn that berating one's partner kills feelings of love! And she could not hope to have a powerful relationship with Ted if she insisted upon 'making him wrong'.

And finally, I taught her that *she* was *responsible* for her side of her relationship with Ted; and that the best way to manage her side of the relationship was to aim to create a 5:1 ratio of positive to negative moments. (This ratio was *scientifically established* by Professor John Gottman, after working with hundreds of couples, over a twenty year period, at the University of Washington).

Once Dotty accepted that she had to maintain a 5:1 ratio of positive to negative moments in her relationship with Ted; and that you cannot collect honey if the bees are swarming, which they do if you kick over the hive; she was better able to manage her jealous rages.

However, I then added one final 'persuader', which really calmed her down.

"Let's assume", I suggested to her, "that this *main Jezebel* (or predatory female) knows exactly how to wreck a relationship, when she wants to move in on the male partner. Let us assume that her strategy is this. She dresses in a provocative way, and makes herself very visible, ensuring that she encounters you and Ted. And when you all meet, she flirts outrageously with him – hoping and praying that this will cause you to go ape-shit and wreck the relationship for her".

"Oh, my God!" gasped Dotty. "You mean, I am playing right into her hands when I become angry and shout abuse at Ted?"

"I mean precisely that!" I told her. "And, not only that, but that instead of moving away from Ted when the 'Jezebel' strikes, you should *move closer* to him, physically; even *touching* him, to demonstrate *who is related to whom* in this triangular situation!"

Next time Dotty came to see me, she told me she had been provoked several times by 'the Jezebel's' cunning movements, but that she had kept herself calm by telling herself: "Ted is my man", and *moving closer* to him, and touching him. Then telling herself, "I will *not* let this Jezebel wreck my relationship by making me angry and jealous and rageful. I will keep calm, and she will soon go away".

Three sessions later, Dotty told me that, not only had she calmed down completely, and that Ted had been very cooperative in finding ways to avoid running into 'the Jezebel'; but that the Jezebel had sold up and moved to a new neighbourhood!

~~~

8.3.3 The law of 'walking your talk'

Many individuals who come to me for couple's therapy are struggling in life because of a particular problem. When they were young, their mother, and/or father, succeeded in 'switching off their *fierceness* switch'. But we each have to retain a certain degree of fierceness – or *appropriate anger* – to fuel our appropriate assertions of our needs, interests, preferences, and desires in the world. When we have our fierceness switched off, we are vulnerable to being used and abused by others, and we even tend to collaborate in that abuse if we don't know how to fight back.

~~~

8.3.3(a) Couple 7: Simon and Erica

Simon was the oldest son of a farmer, who has a big farm in Lancashire. One day, Simon is expected to inherit the farm. Despite being twenty-eight years old, when he consulted me, he still lived on the farm with his parents and two younger brothers.

Simon came to see me because he was in the process of getting married to Erica, who was twenty-four years old, and they were fighting about where they should live after the wedding. Erica attended the session with him, and she was in a very bad mood.

I worked with Simon first, and he told me: "I want to live on the farm with my family, because it's traditional for the eldest son to take over the farm from their father, when he retires. This is my career and my life". I asked him why this was a problem. "Erica says she wants to live in town, in a flat, because she was raised in a town, and likes to be near the hustle and bustle of shops and cafes and pubs, cinemas and theatres and lots of people".

I explained to Simon that this is what we call a 'mutual problem', meaning that, if one partner gets what they want, the other cannot get what they want. And so it's important to find out what *interests* are being served by both partner's *declared positions*, so that a *compromise* can be found.

But Simon was not interested in finding a compromise. He felt strongly that *Erica should join him on the farm*.

I then worked with Erica, and she sulkily told me that Simon was bullying her into living on the farm, but that she wanted to live in a flat in the nearest big town. I repeated what I had told Simon about this being a mutual problem, and that they cannot both get what they want, because their 'declared positions' were mutually contradictory. I suggested that she think about what it was that she was trying to get by living in the town, and to share that with Simon, to see if they could reach a compromise. But she told me *he wouldn't listen* to her, and that he was bullying her into doing what he wanted.

No progress was made with Simon and Erica, because they each had an entrenched position; and so I suggested that they were *incompatible*, and that they should *think long and hard* before deciding whether or not to go ahead with the wedding.

Six months later, Simon and Erica came back. Now they were married, and living on the farm. Erica was very unhappy – downright depressed - because she was treated as *a junior outsider* by the family, while Simon enjoyed being the centre of attention in the family, as the future owner and day-to-day manager of the farm; and, unlike Erica, he was related by blood to the other people in their communal little life.

I asked Erica what she wanted. "I want to live in a flat in town", she told me.

"And what are you doing?", I asked next.

"I'm living in this horrible situation, on a remote farm, with bossy Simon and his bossy family".

"And how well is that going?" I asked her then.

"It's a horrible mess", she said. "We argue all the time. And I feel like a total outsider, and I'm totally depressed".

"So, let's plan a better outcome", I told her.

"But *Simon won't agree* to any different outcome", she told me. (This made Erica seem 'un-coachable' to me!)

When I worked with Simon, he told me the same story. "It's horrible", he told me. "Erica sulks and argues all the time. The family don't like her because she won't try to fit in!" (Again, he was un-coachable, because he would not consider the concept of *mutual problems* and *compromises* based on *interests* instead of *positions!*)

...

Five years later, Erica came to see me to say she had left Simon, and that she was thinking of suing him for five years of mental cruelty. So I told her, "The court will want you to describe *the circumstances under which he kidnapped you*, and held you *against your will* on his farm".

"What do you mean?" she said.

"Well", I said. "My understanding is that you had a *desire* to avoid living on Simon's farm. This was a *boundary issue* for you, and you *communicated it* to him many times, verbally. But he *ignored* your (verbalized) boundary in this area, and proceeded to *assume* that you *would* join him on the farm after the honeymoon. And that is *precisely what you did.* So, any court will likely conclude that *you cooperated* with the idea of you and Simon living together on his father's farm (even though it was not your ideal preference!)".

"But he *knew* I didn't want to!" she blustered, tearfully.

"Well", I said. "My way of thinking about that is this: You *declared* a boundary – 'I do not wish to live on your father's farm' – but you *failed* to *walk that talk.* You failed to get a flat in the nearest town, and to work out a relationship with Simon on that basis: Him living on the farm and you living in a flat in a nearby town".

"But this is unfair..." she began.

"No, it's not!" I told her. "Simon *verbally bullied* you into living on a farm you did not wish to live on. But the court will want to know if he used any *physical* coercion. If he did not use physical coercion, the court will most likely conclude that *you 'unwillingly cooperated with him'* in moving into the farmhouse. But 'unwilling cooperation' is a form of *self-oppression*.

"You, Erica, oppressed yourself, to suit *Simon's* preference. When you have a boundary issue, you have to not only *declare* it, but also to *act upon it*. You have to *walk your talk*. If you do not walk your talk, you will be vulnerable to being abused. And if you refrain from *walking away* in the face of that abuse, it becomes a form of self-abuse!"

"But what's the alternative?" she whined.

"The alternative", I told her, "is to adopt my non-negotiable stance in life".

"And what is that?" she asked.

"My non-negotiable stance in life", I told her, "is this". I stood up, asked her to stand up in front of me, and then I assumed a karate-like stance, with both palms out in front of my body, like a barrier between me and her. And then I said in a loud, serious, non-negotiable tone of voice, with a serious face: "Don't mess with me!"

"And how would that help?" she asked, sceptically.

"It would have helped you to resist Simon's verbal pressure to join him on the farm. He really was *messing with you* – ignoring *your* preferences – and assuming, in a very strong, *male chauvinist manner*, that the 'little wife' should just fit in with 'the big husband'. And because of your stance in life *you failed to walk your talk* in that context".

I then introduced Erica to the Boundary Exercise – pushing her onto the sofa – in much the way I had done it with Sheepish Shawn, as described above. And we kept going until her fierceness switch 'clicked back on' and she pushed me up against the fireplace, with a very determined look on her face!

I smiled at her fierceness, and signalled the end of the exercise by tapping her gently on the upper arm:

"You have to tell the world not to mess with you" I told her. "And when it does mess with you, you have to take *appropriate* **action** to push back. But always use *assertive language,* and not *aggressive* language. The *'Don't mess with me!'* message is communicated non-verbally; and the verbal element might be something like this: 'I am not willing to go along with your suggestion (Simon)!". (See Chapter 7 above).

Actions speak *louder* than words. And if our words and action do not align with each other, *people will not believe our words*! They have to know that we will 'walk our talk'!

~~~

8.3.3(b) Couple 8: Monica and Louis are both disappointed

Monica phoned me from Birmingham to say that she and her husband wanted to consult me about the state of their marriage. It was difficult to find a date in all three diaries that would line up. I had three un-booked time slots in the following week, and in the week after that. Monica was travelling around TV studios four days per week; and Louis was commuting from Birmingham to London three days per week. But we did manage to find a Saturday slot that worked for all of us.

I worked with Louis first. His complaint was that Monica was too close to a male work colleague. She spent a lot of time with this guy, Tom, on the road, and they often shared a hotel. And Monica had recently admitted that she was having an affair with Tom.

"It was not really so much the affair that hurt", said Louis, "as the fact that Monica said she *loved* Tom, and didn't want to give him up!"

"And how do you feel about that?", I asked him.

"Not good!" he said.

"And what do you want to happen?" I asked him then.

"I want Monica to stop seeing Tom".

"So that's your boundary, is it?", I asked him. "You are not willing to have a wife who sees other men, romantically and/or sexually?"

"That's right", he told me. "That's the bottom line".

"And what have you *done* to try to bring that about?" I asked him then.

"Well, I've *told* Monica she has got to stop seeing Tom", he said.

"And what *effect* has that *declaration* of your position had?" I asked.

"None whatsoever!" he told me, looking very depressed. "She is still seeing him!"

...

Next I worked with Monica. I asked her to tell me her side of the story.

She began by telling me that the first couple of years of her marriage to Louis was lovely. They had a baby, and she enjoyed staying at home with the baby. And Louis was home every evening, and paid lots of attention to Monica and the baby, Tanya.

Then Louis's work became busier, and he had to go on the road a few days per week. And then they found they could not make ends meet, and it was decided that she would go back to work, and leave Tanya with a babyminder. Her job had always involved TV studio work, and lots of travel.

"Once I went back to work, two years ago", Monica told me, "the amount of contact between me and Louis was minimal. He was always busy, or travelling, when I was home. I tried to make contact with him. I told him I needed more attention from him, but he always had a work excuse, or reason, to be unavailable. He even told me to ask Tom to take me out, if I was desperate to see a show, or to go for a meal. Louis was happy to stay home with Tanya!"

"Over a period of time, I began to develop feelings for Tom. I told Louis I thought it was bad for our marriage that we spent so much time apart; but he said it would change later, and that he trusted me not to be unfaithful to him".

"And was he justified in this trust?" I asked her then.

"I tried to be a good wife", she said, looking downwards. "But I am only human. Eventually I got involved in sexual activity with Tom. And I had to make do with that arrangement for many months. But then Louis picked up my mobile and saw a message from Tom which was overtly sexual and romantic!"

"What happened then?"

"Louis was upset. He asked me to stop seeing Tom. But I couldn't. I had got too involved!"

...

When I returned to work with Louis, I asked him this: "Suppose Monica never ends the relationship with Tom, what will you do?"

"What *can* I do?" he asked me. "I've done my level best to put pressure on her to end it".

"Well", I told him. "You keep demonstrating a *verbal* boundary to Monica, but she does not see any *action boundary*. Not even the *declaration* of an action boundary".

"What does that mean?" he asked me.

"It means this: If you and I were married (raised eyebrows), and you got involved with another person; I would let you know in no uncertain terms that I will not tolerate that situation. And if you tell me that you are too involved with this other person to be able to give them up, then I would tell you, again in no uncertain terms, that, if the affair is not ended forthwith, I will move out, and begin proceedings for a divorce!"

"But I love Monica too much to let her go!" he whined then.

"So then you have to stay, and put up with whatever you get!"

"But that's so unfair!" he told me.

"It may *seem* unfair to you", I told him. "But it is also *absolutely logical*. It is the *logical consequence* of **two actions** by you.

- The **first** is that you failed to pay sufficient attention to Monica – to spend enough quality time with her, and to be sexually active enough with her – to prevent her being seduced by somebody else.

- And the **second** is this: When you discovered that she was not willing to give up her lover, you failed to do the *brave* and *principled* thing: which is *to walk out!"*

...

A few weeks later I got an email from Tom, saying he had eventually screwed up the *courage* to walk out.

...

About six months later, I got a phone call from Monica, asking for a new appointment for her and Louis. "Louis?" I asked.

"Yes. Louis and I eventually realized that we mean too much to each other to let each other go completely. So we want to get back together, with a new contract, which includes a clause about shared time and attention; and frequency of sex; and both verbal and *physical* boundaries against affairs!"

I was moved to tears, and very pleased.

~~~

8.3.3(c) Couple 9: Mark and Karen and their undeclared boundaries

Mark came to see me about problems with stress at work. He had a bullying boss and some problems with his fellow workers. But I heard nothing about a partner or a relationship. Mark was a keen learner and he made rapid progress in resolving his stress and communication problems at work. Then, one day, out of the blue, he announced that he felt guilty about having left his childhood sweetheart for his current partner.

"*When* did this happen?" I asked him.

"About three years ago", he told me.

"And *how* did it happen?" I asked then.

"We were members of the same walking club", he told me. "My wife, Julie, didn't like walking; and I often talked to Karen as we walked through the Lancashire countryside".

"*Who* took the initiative in getting romantically involved?" I asked.

"She did", he told me. "Karen started telling me I had a boring marriage, and she could offer me a lot more excitement. She knew my wife was depressed, and she thought I shouldn't have to put up with domestic misery".

"So what *happened*?" I asked.

"She started holding my hand, while we were walking; and then when we did a weekend walk across the Lake District, she came to my room on the first night, and one thing led to another".

"And then?" I asked.

"We had an affair for about a year, and then we started living together about two years ago".

"And was it more exciting?" I asked.

"No!" he said. "I just feel *guilty* and *miserable*".

...

So we agreed that Mark and Karen would attend a joint couple's therapy session.

...

At the first I began by explaining that I would work with one of them at a time, and that the other partner was not to speak, gasp, roll their eyes, or otherwise try to communicate anything, negative or positive, about what their partner was saying. They should (if necessary) make a note, and bring it up when it was their turn. I set the timer for ten minutes.

At first, I tried to find out from each of them 'the story of their relationship': what had attracted them to each other. It seemed sex was the main attraction. And the common activity of walking through the countryside at weekends.

...

I then asked Mark what the problem was in his relationship, and he did not seem to be able to say anything other than that he felt guilty; he regretted leaving his childhood sweetheart; and he was very unhappy all of the time.

When I switched to Karen, she had lots to say. She told me she had had to take the initiative in getting the relationship off the ground; she had had to find a place for them to live; she did all the shopping and cooking; and all the planning of leisure time activities. Mark was completely passive.

I asked her if she had tried to communicate with Mark about her feelings of frustration at his apparent passivity. She told me she complained to him till her throat and head hurt, but it did no good!

...

When I switched to Mark, I asked him: "Have you noticed that Karen is often complaining about your passivity?"

Mark looked downwards, and grimaced. "She's always going on about something!" he said.

"Give me an example", I suggested.

"She yaks on and on about all the things I do wrong; all the things I don't do right; all the things I fail to do at all; and calls me bad names, like 'loser', and 'dope'."

"And when Karen is doing these things – which sound more like *criticizing* than *complaining* – what do you do?"

"What do you mean?" he asked.

"Well", I said. "Do you say 'ouch', when it hurts? Do you say 'Hold on a minute' when she goes too far? Do you say, 'Let me explain'?"

Mark looked really grim-faced at this point. "No", he said. "I just go silent, and ... withdraw".

...

When I switched to work with Karen, I asked her why she had chosen Mark as a partner when she clearly had a relationship boundary which should have kept him out, because he was too damned passive.

"If he hadn't been so physically attractive, I wouldn't have looked twice at him!" she told me, with some anger in her voice.

"But you misled him", I told her then.

"I did no such thing!" she told me, angrily.

"Yes you did", I told her. "You *led him to believe* that you wanted somebody *like him* as a partner, and that you would be a *more exciting* partner than his childhood sweetheart!"

"I didn't know how passive and pathetic he'd turn out to be", she told me, defensively.

"Is that like buying a 'pig in a poke'?" I asked her.

They both looked startled by this question.

"Whatever do you mean?" Karen asked contemptuously.

"I mean", I said, "Isn't it your responsibility to 'inspect the goods' before signing for them!"

"Now you're just blaming me!" she said.

"No. Not blaming", I said. "*Describing*. I'm *describing* a situation in which you *apparently* had a boundary which says: 'I want a sexy man, who is full of initiative, and who will take responsibility for his side of our relationship'. Then you met Mark, and you failed to check to see if he was *this kind of man* before you got deeply involved with him!"

"You can't *blame* me for the way things turned out!" she insisted, in an argumentative tone of voice. She seemed to want to fight me.

"I'm not *blaming* you", I said, in a *reassuring* tone of voice. "I'm trying to *describe* a situation in which you had a boundary which you did not declare up front to Mark. And you still have that boundary, and you have failed to act upon it, by ending this painful feud between you, and moving apart!"

"You're not making any sense", she insisted.

"I'm telling you that you failed to tell Mark what you were looking for in a man; you failed to establish if Mark was that kind of man; and you failed to end the relationship when you discovered that he is very far from being that kind of man!"

"I keep hoping he'll change!" she told me then, looking a bit crestfallen.

"Well", I said. "If you want to try to change him, you have to recognize that you have a right to influence him up to, but not more than 50% of the time – or 50% of the change efforts. He also has the right to try to change you, up to, but not more than 50% of the time, or 50% of the change efforts in your relationship".

"And that's what I'm trying to do!" she told me, scornfully.

"But you're *criticizing* Mark; and he's withdrawing; and you're failing to learn this lesson: 'If you criticize your partner, they will withdraw. If you then become contemptuous of them; they will stonewall you. And you are then very close to the divorce exit'!"

I went on to describe the difference between 'criticism' and 'assertive complaining'. (See Chapter 7). And I asked Karen if she would be willing to learn how to communicate assertively with Mark. She said 'yes', but I was far from convinced.

...

When I switched to work with Mark, I told him something similar. I told him he had a *boundary* around his marriage to his childhood sweetheart, but he'd *failed* to protect it, when Karen began holding his hand. He *failed* to tell her he was *committed* to his wife, and that he did not want to complicate his life. And when he and Karen began living together, he *failed* to *complain* when she *criticized* him; and he *failed* to *get out*. So he did not *declare* his boundary which says this: "I want to be in a relationship of mutual respect; and I am not willing to be criticized and told I am wrong all the time (or even any of the time)!"

He did not *respect* his own boundaries; he did not *walk* his talk. Indeed neither he nor Karen *spoke their boundaries*, nor did they *act* upon them. They simply *muddled through* the hell they created by being *unprincipled* about their personal boundaries.

"You have to *speak* your truth!" I told Mark. "You have to *defend* yourself *verbally*; and not allow anyone to *disrespect* you. *Don't let anybody mess with you!* Push back *assertively*! And if you *cannot* influence your partner to treat you with *care*, and *respect*; then *you should walk right out* of that relationship!"

~~~

First reading: ❏

Second reading ❏

Third reading ❏

~~~

Chapter 9: Six ways to build a happy relationship

9.1 Introduction

Over the course of the first ten of my twenty years as a couple's therapist, I collected, evolved or created eighteen principles, or guidelines, which I teach to my couple clients.

These principles have proved their potency over and over again, as guides to action for troubled couples.

In this chapter, I will present the first six of those eighteen principles. The remainder will appear in Volumes 2 and 3 of this series of books.

9.2 Principles, insights and techniques for successful relating

The following six principles will transform your feelings and thoughts about your partner, or future partner, if you learn them thoroughly.

They will also improve your skills and behaviours in relationships.

But to learn these principles thoroughly, you have to review them over and over and over again; to get them into durable, long-term memory.

9.2.1 Exercise 1: Week One

During the first week of this re-learning program, please read (review) Principles 1-3, below, every day, and discuss them with your partner.

It would be ideal if your partner was also engaged in this re-learning program, and reading the principles for themselves, as well as discussing them with you.

9.2.1(a) Principle No. 1: Building the 'house' of your relationship

One of the first principles that I teach is this:

A marriage (or marriage-like relationship) is like a "house" that is built every day.

The most important question for you to consider, in this connection, is this: What *actions* did you consciously take to build the "house" of your marriage (or marriage-like relationship) today?

Did you smile and kiss your partner?

Did you embrace them, or hug them?

Did you greet them as warmly as you did on your first date, or the first day of your honeymoon? (If not, why not? Don't you think it's important to keep up the quality of your interactions?)

When you wake up in the morning, remind yourself that all you have are 'the foundations' of a relationship. You now have to build that relationship all over again; *every single day*. The house of your relationship is *never* complete. You can *never* 'clock off'.

A relationship is not something you HAVE, it is something you DO! It is a process rather than a thing.

If you go to sleep in your relationship, you will wake up to find it has collapsed from want of repair.

Having destructive arguments with your partner about who is right and who is wrong, and especially who is the 'top-dog' and who is the 'under-dog', is equivalent to trying to polish the walls of your "house" with sledge hammers! You will wreck it in no time.

So I ask again:

What actions did you consciously take today to build the "house" of your relationship?

What actions did you take to stop swinging the *wrecking ball* against the walls of your relationship?

Have you made time for leisure activities together?

Have you listened to your partner?

Have you treated them with care and respect?

Have you avoided allowing familiarity to breed indifference or contempt?

~~~

The second principle is this:

9.2.1(b) Principle No.2. Keep your relationship positive

If you want your relationship to survive, then you need to maintain a 5:1 ratio of positive to negative moments.

If you fail to do this, then your relationship is heading for disintegration.

"But what more can I do?" I hear you ask.

Try this:

Hug your partner every morning.

Avoid discussing heavy topics – including bad news about bills and expenses; or bad news from the TV or newspapers – in the early morning. Leave serious conversations for an appointed time after your evening meal. (This is not just our personal preference. It is *a moral question* of recognizing that our partner may have a calm and peaceful mind, first thing in the morning, and *we could **destroy** that calm peacefulness* by mentioning something distressing or agitating. We have a moral responsibility to refrain from dumping agitating ideas into our partner's mind – because we would not wish our partner to spoil our mental peace by mentioning something unnecessarily agitating. [This is another example of the use of the Golden Rule: which requires us to treat our partner at least as well as we would wish them to treat us!] And we would surely wish our partner to keep serious and difficult problems for discussion at the end of the day, when the hard work of the day has been completed!)

Find out how well they slept; and how they feel today.

Share mealtimes, and keep them peaceful and happy.

Avoid *criticizing* your partner. Criticism is corrosive and destroys self-esteem and good feelings in a relationship. (Use reasonable 'assertive complaints' about behaviours, when necessary. These are not 'criticisms', because they are not about your partner's essence, or personhood. [See Chapter 7]).

Remember to set up dates and assignations with your partner, for friendly talk, walks, outings and sex-love encounters. High quality time together counts towards the 5 positives that you need. Ignoring or abandoning your partner counts towards the negative side of the equation.

Demonstrate respect and care for your partner. Take responsibility for your side of the relationship. And develop a deeper and deeper knowledge of 'who' your partner is. Try to find out more and more about their values, ideas, dreams, childhood history, friendships, goals, etc.

~~~

The third principle is this:

9.2.1(c) Principle No.3. Engage in exchanges of love

The best way to get love is to sincerely offer it to your partner.

*In what ways could you **offer** love to your partner which you are not currently doing?*

And again, what I mean is this:

In what ways could you show your partner that you *care* for them? For their happiness and their wellbeing?

In what ways could you show your partner that *respect* them? That you respect their feelings, their time, their energy, their body, and their mind?

And in what ways can you show your love for your partner by taking responsibility for managing your side of the relationship?

So let me now repeat my original question: *In what ways could you* **offer** *love to your partner which you are not currently doing?*

"But", I hear (some of) you protest, "What love do I get from *them*?"

That's a really crazy way to do the sums: (the math(s)).

That response is just like a person sitting in front of a cold and black stove, with a huge wooden log in their hands, and they are saying to the stove: *"If you give me some heat, I'll give you this log!"*

Crazy! All they have to do is put the log on the fire, ignite it, and then fan the resulting flames a little; and – whoosh – up comes the warming heat.

Do not wait for your partner to start loving you before you will love them. That's crazy.

Become the **source** *of love in your relationship, and watch the magical results!*

Take responsibility for the state of your relationship. "If there's a problem here, then I am responsible". Nobody's coming on a cuffing white charger to rescue your relationship. Get stuck in and sort it out.

Successful lovers are 'givers'. Unsuccessful lovers are like vampires. They are looking to suck some kind of benefit out of their partner. This is the wrong way around. Your partner will flee from vampire behaviour.

But if you love your partner, they will (normally) repay you in kind, and to a similar degree!

Give up being a vampire of love, and become what you are: *A potent source of love in the world.*

~~~

This is the end of the Week One exercises. Please go back and review them every day for seven days. To make sure you don't forget, please write this work into your diary or put it on your calendar.

9.2.2 Review

At the end of week one, sit down with your partner and review the week's work in learning the first three principles:

What have you both learned?

What surprised you most?

What pleased you most about the way the week of learning has unfolded?

~~~

And now we enter the second week of this self-directed learning programme, which is described in Exercise 2.

9.2.3 Exercise 2: Week Two

For the next seven days, please read principles 4-6 every day, and discuss them with your partner every single day, and try to reach some kind of mutual understanding, or shared agreement, about the principles.

9.2.3(a) Principle No.4. Love is an other-directed action in the world.

Love is not primarily (at least not initially) a "nice feeling"; and it is definitely not a form of self-indulgence. (Nice feelings may emerge as a result of loving, but *the nice feelings* are *not* 'the loving'!)

M. Scott Peck has defined love as a process of *extending yourself* in the service of another person. That means, *taking action* which contributes to the *happiness* and *wellbeing* of a loved one.

So, in what ways could you extent yourself (or exert yourself) in the service of your partner?

(You do not have to serve them in a 'servile' [or servant-like] manner. You should serve them in an *egalitarian*, or *equality-based* way. When you make the effort to serve them, they are most likely to reciprocate, by serving you also. And if they *don't*, why are you getting into a relationship with somebody who *does not* reciprocate your love?)

So, to repeat: If love is a process of "extending yourself in the service of another person", in what ways could you *extend yourself* in the service of your partner which would increase the flow of love from you to them? (And, later, back again! *Cast thy bread upon the waters, for it shall return after many days!*)

To be successful in love, you need to be able to stand on your own two feet.

You need to be able to live on your own, for a protracted period of time (before settling down with a partner!), and to learn to enjoy your own company.

You should also avoid '*falling* in love' as that will only produce an unstable relationship. Instead, learn how to '*stand* in love'.

At the core of a loving relationship is a *commitment* to (actively) love your partner: which means a *commitment*, a *promise*, to *create* love; *to make it happen!*

Don't hang around waiting for sparks to fly. You are *a potential source* of sparks in the world! And you are *the source of love* in your own life!

~~~

9.2.3(b) Principle No.5. Do not conflate (or combine) your partner with some of their questionable habits

It is important to distinguish between your partner on the one hand and their behaviour on the other!

Up to a certain point, when your partner engages in a bad behaviour, it would be wrong to see them as being wrong, in their essence. However, beyond a certain point, they do become 'bad', especially if they act *illegally* or *immorally*, to any significant degree. A partner who engages in domestic violence, or sexual infidelity, is definitely acting as a bad person, and should be *divorced*!

However, on the other hand, when your partner behaves *inefficiently* or *ineffectively*, they are not thereby found to be a **bad person**. A partner who cannot earn much money, or who cannot keep a tidy home, is not a Bad Person. They may not be culpable at all, but at worst, they are inefficient and ineffective. If you don't like their inefficiency or ineffectiveness, you should get out to the relationship, instead of berating them for being the imperfect way that they happen to be. But you could also, and preferably, learn to *accept them with all their imperfections*, and thus to extend yourself in the service of an imperfect being. (Remember, unless you are the Ruler of the Universe; *you must also be imperfect!*)

If you metaphorically put your partner on a pedestal (with *Great Partner* on the plinth) when they do something you like, and then metaphorically dump them into the rubbish bin (with a 'Bad Partner' label on their feet) when they do something you dislike, that is called 'splitting' – splitting one person into two (the Good One and the Bad One) - and that is a very *destructive* habit in couple relationships.

You have got to learn that *your partner is your partner*. And, once you have got through the dating and mating phase, and have moved into a settled relationship, whether living together or not, it is essential that you recognize that you have to compromise. You cannot re-design or 're-build' your partner, in your own image. You have to accept that there will be traits and habits of theirs that you like, and some that you dislike. This will also apply for them! (You are not, recall, a perfect angel yourself!) You have got to refrain from "making them wrong" when they do things *differently* from the way you would do them. (And even when they do things more *slowly*, or *less efficiently*, or *less effectively*, than you would do them!)

Then you can more easily accept your partner *one-conditionally*[70], while wishing, desiring and even requesting that they please change the specific behaviour that causes you a problem. (The one condition that you have to apply to accepting your partner is this: You do not have to accept their illegal or immoral actions!)

You do not have an absolute right to demand that your partner change *any* of their behaviours, and if you proceed on the assumption that you have such a right, you will have *a great deal of misery* in your marital relationship. (But you are entitled to have a boundary which says: "I will not respect you, and I will not stay with you, if you engage in illegal or immoral actions!")

Can you think of an incident recently where you *condemned* **your partner** (as a whole person) for engaging in behaviour(s) that you did not like, instead of merely objecting to their *behaviour*?

Do you know what you could have done which would have been more effective? (If you answer 'No' to this question, then you could benefit from studying Chapter 7 again, so than you learn how to separate the person from the problem).

~~~

9.2.3(c) Principle No.6. Desiring versus demanding love

It's OK to want to be loved by your partner. It is not OK (not sensible, helpful or effective) to demand that you be loved by your partner, or anybody else!

Are you *demanding* that you be loved by your partner? If so, you'd better stop that!

It is sensible to offer love, and see if they offer love back. The reason this is sensible is that offering love to your partner is one of the things that is within your control. You can do that if you decide to do so, and you should decide to do so, if you want to be loved.

But you cannot determine that your partner will initiate loving actions towards you. That is why it is unrealistic to expect love in the absence of your having initiated it.

If you believe you are actively loving your partner, and they are not loving you back, the first thing to do is to ask them: "Do you experience me as being a loving partner?" And, if not: "Why not?"

If you are not loved by your partner – after you have spent time demonstrating your love for them – by 'extending yourself' in their service - then the reasonable, democratic, loving and personally-effective thing to do is to tell your partner that you cannot easily live on the *thin gruel* that they offer in the name of love, and that you intend to decamp to a warmer environment, if they cannot find it in their heart to love you as much as you demonstrably love them!

But don't play games about this! If you say you are going to decamp, unless something changes, then you had better move out and move on if that thing does not change!

It is not OK to use separation or divorce as a threat-stick to beat your partner with!

Are you straight with your partner about how well your relationship is working, and what you would prefer to do if the relationship does not work out?

Does your partner know *precisely* what it is you are ***asking*** for?

~~~

This is the end of the exercises for Week Two. Please go back and review them every day, for seven days, and discuss them with your partner. Then move on to the Review.

9.2.4 Review

At the end of week two, sit down with your partner and review the week's work in learning the second three principles:

What have you both learned?

What surprised you most?

What pleased you most about the way the week of learning has unfolded?

~~~

This learning programme will be continued in Volume 2 of this book series.

~~~

First reading ❏

Second reading ❏

Third reading ❏

~~~

Chapter 10: Managing your body-brain-mind for successful relationship

10.1 Introduction

To be a good, effective, loving, caring, supportive partner (in a marriage or civil partnership, or cohabiting, sex-love relationship), you have to be in a good state of physical and mental health; emotional wellbeing; and with a good - (meaning happy and resilient) - philosophy of life.

In this chapter, I want to review some general guiding principles about how to relate to your partner from your *'Adult ego state'* (or your *rational, grown-up self*) to their *Adult ego state*. (See also Appendix B, below).

Then I will guide you through a process for coping with unavoidable problems in your life; problems which could have a negative effect on you and your relationship, if you do not manage them well.

And finally, I will briefly review the importance of diet and nutrition; sleep and relaxation; physical activity and exercise; and self-talk or philosophy of life.

10.2 Relating from Adult to Adult

If you - (whether you are a husband or a wife; or male or female partner) - knew yourself well enough, you would have the *courage* to let whatever happens in your relationship happen, and to deal with the consequences; instead of trying to *control* your partner in a vain effort to ensure that certain things won't happen.

This kind of attempt to control your partner, to guide them to your desired outcome, is subject to the law of paradoxical effect: which means, it normally produces the very result you are trying to avoid!

I am not thereby saying that you should let your partner mess you around; abuse you; or to be unfaithful to you. No! In such circumstances you should *end the relationship*, on the basis that this person could not possibly treat you like this if they *really loved you*; and you should not stay in a relationship with a *loveless sadist*! You are worth more than that. You have a right to be loved; cherished; and treated well as an equal partner in your relationship. (And I am also not saying that you have no right to *influence* your partner: You do. See Myth No.7; plus Sections 1.2.4(c) and (d), and 1.2.5; and Roadblock No.5, sub-para (c); plus Sections 7.3.1 and 7.3.2, for clarification).

You should respond appropriately to whatever happens, *after the event*. Do not try to *anticipate* negative outcomes! Especially, do not try to be *a mind-reader* of your partner's intentions.

You and your partner should have *agreed upon goals*, and you should *trust* your partner to honour your joint agreements. (This does not mean that your partner *has to agree to the goals you want to set*; or vice versa. It means *you have your goals*; your partner has *their goals*; and you have also got a *direction* for your relationship, and *a set of boundaries* around each other, and around the relationship – by *voluntary* agreement!)

You should have *boundaries*, which you *communicate* to your partner, so your partner knows who you are and what you are attracted to and what you are repelled by. This would allow them to *choose* their own actions accordingly. If they displeased you enough, you should have a boundary which states, "I will walk away if X happens".

You are not a child. You do not need to *cling* to your partner like a baby to its mother. (If you feel like clinging to your partner like a child, then you probably have an insecure attachment style – from your family of origin – and probably an anxious-ambivalent attachment style. You should see a good counsellor to work on that. [See Section 6.10 to 6.12(b)]).

But you also are not your partner's boss. You do not have the right to *control* your partner.

To have a happy marriage, you must both be free to choose each other, over and over and over again. And the right to **stop** *choosing your partner* is enshrined in the principles of the Protestant reformation – the right to divorce! It seems to me highly likely that no other single innovation has contributed half as much to the quality of married life as the right to divorce has! It seems to me, based on personal experience, that people who are locked into closed marriages will very often experience *enslavement* and *festering* resentment.

The more you try to manipulate your partner from Parent or Child ego states; and the more you try to dominate your partner from Parent or Child states; the more your partner will be **obliged** *to leave you, in order to be free!*

The more freedom you can offer your partner within your marriage, (and within reason!), the more your partner will be free to see your generous heart, and to be drawn to it. When your partner understands how you feel about them exercising certain freedoms, they are likely to adjust their behaviour to cause you less unhappiness. That is a freely chosen act on their part, and not something you have achieved by coercion. (But beware of using manipulation of their emotions to *control them* indirectly! Fair influence is not the same thing as control!)

Your love for your partner should include a good deal of what is called 'agape':

"Agape is love that seeks the welfare of the other. It is love that has nothing to do with how someone is gratifying us at the moment. It has to do with what is good for *the other*. In short, agape is concerned with the good of the other person". Cloud and Townsend, *Boundaries in Marriage,* page 117.

Agape is what underlies M. Scott Peck's definition of love as 'extending yourself in the service of another'.

If you are desperately trying to control your partner's actions out of a sense of insecurity, then you need to stop that, and work on your own insecurities instead.

But you don't give up your efforts to *influence* your partner (as much as you will allow them to influence you); to teach them *what you like* and *what you do not like*; and to do trade-offs with them. (One way to do this is through the use of 'conditional appreciation messages'. [See section 7.3.6 of Chapter 7]). Do not passively sit around waiting for your partner to discover what you would like from them. Tell them up front! But do it fairly, and equally, without any coercion or manipulation! And if what they want is to take their love back; to leave you and move on into a new chapter in their life; you have got to let them do that!

10.3 Coping with unavoidable problems in your relationship

No matter how hard you try, you will never be able to create a problem-free life nor a problem-free relationship. So you have to know how to manage your emotions around unavoidable upsets, so that they will not spoil your relationship by making you overly upset all the time.

One way to do this is to learn to re-frame your practical problems, so they show up as less unbearable than they otherwise would seem. I have developed a process for this kind of re-framing. It's called the Six Windows Model.

~~~

10.3.1 Introduction to the Six Windows for re-framing problems

The Six Windows Model of E-CENT counselling is a way of helping clients to rethink and re-frame their emotionally disturbing problems, without engaging in confrontation and conflictual argumentation.

It consists of an experiment, in which the client is asked to imagine how their problem would look when viewed through six different 'window frames' – each of which provides a slightly different 'context' for the problem.

Here's how it works:

Think about a current problem, which is serious enough to require urgent attention. Look through each of the following six 'windows' in turn, (as if looking at that current problem), and ask yourself the questions suggested below. Let us begin with Window No.5, and then we will go back to No.1:

 **Window No.5**: The slogan around this window says: "There are certain things I can control, and certain things that are beyond my control".

Ask yourself: "Am I currently upset because I am **trying** to control something that is *beyond* my control?"

"If I *give up trying to control* what is clearly beyond my control, how much happier would I feel?" (Normally, a lot!)

"My partner is definitely beyond my control. I have the right to try to *influence* them, but not to control them".

One way to try to influence them is to use appreciation messages, and conditional appreciation messages. (See Chapter 7, above).

"When they behave differently from the way I would prefer, can I think of that as *a trade-off* for something I want from them?"

~~~

Tell yourself this: "If my partner does *a lot of things* that I would like to *resist*, or *control*, or *eliminate*, or *avoid*, perhaps I'm in the wrong relationship; and perhaps I'd better look for somebody with whom I would have *a greater degree of compatibility* (but never *total* compatibility, because that is *impossible!*)"

~~~

Do you feel that you and your partner have achieved a 5:1 ratio of positive to negative moments in your joint life?

Yes or No?

If Yes, then you don't need to change your partner's behaviour in general.

If No, then what can you do – in terms of changing your own behaviour -to try to improve the number of positive moments?

And if you have done everything you can think of to increase the positive contributions that you make to your relationship, and you've done everything you can think of to reduce your tendency to contribute negative feelings and actions to your relationship, then you should think of trying to influence your partner to change. So, what do you need to say to your partner to begin *influencing them* to try harder to promote that essential 5:1 ratio? (Hint: Use appreciation and conditional appreciation messages! [See sections 7.3.5 and 7.3.6, above].)

Think about the problem that you are viewing through Window No.5. Does it seem even slightly less intense when you apply the slogan around this window? Does this way of re-framing the problem make it less of a problem?

~~~

Window No.1: The slogan around this window says: "Life is **difficult** *for all human beings*, at least some of the time, and often much of the time".

Ask yourself: "Is life difficult for me right now, in my relationship? Yes or No?"

And, of course, to some extent your answer has to be 'Yes', because you are looking through this window at a problem in your current relationship.

So, try telling yourself something like this: "Since I am a human being, and life is often difficult for humans, it must often be difficult for me. And this seems to be one of those situations."

You could also add this: "So *I must learn to accept this reality*; to learn to live with this *unavoidable* difficulty; until such time as it passes, or I pass! Or circumstances change enough for me to be able to control it."

Do not expect to find a way of living which eliminates all difficulty!

Think about the problem that you are viewing through Window No.1. Does it seem any less intense when you apply the slogan around this window? Does this way of re-framing the problem make it less of a problem?

~~~

Window No.2: The slogan around this window reads: "Life is **significantly less difficult** when I avoid picking and choosing things that are not easy to get! That means it's less difficult when I *pick and choose more sensibly* or reasonably."

Ask yourself: "How sensible or realistic am I in the things that I pick and choose, to gain or achieve, in my relationship? And is *picking and choosing unrealistically* part of the problem I am viewing through this window?"

Of course, humans cannot avoid picking and choosing between outcomes and circumstances. That is part of our nature. But the bigger the gap between what I choose and what seems achievable, the more upset I am likely to be! (You too!)

Tell yourself this: "If I am experiencing difficulty right now, doesn't that mean I might be (unrealistically) picking and choosing?"

Ask yourself: "What can I give up hoping for, praying for, which seems never to arrive?"

And remember, life would be much less difficult if you were to pick and choose more moderately, more modestly, and/or more realistically.

Think about the problem that you are viewing through Window No.2. Does it seem less problematical when you apply the slogan around this window? Does this way of re-framing the problem make it less of a problem?

~~~

Window No.3: The slogan around this window is this: "Life is **both** difficult **and** non-difficult."

So if you are very upset, might it not be because you are exclusively focusing on *the difficulties*, and overlooking those bits which are not difficult (for which you could be grateful)?

An example would be this: Your partner has some bad habits and some good habits.

And, instead of looking at them in balance, you insist upon focusing your attention upon their bad habits or traits, and thus you tend to overlook their good habits or traits.

If you could keep both their good and bad habits and traits in mind, you would be much less disturbed by their bad habits.

Try this: Every night for a month, write down six of your partner's good habits; and six of your own bad habits, which you partner accommodates, ignores or puts up with!

Think about the problem that you are viewing through Window No.3. Does it seem even slightly less intense when you apply the slogan around this window? Does this way of re-framing the problem make it less of a problem?

~~~

Window No.4: The slogan around this window is this: "Life could always be *very much more difficult* than it currently is for me."

No matter how bad our life circumstances are, they could always be worse. (But do not use this window to justify putting up with domestic violence, or verbal abuse, or infidelity! Nobody should have to ensure such evils! And do not use any of these windows to lecture your partner [or anybody else] about how they 'should' see the world! Or what they *should* be willing to endure!)

So, ask yourself this: "Am I making the mistake of thinking that my life is already (and always) 100% bad? Or as bad as could be?"

Yes or No?

Then ask yourself the following questions:

"What if a crocodile was eating my rear end off, in addition to my current problems, what percentage would that be?"

"Are there any problems I could be working on?"

Yes or No?

If your answer is No, then you should recognize that *life could be worse than it is.* At least it is not as bad as some circumstances that you could easily think of. And that is a *relative mercy!*

~~~

Window No.5 was presented first, above.

~~~

 **Window No.6:** The slogan around this window states that, "If life is a school in which we can learn from our experience, then what positive lesson could I learn from my current negative situation(s)?"

This leads to the following three supplementary questions:

(1) "If there are problems in my life, am I learning from trying to manage them?"

(2) "And if so, what am I learning?"

(3) "And if I am *not leaning anything,* how could I think about this situation more constructively, so that I can learn something from

my life's journey?"

At the very least, your current problem could teach you:

(a) Whether or not it seems to be *controllable*; and how to *endure it* if it cannot be eliminated.

(b) Whether or not it is *the worst problem imaginable*, and if not, it would clarify what would be worse.

(c) How to be *grateful* for the problems you do *not* have, and to *accept* the ones that are unavoidable.

And probably several other lessons.

~~~

Reflection: Did this process, of viewing a current problem from six different 'directions' or perspectives, or through six different 'lenses', or 'frames', change how it looks and feels to you? (Normally it will!)

For a fuller introduction to the Six Windows Model, see Chapter 6 of Byrne (2018a).

10.4 Taking care of your physical and mental health

If you want to be in good enough shape to manage an effective sex-love relationship, then you have to pay attention to the following lifestyle factors:

10.4.1. Diet

Your ability to think straight, to feel calm and collected, and to maintain a reasonable energy output – including sexual energy – is directly related to, and dependent upon, what you eat and drink. As a general guideline, you should eat a balanced and varied diet, mainly based upon vegetables; with some grains (preferably gluten free, if you can in fact tolerate grains, which many people can't); some nuts, seeds and fruits; some meat and dairy products are normally recommended (but many people are vegetarians or vegans; and many people find that they cannot tolerate dairy products). If you have dietary complications, please see a good, qualified nutritional therapist. (See Myth No. 11 in Chapter 2 for an extensive list of foods to avoid and foods to eat for physical and mental health, and sexual vitality).

~~~

10.4.2. Exercise

It is important to avoid a sedentary lifestyle, as this promotes problems of physical illness which will undermine your capacity to be mentally well, to be a good companion to your partner, and to function well in the bedroom. As noted in Myth No. 11 in Chapter 2:

"A study conducted at the University of California-San Diego tracked 78 middle-aged men on an aerobic exercise program. The subjects exercised at moderate intensity for 60 minutes a day, three or four days a week. After nine months of continuous exercise, these subjects reported that their sex life was more satisfying as far as stamina and orgasms. In comparison, 17 male subjects that performed light workout routines such as walking at a comparatively slower pace stated that they had no substantial improvement in their sex lives".[71]

~~~

10.4.3. Sleep

Sleep is hugely important for our physical and mental health. You need to aim to get 7.5 to 9 hours of sleep every single night, without exception; and preferably normally more than eight hours. If you have sleep problems, do not take sleeping pills, as that will prevent you having proper, restful sleep, and the kind of sleep during which you not only process the stresses and strains of the day, but physically clean out the debris from your brain. If you suffer from insufficient sleep, you will not be able to maintain the level of physical and mental health needed to sustain a happy relationship. (See Chapter 5 of Byrne, 2018)[72]. In particular, your emotional intelligence will decline, and you will be more prone to angry outbursts, which are the kiss of death to romantic relationships.

10.4.4. Self-talk, or philosophy of life

Your philosophy of life is hugely important - alongside the lifestyle factors considered above - in helping to shape your feelings and emotions as well as your physical and mental health.   This book aims to teach you a powerful philosophy of married life, including the use of the Six Windows Model, above. By the time you have finished studying this book – not to mention Volumes 2 and 3 – you will have a very helpful philosophy of life which will support you in being a good, effective, loving, caring and successful marriage partner (or marriage-like [civil] partner if you do not formally marry).

~~~

Study guidelines

Tick that you've read this chapter once: ☐ Then, please read this chapter a second time: ☐ And a third time: ☐

~~~

When reading and re-reading this chapter, please underline those points that seem most important to you.

Make notes in the margins, as necessary, as quick reminders of the content of a paragraph or a page.

And turn down the corner of the page, when the content is so important you want to find it again, quickly and easily.

Also, add important points, with their page numbers, in your own index to this book, in Appendix 'L', below.

~~~

Chapter 11: How you were shaped by observing your parents' relationship

11.1 The Inner Couple model

While Werner Erhard emphasised the idea that we each carry around a *definition of relationship* in our mind - and that we measure our current relationship against that non-conscious definition - Anne Teachworth (1999) emphasised the fact that *we learn what a relationship is by watching our mother and father relating to each other*, when we are very young.

By watching your mother and father relating to each other, when you were an infant, and up to the age of about ten years, you formed an **Inner Couple** *image*, as a guide to action in your adult life.

Whatever you saw your mother and father doing with and to each other, in the first five to ten years of your life, gets encoded into your non-conscious wiring for your later, adult relationship knowledge/ skills/ attitudes.

It seems when we are young, we decide that one of our parents (our favourite) will be *our role-model* for *How to Be an Adult*. This is our Adult Role Model. The other parent then becomes *our Mate Model*; or the image we will pursue in (non-consciously) seeking a mate when we grow up.

You can test this idea for yourself with these simple questions:

(a) In your current (or most recent) adult couple relationship, do you, or did you, often find yourself acting as if you were copying one of your parents?

(b) If so, which one? Mother or father?

The answers to these questions should tell you who your inner Adult Role Model is. (And thus, your Inner Mate Model must be the other parent).

In your current (or most recent) adult couple relationship, do you, or did you, tend to relate to your partner as if they were your (hypothetical) Inner Mate Model?

According to Anne Teachworth, you will always seek to find a perfect match, in your adult relationships, to fit your Inner Couple. That is to say, unless and until you *successfully re-wire yourself* with *an Improved or Reformed Inner Couple*, you will keep replicating your parent's marriage.

So how can you re-wire yourself for an Improved Inner Couple?

There are two stages to this process:

Stage 1: Collect all the relevant data that you need in order to think your way through this question: "What would I need to change in my Inner Couple in order to produce a better relationship for me, now that I am an adult?"

Stage 2: Run a little psycho-drama in your mind, to change how your Inner Couple relate to each other; and to your Inner Child.

In the next two sections, I will help you to work through those two stages for yourself.

~~~

11.1.1 Stage 1 – Collecting the childhood data

Here is a series of questions to help you to collect the data you will need to revise your Inner Couple:

1: Think back to your earliest memories. What were you like as a child, in the first ten years of your life? Happy or sad? Angry or anxious? Introverted or extraverted?

2: What did your mother look like, and how did she behave, in her *adult relationships* with others (like father, friends, shop keepers, etc.) when you were a child, under the age of ten years? How would you describe her personality back then? Introverted or extraverted? Loving or indifferent? Angry or passively withdrawn? Depressive? Etcetera.

3: What did your father look like, and how did he behave, in his *adult relationships* with others (like mother, friends, shop keepers, etc.) when you were a child, under the age of ten years? How would you describe his personality back then? Introverted or extraverted? Loving or indifferent? Angry or passively withdrawn? Depressive? Etc.

4. What was your mother like *as a parent* to her children when you were a child – up to the age of ten years?

5. What was your father like *as a parent* to his children when you were a child – up to the age of ten years?

\# 6. Think back to *how your mother related to you* as a child. Was she kind or cruel? Was she attentive? Did she listen and care about what you thought and felt? Could you go to her with your problems (as if she was a 'secure base' for you)? Were you emotionally close to, or remote from, each other? Was she calm or agitated? Did she shout at you, or strike you?

\# 7. Think back to *how your father related to you* as a child. Was he kind or cruel? Was he attentive? Did he listen and care about what you thought and felt? Could you go to him with your problems? Were you close to, or remote from, each other? Was he calm or agitated? Did he shout at you, or strike you? Did he set reasonable boundaries and house rules for you; or was he overly-controlling or too lax; or inconsistent in his rules and boundaries?

\# 8. How did your parents relate to each other? Did they show care and respect for each other? Did they take equal responsibility for their side of the relationship? Did they show an interest in each other? Did they seem to be loving and kind? Or cool and indifferent to each other?

~~~

Once you have answers to all of the eight questions above, you can move on to Stage 2.

~~~

11.1.2 Stage 2 – Creating a Revised Inner Couple

In this part, I will help you to run a little 'psycho-drama' in your mind, to change how your 'Inner Couple' relate to each other; and how they both relate to your Inner Child.

Firstly, make yourself comfortable in a place where you will not be disturbed. Switch off any phones that could distract you. And make sure the temperature is comfortable.

Take a sheet of paper and draw three 'action centres' (or 'locations') as follows:

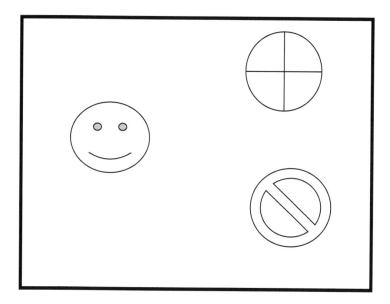

Now, imagine that each of those locations is a chair – an ordinary household chair – like a dining chair.

Next, label each chair, as follows:

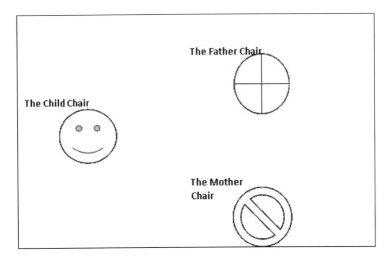

Now, imagine you are in a room with those three chairs in place; and that you are under the age of ten years. (How old are you, and what year is it? Write that down).

Your mother – as she was then (in that year, when you were that age) – is on the Mother Chair. Your father – as he was then – is on the Father Chair. And Little You – as you were way back then (in that year, when you were that age) – are sitting on the Child Chair.

Now, in your mind's eye, follow these instructions:

1. Sit in the Child Chair, and tell your mother how you wanted her to relate to you (when you were a child).

2. Then move over, and sit in the Mother Chair, and tell Little You that you (playing the role of mother) will (from this moment onwards) treat 'Little You' the way Little You wants to be treated.

3. Sit in the Child Chair again and thank mother.

4. Then, still sitting in the Child Chair, tell your father how you wanted him to relate to Little You.

5. Move to the Father Chair, and tell Little You that you (playing the role of father) will (from this moment onwards) treat Little You the way Little You wants to be treated.

6. Move back to the Child Chair and thank your father.

7. Then, still sitting in the Child Chair, tell your mother and father how you want them to relate to each other (for your sake, as a child witnessing their relationship; and building up your Inner Couple from their relationship).

AT THIS POINT, YOU SHOULD **SWITCH ON AN AUDIO RECORDING DEVICE**, FOR THE NEXT SECTION – SO YOU CAN CAPTURE THE DIALOGUE BETWEEN MOTHER AND FATHER, AS AN IDEAL COUPLE, FOR YOU TO LISTEN BACK TO MANY TIMES OVER THE DAYS AND WEEKS AHEAD:

8. Then move to the Mother Chair, and speak (as mother) to father in the way Little You wants and needs them to speak and act.

9. Then move to the Father Chair, and respond to mother (as if you were father) in the kind of loving, caring, respectful, responsible way that Little You needs them to respond.

10. Then back to the Mother Chair to continue that dialogue...

11. And back to the Father chair...

Until that *Positive **Inner Couple** dialogue* is complete, and safely recorded on your audio machine.

~~~

Next, you should listen back to that dialogue between your New Inner Couple, every night for 30, 60 or 90 nights (at bedtime), until you are confident that this new programming has gone deeply into your sub-conscious mind.

You will know how well it has worked by the way you find yourself relating to your current, or a new, partner. If you are disappointed by the way you relate to them, then go back to listening to the New Inner Couple dialogue, for another 30, 60, or 90 nights; until you are happy that you have over-written your old Inner Couple, and now have an emotionally intelligent, caring, respectful and responsible New or Revised Inner Couple running your romantic life!

~~~

Study guidelines

Tick that you've read this chapter once: ❏

Before moving on to Chapter 12, please read this chapter a second time: ❏

And a third time: ❏

~~~

When reading and re-reading this chapter, please underline those points that seem most important to you.

Make notes in the margins, as necessary, as quick reminders of the content of a paragraph or a page.

And turn down the corner of the page, when the content is so important you want to find it again, quickly and easily.

Also, add important points, with their page numbers, in your own index to this book, in Appendix 'L', below.

~~~

Chapter 12: Summary 1 – How to build a successful couple relationship

12.1 Introduction

In this book, we set out with two main goals:

1. To teach couples how to improve their existing relationship, or how to build a new relationship which is happy and successful. And:

2. To help new couple therapists, or counsellors, psychologists and psychotherapists in general, to learn from our experience.

In this summary, we want to present a summary of the key points that are most relevant to couples, rather than counselling practitioners. (Chapter 13 summarizes the key learning points for professional helpers of couples!)

In this chapter, we went back over the territory we covered in the main chapters, above, plus the appendices, below, and pulled out the key learning points that we want to emphasize for couples; and also looked for ways in which you can apply those key points to enhance your own learning about your own relationship, and how to improve it.

We have listed advice that seems reasonable, in an effort to maximize the usefulness of this book to all those readers who want to learn to be happier and more successful in their own couple relationships.

12.2 Key learning points for individuals and couples

In this book we have presented the first one-third of the material we want you to know about, in order to improve your chances of having a happy and successful couple relationship.

If you like, this is your Foundational Course in how to create a happy, successful, committed relationship with your partner.

In the section that follows, we want to sum up some of the most important key learning points that we would like you to remember.

As you read through this list of key learning points, we would like you to make notes of things you think you should act upon in the immediate future.

~~~

Firstly, if you want to be happily married, or related, you should marry, or live with, a *friend* with whom you are willing to always and only act from *loving kindness, fairness,* and *equality.* (This does not preclude the *possibility* or *necessity* of *asserting yourself* from time to time – when things go wrong - but assertion should always be from a place of *constructive problem-solving,* and *reasonable boundary maintenance,* and not from aggressive point scoring, *criticizing the person,* or putting your partner down!)

~~~

Secondly, to break bad relationship habits, you should make a serious study of our definition of relationship. Go over and over and over the following three-part definition, day after day after day, until it becomes part of your most fundamental neurological (or brain cell) wiring.

> 1. *A positive sex-love relationship is a voluntary, bonded attachment to an emotionally significant other, who is equal, respected and cared for; and who reciprocates my egalitarianism, respect and care.*

> 2. *Successful relationships are based on agreed on goals; and mutually satisfying shared activities; in substantial periods of time spent together; resulting in a 5:1 ratio of positive to negative moments.* (That does not mean that my partner must agree to my goals, or vice versa. Instead it means, I support my partner in pursuing her goals; and she supports me in pursuing mine. [Notice there are no "sergeant majors" in this statement; no "directors"; no "leaders" and "led"!])

> 3. If you want to have *a really **powerful** relationship* with your partner, you have got to stop ***making them wrong***. And making

them wrong means describing them as being bad or wrong – or becoming angry and shouting at them, or using verbal putdowns with them - when their ideas/ values/ goals or behaviours deviate from your idea of what they *should* be! (It should go without saying that you must never, ever, push your partner around, or shove them, or hit them, or physically restrain them.) And, crucially, not making them wrong means: *I give up criticizing my partner*; and I discipline myself to only use 'assertive complaining', which does not put them down!

~~~

Thirdly, to make sure you are acting in a loving manner, you should make a serious study of our definition of love. Go over and over and over this definition, for weeks and weeks, on a daily basis, until it becomes a profound part of your understanding of the nature of the world of human relationships.

In his book, *The Art of Loving*[73], Erich Fromm defines love as comprising *care, respect, responsibility* and *knowledge* of your partner. How do these qualities fit with our definition of love as passion, intimacy and commitment? They certainly are not equivalent definitions. And, in my work with couples, I have often found it helpful to emphasize care, respect and responsibility, because those qualities were often missing from one or both sides of the relationship. Therefore, our definition of love has to have Erich Fromm's definition added on. Like this:

Love is defined by the following qualities: Passion (automatic and willed); Intimacy (including care and respect and sharing personal knowledge with each other, to achieve emotional and physical closeness); and commitment (including taking responsibility for our own side of the relationship; and extending ourselves in the service of our beloved [in adult; nurturing; and playful ways]).

~~~

Fourth: During your childhood, you were strongly influenced (and shaped) by your experience of observing your mother and father relating to each other. You probably modelled yourself upon one of your parents –

your favourite one; or the one with whom you shared gender identity – and you most likely now behave in relationships in much the way you saw that parent behave.

It may also be that you tend to choose a partner like the 'other parent', the one you did not model yourself upon. That one is your 'mate model' rather than your 'role model'.

See Chapter 11 for advice and guidance on breaking out of these deeply ingrained patterns of relating, which will be problematical for you if your parents had a less than happy relationship. The guidance in Chapter 11 will help you and your partner to reprogram your 'Inner Couple', so you can begin to relate to each other from healthy inner models.

~~~

Fifth: A marriage, or couple relationship, is "a house that is built every day". It is not a *thing*. You do not *own* it, and can *never* own it. You can only *build* it! And the only way to build a happy and durable relationship is to work at loving your partner every single day, beginning when you get up in the morning, and always kissing goodnight; and never going to sleep on a bad feeling. If necessary, stay up, and talk your upsets through until you are both happy that you are 'friends again'! But if this proves too difficult, make an agreement to solve the problem as a priority tomorrow, and make sure you stick to that. If the communication is too snarled-up, make an appointment to see a couple therapist who can help you both to resolve the problem. (Also, you should commit yourselves, as a couple, to completing the course of training in how to build a happy relationship, outlined in Chapter 9).

~~~

Sixth: To *say* you *love* your partner is not just to say you have *a particular feeling* about them.

Why not?

Because: "By *your deeds* they will know you!" How do you *behave* towards your partner? Do you *demonstrate* love for them?

To demonstrate love for your partner, you must show *care* and *respect*. If your behaviour towards your partner suggests that you are being disrespectful, then they will not experience you as 'loving them', even if you insist, 'But of course I love you!' If you want them to *understand* that you love them, you must always *act from respect*, and never from *disrespect*! If you disagree with some aspect of *their behaviour*, you have to find respectful ways to communicate that disagreement to them. (See Chapter 7).

And does your behaviour show that you *care*? Caring for your partner is often demonstrated by:

> # Showing an interest I how they feel;

> # sharing the work of the relationship on an equal basis;

> # showing an interest in what they think, and what they dream of doing in life;

> # expressing appreciation for their presence; their love; and their contributions to your relationship;

> # being helpful, kind and considerate. And so on.

You must also show that you *take* **responsibility** *for your side of the relationship*, and do not leave the building and maintenance of the relationship to your partner.

And you should try to show *an interest* in your partner: Who they are. Where they came from. What their childhood was like. What their previous relationships were like. What their hopes and dreams are. How they are feeling today. What is going on in their life right now. And so on.

(See Chapter 6).

~~~

Seventh: You should aim to achieve *a relationship of equality*. Do not try to gain any advantage over your partner. And do not allow your partner to gain any advantage over you. Do not cheat or lie. And do not forgive cheating and lying on your partner's part more than once. (Every dog gets *one* bite!) Do not abuse or oppress your partner. And do not allow your partner to abuse or oppress you. It would be better to live alone than to create an abusive or oppressive relationship; or to allow yourself to be abused or oppressed. Never use physical restraint or physical violence against your partner. Never engage in verbal abuse, or angry shouting. Always strive to be calm and peaceful; or to escalate to *reasonable assertiveness*, but not to aggression. Do not engage in any form of aggression, direct or indirect. (See Chapter 7).

~~~

Eighth: Strive to show romantic affection for your partner. You can do this with a smile; a touch; a kind word; a cuddle; a cooperative action; or treating your partner to some little comfort or indulgence. Your relationship probably began on a date, or after a date, or before a date; and probably included a history of dating, or 'going out together'. Do not abandon that practice just because you have 'landed your catch', like a fish in your net. Remember to arrange dates to spend quality time with your partner; at home, or out walking, or out for a tea or coffee break, or a visit to friends, or to a bookshop, or to a museum or art gallery, or a sporting event, or a party; or whatever. This time should be *declared* to be a date; a special outing; a romantic time spent together. (When children come along, this side of the relationship often gets disrupted, for a time; but it is important for the partners to get past this stage, when the child reaches the age of three or four years. Then they should take time for themselves to be friendly, alone, romantic, and affectionate with each other).

~~~

Ninth: Strive to keep up the sexual side of your relationship. Initially, this will be automatic and spontaneous. But, after a couple of years, the sense of *urgency* and *appetite* will tend to decline; and it has to be kept alive by *conscious actions* of the Adult part of yourselves. You need to discuss how often you would both like to make love (or have sexual intercourse together); and then set a day and time aside when you will make this happen! Do not leave it to chance, as it can keep slipping away. So make dates for lovemaking, and keep to them. Make sure that the sexual side of your relationship is completely equal. Both partners need to have pleasure and orgasm. Of course, it normally takes longer for the female partner to warm up (often twenty minutes or more!), so the male partner has to be patient and diligent in the use of foreplay; and the male partner needs to understand the female genitals, and especially the role of the clitoris. (See Appendix G). If the male partner does not understand how to stimulate her clitoris (at the beginning of their relationship), the female partner needs to patiently teach him.

Of course, in homosexual relationships, this problem does not arise because, with gay males, the clitoris is not an issue; and with gay females, they are normally both aware of the seat of the female orgasm.

~~~

Tenth: Make sure you do not subscribe to any unrealistic myths about the nature of relationships; and recognize that your partner has both good and bad aspects; and good and bad features; and you have to take on *the whole package* when you get involved in a relationship.

You and your partner should be *broadly compatible* at the point where you get together. (If you are not, then the relationship is likely to be *short lived*; or *longer lived* but miserable!) And compatibility normally depends upon having a significant overlap between both partners' values, attitudes, beliefs, cultural backgrounds (including social class!), aspirations, and so on.

And you both have the right to strive to *influence* your partner's behaviour and/or values, in those areas where you cannot easily go along with a particular behaviour or value of theirs. But bear in mind: You must avoid *making your partner **wrong**!* If you desire behaviour change from your partner, you need to *request it*, kindly and politely (in the form of a conditional appreciation message [See Chapter 7.3.6]), with the understanding that, if your roles were reversed, you would be willing to accommodate *their request* for behaviour change.

And you must actually **give** *as much as you* **get** in the cut and thrust of your two-way attempts to influence each other. If you *too frequently* request behaviour changes from your partner, and *too infrequently* agree to your partner's requests for you to change some of your behaviour, you will be seen to be *unfair*, and that will most likely *fatally damage* the relationship. So strive for *fairness* and *equality* in your giving and taking of influence. (There are no 'bosses'; 'leaders'; 'head teachers'; or 'CEO's' in happy relationships!)

~~~

Eleventh: Strive to be a good listener, before you attempt to communicate anything to your partner. Learn how to actively listen – using reflection and summarizing skills. (See Chapter 4).

Strive to understand your partner's point of view, before you try to respond to what they are saying. Walk with them in the direction of their explanation and description of their understanding and beliefs. Once they feel they have been fully heard; turn around, and walk them back in the direction of your explanation and description of your understanding of the subject under discussion. Do this as often as is necessary before you can both reach agreement.

Or try this: Separate your partner from the problem. Stand alongside your partner, and put the problem on the table in front of you. Discuss this problem in terms of 'interests' rather than 'positions'.

Here are some questions that will help you to explore your 'interests', and avoid insisting upon your 'positions':

> *For what reason is your take on the problem important to you?*

> *What do you want to get from the situation?*

> *And what interest is 'underneath' that goal?*

> *And underneath that again? (Or why is that important to you?)*

Keep going until you both understand each other's 'interests' in the problem, and then try to find *a mutually satisfactory solution.*

Do not try to *force* your solution on your partner. And do not lose your temper and try to get your own way! Try using conditional appreciation messages. ("I'd really appreciate it if you would agree to do X".)

If necessary, or desirable, set up formal listening times. And just listen! (See Chapter 4). And, if all else fails, make an appointment with a counsellor who agrees to mediate between you to solve your mutual problem.

~~~

Twelfth: Do not send *roadblocks* to your partner, when they are speaking to you. Especially if they are obviously under stress.

> Do not send *solutions* or give *advice* (unless they specifically ask for these kinds of inputs from you; or they agree to receive such inputs from you).

> Do not *ignore* their concerns.

> Do not try to *reassure them*, as if they did not know perfectly well how to evaluate their own situations. (Avoid reassurance, *unless* they *ask* for reassurance; or they seem *open* to reassurance; or you *ask them* if they would like some reassurance, and they say 'yes'!)

> Do not *judge them* negatively.

Remember, under normal circumstances, they are not their behaviour; although they are *accountable* for their behaviour; and if their behaviour goes over certain (moral or legal) lines, then we are justified in seeing them as 'being bad'. (See Appendix F). But for most purposes in our relationship communication, we should not equate *our partner* with *their behaviour*.

If necessary, or desirable, set up formal listening times. And just listen!

~~~

Thirteenth: Make sure you have reasonable boundaries in your relation-ships, and communicate your boundaries to your partner.

Ask your partner about their boundaries.

Our boundaries are our *rules* and *values* which determine what we will admit into our lives (the *good* stuff) and what we will exclude from our lives (the *bad* stuff). (These are sometimes called our 'red lines'. If you have no 'red lines', you will be vulnerable to being abused by others!)

We should *communicate* our boundaries to our partner *assertively*, and not aggressively. (See Chapter 8).

Make sure you understand your own personal conflict style. (See Appendix D.

~~~

Fourteen: You must make sure you grow your Adult ego state; and shrink your Controlling Parent and Adapted Child ego states. (See Appendix B).

Being in 'Adult ego state' means being reasonable, rational, sensible, logical and calm; with *well-regulated emotional responses* to the things that come up to be dealt with in your life. (But do not go for *Permanent* Adult, as you will come across as excessively boring! You also need to engage in Playful Child, Nurturing Parent, and Good Controlling Parent [for health and safety purposes]; but all *regulated by* your Adult state.)

If your emotional intelligence is below par, you should find that studying this book by reading it repeatedly will gradually raise it; and you can also study additional materials, like Claude Steiner's (1999) book on *Achieving Emotional Literacy*[74]. Make sure you use Appendices B and E until you have those ideas and principles, for managing your emotions and your behaviours, strongly encoded in your long-term memory. (This normally takes more than 30 days of reviewing the material, over and over again!)

It is also important, as mentioned above, to keep a good deal of Playful Child ego state in your personality, under the eagle eye of your Adult ego state.

This means that you keep asking yourself: "Am I being *light and easy* enough in my overall communication with my partner? Not too serious, too much of the time? And am I being *playful enough?*"

The other side of this consideration is equally important, and can be addressed by this kind of questioning: "Is this *appropriate* playfulness that I am engaging in, or am I in danger of 'hooking' (or eliciting) my partner's Critical Parent ego state, which would be painful for me to receive. Or am I in danger of not taking the current situation *seriously enough*, which would be a lack of responsibility on my part?"

Partners who are playful can have a lot of fun together, and this makes for a more interesting life than couples who always and only operate from serious and business-like 'Adult to Adult' communications, with *all* Parent and Child influences *excluded*.

You will also benefit from keeping your Nurturing Parent ego state active; again, under Adult scrutiny. (This means that you keep asking yourself: "Is this Nurturing Parent communication, from me to my partner, still *appropriate*, or am I in danger of becoming *patronizing*?") See Appendix B for an improved understanding of these Parent, Adult and Child 'ego states'.

~~~

Fifteenth: Give up passivity and aggression.

It is much more helpful and effective in relationships to operate from the "I'm OK – You're OK" position.

This is a principle of equality and non-judgemental relating. Give up the idea that there are *Top Dogs* and *Under Dogs* in life. These ideas are anathema to the principles of equality, fairness and love.

Learn to *ask* for what you want, openly and directly.

Say 'no', *clearly*, when you do not want to go along with your partner's idea.

Or 'trade off', if you do not particularly *want* to do something, but would be *willing* to do it, provided your partner *did something for you* which they have been resisting doing. (But do not ask your partner to trade-off something that would cause them unhappiness or distress. Do not ask for something which would normally be seen as immoral, illegal, or distasteful to most people; or something that crosses one your partner's 'red lines').

To offer a trade-off with your partner, simply say something like this: "If I do that for you, what will you do for me?" Or: "If I go along with you on that, will you go along with me on [X]?")

Avoid making 'You' statements – like, "You should not have..."; "You always..."; "You got it wrong..." – and especially avoid making 'You' statements with an *accusatory pointing finger*!

Stick to making 'I statements' – like, "I wish..."; "I want..."; "I think..."; "I feel..."; "I would appreciate it if..."; "I would prefer..."; or "It seems to me..."; and so on.

Become a Leveller. Be frank and honest with your partner – but not cruel! (See Appendix D).

Negotiate fairly, by separating your partner from the problem; and negotiating in terms of your mutual interests, instead of fighting about your respective 'positions'.

Let you partner know that *you appreciate it* when they do something kind or helpful or cooperative. Then, when you want to influence their behaviour, tell them *you would appreciate it* if they would do... (X)!

And keep your body-brain-mind strong, by managing your lifestyle well, so that you will normally display assertive body-language, which will encourage your partner to relate to you in a respectful, *Adult* manner.

~~~

Sixteenth: Manage your body-brain-mind well so that you will be happy, healthy and relaxed enough to function effectively in your relationship. When you are physically and mentally healthy, you are better able to be a loving partner: physically and mentally.

Try to set up daily practices of sleeping eight hours every night; eating a healthy, slow-burning breakfast; taking nutritional supplements with your main meals; especially vitamins B, C and E for stress; and a broad spectrum multivitamin for general wellbeing.

Eat a healthy, balanced diet, mainly of vegetables and (less) fruit; with some seeds and nuts; most often in the form of salads; with some protein: like organic eggs; wild Alaskan salmon; some white fish; sardines; and grass fed meats, like lamb, in moderation.

Make sure you drink six to eight glasses of water per day.

And take at least thirty minutes of physical exercise; and move around for about ten minutes every hour. Sitting around for long periods of time is very bad for your health.

Meditation is also a good daily practice for stress reduction, happiness creation, and the promoting of loving kindness. If you and your partner can get in the habit of meditating and exercising together, this will count towards your 5:1 ratio of positive to negative moments, which is essential if you want your relationship to survive and thrive.

(Remember to take turns, if there is any reading to be done before meditation; or if there is any leading role in your exercise system! Equality; equality; equality!)

~~~

Seventeenth: Dr John Gottman found that, having worked with, and conducted research upon, hundreds of couples, that the bottom line of his research data was this:

- Those couples who demonstrated a 5:1 ratio of positive to negative moments, when discussing difficult topics in his marriage lab, were still happily living together five years later, during follow-up interviews.

- Those couples who scored less than 5:1 for positive to negative moments, during those discussions, had separated within the following five years.

So, if you value your relationship, and you want it to last, and be happy, you have to work hard to achieve that magical 5:1 ratio of positive to negative moments.

And you can do that best by showing care and respect for your partner; by taking responsibility for your side of the relationship; by keeping the

...tic and sexual aspects of the relationship going; by sharing the work of the relationship equally; and by creating fun and recreation together.

12.3 Concluding statement

Now that you have reviewed this list of key learning points for the first time, review your list of notes, and construct an action list, to follow up on those points that you want to prioritize. This is the first draft of your *Action List for self-improvement and relationship success.*

By studying this book; and reviewing this chapter; and working on your *Action List* for self-improvement and relationship success; you will, in time, become a great lover and a very happily related individual in a successful relationship. And those outcomes are well worth working towards!

Best wishes to you for a happy and successful relationship.

Jim Byrne,
Doctor of Counselling
October 2018

~~~

Study guidelines

Tick that you've read this chapter once: ❑ Please read this chapter a second time: ❑ And a third time: ❑

When reading and re-reading this chapter, please underline those points that seem most important to you.

Make notes in the margins, as necessary, as quick reminders of the content of a paragraph or a page. Also, add important points, with their page numbers, in your own index to this book, in Appendix 'L', below.

~~~

Chapter 13: Summary 2 - How to teach individuals and couples to have happy and successful couple relationships

13.1 Introduction

In this chapter, we present a range of guidelines which can be used by counsellors, psychotherapists, psychologists, psychiatrists, physicians, social workers and others, to guide individual clients or patients towards a better understanding of the nature of couple relationships, and how to improve any relationship which is not working well.

We have gone back over the territory we covered in the main body of this book, and pulled out the key learning points that are relevant to professional helpers; and also looked for ways in which you can apply those key points to enhance your own professional practice.

We have listed the advice and guidelines that seem most helpful and usable, in an effort to maximize the usefulness of this book to all those professional readers who want to learn to be more helpful and effective in dealing with troubled couple relationships.

There is, however, one complication. Since we do not know how much experience, if any, the readers of this chapter will have, we have little choice but to assume that many readers may be new to this field, and so we have to aim our presentation at that level. However, some readers may have some years, or maybe even many years, experience in this field. Some readers, for example, may have many years' experience in the field of couple's therapy, but want to read this book to compare their approach to mine; or to see if they can find any new ideas that they have not encountered before. We do not wish to insult such readers by pitching our presentation at too low, or simple, a level for them. However, we have little choice but to pitch it at the level of the most basic potential reader: somebody who is relatively new to couple's therapy, and needs to be given the basic insights that we have developed.

13.2 Principal Guidelines for Therapists who want to use this system

Whether you are new to couple's therapy, or a seasoned professional, you will find that my approach is quite distinct.

Here is a form I used to use to structure the first couple's therapy session, with a new couple, up to about three or four years ago.

Names: xxxxxxxxxxxxx

Date: xxxxxxxxxxxxx

Time: xxxxxxxxxxxxxxx

Set the scene: xxxxxxxxxxxxxxxxxxxxxxxxxxxxxxxxxxx

Agree audio recording, or not: xxxxxxxxxxxxxxxx

Decide who will interact with me first: Flip a coin? Or ask them?

Set the timer: xxxxxxxxxxxxxxxxxxxx

Story of relationship: 5 minutes each partner

What issue do you want to work on? 10 minutes each partner

My teaching/facilitation inputs: xxxxxxxxxxxxxxxxxxxxxx

Pulling the session together, and wrapping it up.

Date/time of next session: xxxxxxxxxxxxxxxx

Homework tasks/materials: xxxxxxxxxxxxxxx

The main thing that has changed in that time is that audio recording of sessions has largely dropped out of the process, except when we work on something called 'Inner Couple Work' – see Chapter 11. I usually ask my clients to bring a recording device with them for recording part of the 'Inner Couple' work, which is conducted using Gestalt Chair-work. Most often, clients use an audio recording app on their mobile phone for this purpose.

~~~

Here, then, is my attempt to provide an overview of how I work:

Firstly: Before the clients arrive (if both partners are attending), I set up a sofa with two notepads and pens. The purpose of those tools will become clear in a few moments.

Secondly: When the couple arrives, I greet them, and guide them to be seated, and (assuming it is their first couple's therapy session with me) I ask them if they have any previous experience of counselling or therapy elsewhere; and couple's therapy in particular. I then explain that my approach is *different* from all other systems they may know about.

Third: I explain that I will work with one person at a time (often for about ten minutes, timed on a standard timer). And when I am working with one of them, their partner *must not speak*. There is to be no cross-talk or arguments or verbal exchanges of any kind between them. They are not to turn to each other to make a point; but to focus upon their encounter with me! While one of them is working with me, their partner is to remain quiet; to avoid any gasping or panting; rolling of eyes, or other non-verbal leakage; or verbally objecting to anything their partner says to me. Instead of those kinds of negative responses, they should make a note in their notebook, if they think their partner has said something they need to comment upon when it's their turn to work with me.

This system came out of my early experience of couples coming to my consulting room, and assuming I would sit and listen to them arguing and rowing with each other, and that I would then tell them which one was 'right'!

All humans are creatures of habit; and however they relate to each other at home - or in the car or on the bus on the way to see me - is a good indicator of how they are likely to relate in my presence, unless I *firmly* break up their habit patterns.

On more than one occasion, I have stood up in a couple's therapy session, placed myself in the space between the couple, and told the individuals, who were breaking my rule of no cross-talk, to be silent.

"There is *no fee* you could ever pay me which would encourage me to sit here and passively listen to you abusing each other!" I've told them.

"You can do that outside my door for free!"

Sometimes, a couple will have already agreed who will speak first, in which case I honour that decision. At other times they cannot decide, and then I normally flip a coin and the winner decides who goes first. (This is a simple way in which I model equality of treatment!)

Fourth: As soon as I begin to interact with a member of the couple, *I set a timer for an **agreed** number of minutes,* so the time is divided equally between them. This is another expression of egalitarianism and fairness.

(A forty-five minute session goes swiftly by when it's being shared by a couple. So I often suggest, budget permitting, that we have 90 minute sessions).

However, sometimes what the speaker is saying - at the point that the buzzer sounds for the end of their time - is too important to be cut short. In any such cases, I extend the speaker's time by a couple of minutes or more.

Most often the couple leaves the session feeling that they have had completely equal time to speak; but sometimes they go away feeling that one of them got a little more time than the other (and very rarely this is a lot more time than the other), *by agreement, because that was what the couple **both** needed.* And therefore, although the distribution of time was not quite equal, it was *agreed to be fair!*

Fifth: Their stories of relationship: With a new couple, I normally begin by asking each of them to tell me the story of their relationship, in summary form, in about five minutes each. Specifically, I ask them to answer two questions:

> Q1: *How did you meet?* And:

> Q2: *What attracted you to your partner?*

This is something that Professor John Gottman developed from his research with couples[75]. The degree of positivity of the story of relationship is a good indicator of the medium term (five years!) viability of the relationship.

If either, or both partners spend their five minutes focussing on what is *wrong* with their relationship, this is a very bad sign for the survival of their relationship in the subsequent five years or so.

However, if both of them begin by talking about *the good old days* when they were *in love*, and how *much they liked and enjoyed each other*, even if they then go on to talk about what a hell on wheels their life has been recently, then that is a good prognosis for the survival of their relationship as a loving pair bond – because of the positive early memories.

When the story of relationship presented to me by a member of a couple is primarily negative, I coach the client to dredge their memory-banks for positive memories of the relationship, and to try to rewrite the story of their relationship in much more positive terms; and I advise them that if they cannot achieve that goal, then their relationship is probably heading for the exit (meaning separation and/or divorce). Often, I have asked particularly negative couples to go away and write about the early days of their relationship, and to refine the story until it becomes happier and happier.

Sixth: What issue do they want to work on? When both partners have told their story of relationship, I then give them my appraisal of what this means for the future of their relationship: Either:

(1) their stories are positive, and this is a good sign that the relationship can be saved. Or

(2) their stories are too negative, and they should try to rewrite them, to make them more positive.

I then move on to ten minutes each on the 'burning issue' that they individually want to raise. This could be anything: Lack of affection; insufficient sexual contact; lack of intimacy; unfair fighting; volatility from one partner; poor communication; infidelity; and so on.

This is the point at which I begin to teach the individual partners some of the eighteen principles of couple's therapy that I have collected/developed over the past twenty years. (Six of those principles are presented in this book, in Chapter 9; and the other twelve will be presented, in two blocks of six, in Volumes 2 and 3).

As they work with me, I automatically make connections to some of my key principles of happy and successful relationships, and identify one or two principles as potential solutions to aspects of what I am beginning to perceive as the underlying problem(s) in their relationship.

I would like to present six of those principles here; and the remainder will be split between volumes two and three:

(1). A marriage is a "house" that is built every day. What *actions* did you consciously take to build the "house" of your marriage today? If you go to sleep in your relationship, you will wake up to find it has collapsed from want of repair. Arguing and rowing with your partner about who is right and who is wrong, and especially who is the 'top-dog' and who is the 'under-dog', is equivalent to trying to polish the walls of your "house" with sledge hammers! You will wreck it in no time. So I ask again:

*What actions did you consciously take today to **build** the "house" of your relationship?*

*What actions did you take to **stop** swinging the wrecking ball against the walls of your relationship?*

~~~

(2). If you want your relationship to survive, then you need to maintain a 5:1 ratio of positive to negative moments. If you fail to do this, then your relationship is heading for disintegration.

"But what more can I do?" I hear you ask.

Try this:

Avoid *criticizing* your partner. Criticism is corrosive and destroys self-esteem and good feelings in a relationship. Use reasonable '*assertive complaints*' about *behaviours*, not about your partner's essence, or personhood.

Remember to set up dates and assignations with your partner, for friendly talk, walks, outings and sex-love encounters. High quality time spent together counts towards the 5 positive moments that you need (out of every 6). Ignoring or abandoning your partner – or angrily frightening them - counts towards the negative side of the equation.

(3). The best way to get love is to sincerely offer it to your partner. In what ways could you *offer love* to your partner which you are not currently doing?

"But", I hear you protest, "what love do I get from them?"

That's a really crazy way to do the sums. 'Holding out for love' is just like a person sitting in front of a cold and black stove, with a huge wooden log in their hands, and they're saying to the stove: "If you give me some heat, I'll give you this log!"

Crazy! All they have to do is put the log on the fire, and fan the resulting flames a little; and – whoosh – up comes the warming heat.

Do not wait for your partner to start loving you before you will love them. That's crazy. Become *the **source** of love* in your relationship, and watch the magical results!

~~~

(4). Love is not a "nice feeling" (at least, not initially!). Love is a *process* of "extending yourself in the service of another person". In what ways could you *extend yourself* in the service of your partner which would increase the flow of love from you to them? (And, later, back again! *Cast thy bread upon the waters, for it shall return after many days!*)

~~~

(5). It is important to distinguish between **your partner** on the one hand and **their behaviour** on the other! Then you can more easily accept your partner **one-conditionally**, while wishing, desiring and even requesting that they please change the specific behaviour with which you have a problem. The one condition that you should apply to accepting your partner is this:

Do they broadly try to act in moral ways with you?

If they do, that's great! You can learn to accept them with all their fallibilities and frailties and tendencies towards error.

However, if they *clearly* act **immorally**, as, for example, in using physical abuse or verbal abuse with you, then you should not accept them, but get the hell out of the relationship, as fast as you possibly can run!

If your partner is broadly moral in the way they behave, you might still have some problems with some of their behaviours. But remember, you do have the right to try to influence them to change their behaviours, and/or their values, to the extent that you are willing to allow them to try to change your behaviours and values.

However, you do not have an *absolute right* to *demand* that your partner change *any* of their behaviours, and if you proceed on the assumption that you have such a right, you will have *a great deal of misery* in your marital relationship.

Can you think of an incident recently where you condemned **your partner** *for engaging in behaviour(s) that you did not like, instead of merely objecting to* **their** <u>behaviour</u>? *Do you know what you could have done which would have been more effective?* (If you answer 'No' to this question, then you could benefit from studying one-conditional self-acceptance, and one-conditional acceptance of others. See the brief introduction to this subject in Appendix J, below).

~~~

(6). It's OK to *want* to be loved by your partner. It is not OK, (meaning, not sensible, helpful or effective), to *demand* that you be loved by your partner, or anybody else!

Are you *insisting* that you be loved by your partner? Regardless of how you behave towards your partner?

If so, you'd better stop that!

It is sensible to *offer love*, and see if they offer love back. If you are not actively loved by your partner (assuming you show active love for them!), the democratic, loving and personally-effective thing to do is to tell your partner that you cannot easily live on the *thin gruel* that they offer in the name of love, and that you intend to decamp to a warmer environment! But don't play games about this! If you say you are going to decamp, unless something significant changes, then you should keep your promise, if that thing does not change, or change to your satisfaction!

It is not OK to use separation or divorce as a *stick* to beat your partner with!

Are you straight with your partner about how well your relationship is working, and what you would prefer to do if the relationship does not work out?

*Does your partner know precisely what it is you are **asking** for?*

~~~

End of the six principles. (Principles seven to eighteen will be included in Volumes 2 and 3 of this series).

~~~

Back to the seventh point in my earlier list:

Seventh: The main lessons I am trying to teach my couple-clients are as follows:

(a) If you want to have a happy relationship, you have to treat your partner as an *equal* human being.

(b) You have to *actively love them*. And this means you must show *care* and *respect* for them. You must *take responsibility* for your side of the relationship. And you must show an interest in *gaining knowledge* of your partner: *Who are they? How do they feel right now? What do they like, and dislike? What are their dreams, wants, desires?* And so on.

(c) You must each *work hard* to achieve *a five-to-one (5:1) ratio* of positive to negative moments.

(d) And there must be a good deal of compatibility, but never total compatibility. There has to be a good balance of comfort and passion in the relationship. You cannot substitute more comfort for less passion, or vice versa. Both comfort and passion are important in their own right.

Eighth: I also strive to teach them new, empowering definitions of relationship (as described in Chapter 1); how to explode some myths about relationships (which are outlined in Chapter 2); how to communicate effectively (as described in Chapters 4 and 7, and Appendix B; and how to construct, and communicate about, their personal boundaries.

Ninth: I also teach my clients eighteen ways to build happy relationships, six of which have been presented above. And I teach them to take a holistic approach to self-management, in order to have a positive lifestyle which supports good relationship skills (as explored in Chapter 10).

Tenth: I increasingly use the *Inner Couple* model – of how each of us is shaped by our parents' relationship – and how we end up reproducing their relationship in our own adult lives, unless and until we do some kind of therapy to change how we relate in the here and now. (See Chapter 11).

Eleventh: For an overview of what I try to teach my couple clients, please see Chapter 12.

~~~

Applying these learning points

If you are a couples' therapist, and you want to teach any of the ideas described in this book, please read the section that interests you the most, at least three times, and try to teach one or two points from that section to your first/next couple client.

I have found that it is important to build up slowly. To acquire an idea; to apply that idea in a session with a couple; and then to learn from that application. Slowly, over a period of time, you will expand your declarative knowledge (what you know) and your procedural knowledge (what you can do). There is enough Continuing Professional Development 'meat' in this book to fill one thousand hours of learning and growing!

13.3 Recently revised structure of couple´s therapy sessions

In recent weeks, I have decided to keep my couples even more separated out than before. Up to recently, I would see them together for every session that they wanted to attend. I kept them out of conflict by dealing with one at a time. However, recently, I began to realize that, with some difficult couples in particular, they continue to exert an inhibiting effect upon each other's communication with me, even if they follow my rules of not engaging in any kind of disruption of that communication, verbally or non-verbally. This reduces the possibility of real therapeutic progress with their individual and their relational problems.

So now, I have instituted a new system, which is described on my website like this:

In the light of my recent experiences of providing couples therapy services, I have decided to make the following changes to my service:

1. Instead of an *open-ended offering*, I now offer a *specific structure*.

2. The structure is as follows:

> Session (1): A 45 minute session with one member of the couple. Attendance by one partner only. This will normally be the person who contacted me to set up the therapy series (unless there are very good reasons why it has to be the other partner).

> Session (2): A 45 minute session with the other partner. Attendance by one partner only.

> Session (3): A 90 minute (double) session with both partners present. Both partners attend, but I only work with one at a time, as in my previous process.

~~~

3. If you come to see me; and complete three sessions; and you find this three-session process is helping to heal the problems in your relationship, then you would most likely opt to attend for a further three sessions, following the same structure shown in Sessions (1)-(3) above.

4. There will also be a new emphasis in my revised process upon asking you to complete questionnaires, so I can quickly and reliably come to understand:

> (a) Your *attachment styles*;

> (b) How passive, assertive or aggressive you each tend to be;

> (c) Your *conflict resolution styles*;

> (d) Your *emotional needs* profile;

> (e) The *experiences* that went into shaping your 'Inner Couple';

> (f) And anything else that seems to be needed, or potentially helpful.

13.4 Preparing for your couple's therapy sessions

Next, I want to present a case study of my preparation for a member of a couple, who wanted help for himself and his girlfriend. I wrote these notes in my Morning Pages. (Strategy No. 2B, in Byrne, 2018b).

Case notes:

I need to prepare for a double session with Kevin Clarke (not his real name) – tomorrow morning, at 11.00 am. He is an American financial consultant, working in Manchester; and his girlfriend, Johanna, is a trainee journalist in Birmingham; the city in which she was born. They, obviously, have a long-distance relationship. Kevin contacted me over Skype to set up a series of three sessions: one with him (90 minutes), tomorrow; one with Johanna (90 minutes) next Tuesday; and then a joint session (also 90 minutes), the following week. He seems to be involved in a conflicted relationship with Johanna - (what some would call 'an involvement' or 'entanglement' [especially Werner Erhard – in his audio program: *Relationships, Making them Work*). Kevin tried to persuade me that 'the problem' is Johanna's 'psychiatric condition'.

Initial observations: Kevin seems to be badly overweight, which might suggest that his diet is playing some part in his psychological struggles with Johanna (the *junk food* > *anger* link). He also seems to be convinced that he is right, and the rest of the world is wrong, in any conflict.

Notes for guidance of a couple's therapy session

\# Ask Kevin to describe how he met Johanna, and to say what it was that attracted him to her.

\# Is there enough love and respect left in the relationship, to make it worth trying to save it?

\# What proportion of their shared time is happy/positive and what proportion is unhappy/negative? (Explain the need for a 5:1 ratio of positive to negative moments!)

What exactly does Johanna do, in the relationship, that causes problems for Kevin?

Describe the *Four Horsemen of the Apocalypse* (Gottman, 1997), and check to see if he thinks they have that pattern of relating in their communications. (Criticism leading to Withdrawal; plus Contempt leading to Stone-walling).

Describe the **Controlling Parent** *versus* **Adapted/Rebellious Child** pattern of relating. And ask if this fits his relationship with Johanna.

Ask him how his parents related to each other when he was 0-5 years old; and then 5-10 years old. (Did either of them behave like Johanna? And does he relate to Johanna like one of his parents related to the other?)

How did his mother relate to Kevin?

How did Kevin's father relate to him?

Ask him to describe his previous relationships with women and girls. Were any of them similar in any way to his relationship with Johanna? Or did any of his previous girlfriends cause Kevin to interact in ways reminiscent of Johanna's problematic behaviours?

Ask him to describe the sources of stress in his life, and list them below:

What did he have for breakfast this morning?

What did he have for his evening meal last night?

How much water has he drunk in the past 24 hours?

How much caffeine (tea, coffee, cola) did he consume yesterday, all day?

\# How many units of alcohol did he consume yesterday, all day, up to bedtime?

...

\# When was the last time he did some physical exercise?

What was it, and how much?

...

\# Ask him to complete the Assertiveness Questionnaire.

Pull out any obvious problems...

...

\# Ask him to complete the Emotional Needs Assessment form.

Focus on any obvious problems...

...

\# Ask him to define love, as he understands it:

\# Ask him to read through my definition of love, and tell me how this differs from what he and Johanna have been calling love?

Ask him to define 'relationship' as he understands it, and as he is applying it to his association with Johanna:

Ask him to read my definition of relationship, and tell me how this differs from what he and Johanna have been calling 'a relationship':

Refer to the Couple Relationship pamphlet that I sent to him, as an email attachment. Ask him if he has read about the 'Inner Couple' model, in Part 2 of that pamphlet.

> If he answered 'yes':

>> Does he want to work in his Inner Couple with me?

>> Yes? No? Maybe? Don't know?

>> ...

>> Does Johanna want to work on her Inner Couple with me?

>> Yes? No? Maybe? Don't know?

>> ...

> If he answered 'No' (that he has not read the pamphlet), then describe the *Inner Couple model* to him.

~~~

\# Cover as much of this agenda as is possible in 90 minutes, and then ask him to consider how we proceed from this point:

Q1. Is there any point having a joint session with him and Johanna, in two weeks' time?

Q2. In the light of the answer to Q1, is there any point confirming Johanna's appointment with me for next week?

Q3. How do you, Kevin, want to proceed?

~~~

Postscript: This case study gives some indication of how holistic and integrative my approach to couple's therapy is.

Again, if you are new to the work of being a couple's therapist, you need to build up to this kind of complexity, one building block at a time.

To use an analogy from judo: When you are a 'white belt' (or beginner) you have to move slowly, cautiously, and carefully; and do not expect yourself to be able to move like a 'black belt' (expert). But if you keep training, working at learning more and more; then, eventually, there is nothing to stop you becoming a black belt (in small, graded steps; from white to yellow belt, and from yellow to orange belt; and so on)!

Part of the secret is to keep re-reading and re-reading this text; applying bits and pieces of it with clients; integrating bits and pieces from this system with your current approach; and so on. Inch by inch it's a cinch!

~~~

Study guidelines

Tick that you've read this chapter once: ❒

Please read this chapter a second time: ❒

And a third time: ❒

~~~

When reading and re-reading this chapter, please underline those points that seem most important to you.

Make notes in the margins, as necessary, as quick reminders of the content of a paragraph or a page.

And turn down the corner of the page, when the content is so important you want to find it again, quickly and easily.

Also, add important points, with their page numbers, in your own index to this book, in Appendix 'L', below.

~~~

References

Agnew, T. (1996) Mind & Body: About to be married? You need help... Health: Thelma Agnew on the best part of breaking up – avoiding it. *The Observer* (newspaper). 24th November 1996.

Ainsworth M (1967). *Infancy in Uganda: Infant Care and the Growth of Love.* Baltimore: Johns Hopkins University Press.

Ainsworth M. (1969) Object relations, dependency, and attachment: a theoretical review of the infant-mother relationship. *Child Development, 40 (4):* 969–1025.

Armstrong, J. (2003) *Conditions of Love: The philosophy of intimacy.* London: Penguin Books.

Barnes, J. (2018) *The Only Story.* (A novel about first love). London: Jonathan Cape.

Bargh, J.A. and Chartrand, T.L. (1999) The unbearable automaticity of being. *American Psychologist, 54(7):* 462-479.

Baumeister, R.F. and Leary, M.R. (1995) The need to belong: Desire for interpersonal attachment as a fundamental human emotion. *Psychological Bulletin, 117:* Pages 497-529.

Bean, M. (2009) Master Her Body: Sexy women reveal how to tease them, please them, and make them beg for more. Men's health blog. Available online: https://www.menshealth.com/sex-women/a19545523/sex-tips-for-clitoral-stimulation/. Accessed: 7th August 2018.

Beard, M. (2017) *Women and Power: A manifesto.* London: Profile Books Ltd.

Berne, E. (1947/1986) A *Layman's Guide to Psychiatry and Psycho-analysis.* Harmondsworth: Penguin Books.

Berne, E. (1973/1981) *Sex in Human Loving.* Harmondsworth, Middlesex, UK: Penguin Books.

Berne, E. (1975) *What Do You Say After You Say Hello?* London: Corgi Books.

Blumenthal, J.A., Babyak, M.A., Moore, K.A., et.al. (1999) Effects of exercise training on older patients with major depression. *Archives of Internal Medicine, Oct 25 1999, Vol.159 (19):* Pages 2349-2356.

Blumenthal, J.A., Smith, P.J., and Hoffman, B.M. (2012) Is exercise a viable treatment for depression? *American College of Sports Medicine Health & Fitness Journal.* July/August; Vol.16(4): Pages 14–21.

Bolton, R. (1979/1986). *People Skills: How to assert yourself, listen to others, and resolve conflicts.* Englewood Cliffs, NJ: Prentice-Hall Inc.

Borchard, T. (2015) 10 Ways to Cultivate Good Gut Bacteria and Reduce Depression. Everyday Health Blog. Available online: http://www.everydayhealth .com/columns/therese-borchard-sanity-break/ways-cultivate-good-gut -bacteria-reduce-depression/

Bowlby, J. (1979/2005) *The Making and Breaking of Affectional Bonds.* London: Routledge Classics.

Bowlby, J. (1980) *Attachment and Loss: Vol. 3. Loss, sadness and depression.* New York: Basic Books.

Breus, M.J. (2010) A good night's sleep for good sex: Links between healthy sex life and a healthy sleep life. *Psychology Today Blog.* Online: https://www.psychology today.com/gb/blog/sleep-newzzz/201004/good-night -s-sleep-good-sex. Accessed: 31st May 2018.

Brewer, S. (2013) *Nutrition: A beginners guide.* London: Oneworld Publications.

Brogan, K. (2016) *A mind of your own: The truth about depression and how women can heal their bodies to reclaim their lives.* London: Thorsons.

Bruner, J. (1986) *Actual Minds, Possible Worlds.* Cambridge, MA: Harvard University Press.

Burton, R. (trans) (1883/1991) *The Kama Sutra of Vatsyayana.* Park Street Press.

Buzan, T. (1973) *Use Your Head.* London: BBC Books.

Byrne, J. (2010/2018) The Story of Relationship: Or coming to terms with my mother (and father). E-CENT[76] Paper No.10. Hebden Bridge: The Institute for E-CENT. Available online: https://abc-counselling.org/my-story-of-relationship-with-mother/

Byrne, J. (2016) *Holistic Counselling in Practice: An introduction to Emotive-Cognitive Embodied Narrative Therapy.* Hebden Bridge: The Institute for E-CENT Publications.

Byrne, J. (2017a) *Metal Dog – Long Road Home: A mythical journey through the eye of a needle.* The fictionalized memoir of an improbable being. (A semi-autobiographical novel or extended story). Hebden Bridge: The Institute for E-CENT Publications.

Byrne, J. (2017b) *Unfit for Therapeutic Purposes: The case against Rational Emotive and Cognitive Behavioural Therapy (RE&CBT)*. The Institute for E-CENT, with the CreateSpace platform.

Byrne, J. with Renata Taylor-Byrne (2018a) *Lifestyle Counselling and Coaching for the Whole Person: Or how to integrate nutritional insights, exercise and sleep coaching into talk therapy*. Hebden Bridge: The Institute for E-CENT Publications.

Byrne, J. (2018b) *How to Write a New Life for Yourself: Narrative therapy and the writing solution*. Hebden Bridge: The Institute for E-CENT Publications.

Carnegie, D. (1983) *How to Win Friends and Influence People.* Surrey: World's Work Ltd.

Clinard, H.H. (1985) *Winning Ways to Succeed with People.* Houston: Gulf Publishing Company.

Cohen, D. (1997) *Carl Rogers: A critical biography*. London: Constable.

Comfort, A. (1970/2011) *The Joy of Sex*. (Revised and updated by Susan Quilliam). London: Mitchell Beazley.

Coleman, A.N. (2002) *A Dictionary of Psychology*. Oxford: Oxford University Press.

Corey, G. (2001) *Theory and Practice of Counselling and Psychotherapy.* Sixth edition. Belmont, CA: Brooks/Cole.

Craze, R. (1999) *The Pocket Book of Foreplay*. London: Thorsons.

Croteau, J. and Andrews, C. (2018) Social ties are good for your health. BeWell blog. Stanford University. Online: https://bewell.stanford.edu/social-ties-are-good-for-your-health/. Accessed: 14th June 2018.

Dawkins, R. (1989) *The Selfish Gene.* Second edition. Oxford University Press.

Delvin, D. (2016) The Clitoris. On the Net-Doctor blog at: https://www.netdoctor.co.uk/conditions/sexual-health/a2317/the-clitoris/. Accessed: 12th November 2018.

DePaulo, B.M. and Morris, W.L. (2005) Singles in society and science. *Psychological Inquiry, 16:* 57-83.

Diamond, M. & Sigmundson, H. K. (1997) *Sex reassignment at birth: A long-term review and clinical implications, Archives of Pediatrics and Adolescent Medicine, 152,* Pages 298 – 304.

Diener, E., Suh, E.M., Lucas, R.E. & Smith, H.L. (1999) Subjective wellbeing. Three decades of progress. *Psychological Bulletin, 125:* 120-129.

Doidge, N. (2008) *The Brain that Changes Itself: Stories of personal triumph from the frontiers of brain science.* London: Penguin.

Dovidio, J.F. (1984) Helping behaviour and altruism: An empirical and conceptual overview. In: L. Berkowitz (ed), *Advances in experimental social psychology. Vol. 17,* Pages 361-427. New York: Academic Press.

Duhigg, C. (2013) *The Power of Habit: Why we do what we do and how to change.* London: Random House.

Durbanville (2015) In Romeo and Juliet, Juliet is 13, but how old is Romeo? eNotes, 30 July 2015. Available online: https://www.enotes.com/homework-help/know-that-juliet-13-half-but-how-old-romeo-51141. Accessed 7th July 2018.

Eaker, E. (2007) Bite your tongue, kick the bucket. News report in the *Metro* Newspaper; Tuesday August 21st, 2007. Page 4.

Eisenberger, N.I., Lieberman, M.D., and Williams K.D. (2003) Does rejection hurt? A fMRI study of social exclusion. *Science, Vol. 302, Issue 5643*, pp 290-292. Available online: http://science.sciencemag.org/content/302/5643/290

Ellis, A. (1962) *Reason and Emotion in Psychotherapy*. New York: Citadel/Carol Publishing.

Ellis, A. (1994) *Reason and Emotion in Psychotherapy: revised and updated.* New York: Carol Publishing.

Epston, D. and White, M. (1990) *Narrative Means to Therapeutic Ends.* New York: W.W. Norton and Company.

Erhard, W. (1981) Relationships: Making them work. An audio program. Available at YouTube: https://www.youtube.com/watch?v=pCrCgYgHkm8. Accessed: 10th August 2018.

Erwin, E. (1997) *Philosophy and Psychotherapy: Razing the troubles of the brain,* London, Sage.

Firstein, I. (2010) Barriers to effective communication. Online blog, here: https://www.goodtherapy.org/blog/barriers-to-effective-communication/. Accessed: 11th June 2018.

Fisher, R. and Ury, W. (1997) *Getting to Yes: Negotiating an agreement without giving in.* London: Random House.

Freud, S. (1995) Beyond the pleasure principle. In: Gay, P. (ed) *The Freud Reader.* London: Vintage Books.

Fromm, E. (1995) *The Art of Loving*. London: Thorsons.

Garapick, J. (2014) Committed Relationship - What Does That Really Mean? A blog post. Online here: https://gettingtotruelove.com/2014/06/20/ committed – relationship-mean/. Accessed: 15th August 2018/

Gladwell, M. (2006) *BLINK: The power of thinking without thinking.* London: Penguin Books.

Gordon, L.H. (1969/2016) Intimacy: The art of relationships. How relationships are sabotaged by hidden expectations. *Psychology Today* blog. Available online: https://www.psychologytoday.com/us/articles/196912/intimacy-the-art-relation-ships. Accessed: 21st June 2018.

Gottman, J. (1997) *Why Marriages Succeed or Fail: and how you can make yours last.* London: Bloomsbury Publishing.

Gottman, J. (1999) *The Seven Principles for Making Marriage Work.* London: Weidenfeld and Nicolson.

Gottman, J. (2017) Building a great sex life is not rocket science. A blog post. Available here: https://tinyurl.com/yd4cm95a. Accessed: 13th August 2018.

Gray, J. (2003) *Straw Dogs: Thoughts on humans and other animals.* London: Granta Books.

Greer, G. (2018) The law doesn't know what rape is, and that ruins sex for women. *The Sunday Times, August 26th 2018.* Comment. Page 21.

Greer, G. (2018) *On Rape.* London: Bloomsbury.

Gross, R. (2001) *Psychology: The science of mind and behaviour,* Fourth edition. London: Hodder and Stoughton.

Haas, E.M. (2018) Nutritional Programs: Nutritional Program For Sexual Vitality. An online blog at Healthy.net. Available online at: http://www.healthy.net/Health/Article/Nutritional Program for Sexual Vitality/1273/2. Accessed: 31st May 2018.

Haidt, J. (2001) The emotional dog and its rational tail: A social intuitionist approach to moral judgement. *Psychological Review, 108(4):* 814-834.

Haidt J (2002) The moral emotions. In: Davidson, R.J., Scherer, K., Goldsmith, H.H., (eds) *Handbook of affective sciences.* Oxford: Oxford University Press.

Haidt, J. (2006) *The Happiness Hypothesis: Putting ancient wisdom and philosophy to the test of modern science.* London: William Heinemann.

Harker, L. and Keltner, D. (2001) Expressions of positive emotion in women's college yearbook pictures and their relationship to personality and life outcomes across adulthood. *Journal of Personality and Social Psychology, 80:* Pages 112-124.

Hart, S. (2011) *The Impact of Attachment: Developmental neuroaffective psychology.* London: W.W. Norton and Company.

Hatfield, E., & Sprecher, S. (1986). Measuring passionate love in intimate relationships. *Journal Of Adolescence, 9(4),* Pages 383-410. doi:10.1016/S0140-1971(86)80043-4. Accessed: 21st June 2018.

Hobson, R. (1985/2000) *Forms of Feeling: The heart of psychotherapy.* London: Routledge.

Holford, P. (2010) *Optimum Nutrition for the Mind.* London: Piatkus.

ISSM (2012) What is the normal frequency of sex? International Society for Sexual Medicine. Online blog: http://www.issm.info/sexual-health-qa/what-is-the-normal-frequency-of-sex/. Accessed: 23rd June 2018.

James, O. (2002). *They F*** You Up: How to survive family life.* London. Bloomsbury.

Joines, V. and Stewart, I. (2002) *Personality Adaptations: A new guide to human understanding in psychotherapy and counselling.* Nottingham: Lifespace Publishing.

Kahneman, D. (2012) *Thinking Fast and Slow.* London: Penguin Books.

Kashdan, T. and Biswas-Diener, R. (2015) *The Power of Negative Emotion: How anger, guilt and self-doubt are essential to success and fulfilment.* London: Oneworld Publications.

Kerner, I. (2011) *She Comes First: The thinking man's guide to pleasuring a woman.* London: Souvenir Press.

Kiecolt-Glaser, J.K.; Tamara Newton; John T Cacioppo; Robert C. MacCallum; Ronald Glaser; and William B. Malarkey (1996) Marital Conflict and Endocrine Function: Are Men Really More Physiologically Affected Than Women? *Journal of Consulting and Clinical Psychology, 1996, Vol. 64, No. 2,* Pages 324-332.

Kiecolt-Glaser, J.K., Belury, M.A., Andridge, R., et al (2011) 'Omega 3 supplementation lowers inflammation and anxiety in medical students: A randomised, controlled trial'. *Brain, Behaviour, Immunity, Vol. 25(8).* Pages 1725-1734.

Kiecolt-Glaser, J.K.; Stephanie J. Wilson, Michael L. Bailey; et al., (2018) Marital distress, depression, and a leaky gut: Translocation of bacterial endotoxin as a pathway to inflammation. Psychoneuroendocrinology, 2018; 98: 52 DOI: 10.1016/j.psyneuen.2018.08.007

Kitzinger, C. (1997) Born to be good? – What motivates us to be good, bad or indifferent towards others? *New Internationalist, No. 289, April 1997.*

Klein, M. (1940) Mourning and its relation to manic-depressive states, in *The Selected Melanie Klein.* Edited by Mitchell, J. (1986). London: Penguin Books.

Knapton, S. (2018) Why a marital argument hits you in the gut. *The Daily Telegraph* (newspaper, UK): 16th August 2018. Page 11.

Koedt, A. (1968/1970) *The Myth of the Vaginal Orgasm.* New England Free Press.

Lee, J.A. (1973) *The Colours of Love: An exploration of the ways of loving.* New Press.

Levine, A. and Heller, R. (2011) *Attached: Identify your attachment style and find your perfect match.* London: Rodale/Pan Macmillan.

Lewis, T., Amini, F. and Lannon, R. (2001) *A General Theory of Love.* New York: Vintage Books.

Liverpool, L. (2018) A bad marriage can seriously damage your health, say scientists. *The Guardian,* Online: https://www.theguardian.com/lifeandstyle/2018/jul/16/a-bad-marriage-is-as-unhealthy-as-smoking-or-drinking-say-scientists?CMP=share_btn_fb. Accessed: 28th July 2018.

Lucas, R.E., Clark, A.E., Georgellis, Y. and Diener, E. (2003) Re-examining adaptation and the set point model of happiness: Reactions to changes in marital status. *Journal of Personality and Social Psychology, 84:* Pages 527-539.

Lyall, S. (2008) Revising 'Sex' for the 21st century. *Fashion and Style: New York Times online.* ('The Joy of Sex', revised for today). https://www.nytimes .com/2008/12/18joy.html. Accessed: 22nd June 2018.

Lyubomirsky, S., King, L., and Diener, E. (2005) The benefits of frequent positive affect: Does happiness lead to success? *Psychological Bulletin. Vol. 131, No. 6,* Pages 803– 855.

Mahler, M.S., Pine, F. and Bergman, A. (1975/1987) *The Psychological Birth of the Human Infant: Symbiosis and individuation.* London: Maresfield Library.

Mastekaasa, A. (1994) Marital status, distress, and well-being. An international comparison. *Journal of Comparative Family Studies, 25:* 183-205.

McLeod, S. (2015) Piaget's Theory of Moral Development. Online blog. Available here: http://www.simplypsychology.org/piaget-moral.html. Reviewed on 12th June 2018.

Mercola, J. (2013) 'Vitamin D — One of the Simplest Solutions to Wide-Ranging Health Problems'. Available online: http://articles.mercola.com/sites/articles/ archive/2013/12/22/dr-holick-vitamin-d- benefits.aspx. Accessed 15 June 2016.

Michael, R.T., Gagnon, J.H., Lauman, E.O., and Kolata, G. (1994) *Sex in America: A definitive study.* New York: Little Brown and Co.

Milgram, S. (1974) *Obedience to Authority.* New York: Harper and Row.

Money, J. & Ehrhardt, A. A. (1972) *Man and woman, boy and girl: Differentiation and dimorphism of gender identity from conception to maturity.* Baltimore: Johns Hopkins University Press.

Natural Partners (2018) Eating for sexual vitality. An online blog. Available here: https://blog.naturalpartners.com/eating-for-sexual-vitality/. Accessed: 31st May 2018.

Nelson-Jones, R. (1986) *Human Relationship Skills: Training and self-help.* London: Cassell.

Nelson-Jones, R. (2001) *Theory and Practice of Counselling and Therapy.* Third edition. London: Continuum.

NHS Choices (2016) Moodzone: Exercise for depression. https://www.nhs.uk/ conditions/stress-anxiety-depression/exercise-for-depression/. Accessed: 1st August 2018.

Northrup, C., Schwartz, P., and Witte, J. (2014) *The Normal Bar: The Surprising Secrets of Happy Couples and What They Reveal About Creating a New Normal in Your Relationship.* New York: Harmony Books.

Ohio State University (2018) How ugly marital spats might open the door to disease: Study links couples' hostility and gut bacteria, inflammation in bloodstream. *ScienceDaily. ScienceDaily, 15 August 2018.* Available online: www.sciencedaily.com/ releases/2018/08/180815085903.htm. Accessed: 16th August 2018.

Olds, J. and Schwartz, R.S. (2010) *The Lonely American: Drifting apart in the twenty-first century.* Boston, MA: Beacon Press.

Panksepp, J. (1998) *Affective Neuroscience: The foundations of human and animal emotions.* Oxford University Press.

Peck, M. S. (1998) *The Road Less Travelled: A new psychology of love, traditional values and spiritual growth.* London: Arrow Books.

Perlmutter, D. (2015) *Brain Maker: The power of gut microbes to heal and protect your brain – for life.* London: Hodder and Stoughton.

Piaget, J. (1952) *The Language and Thought of the Child.* New York: Humanities Press.

Piaget, J. (1954) *The Moral Judgement of the Child.* Glencoe, Ill: Free Press.

Popova, M. (2018) John Steinbeck on Falling in Love: A 1958 Letter of Advice to His Lovesick Teenage Son. In the BrainPickings blog: https://www. brainpickings.org/ ?mc_cid=40c48c0405&mc_eid=204f4a8f33. Accessed: 28th June 2018.

Prochaska, J.O., Norcross, J.C. & DiClemente, C.C. (1998). *Changing for Good.* Reprint edition. New York: Morrow.

Ratey, J., and Hagerman, E. (2009) *Spark: The revolutionary new science of exercise and the brain.* London: Quercus.

Redfern, R. (2016) The importance of nutrition for mental health. *Naturally Healthy News. Issue 30,* 2016.

Reiss, J. (2017) Hand stimulation techniques for explosive orgasms. The Rebel Circus blog. Available online: http://www.rebelcircus.com/blog/hand-stimulation-techniques -explosive-orgasms/. Accessed: 7th August 2018.

Rilke, R.M. (2011) *Letters to a Young Poet.* CreateSpace Independent Platform.

Rogers, C.R. and Stevens, B. (with Eugene T. Gendlin, John M. Shien and Wilson Van Dusen) (1967/1998) *Person to Person: The problem of being human; a new trend in psychology.* Lafayette, CA: Real People Press.

Ross, J. (2003) *The Mood Cure: Take charge of your emotions in 24 hours using food and supplements.* London: Thorsons.

Sarbin, T. R. (1989) Emotions as narrative emplotments. In M. J. Packer & R. B. Addison (eds.) *Entering the circle: Hermeneutic investigations in psychology* (pp. 185-201). Albany, NY: State University of New York Press.

Sarbin, T. R. (2001) Embodiment and the narrative structure of emotional life. *Narrative Inquiry, 11,* 217-225.

Satir, V. (1972/1983) *Peoplemaking.* London: Souvenir Press.

Schore, A.N. (2015) *Affect Regulation and the Origin of the Self: The Neurobiology of Emotional Development*. London: Routledge.

Shackleton, F., Barlow, A., Ewing, J., and Janssens, A. (2018) Asking ten 'critical' questions before embarking on a serious relationship can help couples thrive. Research News. University of Exeter. Available online: https://www.exeter.ac.uk/ news/research/title_672700_en.html. Accessed: 3rd August 2018.

Shealey, G. (2018) Can exercise improve your sex life? Online blog: HowStuffWorks. Available here: https://health.howstuffworks.com/wellness/ diet-fitness/exercise/can-exercise-improve-your-sex-life.htm. Accessed: 31st May 2018.

Siegel, D.J. (2015) *The Developing Mind: How relationships and the brain interact to shape who we are*. London: The Guilford Press. Pages 152-153.

Skynner, R. and Cleese, J. (1987) *Families and How to Survive Them*. London: Methuen.

Smith, P.K., Cowie, H., and Blades, M. (2011) *Understanding Children's Development. Fifth edition*. Chichester, West Sussex: Wiley.

Spector, T. (2013) *Identically Different: Why you can change your genes*. London: Phoenix.

Spiegelhalter, D. (2015) *Sex by Numbers: What statistics can tell us about sexual behaviour*. London: Profile Books.

Steinbeck, E. and Wallsten, R. (eds) (1989) *Steinbeck: A Life in Letters*. London: Penguin Books.

Steiner, C.M. (1990) *Scripts People Live: Transactional Analysis of Life Scripts*. Second edition. New York: Grove Press.

Steiner, C.M. (1999) *Achieving Emotional Literacy*. London: Bloomsbury.

Stewart, I. and Joines, V. (1987) *TA Today: A New Introduction to Transactional Analysis*. Nottingham: Lifespace Publishing.

Stewart, I. (1989) *Transactional Analysis Counselling in Action*. London: Sage.

Storr, A. (1989) *Freud: a very short introduction,* Oxford, Oxford University Press.

Taylor-Byrne, R.E., and Byrne, J.W. (2017) *How to Control Your Anger, Anxiety and Depression, Using nutrition and physical activity*. Hebden Bridge: The Institute for E-CENT Publications.

Teachworth, A. (1999) *Why We Pick the Mates We Do: A step-by-step program to select a better partner or improve the relationship you're already in.* Metairie, Louisiana: The Gestalt Press.

Templar, R. (2016) *The Rules of Love: A personal code for happier, more fulfilling relationships.* London: Pearson.

Teychenne M, Costigan S, Parker K. (2015) The association between sedentary behaviour and risk of anxiety: A Systematic Review. *BMC Public Health, 2015.* Cited in *Medical Daily*, here: http://www.medicaldaily.com/constantly-sitting-down-being-sedentary-could-worsen-anxiety-and-mental-health-338952

Triggle, N. (2016) Alcohol limits cut to reduce health risks. BBC News. Online: https://www.bbc.co.uk/news/uk-35255384. Accessed: 11th August 2018.

Turner, J.H. (2000) *On the Origins of Human Emotions. A sociological inquiry into the evolution of human affect.* Stanford University Press.

Umberson, D., Williams, K., Powers, Daniel A.; Liu, Hui; and Needham, Belinda (2006) You Make Me Sick: Marital Quality and Health Over the Life Course. *Journal of Health and Social Behaviour, Vol 47, Issue 1*, pp. 1 – 16. March 2006. Available online: http://journals.sagepub.com/doi/10.1177/002214650604700101. Accessed: 13th August, 2018.

Vitale, J. (2006) *Life's Missing Instruction Manual: the guidebook you should have been given at birth.* Hoboken, NJ: John Wiley and Sons Inc.

Waite, M. (ed) (2012) *Paperback Oxford English Dictionary. Seventh Edition.* Oxford: Oxford University Press.

Waite. L.J. and Gallagher, M. (2000) *The case for marriage: Why married people are happier, healthier, and better off financially.* New York: Doubleday.

Wallin, D.A. (2007) *Attachment in Psychotherapy.* New York: Guildford Press.

Watts, A. (1962/1990) *The Way of Zen.* London: Arkana/Penguin.

Westheimer, R.K. (2000) *The Encyclopaedia of Sex.* Second Edition. London: Bloomsbury Academic.

Whitbourne, S. K. (2012) What is the passion in passionate love? Does – and should – passion matter for long-term relationships? *Psychology Today* Online blog. Available here: https://www.psychologytoday.com/us/blog/fulfillment-any-age/201212/what-is-the-passion-in-passionate-love. Accessed: 21st June 2018.

Whipple, T. (2018) Even babies can spot a bully ... and disobey them. London: *The Times, September 4th* (newspaper). Page 13.

WikiHow (2018) How to improve sexual health through diet. An online blog. Available here: https://www.wikihow.com/Improve-Sexual-Health-Through-Diet. Accessed: 31st May 2018.

Wolinsky, S., with Margaret O. Ryan (1991) *Trances People Live: Healing approaches in quantum psychology.* Las Vegas, NV: Bramble Books

Zilbergeld, B. (1995) *Men and Sex: A guide to sexual fulfilment.* London: Harper Collins Publishers.

Zimbardo, P. (2007) *The Lucifer Effect: How good people turn evil.* London: Rider.

~~~

Appendix A: The twenty core beliefs of our emotive-cognitive philosophy of counselling

Copyright (c) Jim Byrne, 2018

A1 Twenty core principles

Firstly, I do not make the mistake of extrapolating from *adult functioning* in order to understand the psychology of human nature. Instead, *I begin with the baby* in the mother's womb (where the mother may be more or less stressed, and more or less well nourished, depending upon the actual circumstances of her life). I then move on to the baby post-birth, which is colonized by a carer (normally mother) who may be more or less sensitive to the baby's signals of comfort and discomfort; more or less responsive to the baby's needs; and more or less caring. And I also take account of how stressed the mother was, by her life circumstances, even *before* the baby was conceived. These are the *foundations* of human emotional and general psychological functioning.

~~~

Secondly, I accept the *Attachment theory* proposition, that the baby is born with an innate attachment drive, which causes it (after period of about twenty to twenty-four weeks of development) to seek to attach itself to a main carer. The attachment bond that is formed becomes either *secure* or *insecure*, depending upon whether the mother (or main carer) is "good enough" – meaning sensitive, responsive, and caring enough to soothe the *affective states*[77] of the baby.

Later father and siblings become important attachment figures for the baby. And the baby forms a set of internal working models of relationship based upon those earliest relationships.

~~~

Third, the first five or six years of life are taken to be the *prime determinants* of what kind of life the individual will live. Very largely, the emotionally significant narratives (stories), scripts (maps) and frames (lenses) that the child learns and forms during this period – which manifest in the form of moods and emotional states, expectations, beliefs and habitual patterns of behaviour - will determine its trajectory through life, *all other things being equal.* There is, of course, some degree of malleability of the human brain-mind, and so what was once shaped badly (by negative relationship experiences) can *to some extent* be reshaped into a better form by subsequent 'curative experiences', with a love partner, or with a counsellor or psychotherapist. (Wallin, 2007; Doidge, 2008).

~~~

Fourth: With regard to the narratives, stories, schemas, scripts and frames that the individual learns and/or creates: these are, as J.S. Bruner said[78],

- *Enactive* (or experiences of *doing*);

- *Iconic* (or experiences of *seeing* or *visualizing*); and/or:

- *Semantic* (or *language based* abstractions; *verbal* meanings; and *spoken interpretations* of events and objects).

In cognitive psychology, the development of the child and later adult is mapped through studies of *attention, perception, memory, language and thinking.* And *emotion* only gets a brief mention at the end of standard textbooks – as an afterthought. However, in E-CENT, I teach that a *human* being is **essentially** and **unavoidably** an *emotional* being.

It is *an emotional being* that pays attention, when a *human being* pays attention.

It is *an emotional being* that perceives, when a human being is perceiving. Perception is never 'purely cognitive' (if by 'cognitive' we mean 'thinking in words, without any feelings').

It is an *emotional being* that forms memories, when a human being forms memories. We probably have no memories about which we have absolutely *no feelings* whatsoever! Even the equation e = mc^2 is likely to come with some degree of attendant feeling.

It is an *emotional being* which uses language. The coolest languaging does not allow us to escape from our emotional foundations. (If you imagine that a child leaves their feelings at the door of the school to which they go to learn to think, you have never tried to control a classroom of emotionally volatile 'learners'!)

It is an *emotional being* that thinks: or should I say 'perfinks'; because we do not think *separately* and *apart* from our perceptions and feelings. *We* **apprehend** *the world in* **one** *perceiving-feeling-thinking (or perfinking)* **grasp** *of the body-brain-mind!*

And even the most abstract of academic thinking cannot be **totally** **separated** from the (strong or weak) emotionality of the person engaging in it.

In other words, **the human brain-mind is an emotional brain-mind**. Human beings are emotional beings, at their very foundations, and they can also think (to some limited extent! [Thought it is perhaps better to always stick to the concept that we 'perfink'!])

Humans are not 'cognitive beings', if by *cognitive beings* we mean 'computer like'. Computers do **not** have emotions. And humans are not computers! (This is why I developed *emotive-cognitive* therapy, because cognition and emotion cannot ever be *separated*; and emotionality precedes cool processing experiences [in the form of innate capacities to evaluate sensations as well as via attention, perception, memory, language, and analysis], and then again, emotionality also *supports* cool processing of experiences!)

Indeed, we could say that human beings are not thinking beings at all. They are, as suggested above, actually *perfinking* beings (Glasersfeld, 1989): or beings who *perceive-feel-and-think* all in one grasp of the mind. And the feeling component never sleeps! You cannot leave it at the door on your way into school or work.

~~~

Fifth: We accept that temperamental differences are detectable in new born babies; that an individual may be born with a tendency towards introversion or extraversion; and that a particular new born baby may also be *more* emotionally disturbable, or *less* emotionally disturbable than average. We accept that there are fundamental differences (emotionally and behaviourally) between boys and girls. (For example, the case of John Money and David Reimer)[79]. We accept that the innate nature of the baby will influence and impact the mother in how she relates to the baby; and the mother's personality and character and temperament will also influence and impact the baby.

But in general the mother has much more influence than the baby. "Genetic determinism" has been replaced by "epigenetics", which accepts that genes have to be "switched on" by an environment, and that the genes of identical twins can be changed – as often as not - by placing them in two different home environments. And even where identical twins are raised in the same home, they may well develop different personalities. (See the case of Ladan and Laleh, who were monozygotic [single egg] twin sisters, with significant personality differences: [Spector, 2013)][80].

Returning to the dialectical (or interactional) cross-influence between mother and baby: this will eventually settle down into a stable pattern of relating, which will be experienced by the baby (and the mother) as more, or less, satisfactory.

Depending upon whether or not the mother can function as a 'good enough' mother (in terms of being sensitive, caring, responsive and in good communication with her baby), the child may develop either a *secure* or an *insecure* 'attachment style'. And these attachment styles play out in all significant future relationships.

~~~

Sixth: E-CENT theory takes into account that we are bodies as well as minds, and so diet, exercise, sleep, relaxation/ stress, social connection and relatedness, meditation/ mindfulness/ detachment, personal history, drugs and other physical inputs and stimuli, are seen as important factors in determining the *emotional-thinking-perceiving state* of the individual client. That is to say we are body-minds, and our body-mind has needs – both physical and emotional. It is *wrong* to assume, as the CBT and REBT theorists assume, that *the only factor* which intervenes between a *noxious stimulus* - (meaning a *negative experience*) - and a negative emotional or behaviour reaction, is the client's *thoughts* and *beliefs, attitudes* and *values*. The fact is that *whole* body-brain-mind of the client plays a role in the processing of significant incoming stimuli, or feedback from the environment.

~~~

Seventh: We need to be loved, liked and accepted by some significant others, if we are to live fulfilling lives. (This need is very strong when we are babies, and it continues to strong throughout our lives. However, it is not as strong as our need for oxygen or food. If we fail to get oxygen, we will die in seconds; if we fail to get food, we will die within days; and if we fail to give and get love, we will wither and die more quickly than those individuals who do learn how to give and get love. This fundamental reality was denied by Dr Albert Ellis, who had a very severe *insecure attachment style*, which caused him to deny his own need for love, and then to generalize that to all other adults! (Byrne, 2013; and Byrne, 2017b).

~~~

Eighth: E-CENT starts from the assumption that we are primarily *social animals*, and not solitary individuals. We are social to our very roots, especially from the moment of birth, when we are handed into the arms of our mothers. Everything that happens from that point onwards - and also including the original birth trauma - is significant for the development of the so-called 'individual' (who is really *a psychological amalgam of* significant other 'individuals' with whom the baby is related from birth onwards, and who we [the baby] 'internalize' as 'models'). In particular, our mothers and fathers are electro-chemically braided into the very foundations of our personality and character (in networks of neurons): Byrne (2009b).

~~~

Ninth: From the Object Relations school, E-CENT takes the view that the first three phases of development of childhood can be disrupted, between birth and about the age of six years - or the first four sub-phases from birth to age three - resulting in specific forms of relationship dysfunction in later life. (Mahler, Pine and Bergman, 1975/1987). The solution to these problems tends to include a mixture of:

- 'being with' the client in a warm, accepting and responsive relationship;

- 'holding' the relationship in a suitable, warm dialogue, which regulates the client's emotional states;

- teaching the client how to re-frame their difficult problems and challenges;

- helping the client to make conscious, and then to process, their un-experienced or resisted emotions about difficult experiences from the past;

- providing analysis and models as feeling-thinking ways forward; and:

- providing a 'safe harbour' and a 'secure base' for the client, so they can learn how to have a secure relationship, perhaps for the first time.

~~~

Tenth: E-CENT theory represents the new born baby as containing two fundamental potentials:

(1) To develop pro-social and caring attitudes (or virtues); and

(2) To develop anti-social and destructive egotistical attitudes (or vices).

One of the functions of the process of socialization is to ensure that the new person mainly develops their 'good side' (or what the Native American Cherokee people called the 'good wolf') through the moral teachings of their parents, teachers and others; and that their 'bad wolf' is constrained and contained. (It cannot ever be totally or permanently eliminated. We each contain the capacity for significant levels of evil [or immoral and criminal acts] to the ends of our days!)

The happy functioning of humans (as social animals) depends upon the extent to which we develop our pro-social, moral virtues, and resist our anti-social, immoral or amoral vices.

Some counselling clients are clearly operating mainly from 'good wolf' and some are significantly operating from 'bad wolf'. That latter client group often needs direct or indirect coaching in moral philosophy; and encouragement to operate mainly from 'good wolf', for both the sake of their community and the sake of their own happiness and personal success.

~~~

Eleventh: E-CENT theory sees humans as *primary non-conscious beings*, who operate tacitly, automatically, from layers of cumulative, interpretative experience - stored in the form of schemas and stories, and non-narrativized experience, in long-term memory - and permanently beyond *direct* conscious inspection. At least 95% of all of our daily actions are executed non-consciously and automatically[81]. So change is not easy; delusion is our normal state (i.e. our perceptions of ourselves, others and the world are not 'snapshots of reality')[82]; and we project our own 'stories' onto our environments, and judge them accordingly[83]. To wake up to a more accurate understanding of life - with our Adult-functioning (or Adult ego state) in the driving seat of our behaviour - is not easy, but it is possible, at least to some degree.

~~~

Twelfth: We mainly operate from one of three so-called 'ego states', or 'ways of being' (as described in Transactional Analysis [TA])[84]. See Appendix B, below). These are:

(P) **Parent** ego state: When we are operating from this ego state - where we think, feel and behave just like some parent figure from our past life experience - we are said to be *'in' Parent ego state*;

(A) **Adult** ego state: This is the logical, reasonably cool and rational, or language-based, 'computing' part of the personality - (but still *somewhat* emotive/evaluative. Remember, we can never separate thinking rom feeling; but we can learn to perceive/feel/think more analytically [as in 'critical thinking']). Most of us strive to be 'in Adult ego state' when we are studying, and/or teaching, and or trying to be reasonable. But our Adult ego state always has a contribution from the emotional centres of our brain. And, finally:

(C) **Child** ego state: This state of being is characterized by our thinking, feeling and acting (or perceiving-feeling-thinking) just like we once did as a young child. We are said to be 'in Child ego state' when we are playful, rebellious, creative, or (more controversially) amorous.

The aim of E-CENT counselling, (in relation to ego state functioning), is to try to help the client to get their Adult ego state into the *Executive position* of their personality; aided and abetted by their Nurturing Parent ego state; and their Free Child. But we also need some elements of Adapted Child, for good manners and social responsibility; and some Rebellious Child, for the sake of self-assertion and self-defence. But the bigger the Adult ego state grows, the more we can (theoretically) take conscious control of our lives (to the degree that that is ever possible for a *largely non-conscious, feeling being!*)

~~~

Thirteenth: We seem to be emotional story-tellers in a world of stories. Language is the sea in which we swim, unknowingly; as fish swim in water without ever 'spotting' the water. And so our neurotic reactions *often* tend to be outgrowths of old, illogical, unreasonable and unhelpful narratives and stories, scripts, schemas, beliefs and attitudes – all of which have feeling components.

The exceptions to 'narrative disturbances' tend to be:

1. When our neurotic feelings are a result of **unprocessed** *experiences* from the past (which are stored as *images* or *sensations*); or:

2. When we are trying to *control the uncontrollable*; or:

3. We are *rejecting the truth* of our situation. Or:

4. When we are sleep deprived; or:

5. Stressed by *low* or *high* *blood* *sugar* (from dietary mistakes or transgressions); or:

6. When we abuse alcohol or 'recreational drugs'. (Alcohol knocks out the Parent ego state, which contains our conscience. If we continue drinking we next knock out the Adult function; and then we are operating from pure [playful/irresponsible] Child motivations and urges!)

7. When we suffer from Non-Celiac Gluten Sensitivity (NCGS) whereby toxins leak through the gut wall (which is made permeable by consuming gluten, in the form of breads, cereals, etc.), and bypass the so-called blood-brain barrier, causing havoc with our brain chemistry; or:

8. We are deficient in particular nutrients which affect our moods; or:

9. We have not done enough physical exercise to move our lymphatic fluid around and to eliminate stress hormones from our body. Or:

10. We are stuck in a high stress situation, such as an unworkable relationship; an overburdening job or business; or financial difficulty; or homelessness; or the threat of any of those kinds of serious socioeconomic problems.

~~~

Fourteenth: One of the major sources of emotional disturbance among humans is *unmanageable* stress and strain. Throughout the whole of the life of the individual, the external environment will continue to exert an impact on the moods and emotions of that individual. Only the most highly trained and committed, and extreme, Stoic or Zen Buddhist practitioner, could ever come *anywhere near* to ignoring (or being largely unaffected by) their external environment! Indeed, only a **rock**, or lump of **wood**, or other inanimate object, ever achieves *complete indifference* to its environment. (And the more extreme statements of the Stoics – such as "Nobody can harm me!" - are *easy to utter* but largely **impossible** to live!)

People *are* upset by the negative experiences they have, day by day, and hour by hour.

~~~

Fifteenth: It may be that we each have a (socially induced) vulnerability towards angering, panicking or depressing ourselves, when we are stressed by external events or objects; and E-CENT counselling and psychotherapy tries to help the client to work at gradually reducing those vulnerabilities, by:

1. Re-parenting the client, so they *rewire their orbitofrontal cortex*, which is where they have stored their 'personality adaptations' and *attachment styles* in response to their childhood parenting experiences; and/or:

2. Encouraging them to change elements of their stories, attitudes, beliefs and schemas (about themselves, other people and the world); and/or:

3. By learning to reframe problematical activating stimuli; and/or:

4. By *'completing their (unprocessed, or traumatic) experiences'* from the past; and/or:

5. By integrating the left and right hemispheres of their brains, which are often thought of as the (primarily) *feeling* (right side) and the (primarily) *thinking* (left side) of the brain. (We try to identify those clients who lead with thinking; those who lead with feeling; and those who lead with action, or behaviour. We try to help them to integrate their leading modality with their 'missing ingredient' – so sometimes to integrate their feelings with their thinking; or their thinking with their behaviour; etc. [Joines and Stewart, 2002]).

Significant stories, which we explore with clients, include: The story of origins, including birth and birth-family; The story of personal identity; The story of key relationships (mother/ father); Stories of transitions; The story of career/ wealth/ success/ poverty/ failure; The story of present problems; The connections between the story of origins, the story of relationships, and the story of present problems; and so on.

~~~

Sixteenth: Our clients may be distressed because of their illogical, unreasonable, unrealistic or insupportable beliefs and attitudes about themselves, other people and the world, and we try to get them to reframe those beliefs and attitudes, using the Six Windows model. (See Chapter 10, Section 10.3.1). From the (moderate) teaching of the Buddha and (moderate) Stoicism we learned that people often disturb themselves by having *unrealistic desires; goals* that cannot be achieved; and those goals might be about self, other people, or the wider world. For examples:

"I want to be more like this..." which is beyond my reach.

"I wish I could be less like that..." which I have tried, and failed, to do.

And "The world should be different from the way it is!"

But we do not make the simplistic mistake of thinking that the problem here is the word "should". The problem is *desire or appetite, taken to unachievable levels.* (As the Buddha is reputed to have said: "One hair's breadth difference between what you want and what you've got, and heaven and earth are set apart!") And, besides, *we **need the** word 'should'* to define our moral rules! So we do not fetishize the world 'should', or any other word. We mainly focus on *meanings* and *emotions!* And on *concrete realities!*

For example, we often use the WDEP model to explore these issues:

W = What do you want?

D = What are you doing to get what you want?

E = Let's evaluate how well your D (Doing) serves your W (Want or goal).

P = Plan or re-Plan. Very often, there is a mismatch between the W and the D which, once understood, resolves the problem.

We might also use the Egan model:

Where are you now?

Where are you trying to get to?

And what action could you take to build a bridge to your desire destination?

And, very often, we use the Six Windows Model to help the client to re-frame their problem.

~~~

Seventeenth: Our clients may be distressed because they have failed to process some earlier emotional experience, which is now stuck in the basement of their mind, causing neurotic symptoms to emerge in the form of distorted thoughts, feelings, behaviours, relationship conflict, or physical symptoms. In this kind of situation, the E-CENT therapist's role is to help the client to dig up that part of their past; to process the unprocessed experience - which we call *'completing your experience' of what happened*, or what *failed* to happen. In order to do this successfully, we have found that they need to be able, simultaneously, or concurrently, to *reframe those previously unprocessed experiences*, so they do not merely re-stimulate the distressing feelings which caused those felt experiences to be denied, rejected and buried in the first instance, all those years ago. In practice, we teach our clients to reframe their problems before we ask them to engage in digesting old traumatic experiences. (See Chapter 10, above; and Byrne, [2018a], Chapter 6).

~~~

Eighteenth: Our adult relationships (such as marriage and living together) are strongly coloured, shaped and driven by the original drama between our babyhood-self and our mother and father, and sometimes key siblings. We repeatedly re-enact our family-of-origin drama, until we work on it and resolve it.

We have to 'complete' our relationships with our parents (and sometimes key siblings) before we can grow up and move on. And completing those relationships means *allowing them to be, exactly as they were* - accepting them, feeling the related feelings, and getting over our judgemental attitudes and hurt feelings about our parents, who were just 'blokes and birds doing their (highly imperfect) jobs'.

And our *most oppressive* siblings were little, ignorant kids! (But it can take a lot of processing time to get to the stage of *forgiving* them all).

A further complication arises from the fact that our definition of relationship comes from what we saw our parents do to and with each other, when we were less than five years old; and somewhat beyond that age, say up to the age of ten years. Unfortunately, that 'relationship modelling' means we copy one of our parents as our *Adult Role Model*; and we go out and seek a life partner on the basis of the other parent, who becomes our *Mate Model!*

In E-CENT practice, we now help clients to revise those old 'movies' of inadequate relationship skills; and to replace them with healthier modelling. This involves helping the client to revise their *Adult Role Model* and their *Mate Model*.

~~~

Nineteenth: When the relationship between the client and his/her parents is too damaged, E-CENT counselling offers the client the option to engage in a 'puberty rite', in which they 'cut their ties' to their parents – *divorce them*, as it were – and in this way clean up their psychological baggage about their parents. (This is a fourteen day process of visualization of cutting the ties with the parent[s] – one parent at a time - and allowing both the client and the parent[s] to be free to live their own lives).

After the cutting the ties process is over, the client feels much freer to run their own lives from their *Adult ego state*, based on present time realities, instead of constantly wrestling with emotional ties from the past. And the relationship with the parent from whom the client has cut their ties – if they are still alive - often becomes much better and more satisfactory in the present moment. (But even if the parent or parents are dead, it is still *possible*, and often *necessary*, to cut the ties in the case of relationship damage).

~~~

Twentieth: When the client is very distressed about their early childhood experiences, we deploy a process of *'externalizing' the inner child*, so the client can nurture and heal their own childhood self in the present – in the form of a *physical referent* or *symbolic self*. This process gradually changes the perceptions-feelings-thoughts of the client, as the inner child gradually 'grows up' and becomes more content with its lot.

~~~

These twenty principles are the bare bones of E-CENT theory. We could probably identify a few sub-principles or supplementary processes within each of those main principles/processes. We could also identify some intermediate principles, processes or propositions that reside between those core principles/ processes/ propositions. And we may well keep expanding this list as the theory unfolds. However, we also recognize the value, in terms of human memory, of keeping lists as short as possible, and no shorter. As lengthy as necessary, and no longer.

~~~

Appendix B: Transactional Analysis will help you to understand your relationship communication problems

By Dr Jim Byrne

Copyright (c) Jim Byrne, 2009-2018

B1(a) Prelude

If you have problems in your communication with your partner, it's important to figure out where those problems are coming from, and how to begin the process of fixing them. Using your 'common sense' is not likely to result in very much progress, because 'common sense' includes so many myths (as shown in Chapter 2, above). For this reason, you need a more scientifically reliable model of human communication, against which you can measure your own communication style.

In terms of 'common sense', it often seems to most uninformed individuals as if we are 'unified adults', with 'free will', and a capacity to *do no wrong*. Other people 'show up' for us as *being wrong*, but we are *always right*. (Of course, some people have that in reverse, and they see themselves as always wrong, or always inferior, and other people as always right and/or superior).

In many scientific psychology studies of human beings, it seems we are not unified beings at all, but fragmented beings. According to Robert Hobson (1985/2000), we (so-called 'individuals) are actually *communities of sub-personalities*. If you think about it, you are sometimes playful. "Let's get out to the seaside for the day!" you might declare excitedly, to your partner, on a bright, summer morning. (This sounds and feels like a childlike expression of joy and fun).

On another occasion you may angrily wag your finger at your partner and say, "Stop disrupting my work. I've got to get this finished by a strict deadline!" (This sounds more like a controlling parent).

And in yet another context, you may embrace your partner and murmur, "Never mind, darling. It'll all work out okay in the end" – to reassure them when they are feeling down or defeated by some serious problem. (This sounds like a nurturing parent part of you).

1. "You (my partner) should not have made that mistake!" (You must be perfect!)

2. "I realize you will make mistakes occasion-ally, because you are human". (It's okay to be imperfect!)

3. "You should accept yourself just the way you are!" (I'm OK, and you're OK!).

4. "Let's forget everything, and get out and have some fun!" (Let's create some positive experiences!)

Figure B1(a): The fragmented nature of our moods and emotions

In Figure B1(a) above I have presented four different positions (from a range of at least ten such positions) to show just how differently a person may perceive their partner form one day to another; or from one context to another. Those four statements are in significant tension, or even outright contradiction with each other, and cannot be thought to come from a 'unified individual'; but rather from a fragmented, or variable, individual. If you witnessed the person in Figure B1(a) as they uttered those four statements above, you would also notice that their body language was different on each occasion; including their posture, facial expression, and hand gestures. Also, their tone of voice would be significantly different from one statement to another. This shows that the person is operating from clearly distinct parts of themselves – clearly distinct parts of their personality – or distinct states of their 'ego' or 'self'.

In this current appendix, we will explore Transactional Analysis, which is a way of understanding *positive* and *negative* aspects of human personality; and *helpful* and *helpful* ways of relating to your partner. And then, in Appendix D, we explore five different styles of handling conflict in relationships.

One example of the way Transactional Analysis (or TA) helps us to understand relationship problems is as follows. In many troubled or conflicted couples, we see the following pattern repeated over and over again:

One partner tends to *control* the other, for *bad* reasons; and the controlled partner *adapts* to this control for a while, and then *rebels* with some aggressive force.

In TA language, this is described as follows:

One partner tends to operate (too often, or too much) from what is called the 'Critical Parent' or 'Bad Controlling Parent' part of their personality; and this causes their partner to slip into operating from the 'Adapted (or Conforming) Child' part of their own personality. But this does not last, and after a while, the one in 'Adapted Child' flips into 'Rebellious Child' and fights back in what is experienced as a stressful and unpleasant backlash!

If you study this system, you can learn, over time, to *mainly* operate from the more reasonable 'Adult' part of your personality, and to avoid 'hooking' (or *triggering*) the (volatile) 'Rebellious Child' part of your partner.

But 'Permanent Adult' functioning is relatively boring, for the other partner, so it is also important to know how to add in elements of 'Good Nurturing Parent' and the 'Playful Child' parts of your personality, to produce a more rounded, more loving, caring and fun personality profile.

In this appendix, I provide you with all the nuts and bolts you will need to build a more balanced personality profile for yourself, which has your 'Adult' part in the 'executive position', meaning the driving seat of your communication with your partner.

Your reward for studying this material will be that you will have a much happier, relatively conflict-free relationship! And it will help you to maintain the 5:1 ratio of positive to negative moments that your relationship needs in order to survive and thrive.

B1(b) Introduction

Sigmund Freud created the insight that the human individual has three main components to their being. These are:

(1) The part that was born (the body-brain [which has an embryonic 'mind']. Freud called this phenomenon 'the It' [which anglicized psychoanalysis calls the 'id');

(2) The 'internalized others' (mainly memories of encountering mother and father, etc.; which Freud called the over-I [and which anglicized psychoanalysis calls the 'superego']); and:

(3) The 'socialized personality' – or the shape we take on because of how we are treated in our social encounters - (which Freud called 'the I', [and which anglicized psychoanalysis calls 'the ego').

Freud argued that part of every person was conscious and part was non-conscious; and that idea is no longer contested. However, today, we think of the non-conscious part of the brain-mind as 'the adaptive unconscious', which allows us to process our encounters with our environment without having to take conscious thought, most of the time. (Gladwell, 2006).

Freud's system of psychoanalysis was slow and difficult, and involved trying to externalize the contents of the non-conscious part of the mind of the patient/client. He also over-emphasized the role of our sexual development in the emergence of psychological difficulties; and failed to take account of the importance of the relationship of attachment between the mother and her child. But that relationship plays a crucial role in shaping the future personality and emotional stability of the child.

Then along came Dr Eric Berne. Berne was born in Canada, and moved to America at the age of twenty-five years, to pursue his medical internship. He became a medical doctor and trained psychiatrist, who, at the end of the Second World War, was interested in finding ways of making psychoanalysis more accessible to ordinary people, in a way that was simpler, quicker, more user-friendly and more efficient than Freud's approach.

B2 Origins

Dr Eric Berne began to develop his popularized approach to psycho-therapy somewhere in the 1940s, when he was a US Army medical officer; but his first paper on Transactional Analysis (TA) proper did not appear until 1957 (according to Stewart, 1989)[85]. Much work was done in the 1950's and '60's, with his famous book, *Games People Play,* which appeared in 1964; and *What Do You Say After You Say Hello? –* which appeared in 1972 (after Berne's early death in 1970).

Transactional Analysis (TA) really began when Dr Berne was working with a successful lawyer as a therapy client. This lawyer felt very much like a competent adult in his work, but he had an occasional tendency to say; "I'm not really a lawyer. I'm just a little boy!"[86]

Eventually Berne realized that the lawyer operated from 'different places' within himself; or 'different states of the ego' – meaning different parts of his personality.

Berne and a group of collaborators began to investigate those 'ego states', listening to audio recordings of psychotherapy sessions, and identifying the 'places' that the patient and the therapist were 'transacting' from.

Out of this research/practice process came the insight that we humans operate from different ego states, depending on the external circumstances of our social encounters, and our personal life histories.

B3 The development of ego states over time

Berne focused his system mainly on the 'I', or 'ego', and came up with the inspired insight that each individual begins life as a child, grows and develops (through a *Little Professor* stage, and then a more Adult stage), and that we *internalize* experiences of our *actual parents* relating to us.

In the process, all of those stages of development, and all of those experiences, are stored in the individual's memory banks, so that we each have

- a Child part to our ego (or childlike-I);

- an Adult part to our ego (or adult-like-I); and

- a Parent part to our ego (or parent-like-I).

And, in our encounters, or transactions with others, we operate from one such part of our personality, to another such part of the other person's brain-mind: (See Figure B1(b) below.

The Adult part of us is partly a result of innate psychological development (as argued by Jean Piaget), and partly a result of our socialization (as argued by Lev Vygotsky). It uses language-based logic and reason to 'compute' the world of experience (but it also uses intuition, and emotional information). And it is largely non-conscious, and capable of being conscious; but not conscious of *everything* which is stored non-consciously!

The Parent part of us is copied from our parents, so that, when we are 'in Parent ego state' we are most often thinking, feeling and acting just like some parent figure from our family: mother, father, granny, granddad, etc.

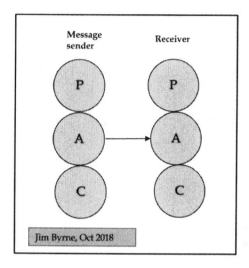

Figure B1(b): Adult-to-Adult functioning

This is how Berne described TA and his ego state model, back in 1975, in his book entitled, **What do you say after you say hello?**

"The basic interest of transactional analysis is the study of ego states, which are coherent systems of thought and feeling manifested by corresponding patterns of behaviour. Each human being exhibits three types of ego states.

"(1) Those derived from parental figures, colloquially called *the Parent*. In this state, s/he feels, thinks, acts, talks and responds just as one of his/her parents did when s/he was little. This ego state is active, for example, in raising his/her own children. Even when s/he is not actually exhibiting this ego state, it influences his/her behaviour as the 'parental influence', performing the functions of a conscience.

"(2) The ego state in which s/he appraises his/her environment objectively, and calculates its possibilities and probabilities on the basis of past experience, is called *the Adult ego state, or the Adult*. The Adult functions like a computer". (But, remember, computers do not have feelings and emotions, and your Adult ego state *does*!)

"(3) Each person carries within (themselves) a little boy or little girl, who feels, thinks, acts, talks and responds just the way he or she did when he or she was a child of a certain age. This ego state is called *the Child*. The Child is not regarded as 'childish' or 'immature', which are Parental words, but as childlike, meaning like a child of a certain age, and the important factor here is the age, which may be anywhere between two and five years in ordinary circumstances. It is important for the individual to understand his/her Child, not only because it is going to be with him/her all their lifetime, but also because it is the most valuable part of his/her personality". (Pages 11/12, Berne 1975).

Berne further theorized that, to be optimally effective, an individual needs to learn to function mainly with their adult-like-I (or Adult ego state) in the driving seat of their life - or what he called *having the Adult in the Executive Position*, or running the show.

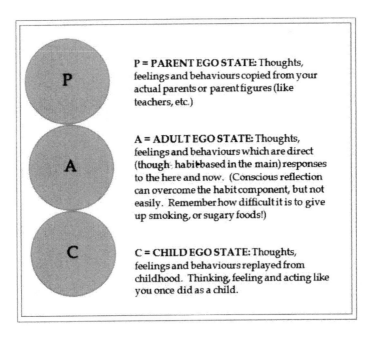

P = PARENT EGO STATE: Thoughts, feelings and behaviours copied from your actual parents or parent figures (like teachers, etc.)

A = ADULT EGO STATE: Thoughts, feelings and behaviours which are direct (though habit-based in the main) responses to the here and now. (Conscious reflection can overcome the habit component, but not easily. Remember how difficult it is to give up smoking, or sugary foods!)

C = CHILD EGO STATE: Thoughts, feelings and behaviours replayed from childhood. Thinking, feeling and acting like you once did as a child.

Figure B2: The basic PAC model

The *Parent* ego state was seen as having good and bad aspects, and so it was important to learn to distinguish between those aspects, and to mainly utilize the good (healthy and helpful) aspects of that ego state.

The Child ego state was also seen as having good and bad aspects, and the good (healthy and helpful) aspects were to be promoted, and the bad aspects controlled or regulated.

Thus it became possible for a psychoanalyst to talk to virtually any emotionally disturbed former soldier, demobbed from the US Army, about whether they were functioning in an appropriately Adult way, or an unhelpful Child or Parent way.

One of the things Berne overlooked was this: The Adult ego state can be used to set up a helpful charitable cause (which I call Good Adult), or to rob a bank (which I call Bad Adult)! That is to say, the Adult ego state, just like Parent and Child, has a good side and bad side!

B4 A review of the ego-state model of TA

Revision is the key to sound learning. We need to get the same information in various ways, with variations, in order to build up a three dimensional sense of the field we are studying. Let us begin by reviewing the basic theory of ego states. I want to do this by presenting two questions from TA Mini-paper No.6, which I completed in 2002 as part of my Diploma in Counselling Psychology and Psychotherapy.

B4.1 Exactly what is an ego state?

Ego states are patterns of thinking, feeling and behaviour - the main ones being Parent, Adult and Child - abbreviated to P, A and C.

⊙ **P. The Parent ego state** is normally shown as split between Controlling Parent (CP) and Nurturing Parent (NP). But both CP and NP also have a good and bad side. (See Figure B3 on the next page).

Parent ego state is copied from actual parent figures from the past.

⊙ **A. The Adult ego state** is assumed to be based on age-specific 'reality appraisal', which tends to be *fairly logical* and *rational* (but underpinned by emotional evaluations, and cultural conditioning!) And again, split between a Good [pro-social, empathic] side and a Bad [antisocial, selfish] side);

And Finally:

⊙ **C. The Child ego state** is a relic of childhood, whereby we think, feel and act as we once did as a child. (Sometimes we are in [good or Bad] Adapted Child [AC], and sometimes in [Good or Bad] Free Child [FC]).

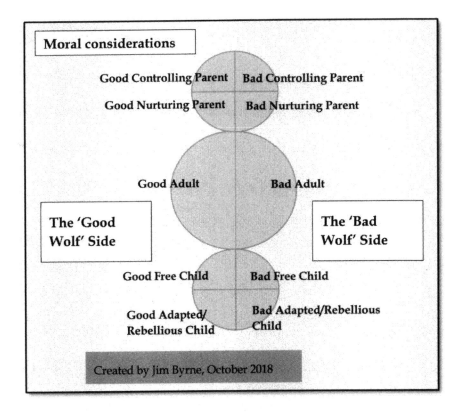

Figure B3: Elaborated model of the ego states

We tend to move around between ego states, depending upon the incoming stimulus (or what is impinging upon our attention); and we tend to have a set pattern of relating in particular situations, which may be high on Parent; high on Child; or high on Adult; where 'high on' means that we spend a lot of time/energy in that particular ego state. When we communicate with each other, we operate from a specific ego state each time, and we also tend to address a specific ego state in the other person.

However, sometimes we may speak to another person, intending this to be an Adult-to-Adult communication, but they, for whatever reason, hear it as a Parent-to-Child communication, and either rebel (from RC) or adapt (from AC).

And it is also possible that the person you speak to (from your Adult ego state) is so locked into their Parent ego state, that they will reply from Parent, and try to (or tend to) hook our Child ego state.

The possible combinations of potential transactions are shown in the next illustration:

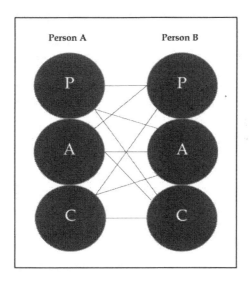

Figure B4: Potential transactions between ego states

Person A can speak or act from their Parent, Adult or Child ego states, to any of Person B's ego states; and vice versa. And, in practice, they can operate from any of the subdivisions of their ego states (for example Good Nurturing Parent to Bad Rebellious Child).

For most purposes, *Adult-to-Adult interactions* are *best*; but we need to use the (Good) Controlling Parent ego state when we are in parenting or supervising roles. And our good manners mainly come from our (Good) Adapted Child ego state. However, it is our aim to have our Adult ego state in the Executive Position of our personality, and to use the other good ego states under the general management of our Adult ego state.

~~~

B4.2 A more detailed description of the ego states

(P) Parent: The Parent or extero-psychic ego state is a set of feelings, thoughts, attitudes and behaviours which resemble those of parent figures. It contains controlling and nurturing aspects.

When I am 'in Parent ego state', I am thinking, feeling and acting just like some real parent figure from my past (my mother, father, grandparent, teacher, etc.)

There are two main subdivisions of the Parent ego state: identified as the Nurturing Parent (NP) and the Controlling Parent (CP). Then there is something called the 'Critical Parent'. In E-CENT counselling, we think of the Critical Parent as the Bad Controlling Parent. It is negative, destructive criticism, or criticism which is not aimed at either the best interest of the child, nor at the best interests of society, but rather at some selfish, personal interest of the person doing the criticizing. On the other hand, the Good Controlling Parent acts in the (ultimate) best interests of the child and the family/community/society; and the Good Controlling Parent tends to be assertive rather than aggressive.

(A) Adult: When in the Adult or neo-psychic ego state, the person (relatively) autonomously and (relatively) objectively appraises reality and makes judgements (but not without any emotional component!) The Adult ego state functions like a partially self-programming probability computer, which computes on the basis of socially agreed rules of behaviour, social understandings, and well-regulated emotional appraisals.

When I am in my Adult ego state, I am functioning like a 'fleshy, cool-emotional computer', by being relatively logical, rational and reasonable, in the here and now.

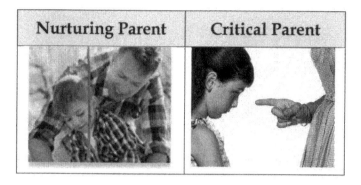

Nurturing Parent	Critical Parent

Figure B5: Nurturing and critical parent ego states

Adult language involves the use of 'I-Statements': "I think..."; "It seems to me..."; "I am willing (or not willing)..."; etc.

Parent language, (and especially Controlling Parent, and Critical Parent), is based on 'You-Statements'; for examples: "You should..."; "You must..."; "You have to..."; "You are wrong, and I am right about...", etc.

Another way of saying the same things is this:

Adult language normally consists of making *preferential* statements: "I would *prefer it* if you would... (do X instead of Y, [for example])". An exception would be when it comes to *defending your boundaries*, in which case you would use **a stronger I-statement**, like this: "I am *unhappy* about that behaviour, and I **will not** go along with...(X)".

~~~

(C) Child: The Child or archaeo-psychic ego state is a set of feelings, thoughts, attitudes and behavioural patterns which are historical relics of an individual's childhood.

When I am in my Child ego state, I am thinking, feeling and behaving just like I once did as a little boy. I may be adapting to others (Adapted Child ego state), rebelling against them (Rebellious Child ego state), or operating more authentically and autonomously (Free or Natural Child ego state).

And each of those states can be either good or bad, as follows (where + means Good, and – means bad):

+FC = Good Free Child ego state.

- FC = Bad Free Child ego state.

+AC = Good Adapted Child ego state.

-AC = Bad Adapted Child ego state.

To quote an online description: "Child Ego State can be inferred from (i) the Physical state such as emotionally sad expressions, despair, temper tantrums, whining voice, rolling eyes, shrugging shoulders, teasing, delight, laughter, speaking behind hand, raising hand to speak, squirming and giggling and (ii) the Verbal cues such as baby talk, I wish, I don't know, I want, I'm going to, I don't care, oh no, not again, things never go right for me, worst day of my life, bigger, biggest, best, many superlatives, words to impress." Source[87].

Note: The Adult ego state should also be seen as split down the middle, between a Good side (or Good Wolf side) and a Bad side (or Bad Wolf side).

~~~

To find out more about your own ego states, you could complete a TA Quiz which can be found by searching on the Internet for this web address: **https://tinyurl.com/he4f2sb**

The value of TA questionnaires was brought home to me way back in 1984, when my wife (Renata) and I completed brief questionnaires during marriage guidance counselling, with a TA therapist, and we discovered that, while I scored higher on Controlling Parent than I did on Adult, Renata scored higher on Adapted/Rebellious Child than she did on Adult. This allowed us both to see that we would have to figure out how to become **more** *Adult* in our day to day functioning. Or as Renata wrote recently:

"In a strong marriage, there's a transition from Child ego state, and Parent ego state, to Adult function. We have to keep the Adult ego state in the Executive Position, or in control of our interactions". Renata Taylor-Byrne

The aim of TA is to help you to get your Adult ego state in the Executive Position of your personality, which allows the Adult to control your decisions as to when it is appropriate and/or inappropriate to operate from Parent; and when it is appropriate and/or inappropriate to operate from Child ego state. Also, to review your life position, and opt for the 'I'm OK - you're OK' position (which is described further down this page). The third major aim of TA is to help the client to 're-decide' about any childhood decisions (or 'scripts') which are not serving them well as adults.

One way to *grow your Adult ego state* is to study the Six Windows Model of E-CENT counselling, and/or **Critical Thinking** skills.

~~~

B4.3 Revision:

The Parent ego state has two sub-divisions: the *Nurturing Parent* ego state, and the *Controlling Parent* ego state. Both of these states has a positive and a negative side.

Nurturing Parent ego state can be helpful to others, and supportive, loving and caring; but it can also come on as the 'smother mother' or the over-solicitous, rescuing dad (and *rescuing* can be depowering to children seeking to achieve autonomy).

The Controlling Parent ego state is needed in parenting, in the process of setting reasonable boundaries for children; and teaching them a moral code. However, it can be overused in adult relationships, where it shows up as domination and lack of democratic sharing.

The Child ego state also has two subdivisions: the *Natural (or Free) Child* ego state, and the *Adapted/Rebellious Child* ego state. Again, both of these states have a good and bad side.

The *Free Child* ego state is the source of play and creativity; but it is also capable of engendering risky behaviours (fast driving, hard drugs, unprotected sex) which threaten the survival of the individual.

And the *Adapted/ Rebellious Child* ego state has the positive tendency to be pro-social and cooperative, and the negative tendency to be too conformist and weak in relation to bullies.

In E-CENT counselling theory, we argue that the Adult ego state is as split as the Parent and Child. For example, the Good Adult ego state might design a new approach to bridge building, and make bridges safer for public use; while the Bad Adult ego state might spend a lot of time trying to figure out how to break into the Bank of England to steal all the gold bullion stored there. Both states might be equally logical and effective in their strategic thinking, but one is immoral and the other is moral. (More below).

~~~

B4.4 Revision exercises:

Recall a time when you were clearly operating from your Controlling Parent ego state. What were you thinking, feeling and doing? Describe the situation and the people involved, and the ego states of those other individuals. What were the consequences for you of acting in that way?

Recall a time when you were clearly operating from your Adapted or Rebellious Child ego state. What were you thinking, feeling and doing? Describe the situation. Who else was involved? What ego states were they in? What were the consequences for you of acting from Child ego state?

Recall a time when you were clearly operating from your Adult ego state. What were you thinking, feeling and doing? What was the situation; who else was involved; and did you benefit from being in Adult?

~~~

Recall a time when somebody, to whom you were related, was operating from Child ego state. What happened? Was this because you were operating from your Parent with them? If so, how could you have switched to Adult, and invited an Adult response from them?

Recall a time when you seemed to be stuck in Child ego state with somebody to whom you were related. What happened? Was this because they were operating from Parent with you? What could you have done to get out of Child ego state? (If you cannot think of any way to get out of Child when somebody is relating to you from Controlling Parent, read on).

~~~

B4.5 'Parent-stoppers' as self-protection

In general, in order to get out of Parent or Child ego states, you need to ask yourself a question?

What am I doing here? Why am I responding like this? What would be a more Adult way to behave?

To block somebody who keeps coming at you from Parent, it is not a good idea to simply react against them. That puts you in Rebellious Child ego state, and encourages them to keep trying to dominate you. What you could do instead is:

(1) Acknowledge their message by responding from your Adapted Child ego state. (You could say: 'I got that'; or 'I hear what you are saying'); then:

(2) Ask yourself a question, like this: 'How can I get them into Adult?' This question will move you to Adult (because you can only think about the answer to a question when you are in Adult ego state); and:

(3) From there you can figure out an Adult-to-Adult statement to make to them, thus escaping from the Child state in you, which they were (consciously nor non-consciously) addressing, and/or trying to 'hook'.

Another way to block somebody who is in Critical Parent with you is to find something to agree with about what they are saying - e.g. 'You might be right about that'. Or: 'Perhaps I could have done it better...', or whatever. This process is called 'fogging'. (See Appendix C, below).

~~~

B4.6 Staying in Your Adult ego state

One of the challenges in life is to stay in your Adult ego state when somebody is trying to hook your Adapted Child ego state from their Controlling Parent ego state. Using what you learned above, how would you respond (from Adult) to somebody who came at you like this:

Authoritarian statement 1. "Just look at the state of this room. You should keep it much cleaner than this!"

Your response (from Adult):

~~~

Authoritarian statement 2. "What do you think you are doing (with that work task)? You ought to know better than to do it like that!"

Your response (from Adult):

~~~

Authoritarian statement 3. "You don't want to do it like that. Do it like this!"

Your response (from Adult):

If you're not sure how to respond, remember the skill of Fogging. Remember how to cross a transaction. (Crossed transactions come to a halt). Or use reflective listening: (for example: "You think I should do it your way!".)

~~~

B4.7 What are games and how do people develop them?

A game (or psychological game), in TA, is a repetitive sequence of transactions in which both parties end up feeling a 'racket feeling' (or *substitute* feeling). It always includes a switch[88] and a payoff, and one or both parties end up feeling bad.

We develop games as young children when we notice in our family that certain feelings are encouraged while others are prohibited. To get our *strokes* – or signs of acceptance/affection and/or recognition from significant others (like parents, etc.) - we may decide to feel only the permitted feelings, and to relate from the set piece positions of *Victim, Persecutor,* and/or *Rescuer.* According to Stewart and Joines (1991): "People play games without being aware they are doing so". (Page 6).

In his early book, 'Games People Play', Dr Eric Berne presented a long list of common psychological games that people play, with various degrees of intensity. The most memorable of those games for me were:

Now I've got you, you sonofabitch.

Ain't it awful.

Wooden leg.

#*Why don't you...? Yes, but...!*

Cops and robbers.

Kick me.

And many, many others. He presented an analysis of each game, including (sometimes!) its antidote. But this all proved too complex for me. I later discovered Claude Steiner's model, whereby all psychological games can be understood as being played form one or other of the three dysfunctional quadrants of the OK corral, as follows:

I'm OK - You're Not-OK!

I'm Not-OK - You are OK!

I'm Not-OK - And you're Not-OK!

Any sequence of moves, normally involving the identification of a Victim, Persecutor and/or Rescuer, which is clearly played from one of the three

Not-OK positions, is by definition a dysfunctional psychological game.

~~~

The main clues that we are stuck in playing a game, based on the definition above, include:

1. The fact that it is repetitive. It happens to us over and over again, often with different partners.

2. It is predictable. Anyone watching would be able to predict the sequence of events and the outcome (the payoff).

3. It involves ulterior (or hidden) transactions, as well as the visible, social-level transactions. We know we are not saying what is really going on.

4. There is a switch. At a certain point the communication shifts and the ulterior element is revealed.

5. One or both parties involved get a negative payoff. We feel bad feelings (of being not-OK.)

~~~

Games are fundamentally unhealthy (psychologically), but they are played for certain unhealthy *advantages* they provide. Essentially, *negative* strokes are better than *no strokes* at all. And so the 'advantage' of the game is that *at least* you get a negative stroke. But it is far better if we can learn to operate from the "I'm-OK/You're-OK" position; and to aim for *intimacy* with others – which means revealing who we are, and relating honestly to the other person.

~~~

The quickest and easiest way to get out of playing psychological games with others is to operate from the life position which says 'I'm OK' (or acceptable to myself), and 'You're OK' (or acceptable to me), exactly the (imperfect) way we both happen to be right now. (More below - when we talk about the OK Corral).

If you can learn to operate from intimacy with the people in your life, you can have a much happier and healthier life than if you play psychological games.

~~~

According to Claude Steiner, psychological game playing is the essence of how we keep our 'life script' going. Our *life script* is a *story* we made up when we were very young, about who we are, and how our life will unfold, and what our ultimate destination in life is going to be. Abstracting the elements which have been targeted by Teachworth (1999), we could say that your life script, in the area of relationships, is some version of the story of what you saw going on between your parents when you were very young. And the games you play with your partner today are building blocks to make that script a reality in your relationship today. For examples, two popular games are: "Now I've got you, you sonofabitch!"; followed by "Poor me!"

Karpman (1968) narrowed the roles played in those nasty psychological games to the three mentioned above: Victim, Persecutor, and Rescuer.

You might be sceptical of the role of scripts and games in shaping human behaviour, *because they are **invisible***. But remember, the strings of ones and zeroes - which are mediating between the keys I am striking on this keyboard and the words that appear on the screen in front of me (and the page in front of you) – are also invisible. And there is lots of research which suggests that our emotions are 'narrative emplotments', or stories. (See Sarbin, 1989 and 2001).

Corey (2001) makes a similar point - summarizing the Narrative Therapy position developed by Epston and White (1990):

"...individuals construct the meaning of life in interpretive stories, which are then treated as 'truth'. The construction of meaning can happen monologically (by oneself) or dialogically (with others), with the latter having the greater power in our lives because we are social beings. In this sense, an individual is most often a socially constructed narrative system".

Although we normally are strongly influenced by socially constructed narrative schemas (or scripts, stories, frames, etc.), which means that we live inside of individually constructed and socially constructed stories in our heads and bodies, we also live in a _real_ world – a *concrete reality* – and our negative or depowering stories produce negative and depowering *consequences* for us in our lived experience. Or as Corey (2001) puts it: "The process of *living our story* is not simply metaphorical; it is very real, with real effects and real consequences in family and societal systems. Families are small social systems with communal narratives that express their values and meanings, which are embedded in larger systems, such as culture and society". (Page 431).

See also Byrne (2018b) on scripts and stories.

(Section B4.9.2 below provides a good definition of a life script. See also section B4.9.2 below, on how to analyze your life for evidence of scripting. Then, section B4.9.4, on how to break out of a negative life script. And then section B4.9.3 on the importance of writing stories about aspect of your life, in order to process your negative experiences, and to get a better life script, and thereby a better future.)

Games, as such, are not well researched, because of lack of interest in the field of psychology in general. However, it is intuitively obvious that some people approach others from the position of trying to Rescue them; some try to Persecute others; and some people come on like perpetual Victims. And working on the writing of our life stories, in the form of writing therapy, very reliably changes human behaviour.

A minority of people seem to be able to get to the position of thinking of *themselves _and_ others* as being basically OK, or acceptable. Most people find that very difficult.

We promote the idea that everybody is born basically equal; that some become *more unequal materially*; or *academically*; or in terms of *social capital*; but we retain a basic equality given by our humanity. We accept others as OK, so long as they are basically moral and acting in accordance with reasonable legal systems.

~~~

B4.8 TA in E-CENT counselling

This is a brief overview of the elements of TA that we teach in E-CENT counselling:

(1) It is important for each client to 'grow their Adult ego state'; to shrink their Good Controlling Parent; and to exclude their Bad Controlling Parent ego states. It is also important to shrink their Good Adapted/Rebellious Child ego states, and to exclude their Bad Adapted/Rebellious Child ego states. They also need to eliminate their Bad Nurturing Parent (smother mother; rescuing dad; and other versions of 'nurturing' for bad motives, or with bad effects!)

(2) That one of the best ways to grow the Adult ego state is to learn the Six Windows Model of E-CENT. Another is to study Critical Thinking skills (e.g. Bowell and Kemp, 2003)*.

(*Bowell, T. and Kemp, G. [2005] *Critical Thinking: A concise guide. Second edition.* London: Routledge.)

(3) It is important to 'filter' Nurturing Parent behaviour through the Adult ego state (to make sure it is appropriate, and not some form of self-defeating or other-defeating Rescuer behaviour); and to keep the Adult ego state in the 'executive position' at all times.

(4) It is important to 'play' (or engage in recreational relating), from Natural (or Free) Child ego state, but again this should be 'filtered' through the Adult ego state, which should monitor the appropriacy/riskiness of particular acts of play.

(5) It's important to operate from a life position that *'I'm OK (or acceptable to myself), and You're OK (or acceptable to me)'*, exactly the way we both are at the moment - even if we both could benefit from some improvements in our behaviour. (See the OK Corral below). However, unlike person centred (Rogerian) counsellors, and Rational Emotive Behaviour Therapists, we in E-CENT do not accept ourselves or other people _unconditionally_. We teach the importance of moral behaviour, and we teach that a person does indeed become 'a bad person' if and when they cross a particular line in terms of 'growing their Bad Wolf', and

neglecting the influence of their 'Good wolf' side. (See Appendix F).

(6) In keeping with the concept of the "innate Good and Bad wolf" aspect of each individual, which is central to E-CENT, we also teach that the TA model should be subdivided as follows, between the 'good side' and the 'bad side' of each of the five ego states:

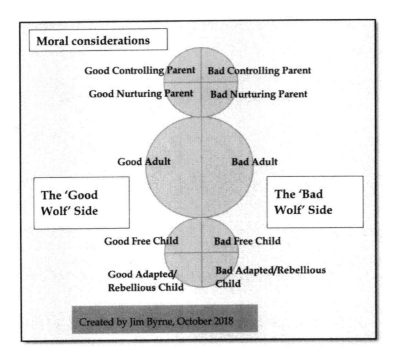

Figure B6: The good and bad sides of human functioning

Every ego state, including Nurturing Parent and Adult, can be operated from the good or bad side of the individual, with good or bad motives, and with good or bad consequences.

There is an objective case that can be made that each of us has to learn how to become a 'good citizen', a 'good character', in order to facilitate the smooth running of our family, local community and work environment.

~~~

The other aspect of the TA model that we use in E-CENT is the OK-corral, which has four 'life positions', as follows:

Figure 3		Your Decision About Others	
		OK	Not-OK
Your Decision About Yourself	OK	1. I'm OK - You're OK	2. I'm OK - You're Not-OK
	Not-OK	3. I'm Not-OK - You're OK	4. I'm Not-OK - You're Not-OK

Figure B7 - The OK-corral showing the four life positions

Of the four positions that an individual can adopt towards themselves and others, only that shown in box 1 is emotionally healthy. That is the "I'm OK - You're OK" life position, which leads to good human relations.

All of the others lead to poor human relations outcomes.

Operating from Box 2 can lead to exploiting and abusing others, or being angry or dismissive towards them.

Operating from Box 3 can result in the individual becoming a 'door mat' for others, by being too passive and compliant.

And operating from Box 4 is a dark, nihilistic place which is likely to be found among sociopaths and suicides and very angry, self-loathing depressives.

~~~

Learning how to operate from the **I'm OK- You're OK** position is the quickest and easiest way to avoid engaging in 'psychological games'. Games are a nasty form of interaction which are played on the Drama Triangle, which involves three players, or two players playing three roles. Those roles are Victim, Persecutor and Rescuer.

~~~

So, in E-CENT counselling and therapy, we teach at least four aspects of TA:

- The ego state model (or 10-part PAC model shown in Figures 3 and 6 above);

- The OK-corral (or Four Life Positions);

- Script theory (or self-narratives); and:

- The Drama Triangle.

We do this to some degree via work in sessions; but also by the use of educational pamphlets and handouts, and follow-up discussion. We also use the chair-work approach developed in Impact Therapy, where we use three chairs to represent the Parent, Adult and Child, and teach the client to reflect on this question: "Which chair am I on right now, and how can I get back to the Adult chair?"

We teach the "I'm OK - You're OK" position, by getting the client involved in enactive exercises with others to unlearn their "habitual box (or Life Position [Ok, Not-OK])" and to learn how to get into and stay in Box 1, above - the "I'm OK - You're OK" position.

~~~

B4.9 Scripts and stories

We also teach our clients that they "live inside of stories" about who they are, where they are, who the other players are, and how life will or must proceed. This has a lot in common with the TA concept of 'script decisions'. Just as in E-CENT, in TA scripts are seen as decisions made in early childhood about who I am, what my life is like, and how my life is going to unfold. These scripts or stories are stored below the level of conscious awareness - as part of the 'adaptive unconscious' - which effectively puts them in the driving seat of our lives. Elements of the script come from parental injunctions, and some from observational learning, or modelling ourselves on people inside and outside the family home. Those social learning elements interact with innate, genetic elements of drives, urges and predilections.

B4.9.1 What is a script?

A script, in TA, is an unconscious life plan or life story based on a decision made in childhood, reinforced by the parents, justified by subsequent experiences, and culminating in a chosen life course or destiny. Our scripts (non-consciously) control our approach to relationships and to tasks. They are based on childhood illusions or delusions which may persist throughout life. They include parental programming and individual decisions in response to parental programming.

According to Stewart and Joines (1991): "By the time you were four years old, you had decided on the essentials of the plot". (Page 99). You continue to revise it through the milestones of reaching the age of seven, with greater ability to reason; and on through puberty into the teenage years, when we (or many of us) reach the stage of 'formal operations' (to use Piaget's term) when we become more adult in our reasoning. But the non-conscious script may still contain a lot of illogical and delusional aspects which were decided upon by the individual during the emotionally turbulent experiences of infancy. And, at the very least, our earliest life decisions colour and shape our later life decisions.

~~~

B4.9.2 Script analysis

The classic TA approach to script analysis consists of finding out the answers to various questions which help the therapist to reconstruct the original 'script matrix' - comprising the sources of the client's script. A classical TA therapist might use some questions like these:

1. Think back to when you were a child, at home with your mother.

What did she say to you about the ways in which you made her happy?

What did she say about the ways in which you made her unhappy?

Are you still conforming to what she wanted from you in the way of 'good behaviour'?

2. Think back to when you were a child, and spending time with your father.

What did he say to you about the ways in which you made him happy?

What did he say about the ways in which you made him unhappy?

Are you still conforming to what he wanted from you in the way of 'good behaviour'?

3. Was your mother upset or scared by any of your childhood behaviours?

Did her fear or upset influence your behaviour?

4. When your mother disapproved of any of your behaviours, how did you feel?

Do you still try to avoid feeling those feelings today?

5. Was your father upset or scared by any of your childhood behaviours?

Did his fear or upset influence your behaviour?

6. When your father disapproved of any of your behaviours, how did you feel?

Do you still try to avoid feeling those feelings today?

7. Who was your main childhood hero?

What kind of life would you have to live to be like your hero?

Are you still living your life as if you were your hero, and how well is that serving you?

8. If a Martian (or perhaps Agatha Christie's detective, Hercule Poirot) looked at the journey you have been on through life, what might they infer about the 'life plan' that is guiding your life?

The purpose of these questions is to identify dysfunctional beliefs about life and how to best live it, so you can reflect upon, and re-decide about, the details of your life plan.

Reflective assignment: Try asking those 8 questions of yourself, and write down your answers. What do your answers tell you about your own life script?

~~~

B4.9.3 Writing key developmental stories

I encourage some of my clients (as appropriate) to write

(1) Their Story of Origins: (Key questions include the following):

- *Where were you born?*

- What were your early years like?

- Were there any childhood traumas?

And:

(2) Their Story of Early Relationships:

- How did you get along with your mother? Do you feel securely attached to her?

- How well did you relate to your father? Do you feel securely attached to him?

- Who else were you close to?

I promote the writing of these stories in order to discover any traumatic events during which my client may have made unhelpful decisions, and to get them to re-decide about that trauma in the here and now. This works well, because now they are grown up, and are less vulnerable than when they were children, and thus they are able to make *more sensible decisions* about the *meaning* of their childhood experiences.

~~~

Parents not only give us injunctions to follow, but they also tend to make attributions regarding who they see us as being, who they think we are, how they think we will grow and develop. Those attributions act like forms of hypnotic suggestion to us, in shaping our own self-concept. Parents can also discount our concerns, our actions or our attributes. We tend to be able to integrate only those things which our parents allow - and to dump those aspects of our thinking, feeling, behaving that they discount.

What aspects of your childhood conditioning are you still carrying around in your head and your heart, which may be negatively affecting your current relationship?

The scripts you made up when you are a child may be still running your life, and destroying your chance of a happy relationship today!

~~~

It is commonly held in some TA circles that scripts can be identified by a core belief, which shapes the individual's life journey. Ten common examples are:

I must not exist;

I must not be me;

I must not be a child;

I must not grow up;

I must not make it in life;

I must not do anything;

I must not be important;

I must not belong;

I must not be close to others;

I must not be well (physically or mentally).

The way to identify whether you or another person has any of those beliefs driving your life is to ask yourself: *Is this the result I am repeatedly getting, despite consciously wanting a different outcome?*

If so, then it may well be that you have such a script driver operating at non-conscious levels of mind.

B4.9.4 How to break out of a negative script

To break out of any script, you need to take these steps:

1. Identify the ways in which your life is not working;

2. Identify the potential sources of apparent script beliefs in your early childhood;

3. Re-decide regarding the kind of life you want to live: to be OK; to treat others as OK;

4. Work hard to change your dysfunctional behaviours, so you are clearly operating from healthy goals and beliefs.

None of this is easy. It will take time. It might require one-to-one counselling or psychotherapy. It might require some group therapy. It might require active learning from reading. It might require extensive writing therapy.

~~~

Another way to unearth your script is this:

Imagine your life is a drama, which was authored by you when you were a very young child. Ask yourself these questions:

1. What is it called?

2. Is it a tragedy or a comedy; or a soap opera; or a romance; a thriller; a black farce?

3. Where is it set?

4. Imagine you have just been born. Who is present? How do they feel about you? How do you feel about them?

5. Now move to your school days. Who are the key actors? How do they relate to you? How do you relate to them? How do you feel? What are your dominant thoughts and actions?

6. Now move up to the present day. What is the scene at the core of your life? Who are the important actors or key players? Who dominates the action? What is the main action? What do you think, feel and do in this situation?

7. Now project into the future. What is the journey from here to there? Have the characters changed? Who are the leading characters? How happy or unhappy are you in this future scene? What is the main action?

How do you think, feel and act in relation to the main action?

8. Now move to the final scene. You are on your deathbed. Who is there with you? Or are you alone? How do others relate to your impending death, and to you? And what are your last words?

9. As the play ends, and the audience gets up to leave, what do they say to each other about you and your life?

~~~

If you do not like the shape of this drama, then you can redesign the future and the outcome. You cannot change the past - although you can change your impressions and interpretations of the past. To change your future, you need to commit to changes in your thinking, feeling and behaviour.

Assignment: If you do not like the drama of your life, as explored above, then please write a new script for your (improved) future life.

~~~

To learn this system of TA, please read this chapter three times:

First reading ❏

Second reading ❏

Third reading ❏

~~~

Appendix C: A description of the skill of fogging

By Dr Jim Byrne

Copyright (c) July 2013-2018

~~~

The skill of fogging is designed to give you an advantage in conflicted conversations by causing a fog to descend upon the mind of your adversary, so they don't notice too clearly the arguments you are using to defend yourself against their aggressive comments.

The idea is to prevent the **Critical Parent** *ego state* of your adversary from browbeating you.

In addition, the idea of using fogging in self-assertion is to remain calm when somebody is criticizing you, and to try to defuse their barrage of criticism; or to draw the sting of their aggressiveness. It is also a refusal to go into **Child** *ego state* under pressure of criticism.

Your aim should be to avoid becoming upset by their criticisms. The Bill of Assertive Rights reminds you that you have the right to be independent of the goodwill of other people before interacting with them. So do not make the mistake of thinking they must like you; or must be kindly disposed towards you. That would be nice; but if it is not happening, it is not happening.

You could walk away, if that was an effective option. For example, you could say something like this: "If you are going to speak to me in an abusive manner, then I'm walking away!" And then go!

But if you feel compelled to stay in the encounter, then you need to *defuse* their aggressive criticism in some pragmatically useful or helpful way.

One way to proceed is to find something in what they say, no matter how small, with which to agree. For example, if they call you a fool, you could agree that there *"probably are **times**"* when you behave foolishly (which is probably true of all humans!) A relevant example here might be this:

Getting into conversations with people who want to give you a hard time.

Or if they say you are stupid, you could agree that we all do stupid things some of the time; and none of us can be perfectly clever all of the time. But the way to say it, as a fogging exercise, would be this: "You are probably right, that I sometimes do stupid things!" (But, silently in your mind, you note that doing stupid things, some but not all of the times, does not make you, a whole person, stupid!)

If it's a heavy male game of "Mine's bigger", in which your adversary is arguing that his much bigger, more powerful car is much better for most purposes than your little car, you could say: "I agree that your car is far superior for those kinds of long and rough journeys which I almost never make!"

Or: "I agree that if I wanted to really impress my neighbours with my material possessions, then it would be better to have a car like yours!"

This kind of response takes the sting out of their criticism, and helps you to feel okay about yourself.

You avoid submitting to the bullying attitudes of your interlocutor (or conversation partner); you refuse to be intimidated; and you certainly do not feel disempowered. If they are the type who enjoys intimidating others, they will quickly become tired of trying to upset you, and move on to somebody else.

Some useful openers for fogging include:

"Perhaps you have a point...

"You may be right...

"You are right, in this sense...

"Maybe I could (do X) better...

"There could be some small amount of truth in what you say about...

"I got that (message)..."

These kinds of responses are also called 'Parent Stoppers' because they thwart the Critical Parent ego state of your adversary or opponent.

The trick is in the sentence ending, whereby, instead of agreeing that you are a complete and utter dolt, you agree you are a fallible, error-prone human, just like him (or her). Instead of agreeing that you are a failure, you simply agree that there is no doubt you could have been more successful in certain areas.

But the *emotional tone* of your response should always be: Perhaps you have *a limited, relatively unimportant* point here; but what of it? What real significance does this little point have?

But don't ask those questions. (That would just extend the argument; and the point of fogging is to *close down* a particular line of argument [in which you are being treated as the **victim** of a **persecutor**!)

But do keep that attitude - (of appearing to agree, but to nothing significant!) - non-verbal. (By keeping it non-verbal, your persecutor cannot respond to it, and take it away from you!). And keep using the types of fogging 'agreements' outlined above.

Warning: Do not use fogging in court; or in academic arguments; as it will show up in those contexts as dishonesty, waffling, or failure to adequately engage with serious arguments. And do not use fogging as a basis for staying in an oppressive relationship. If the other person repeatedly operates from Persecutor to your Victim- or Rebel-role, then it's time to move on; to move away from this emotional abuse!

Fogging is best used as an occasional strategy, to keep from either agreeing to be put down; or from flipping into Rebellious Child ego state. (See Appendix B).

~~~

Appendix D: Handling conflict skilfully – Knowing your personal style

By Renata Taylor-Byrne, Copyright (c) November 2018

~~~

D1 Introduction

"Communication is to relationship what breathing is to living..."

Virginia Satir (1972/1983)[89]

In this appendix, I want to present a simple quiz that helps us to understand how we handle conflict in our current relationships. This quiz will give you a clear picture of how you deal with pressure in situations of interpersonal conflict.

The related descriptions and explanations will also clarify what is wrong with particular ways of communicating, and which approach to communication is best for the health and happiness of your couple relationship (and indeed of all of your relationships).

The quiz, created by Virginia Satir (1972/1983), outlines the five main ways of handling conflict with others. Four of these are unhealthy, or unhelpful, and one is healthy, effective and helpful.

Satir created a system of *conjoint-family-therapy*, and was a pioneering therapist who showed that families play a significant part in the development of the problems of individuals, and that blaming individual family members for their problems was unfair, because the problems that counselling and therapy clients showed up with were learned and created in their family of origin.

Understanding how we deal with conflict at the moment

The helpful thing about this quiz is that it shows you a range of patterns that people play out when they are dealing with interpersonal conflict.

The strategies used vary from constructive to really unhelpful and ineffective.

If you complete the quiz below, and you look at your results, you'll be able to see your current favourite approach, and how to change your behaviour if you are not happy with the result.

D2 Five ways of handling conflict

Here are the five ways of handling conflict which Satir identified:

(1) PLACATING – This involves: Pacifying, calming or appeasing behaviour. (Appeasing means to make someone calm and less hostile by giving in to their demands). The aim here is most obviously to stop the other person becoming, or remaining, angry and aggressive. The placator tends to feel relatively worthless, or weak, and to go along with the idea that their adversary – or the person challenging them - is superior, or significantly stronger, in some way.

Your *'placating'* score shows how much you tend to *placate* or *appease* others to calm them down, instead of dealing with what they are saying, doing or presenting to you.

~~~

(2) BLAMING – This approach is about: Holding someone to account, in a *condemning* or *accusatory* way. The aim here is most often to get the other person to regard you as strong; or to deny your own responsibility. The blamer finds fault with others; dictates to them; and is relatively bossy.

Your *'blaming'* score shows how far you are liable to *blame* other people when under stress.

(3) DISTRACTING – This style of conflict management involves: Diverting, changing the subject, cracking a joke for entertainment, etc. The aim of the distractor is most often to deny the threat by ignoring it; pretending it does not exist.

Your *'distracting'* score shows how much you tend to *distract* yourself and other people from the problems being presented.

~~~

(4) COMPUTING – This approach is about: Assessing, analysing, and theorising about what you are experiencing.

The aim here is most often to *deny a felt sense of threat,* and to relate to the problem *as if it was totally harmless.*

It can also be an attempt to restore you sense of self-esteem by using big words and fancy ideas.

Your *'computing'* score shows how far you tend to *cut off from* your feelings.

This is also sometimes called intellectualizing (with the implication that you use intellectualizing when you should be dealing with your feelings!)

~~~

(5) LEVELLING – Being frank, open, honest, and above board. Telling the truth as you see it. The aim here is most often to be fair, equal and/or *human-growth promoting.*

Your *'levelling'* score shows how far you tend to react *creatively* and *flexibly* and *humanely.*

It is about being reality-oriented, appropriate, and constructive.

~~~

This quiz tests how you react when life gets difficult: particularly during interpersonal conflict.

D3 The Personal Styles Quiz:

Here is the quiz:

Read through the following list of 20 statements.

Place a tick (☑) against the statement number of any statement with which you *strongly* agree. (You will need these numbers to mark your resulting score).

Choose *as many statements as you like from the list* if you think they reflect you or your views.

You should choose *at least* seven statements, but more if you like.

☐ 1. Conflict is something I try to reduce as soon as possible.

☐ 2. If someone's going to tell me something I don't want to hear, I'll quickly and smoothly try to change the subject.

☐ 3. Conflict is healthy if it means the people involved solve a problem.

☐ 4. It's important that people know who's responsible for a mistake.

☐ 5. Catching people off-guard with a compliment is a good way to ease tension.

☐ 6. I've been told I can be unemotional.

☐ 7. I've been told that sometimes I let people take me for granted.

☐ 8. I can get stressed but I try not to let it affect my life too much.

❏ 9. Avoiding taking responsibility for my actions is a good way to shift blame.

❏ 10. In the past, I have taken the blame for something when it wasn't my fault.

❏ 11. I can keep my head clear by distancing myself when those around me are getting edgy.

❏ 12. Hopefully, people know that once a conflict with me is finished, we can then move on.

❏ 13. I'll fight my corner at all costs to make sure I can hold my head up high.

❏ 14. I dislike being shouted at, so I'll usually try to soothe the situation.

❏ 15. If I'm clever and funny enough I can keep conflict at bay.

❏ 16. If something bad happens, I cut off from my emotions; it feels safer to not let my guard down.

❏ 17. I'm not scared to confront someone – but I try to do so without making the other person feel bad.

❏ 18. Becoming overly-emotional during conflict is no way to solve problems.

❏ 19. I have a long memory when it comes to remembering others who've crossed me in some way.

❏ 20. If I've forgotten to do something I said I would, some 'social flirting' keeps people off my back.

D4 The quiz mark sheet

Now that you've chosen at least seven statements as being ones that you agree with, take a look at the grid below. Then tick those numbers in that grid that correspond to the statement numbers that you've ticked in the list above:

Tick the option numbers below that you chose above					
	1	4	2	6	3
	7	9	5	11	8
	10	13	15	16	12
	14	19	20	18	17
TOTAL >					
Inter-personal style →	PLACATING	BLAMING	DISTRACTING	COMPUTING	LEVELLING

Next, add up the number of ticks in each column, and place the total in the **TOTAL** row.

~~~

The next table shows a worked example:

Tick the option numbers below that you chose above				
1	4☑	2☑	6☑	3
7	9	5☑	11	8
10☑	13☑	15☑	16	12☑
14☑	19	20☑	18	17
TOTAL > 2	2	4	1	1
Interpersonal style →	PLACATING	BLAMING	DISTRACTING	COMPUTING	LEVELLING

D5 Scoring

Which column has the highest score? Count the number of ticks (☑) in each column. The one with the *highest score* is your favourite strategy. In the example above, it's the 'Distracting' column.

Which one is highest for your score-grid? Whichever one it is, than that one is your *dominant* conflict management style.

You could also have a 'close second' style, if two scores are close to each other.

In the example in the grid above, we can see that 'distracting' is the style most often chosen by the person who completed that grid, followed by 'placating' and 'blaming'. So this person would be called 'a distractor', as a shorthand description.

D6 Exploring the conflict styles

When things get tough in our lives we choose one or more of these personality patterns. Here is more of an explanation of these styles of behaviour:

D6.1 Placating

Step on a *placator's* foot and they will be the one to apologise. Placators know that peacemakers get blessed – or at least don't get trashed. And so a typical placator will soothe, please and pacify those with whom they come into conflict.

More females than males tend to be placators. They tend to dislike disagreeing with people – even if they are being criticized.

The aim of the placator is to get others to be nice to them – and, as placators tend to be externally influenced, they'll therefore probably go along with whatever the other person wants. They'll hold eye contact, smile a lot, and nonverbally ask for forgiveness. They apologize a lot, which means they tend to overdo it.

To apologize a lot *from a position of weakness* – (suggesting that 'I'm Not OK') is bad for your sense of self-esteem. But to apologize reasonably frequently, *from a position of* **strength** – suggesting that 'I'm OK, and so are you' - for *accidental* and *unintended* negative impacts upon others, is **not** bad for your sense of self-esteem, and could be good for your relationships.

~~~

D6.2 Blaming

If a *blamer* steps on someone's foot, they will expect the other person (whose foot they stepped on) to apologize. This is because a blamer's classic move is to shift the responsibility away from themselves.

There are many ways in which they can do this: They can nag; they can sulk; they can shout; and they can hit out. Or they can pretend that it's not a problem and then launch a surprise attack a few hours later when everyone thinks the worst is over.

~~~

D6.3 Distracting

Did they step on someone's foot? No! A *distracter* will state that they weren't even there. They'll smile, or crack a joke, or say what lovely weather it is today, and do everything they can to deflect attention from the issue at hand. Their favourite phrase is this: 'It wasn't me'.

~~~

D6.4 Computing

When a *'computer'* steps on someone's foot, they simply won't register the fact. They are the one who just doesn't seem to feel anything, and they don't respond emotionally to what's happened. They simply shut down their feelings – and can't understand the suffering of others, if it is (or seems to be) illogical or irrational. Or just plain 'emotional'! (They may seem somewhat autistic, or alexithymic [not understanding feelings], or emotionally unintelligent).

When a *computer style* is used by a person, it may seem like they are simply responding calmly to a crisis. But they are panicking just as much as anyone else. It's just that they are trying to handle their panic by cutting themselves off at the neck. And actually, that's just as bad an idea as placating, blaming or distracting, because they are missing out on the information or motivation their body is trying to give them.

So they will take action, but over-rationally. And they will respond, but insensitively. (This is a common side-effect of studying 'rational therapy' and CBT!)

~~~

D6.5 Levelling

The final personal conflict style is the only healthy one: *Levelling*, or straight communication!

A *leveller* who steps on someone's foot will notice. Then they'll move back, and apologize appropriately. Then they'll ask if there's anything they can do. They won't grovel, dump the information, or look the other way – and they won't cut off from their feelings. They'll be genuinely regretful – but unlike people who run the other four personality sub-patterns, they won't go into a spiral of defensive responses.

So *a leveller* is going to be the one to hang in there under stress or in conflict, and simply get things sorted out. They will strike a balance between thinking and feeling – and that means that they will:

(a) Face up logically to the problem; and:

(b) Have the emotional energy to sort it out.

Whether at home or in the wider world, they'll have the space to listen to other people, take into account everyone's needs, and find a solution.

Anyone who works with a leveller, marries a leveller, or has a leveller for a friend, therefore has an easy life. They know exactly where they stand with a leveller, and consequently feel secure. They know that if any problems arise in their relationship, then the leveller will tell them. (They will not whine, sulk, push the problem away or deny their feelings).

The bottom line is that the more positive your upbringing, the more likely you are to be a leveller. (If you were not raised in this way, you could still be a leveller, if you had some corrective experiences, in social relationships or therapy, or assertiveness training, later in life).

~~~

D6.6 Learning to level

It might now be obvious that the first four 'types' listed above could benefit from learning how to level with others: or to speak up and describe what is happening, and how they experience it.

Being a heavy-duty *placator, blamer, distracter,* or *computer,* isn't a particularly good idea. Not only do these personality sub-patterns feel uncomfortable to use in practice, but they also will not be appreciated by your partner, your work colleagues, or by your friends and family.

Of course, everyone runs a bit of the four unhelpful personality sub-patterns, at least some of the time. This is not surprising, because, when we are young, in our family of origin, we learn ways of behaving that *seem* to work; or that seem to be normal. And at school, skills at maths and English and other subjects are rated much more highly than the ability to deal with people effectively and skilfully.

IQ (or the ability to take logic tests) is rated much higher than EQ (or the ability to read one's own emotions; the emotions of others; and to communicate about both). But when we grow to adulthood, the limitations of our lack of skill in handling conflict do begin to become much clearer. Virginia Satir's therapeutic advice was to shift your behaviour towards *helpful 'levelling'*.

D6.7 Some tips on the various styles

The limitations of the different ways of handling conflict will now be outlined:

1. If you tend to be a placator:

   (a) You may think it's a good sub-pattern as it seems to smooth things over.

   (b) However, you won't get what you want. And you can drive people crazy by always apologising.

(c) To move towards being a leveller, you have to learn to have strong personal boundaries; and higher self-esteem; and to know how to communicate assertively.

~~~

2. If you tend to be a blamer:

(a) You may think it's a good sub-pattern because at least no one shouts at you.

(b) In fact, it alienates people. And, by shifting responsibility, you give away your power.

(c) On the other hand, to move towards being a leveller, you have to realize that the world is not out to get you; and that temper tantrums don't work. You need to move back from aggression towards more reasonable self-assertion.

~~~

3. If you tend to be a distracter:

(a) You may think it's a good sub-pattern because it gets you off the hook or out of the soup.

(b) In fact, you never get to face problems. And you never take responsibility for things. (And taking responsibility is the first step towards solving most of your problems!)

(c) Instead, to move towards being a leveller, learn to face up to it when other people challenge you. Then either take their criticisms on board, or stand firm in believing their criticisms are invalid. Face the truth!

~~~

4. If you tend to be a computer:

   (a) You may think this is a good way to behave, because it keeps you clear of 'messy emotions'.

   (b) In fact, you miss out by ignoring your own feelings and the feelings of significant others. And you may come across as hard-hearted, or cool, or cold and detached. If you cannot read another person's emotions, then you cannot really understand them or communicate effectively with them.

   (c) To move towards being a leveller, allow yourself to pay more attention to what you are feeling, and what those feelings tell you about the value of what is happening to you. Allow yourself to pay attention to what other people are feeling; and take their emotions into account. (You might need some coaching in the labelling of emotions; and understanding how to manage them in yourself. [See Appendix E: Understanding and managing human emotions]). Try to grow your emotional intelligence.

   ~~~

One of the primary aims of being a leveller is to preserve feelings of self-worth all round; and to protect the dignity all the participants in communication with each other. According to Virginia Satir:

"Feelings of worth can flourish only in an atmosphere where individual differences are appreciated, mistakes are tolerated, communication is open, and rules are flexible - the kind of atmosphere that is found in a nurturing family".

Satir's approach is also designed to promote 'the five freedoms', which are defined like this:

1. To see and hear what is here, now; and not what should have been here; what was (previously) here; or what may be here in the future.

2. To say what one thinks and feels, instead of feeling constrained by unreasonable rules imposed by others.

3. To feel what one actually feels, instead of working to substitute 'racket feelings' imposed by others in the past.

4. To ask for what one wants, instead of passively waiting for permission from others to do what they want you to want.

5. To take calculated risks on your own behalf, instead of choosing to play it ultra-safe in a tiny 'comfort zone'.

D7 Conclusion: Learning new behaviours

As you can see from the description above, the behaviour of someone who is a 'leveller' is the ideal style of communication that we can work towards, if we want to work well with other people, and have a healthy, loving relationship with a significant love-partner.

But it isn't easy! You have to put in some considerable effort to bring about personal change.

We never stop learning how to deal with people. The quiz and descriptions shown above should help you to know the strengths and weaknesses of your personal style. And this document makes the case for moving towards being a leveller, and provides some guidelines for doing so.

The 'levelling' approach;

> - reduces conflict (in the long-term, and overall; though the best relationships exist on the other side of conflict [provided the conflict is based on 'fair fighting']). It also

> - reduces stress in our bodies, because we are dealing with problems *as they arise*, by facing up to them.

The reality is that we can't change other people – only ourselves! (And that, as you most likely know already, is not easy – but it's often possible, with enough effort and commitment to change!)

By moving increasingly towards being a leveller, we can earn our own self-respect - (which as Lord Roseberry said, is worth fourteen times more than the approval of other people) - and we can become a really good role model for our children (if we have them) and other people in our environment.

Virginia Satir's model helps us to see where we are operating from; and also what works and what doesn't, when it comes to dealing with conflict constructively.

In the context of the present book, levelling is the foundation of a more constructive, positive, helpful approach to communicating with your partner; of showing respect, care and responsibility; and of protecting the self-worth of both of you as equal human beings.

When you level with your partner, you may feel nervous. And 'the boat' of your relationship may *rock* for a little while - (a few minutes to a few hours).

But this rocky period will pass; and in the process you will be moving through the conflict, and out the other side: which is the gateway to better relationships. Because, as Robert Bolton (1979) writes:

"The best relationships exist on the other side of conflict"!

You cannot get there if you resist conflict – or if you resist levelling with your partner!

~~~

Copyright (c) Renata Taylor-Byrne, Hebden Bridge, November 2018.

~~~

Appendix E: How to understand and manage human emotions

By Jim Byrne and Renata Taylor-Byrne

E1 Introduction

In this appendix we will present an extract from our earlier book on Lifestyle Counselling: (Byrne, 2018)[90]. This will help you to understand and manage your own emotions of anger, anxiety and depression, which will make you a more congenial partner to live with, which will enhance your marriage relationship and help to keep you both happy.

E2 Managing human emotions

Like Panksepp (1998)[91] and Schore (2015)[92], Daniel Siegel, in his (2015) book on the developing mind, emphasizes that what we call 'appraisal' is an *emotive* rather than a *thinking* process. The emotional centres of the brain can appraise an incoming stimulus as either 'good' or 'bad' from the beginning of life, long before we have any form of language labels. (This has been tested empirically, with either a sweet or a sour drink for the baby's first drink after birth, combined with observation of their facial responses!)[93] And from this innate appraisal process, and using our emotional control systems (described by Panksepp, 1998), we elaborate some basic emotional reactions, of anger, sadness, fear, surprise and/or joy[94].

In E-CENT[95] theory we see that slightly differently.

In the beginning, the baby uses its innate, basic emotions (or 'affects') to evaluate the goodness or badness of a situation.

But over time, and especially in the first two or three years of life, the new child is taught by its carers (normally mainly its mother) to modulate its *affects* (or *emotions*) – through rewards, penalties, modelling, soothing, and so on, and it may be that that integration of socialized-emotions, or higher cognitive-emotions, are stored in the Orbitofrontal Cortex (OFC) at the front of the brain (behind your eye sockets).

Thereafter, appraisal becomes *a learned emotive-cognitive process*. And it should be thought of as a function of *perfinking*, (which means *perceiving-feeling-thinking*, all in one grasp of the brain-mind), rather than either *thinking* (which is the CBT preference) or *emoting* (which is the Affect Regulation Theory preference).

Thus it is clear that E-CENT counselling theory does not follow either of the extremes – the *cognitivists* or the *emotivists* – but rather that we have *'perfinked'* – or *perceived/felt/thought* - our own way to a *novel, balanced* solution, which takes account of the innate (emotive) affects, and the later (linguistic-cultural) shaping, both of which are woven together into the *perfinking body-brain-mind*.

~~~

Siegel's (2015) argument is that the baby's 'primary feelings' - (which can be expressed by us (once we have acquired language!) as 'this is good'; 'this is bad'; or 'this feels good'; 'this feels bad') – are elaborated over time into (categorical) emotions (of anger, sadness, joy, fear, etc.).

Furthermore, babies need external affect (or emotion) regulation (soothing and/or stimulation), and it's the quality, quantity and timeliness of that soothing (and/or stimulation) that shapes the baby's dominant mood and habitual emotional profile. (Siegel, 2015, page 183).

As we grow and develop, interact with our care-givers, learn to read their nonverbal emotional states, and increasingly acquire language, we also evolve/ acquire higher cognitive emotions (like guilt, shame, pride, love, embarrassment, elevation, envy, and jealousy, etc.): and the flow of basic emotions, and socially-shaped emotions, is what *creates meaning in our lives*, and allows us to appraise our situations in life.

According to Siegel (2015): Emotions do not follow from thinking. Thinking follows from socialized-emotion. Attention and perception are also modulated by emotion. Emotions are basic to who we are and who we become. And the central features of emotion are *(non-conscious) appraisal* and *(non-conscious) arousal.* (Siegel, 2015. Pages 184-185).

Our ability to manage our emotions, to "regulate our affects", is a function of our history of attachment with our primary carers and subsequent significant others. (Bowlby, 1988/2005; Schore, 2015; Siegel, 2015; Wallin, 2007[96]).

In E-CENT theory, we see that slightly differently. Firstly, innate feelings precede, and are the foundation for, subsequent socialized 'perfinking' (or perceiving-feeling-thinking).

What we call 'thinking' never was a separate function of the brain-mind. *It is one of our delusions* (Gray, 2003) that we are *thinking* beings; that we *think*; that we have *thoughts* (which are not at the same time feelings); that we can *reason, separately* and *apart from* feelings and automatic perceptions!

...

E3 Managing anger, anxiety and depression

So let us look, briefly, at those three common emotional problems mentioned above.

E3.1 Anger:

The E-CENT theory of anger says that anger is one of our basic emotions. It's innate. It was selected by nature for its survival value. We would not survive for long without an innate sense of *angering* in response to abuse or neglect. We also would not survive for long if we did not quickly learn how to *moderate* our anger as young children. My anger is a two-edged sword. It can help to protect me, and it can attract hostile reactions from others.

My **basic** emotion of anger is elaborated into a *higher cognitive emotion* through modelling by my mother and father and significant others in the first few years of my life. My ability to become *emotionally intelligent* in relation to my innate anger urges depends on the emotional intelligence of my parents. My first angry outbursts are with them. How successfully I and they handle those angry episodes will shape how I manage my anger in the school playground. And those *socialized anger management strategies* continue to evolve through my successful and my unsuccessful experiences of engaging in conflict with others: siblings, school peers, and so on.

I may become an *exploder*, who erupts in the faces of others.

I may become an *imploder*, who keeps his anger inside.

Or I may hide my anger from myself (repress it) and then project it into my environment where it may frighten me.

So anger is a socialized emotion, and if you grew up with angry people, you are likely to be prone to angering yourself when provoked; or you might feel fearful of your own anger, or the anger of others.

~~~

Healthy anger is present-time defence of your legitimate rights in the face of inappropriate behaviour by another person. Healthy or *reasonable* anger is the fuel that drives our **assertive** behaviours. It pushes us to engage in *constructive conflict*, when that is *necessary*!

To ask for what you want, which is legitimately yours to request, requires a certain level of 'fire in your belly'. If you lack that fire (that *reasonable* level of anger), then you will tend to 'wimp-out'; to act passively and let other people control you, or intimidate you, or deny you your reasonable share of the social stage.

One of the problems that we encounter in therapy is this: Some parents, anxious to socialize their children to be 'nice' and 'civilized', go too far in 'switching off their fierceness' – instead of teaching them to manage their fierceness appropriately. And one of the things we do for passive clients is to help them to switch on their 'fierceness switch' – but we also try to teach them to only use their fierceness *assertively*, up to the boundary of their personal space – and never to invade the personal space of another – or to use their fierceness aggressively!

Unhealthy or *unreasonable* anger is an over-reaction to a frustrating or insulting stimulus from (or action by) another person; or frustration of goals and desires by an external force. Unhealthy or unreasonable anger leads to **aggressive** actions and destructive conflict; or unhelpful sulking. It is an excessive use of fierceness, and an under-use of honest communication and fair negotiation strategies.

We teach various principles to our anger management clients, including the following eight insights:

1. You were born with *an innate capacity to develop angry*, anxious and depressed responses to your social environment - in response to frustrations, threats and losses.

2. You then encountered your mother, who already had a 'style of relating', based on her attachment experience of her own mother and father. She would inevitably have shaped your emotional expression by:

(a) Modelling an approach to relationship and emotions; and:

(b) Rewarding and penalizing you for your daily emotion expressions, including your angry outbursts in the first couple of years of your life.

3. Your father's approach to relationship, including emotion expression, especially his way of expressing (or suppressing) anger, would have been the next major influence on the development of your emotion expression, including your way of being angry - implosive or explosive; appropriate or inappropriate.

4. If both of your parents had a secure attachment to their own parents, they would have had a warm but assertive approach to relating to you. From them you would have learned to be secure in your relationship with them, and, by extension, in virtually all subsequent people-encounters. You would have learned to express healthy or appropriate anger in an *assertive* way - to ask for what you want, and to say 'no' to what you do not want. And to strive to be treated with respect as an equal human being. You would not have any significant problems with anger.

5. However, if one or both of your parents had an insecure attachment to their own parents, they would have had an insecure attachment to you,

and been either explosively or implosively angry with you when you frustrated them or broke their *personal* rules, or their *culturally shaped moral rules*. From them, you would have learned to engage in unhealthy or inappropriate anger expression of an explosive or implosive type, or a mixture of the two, varying from situation to situation. (Or you might have learned to be *passive* in those situations in which you felt frightened or fearful of reprisals, but *aggressive* in those situations where you felt no constraint of fearfulness!)

6. If you want to change your relationship style today, you need to experience secure relationship with another person - possibly a romantic partner; a very good friend; or a good therapist who understands how to build a secure relationship with you. You need to learn the difference between **appropriate** and **inappropriate** anger. And also, to understand that **explosive** anger - (like shouting and using aggressive body language) - costs you, in terms of damage to relationships and careers, for examples; and that *implosive anger* – (like sulking and stewing in your own angry juices, or withdrawing aggressively) - damages your ongoing happiness, your relationships at home and at work, and ultimately your physical and mental health.

7. You can improve your relationship and attachment style by studying and applying new ideas from emotional literacy and self-assertion. And I (and/or other counsellors) can teach those ideas and skills to you.

8. But you are also a body-mind, and so your approach to managing your diet, physical exercise, sleep pattern, self-talk (or inner dialogue), and relaxation/ meditation, are also important. And it is easier to develop a secure attachment style if your romantic partner is already secure.

9. See Chapter 4 of Taylor-Byrne and Byrne (2017) – sections 4.3 to 4.7 - for specific dietary guidance and advice.

~~~

When an E-CENT counsellor works with an angry client, they may work on deep, emotional and attachment issues from early childhood; or on present-time assertiveness skills; or advice on important dietary changes; or recommendations regarding regular physical exercise, or improvements to sleep patterns; or teaching the client how to reframe their anger-inducing experiences; or changing some elements of their philosophy of life (as they show up in their inner dialogues about anger-inducing situations) – and even to change some aspect of their social or physical environment with which they have been putting up, or tolerating unnecessarily!

~~~

E3.1.1 Managing anger with diet and nutrition

In Taylor-Byrne and Byrne (2017), we explored - among other things - the key ways in which *diet can influence anger*. Some of the key findings were as follows:

Firstly, (unlike in the case of depression) there is at least one study which supports the idea that there is a link between low serotonin levels and the expression of anger, annoyance and irritation (specifically, low serotonin was linked to a reduced ability to self-manage rising levels of anger). We also presented evidence which showed that 5HTP, a natural nutritional supplement (from a West African medicinal plant called *Griffonia simpicifolia*), can be effective in restoring serotonin, an important neurotransmitter within the brain, thus reducing the expression of angry and hostile behaviour, as evidenced by a case study example from Julie Ross's (2002).

The levels of copper and manganese in the client's body can have an effect on levels of anger; so vitamin and mineral supplementation seems to be important to address.

The link between violent behaviour - by young offenders (in prison) - and the condition known as 'reactive hypoglycaemia' (where blood sugar levels fall too low after eating high carbohydrate meals) - has been established by scientific research. There is thus an obvious connection between fluctuating blood sugar levels and anger management problems, and this can guide us in recommending particular (low sugar, slow-burning) foods to our angry clients.

A number of studies have established a definite link between a reduction in the consumption of sugar and refined foods, (on the one hand), and reduced anger and anti-social behaviour, (on the other). In a similar vein, reductions in diets containing trans-fats, mainly involving hydrogenated fats in processed foods, led to a reduction in impatience, irritability and aggression in research participants.

Conversely, the link between pro-social behaviour and a healthy diet has also been evidenced by research. Dietary changes which increase the nutritional content of people's diets (especially introducing omega-3 fatty acids, as found for example in oily fish; plus vitamin and mineral supplements) result in improvements in pro-social behaviour, and better emotion and mood control. Anger levels declined in prisoners whose diet had been supplemented with fish oils, vitamins and minerals: and it has been shown that omega-3 fats have a rapid and significant impact on aggression in children and adults.

For further information, please see sections 4.3 to 4.7 above; and also Taylor-Byrne and Byrne (2017), for specific dietary guidance and advice.

~~~

E3.1.2 How anger can be reduced by exercise:

According to the British National Health Service website, anger is effectively reduced in intensity by exercising, including walking, swimming and yoga. Research studies have supported this view, and here are some examples which have provided valuable evidence on the role of exercise in anger reduction:

Research conducted by Joseph Tkacz, et al., (2008), found that aerobic exercise regimes reduced anger expression among obese children. It was the first study which had been conducted to assess the value of having structured aerobic exercise sessions for overweight children, and the findings pointed to the value of exercise sessions after school.

Also, there was a study which investigated levels of anger amongst undergraduates at the University of Georgia. It looked at whether physical education (exercise) could moderate anger: (Reynolds, 2010); and it was reported in the *New York Times* magazine.

The 16 students selected were regularly oversensitive to provocations, and their anger was easily triggered.

They were subjected to different research conditions (*provocations*), designed to arouse their anger.

Firstly, those provocations were experienced without the benefits of exercise;

Secondly, they were experienced after the benefits of exercise.

The research results revealed that, the provocations had a stronger angering effect – producing a higher level of anger - *before* the exercise than they did after the participants had engaged in physical exercise.

After they had exercised, they were able to show composure and self-assurance in the face of emotional provocation. The physical exercise program did reduce their levels of anger, prompting the lead researcher, Nathaniel Thoms, a stress physiologist, to say:

"Exercise, even a single bout of it, can have a robust prophylactic (therapeutic) effect against the build-up of anger...it's like taking an aspirin to combat heart disease. You reduce your risk".

This result is echoed by the advice of the Mayo Clinic Staff, who have written that the higher the levels of stress a person is experiencing, the more likely they are to have high levels of anger, and that these effects can be diminished by vigorous and pleasurable exercise.

For further information, please see section 4.10 above; plus Taylor-Byrne and Byrne (2017), for more specific information on research into different forms of exercise.

~~~

E3.2 Anxiety:

The E-CENT counselling theory of anxiety says that we are born with an innate sense of fear: (Darwin, 1872/1965; and Panksepp, 1998). Babies begin to display a pronounced sense of fear from about the age of six or seven months. This sense of fear is of something that is *present* – like loud noise; a furry animal; something that looks like a snake; etc. In time, we learn to feel anxious, which is to say, fearful about things that are *not* present, but which we 'think-feel' (consciously and/or non-consciously) might represents threats and dangers just a little while in the future.

People feel different intensities of anxiety, depending upon the seriousness of the threat or danger that they are anticipating, and how that degree of seriousness interacts with their felt sense of 'coping capability'. That is to say:

1. *The less serious the inferred threat is assumed to be* - and the more coping capability we sense that we have - then the *lower* our intensity of anxiety is likely to be.

(Our coping capability seems to be a combination of physical solidity or confidence; emotional stability and optimism; and security of attachment. And these capabilities are fed by healthy diet, regular physical exercise, relaxation/ meditation, social connection, adequate sleep, and so on)

2. *On the other hand, the more serious the inferred threat is assumed to be* - and the less coping capability we sense that we have - then the *higher* our intensity of anxiety is likely to be.

~~~

REBT theorists distinguish between anxiety (which is intense) and concern (which is much less intense); and some other theorists distinguish between anxiety (which is helpful) and panic (which is unhelpful: See Kashdan and Biswas-Diener, 2015)[97].

In E-CENT counselling we do not go along with those kinds of distinctions. We see our clients as having a range of anxious-feeling potential, from very low to very high; and we normally work with clients whose anxiety level is high or very high, and our aim is to help them to reduce it until it is low, or very low. But they will never get rid of it; nor should they try to do so, as we **need** each of our basic emotions. *What needs to be reformed is* **how those basic emotions became socialized!** If we come from *emotionally less intelligent families*, then we will need to **re-learn** how to *emote*, as we become adults, so that we behave ***appropriately*** with those people with whom we work, rest and play.

We also work with clients whose anxiety gets out of control, and becomes panic – which we conceptualize as *anxiety **about** anxiety **about** anxiety* – spiralling out of control.

And we teach panicky clients the following guidelines:

(1) Accept your panic as your own creation (embrace it rather than trying to push it away. You **cannot** push your **own** *agitated lungs and guts away!*)

(2) Recognize that panic passes in a matter of a couple of minutes, so 'play a waiting game'. And:

(3) Take yourself outside and lean against a wall; focus on your breathing, and make your out-breath longer than your in-breath.

> - You can guess at that, or you can count your outbreath to the count of eleven, and your in-breath to the count of seven.

> - Or, if that's too complex, *breathe **out** for a much **longer** period that you breathe in.*

> - Try to empty your lungs completely, before allowing the in-breath to return.

Here is some advice for managing anxiety in general:

Practical strategies for managing anxiety

1. Make sure you get enough sleep.

2. Arise in a timely manner to get on top of the challenges of the day.

3(a) Eat a hearty breakfast of either complex carbohydrates, or protein, but it is perhaps best not to mix them (according to Dr Hay; although Patrick Holford advises mixing them!) (We, Jim and Renata, have chopped salad in a bowl, at least four mornings per week). If you do have cereal for breakfast, make sure it's gluten free, and low GI (Glycaemic Index [or low sugar content]).

3(b) Avoid caffeine drinks and sugary drinks. (One mug of real coffee each day is a good upper-limit guideline. But if you are particularly sensitive to caffeine, avoid it completely!)

3(c) Avoid junk foods because they are high in sugars and bad fats (trans-fats).

4. Make sure you have a mid-morning snack – e.g. a piece of fruit, or some nuts and seeds (assuming you are not allergic to fructose and seeds.) If you have to have some form of bread or cereal, make sure it's gluten free and low in sugar content.

5. Do not skip lunch or evening meals. Eat a healthy, balanced diet, if you can tolerate the grains and dairy. But many people find they have to avoid all gluten (in wheat, rye, oats and barley), and they use gluten free products instead.

The Mediterranean diet is widely recommended. As is the Nordic diet; and, to a lesser extent, the Paleo diet. But we recommend that you develop a personalized diet, by trial and error; perhaps with the support of a nutritionist. But make sure you eat oily fish twice each week; and/or take omega 3 fatty acid supplements.

6. Meditate after breakfast, and then do about thirty minutes of physical exercise at the start of each day. (If it helps, you could start off doing five or ten minutes of each, and then gradually increase the time over the first couple of years, until you reach thirty minutes of each [meditation and exercise], every day – or at least five or six days per week). These two processes tend to calm your central nervous system, making it less reactive.

7. Whenever you feel tense, take a mental break, and take five deep, slow, relaxing breaths. If that does not relax you, then stand up and walk around, counting to twenty silently in your mind. (Sitting around for too long can increase your anxiety level. Sedentary lifestyle is bad for both physical health and emotional wellbeing. So, take frequent breaks and walk around)[98].

8. Set a few (3-6) *realistic* goals for the day, and try to achieve them. Do not aim for perfection. Only try to control what seems likely to be controllable, and leave the rest. Accept the things you cannot change.

9. Watch comedy shows on TV or DVDs, when you get home, instead of *bad News*, or stressful *Current Affairs*. Have a hobby. Read something enjoyable before bedtime.

10. Work at developing good, supportive relationships, at home and at work, and in your community.

11. Keep a journal, and write about your anxiety symptoms. What are the triggers? Which aspects of those triggers are controllable? What could you do to problem-solve in that area of your life? Set goals to change those changeable aspects of your life that cause you anxiety. And accept the rest!

12. Identify a good counsellor or psychotherapist to whom you can talk about your anxiety problems, with a view to changing what can be changed, and learning to accept what is beyond your control.

13. Additional dietary advice could include the following:

- You might need to supplement your vitamin intake from food with a good multi-vitamin and mineral tablet; plus B-Complex; plus omega-3 fatty acid capsules (or strong cod liver oil; or Krill oil capsules); and perhaps *kava kava*.

- Drink lots of water, (six to eight glasses of filtered or glass-bottled water per day), and limit alcohol consumption to one unit every other day, or less.

- Drink herbal tea instead of caffeinated drinks, especially if you have difficulty reducing your anxiety by other means. Camomile tea is soothing of the nervous system.

~~~

E3.2.1 Anxiety management: The impact of diet and nutrition

It has been proven empirically that dietary changes can reduce the experience of anxiety: as demonstrated in Taylor-Byrne and Byrne, 2017.

Firstly, 2011 was the first year in which there was a double-blind trial establishing that there was a link between omega-3 fatty acids and a reduction in anxiety: (Kiecolt-Glaser et al, 2011). This connection has been confirmed by many hundreds of anecdotal accounts by clients (to their professional practitioners) in which those clients have attested to the benefits in anxiety reduction, which they personally gained from omega-3 fatty acids.

~~~

Secondly, both magnesium and GABA (gamma-amino-butyric acid) are very valuable for the body-brain-mind in terms of reducing tension, anxiety and hyper-arousal. The recommended foods are as follows: dark green leafy vegetables, (like spinach and kale); nuts (walnuts and almonds); and seeds; fruit (e.g. bananas); and oats (gluten free); and extracts of Reishi (described as the power mushroom).

~~~

Thirdly, the management of our blood sugar levels can stop the following vicious circle happening:

(1) A person (ill informed) eats white bread, or white pasta, white rice, chocolates and drinks fizzy drinks;

(2) As a direct consequence of this ill-advised activity, this person experiences a rapid rise in blood sugar.

(3) Soon afterwards, this is followed by a big drop in blood sugar levels, as the person's body releases insulin to cope with the sudden influx of sugar. And then,

(4) *Because* of the sudden drop in blood sugar, the hormone, adrenalin, is released into the bloodstream. This results in experiencing a racing heart

and rapid breathing, and negative *perfinking* (or perceiving-feeling-thinking) processes, which create the symptoms of anxiety.

(The vicious circle, of course, is this: When some people feel anxious, they reach for 'comfort foods', which boost their blood sugar levels – and the whole cycle begins all over again!)

The recommended solution is to alter the combination of foods that you eat, so that the release of energy, from the digestion of the food, is slowed down. Also it is recommended that people avoid refined carbohydrates, and simple sugars. Eating vegetables, oily fish and reducing meat consumption; plus eating nuts and seeds; would mean that the blood-sugar roller-coaster effect would be avoided. (This is called 'eating slow-burning fuels').

~~~

Fourthly, there is growing evidence that the state of our guts, including our gut bacteria, is very important in managing the experience of anxiety. This view is expressed by Dr David Perlmutter (2015). He cites many research studies which establish several facts:

(1) When we eat foods containing gluten, this affects the junctions between cells in the intestines, called the 'tight junctions'. This makes them leaky, and this enables toxins that come from within the bacteria in the intestines to enter the bloodstream. As a consequence they bring about a massive inflammatory response in the body-brain.

(2) Perlmutter (2015) also considers that there are physical vulnerabilities which can precipitate high levels of inflammation in the body, such as antibiotic use, manner of birth (i.e. Caesarean section), and the balance of bacteria in the gut.

(3) Dietary changes therefore are necessary to heal the gut, such as:

(a) Giving up gluten-containing foods (like: wheat; rye; [non-organic] oats; and barley – and any foods containing those grains); and:

(b) Consuming oral probiotic supplements, and vitamin supplements. (Specific probiotics [e.g. *lactobacillus* and *bifidobacterium*] reduce anxiety and return the intestines to full health and proper functioning.)

(4) But he also considers lifestyle changes such as sufficient sleep and aerobic exercise as necessary to complete the process.

PS: We have also found that supplementing with the amino acid, L-Glutamine, between meals, quickly heals a leaky gut.

~~~

There is also research supporting the conclusion that the consumption of caffeine, sugar, artificial sweeteners and alcohol actually *create* anxiety in the human body. Two relevant examples to mention are the consumption of caffeine and sugar. High levels of caffeine in coffee bring about a sudden increase in tension and anxiety, and sugar causes an initial spike in our blood-sugar levels, but then an ultimate drop in our blood sugar as the body tries to cope (by removing sugar and storing it – resulting in the removal of too much!), and this results in feelings of anxiety and weakness in the body.

For further information, please see Taylor-Byrne and Byrne (2017), for specific dietary guidance and advice. (But also remember to 'find out for yourself'; perhaps by consulting a nutritional therapist or an alternative or lifestyle medical practitioner).

~~~

E3.2.2 Anxiety management: How anxiety can be reduced by exercise:

If we do not exercise, we are asking for trouble, for our body-brain-minds. This is because, as human animals, we have evolved to handle threats and dangers *by taking physical action*. If we don't take physical action when presented by a threat, we will experience anxiety and a build-up of stress hormones in our body-mind.

We need to process the stressors in our daily lives and remove the stress hormones from our body-mind by taking physical action. Exercise is a form of managed stress, exerted on the body-brain-mind, which actually reduces stress hormones, thereby reducing the feeling of anxiety.

Joshua Broman-Fulks proved this in 2004 with students suffering from anxiety. Two weeks of exercise reduced their anxiety levels, and made the students less sensitive to anxiety. (See Ratey and Hagerman, 2009 for a summary of this research).

If our bodies are tense, the brain-mind registers this and starts to go on 'red alert'. But if we exercise, this action reduces the tension in our muscles – and if our bodies are relaxed the brain-mind does not worry. So exercise stops *the anxiety 'feedback loop'*, whereby we become anxious about being anxious, which then activates the brain into starting the 'fight or flight' response.

Exercise works by making chemical alterations in our bodies. As our muscles move, fat molecules are broken down to provide energy for this extra demand on the body. This then releases fatty acids into the bloodstream; and, as a consequence, tryptophan and serotonin - (which some theorists call **the 'feel-good' hormone**) - increase, and (it is thought by some), serotonin calms us down and also increases our feelings of safety.

For further information please see sections 4.9, 4.12, and 4.13 of Byrne (2018a); plus Taylor-Byrne and Byrne (2017), for information about exercise benefits.

~~~

E3.3 Depression:

The E-CENT counselling theory of depression says we have to distinguish between **transient grief** and **stuck depression**.

Our primary stance on depression and grief is this:

Grief is 'depression' which is *appropriate* to some significant loss or failure in the recent past. While **depression** is stuck-'grief' which is *inappropriate* to loss or failure in the more distant past.

But we also have a secondary stance:

Inappropriate depression can also come from *exaggerating* the degree of badness of a current or recent loss or failure; or refusing to accept its inevitability; or trying (in your mind) to reverse an irreversible loss or failure.

Our (primary stance) distinction (between grief and depression) is equivalent to saying that there is *appropriate depression* (called 'grief', which *gradually* heals itself) and *inappropriate grief* (called 'depression', which *gets stuck* and needs some kind of psychological intervention).

Grief and depression are intense forms of sadness about real or symbolic losses (or failures), combined with a sense of hopelessness and helplessness.

Grief is a helpful emotion which has enhanced human survival; while there is also a kind of *inappropriate-depression* which indicates a grief process that is stuck, and which is not being processed over time; or an *exaggerated sense* of recent loss.

When clients present with grief about a recent (significant) loss or failure, E-CENT counsellors offer sympathy and understanding, and sensitive attunement to their emotional state. Over time, we encourage the client to cry, to grieve, and to heal. There is only so much crying that a person can do about a loss (or failure), if they are gradually *completing their experience* of that loss (or failure).

Stuck-depression is an unhelpful emotion: When client-grief goes on for more than about eighteen months, as an *intense, debilitating* state, we consider that the process is *stuck* and needs to be moved forwards. Two common scenarios are encountered by us:

Scenario 1: Sometimes that stuckness is caused by *trauma* – arising out of the fact that the client was already overly stressed when they experienced the loss or failure in question. So we assist this client by suggesting that we help them to work through our *desensitization process* (outlined in Appendix C of Byrne, 2016).

Or we guide them through a process of getting in touch with their depressed feelings; *naming them*; describing them in words; and reflecting upon their growing understanding of *what it means* (to them) to have these feelings (about their loss [or failure]).

Scenario 2: On the other hand, sometimes the process of grieving gets stuck because of temperament/character problems within the client. This normally takes the form of *excessively strong **demands** or unrealistic expectations that the loss or failure **must be reversed***, somehow – even if somebody has died, or the lost thing no longer exists.

And it does not even have to extend to *strong **demands***. It can simply be *an **unrealistic** desire* which is so important to the client that they cannot let it go, even when it clearly cannot be achieved! ("One hairsbreadth difference between *what you want* and *what you've got*, and heaven and earth are set apart!" Buddhist saying.)

In this latter kind of stuck-depression, (which we have labelled as **Scenario 2** above), we might use the *Six Windows Model* to teach the client to *reframe* their depressing loss or failure: (See Chapter 10, Section 10.3.1, above).

And/or we might recommend that they write out a Gratitude List, every night, for thirty or sixty nights, containing five or six items for which they can be *grateful*. Thus, they can learn to focus upon *what they've **got***, for which they can be grateful, instead of *what they have **lost***, which they cannot (presently) retrieve!

And we would tend to give the following dietary advice: Avoid sugary foods, but do have complex carbohydrates, from vegetables, fruit and (some experts say) whole grains. (However, the Paleo Diet theorists claim that *all grains* cause inflammation in the body-brain, beginning in the guts: and anything that causes physical inflammation will make our emotional well-being worse, not better!) Gluten-free oats might be a good compromise. And brown rice seems to be a safe grain.

Lots of nutrient-rich salads can help; plus good fats, like olive oil, and coconut oil (if you can tolerate fats!) Salmon, sardines, trout and other oily fish are good for brain health. (All of these foods provide a good supply of omega 3 fatty acids).

Avoid factory-farmed chicken, as it contains lots of antibiotics, which tend to kill off your friendly gut bacteria, and there is a link between healthy gut bacteria and emotional well-being. (Borchard, 2015)[99].

Also, avoid trans-fats (which are super-heated, hydrogenated fats).

And make sure you get lots of vitamin D, mainly from daily exposure to sunlight, but supplement with tablet form if necessary: (Mercola, 2013) And a good, full spectrum multivitamin and mineral, plus B-Complex, are also recommended by many theorists. (E.g. Ross, 2003).

For more information on diet, nutrition, and healthy gut bacteria, please see Part 1 of Taylor-Byrne and Byrne (2017).

~~~

E3.3.1 Depression: How diet and nutrition can reduce and eliminate it

In Section 10.4.1 above, we presented a lot of research evidence for the link between diet and depression. For examples:

Both Dr Kelly Brogan (2016) and Dr David Perlmutter (2015) are convinced that depression doesn't come from chemical imbalances in the brain. They consider that the health condition of the gut, if addressed, can eliminate the experience of depression. The main culprit in the creation of mental disorder (or emotional distress) is inflammation in the body; and specific dietary strategies can eliminate this.

Reducing (or, preferably, eliminating) sugar consumption - and getting rid of processed or refined foods - is considered to be very important. So dietary changes which improve nutrition are essential, as well as meditation and exercise. These are daily strategies for the reduction of depression.

Apparently, according to Dr Perlmutter (2015), the health and balance of our gut microbes are very important, as they regulate cortisol and adrenalin (which are the major hormones of the stress response). Interestingly, our guts contain about 70-80% of our immune system (and about 80% of our serotonin – which some theorists see as intimately linked to controlling depression; but other theorists disagree).

The ways in which depression can be reduced, according to Dr Perlmutter (2015), include following these dietary recommendations:

Switch to gluten-free foods;

eat healthy fats (and get rid of and avoid trans-fats);

take *prebiotics* (like psyllium husk, and fibrous vegetables), and *probiotics* (like Acidophilus);

eat fermented foods, like sauerkraut, kimchi, etc.;

and stick to low-carb foods.

Patrick Holford (2010) and Dr Sarah Brewer (2013) are of the opinion that fish oils (which contain lots of omega-3 fatty acids) are very important to help prevent depression. Holford recommends supplementation with natural herbs, minerals and chemicals which balance our neuro-transmitters. He further considers that there are also psychological factors present in depression, which are related to a person's life, and whether they are living it in a way which is true to themselves. These latter issues benefit from talk therapy.

Finally, Robert Redfern (2016) cites evidence that the nutrient B9, which is folate, is one of the main nutrients in a healthy diet that can reduce the risk of depression. The research which he quotes, which was conducted at the University of Eastern Finland, showed that eating a healthy diet, free from processed foods, reduced depressive symptoms and created an overall lower risk of severe depression.

For further information, please see Taylor-Byrne and Byrne (2017), for specific dietary guidance and advice.

~~~

E3.3.2 Depression: How it can be reduced by exercise

The value of exercise for reducing depression is very well-proven, and this has been confirmed by Blumenthal *et al.* (1999), and Blumenthal *et al.* (2012). They carried out what became known as a landmark study, which contrasted the value of exercise with the drug Sertraline, (which is also called Zoloft).

There were three different patient groups for the research procedure:

a group of patients on Zoloft;

an exercise group,

and a group on a combination of exercise and Zoloft.

The exercise group had supervised exercise three times a week.

All three groups showed a marked reduction in their levels of depression, after the research experiment, and approximately half of each of the groups went into remission.

The results showed that *exercise was as beneficial as medication*, and led Dr John Ratey and Eric Hagerman (2009) to recommend exercise for depression. Their conclusion was that exercise altered the brain chemistry of the exercisers, in positive ways, which would help patients with depression.

Ratey and Hagerman (2009) declared that:

"The results should be taught in medical schools and driven home with health insurance companies and posted on the bulletin boards of every nursing home in the country, where nearly a fifth of the residents have depression."

(Ratey and Hagerman, 2009: Page 122).

They also mention the follow-up survey Blumenthal and his colleagues (2010) did six months later. *The researchers found that exercise performed more effectively than medicine in the long term*: About 30% of the exercise group were still depressed, as opposed to 52% of those on medication, and 55% in the combined treatment group.

This means that *70% of those on exercise alone got better*, compared with just 48% on Zoloft alone.

Blumenthal and his researchers found that the most revealing indicator of whether someone would have increased feelings of well-being, was the extent to which they exercised.

"Specifically, every 50 minutes of weekly exercise correlated to a 50% drop in the odds of being depressed."

(Ratey and Hagerman, 2009, Page 124).

These research results refer to major depression – not just mild depression.

Both the British National Health Service and the Mayo Clinic recommend physical exercises as being effective in treating depression.

A valuable reminder is also given by Dr Alan Cohen (a GP with a special interest in mental health: NHS Choices (2016))[100]. He considers that in order to have the *motivation* to perform exercise regularly, we need to *enjoy* it, and he recommends 150 minutes of moderate-intensity exercise every week.

For further information about exercise for depression, please see section 10.4.2 of Chapter 10; plus Taylor-Byrne (2017)[101].

And, for a more thorough grasp of how to understand and control your own emotions, and how help your partner to understand themselves, please see Chapter 7 of Byrne (2018a)[102].

~~~

Appendix F: The Good and Bad sides of human nature: Sometimes called the *'Good & Bad Wolf'*

Copyright (c) Dr Jim Byrne, 2016-2018

~~~

> *"If only there were evil people somewhere insidiously committing evil deeds, and it were necessary only to separate them from the rest of us and destroy them. But the line dividing good and evil cuts through the **heart** of every human being".*

> **Alexander Solzhenitsyn**

F1 Introduction

One of the most important things we each need to learn about a potential life-partner, marriage partner, etc., is this: How moral does this person seem to be in various situations. If you overlook and excuse immoral tendencies in areas of life that do not directly affect you, in the early stages of your relationship, you may come to regret that later on, when their evil tendencies are turned against you!

One of the earliest principles of E-CENT counselling theory was this:

> *We think of every new born baby as containing two potentials: (1) to develop pro-social and caring attitudes; and (2) to develop anti-social and egotistical attitudes.*

Part of the process of normal socialization of every child involves ensuring that the new little person mainly develops their 'good side' - (or what the Native American Cherokee people call the 'good wolf') - through the moral teachings of their parents, teachers and others; and that their 'bad wolf' (or evil or anti-social tendency) is constrained and contained. (It cannot ever be totally or permanently eliminated. We each contain the capacity for significant levels of evil to the end of our days!)

However, the happy functioning of humans as social animals depends upon the extent to which we develop our pro-social, moral virtues, and resist our anti-social, immoral or amoral vices.

Some counselling clients are clearly operating mainly from 'good wolf' and some are significantly operating from 'bad wolf'. That latter client group needs coaching in moral philosophy; and encouragement to operate mainly from 'good wolf'.

The two main arguments we use in this connection are: (1) the importance of following the Golden Rule; and (2) the inescapable Law of Karma, which means that – in addition to bad luck and biological and social heritage - *we reap what we sow!*

The Native American Cherokee concept included the idea of a *war* going on inside each human being. That war is between two 'wolves': the *good wolf* and the *bad wolf*.[103] And the wolf that wins the war is the one that is fed the most!

References to the Good and Bad Wolf, or the good and bad sides of human nature, can be found in various places in the papers and books published by the Institute for E-CENT. However, there is not yet a fully developed E-CENT paper on this topic which pulls all those ideas together. This appendix assembles just a small number of the key ideas that have been developed so far.

F2 The E-CENT theory of good and evil

This idea of innate goodness and badness is reminiscent of the Christian concept of 'original sin' (or innate tendencies towards evil) and 'the state of grace' (a condition described as being "...free from sin" [or free from evil intent], which is achieved through spiritual or religious practices).

The distinction between good and evil is a distinction between actions that contribute to the *welfare* of others, and actions that *harm* the life of others.

However, the E-CENT theory does not rely upon God or the Devil, but rather on innate tendencies towards pro- and anti-social behaviours on the part of the normal human child, and the ways those tendencies are managed during the early socialization of the child.

Sigmund Freud had a similar distinction – the distinction between *the Life urge* (or *Eros*) and *the Death urge* (or *Thanatos*), which he believed were innate and universal drivers of human behaviour[104].

Some counselling clients are clearly operating mainly from 'good wolf' and some are significantly operating from 'bad wolf'.

That latter client group needs coaching in moral philosophy; and encouragement to operate mainly from 'good wolf'.

F3 The concepts of selfishness and altruism

The content of this appendix, and the general theory of the Good and Bad Wolf states, is underpinned by a great deal of research I did during my doctoral studies, including reviewing psychological studies designed to test various theories of morality. It also draws upon academic writing I produced when studying for my Diploma in Counselling Psychology and Psychotherapy.

The E-CENT model of the human psyche includes conflicting urges, attitudes and orientations at the level of the biological organism, as originally posited by Freud. I think I probably emphasize *positive urges* more than Freud did, and especially urges to be social and pro-social, as suggested by Kitzinger (1997) and others.[105] However, as I shall show later, these innate tendencies to behave well and badly are strongly influenced by social shaping, which produces either a strong, weak or benign conscience.[106] The tension between the conscience and the inborn urges create the space in which the self-constructed self (or ego) becomes constructed; and this self is fragmented into a number of self-states (or ego states). And, finally, the resulting "urge to be good" (at the ego level) can break down very badly under certain types of circumstances, especially *strong, external controlling situations*, like Zimbardo's[107] simulated prison experiment; and Milgram's[108] electrocution experiments.

F4 Altruism and egoism

There is a popular theory of "universal egoism" – (Dovidio, 1984) – which claims that humans are fundamentally *selfish,* and that altruism "is an impossibility".[109] This appears to be the dominant view in mainstream psychology. And any act of "apparent altruism" is seen as "selfishness in disguise" by the sociobiologists. (This is not quite the position of Richard Dawkins who, in *The Selfish Gene,* had this to say: "Be warned that if you wish, as I do, to build a society in which individuals cooperate generously and unselfishly towards a common good, you can expect little help from biological nature. Let us try to *teach* generosity and altruism, because we are *born selfish.* Let us understand what our own selfish genes are up to, because we may then at least have a chance to upset their designs, something that no other species has ever aspired to do". [Chapter 1].

So for Dawkins, there can at least be "learned altruism", whereas for me (and Piaget before me) there is an *innate tendency* towards altruism, and an *innate tendency* towards *selfishness,* both of which can have survival value, and both of which can be enhanced or inhibited by the social environment of the individual's childhood.

Beings which were *purely selfish* would most likely not have been 'selected' for survival, as they probably could not have **competed-cooperatively** in any niche which was competed for by *a socially cohesive group.* And it makes no sense to assume, as is implicit in Dawkins' ideas, that non-human primates were "trained" to be sociable, against their "selfish" natures. It makes a lot more sense to assume that their social troops arose naturally, based upon biological drives, enhanced by changing environmental niches which dictated the need for greater cooperation (Turner, 2000).

Of course Dawkins could then move the goalposts and claim that those groups of primates coalesced *to serve their selfish genes,* since they are just "disposable gene machines".

However interesting this may be as *philosophical speculation*, there is no way that Dawkins [or O. Wilson] could ever *validate* that assertion. In what way can it be investigated? I can think of no *suitable experiment* that could be undertaken).[110]

And even if innate altruism is recast as a form of selfishness, it is still *innate altruism!*

F5 Sociological evidence

History and philosophy also mainly seem to point towards the *bad behaviour* of humans. For example, from ancient Greece to this very day, the lives of the majority of humans have been deformed by the insistence of the most powerful property-owning groups to run society as a class-based hierarchy of 'haves' and 'have-nots'. (This is the critique developed by Marx and Engels, the anarchists and Christian Socialists; while the Christian Conservatives supported the bad behaviour of various ruling classes, while castigating the significantly less bad behaviour of *powerless* individuals).

However, it is important to distinguish between what is *innate* and what is *developed*, or *induced,* in humans. And amidst all the exploitation and greed of modern societies, we see also examples of altruism and self-sacrifice; mainly amongst the "lower orders" – although wealthy benefactors have been spotted from time to time. These altruistic acts are said by some to result from "sympathetic instincts". See McDougal, 1908, in Gross 2001, page 434. And Piaget supported the view that both innate and environmental factors shape the development of moral reasoning.[111]

F6 Acceptance or non-acceptance of immorality

The traditional Christian perspective is that humans are born evil – with 'original sin' on (or in) their souls; and that they remain evil unless they are redeemed by Christianity. By contrast, both Carl Rogers and Albert Ellis - (two of the most famous psychotherapists of the twentieth century) -

argued that we should accept individuals *unconditionally*, regardless of how immorally they perform in the world. This is a crazy idea, which would negate all morality and all legal rules about bad behaviour.

I will not *unconditionally* accept anybody, (including myself), if that person is behaving immorally. I will describe that as immoral action, and will I judge the perpetrator of immoral actions as (at least temporarily) a 'bad person'; meaning *a person of bad character* (in at least some *specific* respect)! It is only after they admit their immoral action, repent and make amends, that I will consider that they have resumed being a 'good person' - which means 'a person who has their Good Wolf in the driving seat of their life'. My approach is therefore called **'one-conditional** self-acceptance' and **'one-conditional** acceptance of others' (as distinct from wholly amoral **'unconditional acceptance'**.)

And I also subscribe to 'radical acceptance' of life, but not including immoral aspects of life.

I accept those aspects of life which are beyond my control, and only try to control those which seem likely to be controllable.

~~~

My own experience of life, including my reading and studying activities, supports this one-conditional approach, in opposition to what I see as a tendency towards the naïve view expressed by Nelson-Jones (2001) to the effect that we all have a 'core of goodness'. (Pages 392-393)[112].

Nelson-Jones' position is quite muddled in that he acknowledges that human behaviour can be positive or negative, but he seems to blame the world, and/or the individual's choices, rather than innate tendencies, for the emergence of what Freud called 'the bad animal', or 'wolf', aspect of human behaviour.

This naïve view of human nature - which is hard to credit in a post-Nazi world - was also shared by Carl Rogers, the founder of person-centred counselling: (Nelson-Jones, 2001, page 96).

On the other hand, as mentioned above, the Native American Cherokee people had the concept of a war going on inside each human being; a war between the Good and Bad Wolf. And the wolf that wins the war is the one that is fed the most!

So, one of the most important developmental challenges for every human being is to learn how to starve our bad wolf tendencies, and to feed only our good wolf tendencies.

The core of the good wolf is love, empathy, charity and a range of other virtues (or what Freud called Eros, or the love instinct); while the core of the bad wolf is inappropriate anger, rage, resentment, envy, jealousy, meanness, and other vices (which Freud called Thanatos, or the death urge).

These insights led me to make a modification to the basic E-CENT model of the mother-baby dyad. This is shown in Figure F.1, which follows, below:

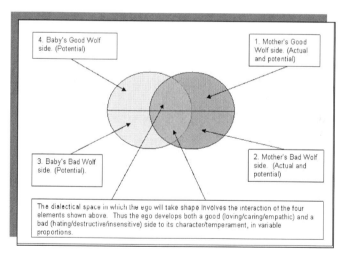

Figure F.1 - The good and bad wolf are inherent in human nature, and in human culture, and the proportions are variable in each individual over time, and from situation to situation

Of course, the line between good and evil is not fixed, as shown in Figure F.1, above, but variable from individual to individual and from situation to situation.

F7 Conclusion

The dividing line between good and evil runs right down the centre of the human heart.

Some individuals, because of their good, moral education in early childhood, tend to mainly operate from their good side[113].

Other individuals, because of their poor socialization into having a set of reliable 'moral intuitions', tend to act from their bad side; and almost anybody will tend to operate from their bad side if put under significant pressure by 'authority figures' to do so.

Counsellors and psychotherapist have an absolute moral duty to make sure they do nothing to give permission to a client to act immorally. And, as good re-parenting figures, they owe it to their clients to correct any moral weakness on the client's part.

And members of sex-love couples have a duty to each other to restrain their Bad Wolf, and to grow their Good Wolf. This mainly entails manifesting love for your partner, and eliminating any manifestation of angry, rageful hatred that emerges in conflict situations.

~~~

Copyright (c) Jim Byrne – November 2018

~~~

Appendix G: The importance of the clitoris

G1 The myth of the vaginal orgasm

In this appendix, I will write about Daniel O'Beeve's first love affair:

His girlfriend, Belinda, informed him up front how bored she became with sex, when she had been involved with a new man *for a few weeks*! He assumed (for a completely unknown reason), that this would not apply to him.

Six weeks later she had betrayed him with another man.

He left, found a copy of a book entitled *The Myth of the Vaginal Orgasm* on the railway platform, as he left town, and studied that book on the train.

What did he learn form that reading?

1. That the male theory of human sexual relations, which he had picked up from his culture by osmosis, was false. It was not enough to insert one's penis into a woman's vagina, and to thrust it in and out, in order to produce mutual pleasure. (It produced undoubted pleasure for the man, and most men failed to ask the woman: 'How is this for you?')

2. Sexual intercourse is the most enjoyable part of sexual relations *for the man* – but for the man *only*! It does not produce an orgasmic experience for the woman - (or *not reliably*, in some cases; and *not at all* in perhaps most)!

For example, in an article about her new book, Germaine Greer (2018) quotes the "statistics of sexologists" as showing that "46% of women *fake orgasm* **every time** they have sex". And they do this to bring the experience of intercourse to an end.

3. For most women, on most occasions, only *direct stimulation of the clitoris*[114], by digital (finger) or lingual (tongue) massage, will bring her to orgasm. (And any man can ask his partner to *teach him* how to do that!)

And just in case some readers insist that my data are not up to date, and that things must have improved in recent years, I offer you this extract from the Metro Newspaper of Thursday November 22nd 2018:

"...A study conducted by Durex in the Netherlands last your (2017) showed that almost 75% of women do not orgasm during sex, whereas only 28% of men don't climax... And it's getting no better: this month a study in The Journal of Sexual Medicine revealed that of 1,700 US newlyweds, 43 per cent of husbands had no idea how often their wives orgasm. So, in straight sex, there does seem to be an Orgasm Gap." (Page 39)[115].

Part of the problem may be the difficulty of communicating about sex: "Sex is still a taboo subject for many and therefore, talking about it is tricky. So first and foremost, communication or lack thereof is a huge contributor to the orgasm gap". (Lynch, 2018, Page 40).

One of the most important point made by Bibi Lynch in this newspaper article is this: Do not fake an orgasm to in order to avoid the embarrassment of talking about it. Once you begin to fake orgasms, the road back to honest communication becomes more and more difficult, and often impossible!

G2 'Rubbing the clitoris' is *necessary but not sufficient*

Back to Daniel O'Beeve's story: For his next sex-love relationship, Daniel at least knew *what* he was "looking for". When he found it (her clitoris), he learned, from his partner, that it has to be handled *gently*, because it is *super-sensitive*. (Some men seem to want to 'erase the clitoris', which is painful and not pleasurable!) So he *studied*, with her guidance – and she actually guided his finger, to show him how it "worked" - and he quickly learned how to give her very enjoyable orgasms. *("Keep your finger straight; do not touch the underside of my clitoris; move up and down; slowly at first; rising to a crescendo!")* It took time for her to reach her orgasm, perhaps ten or fifteen minutes (from start of foreplay to end of orgasm) each time; but she got there in the end, each time.

Unfortunately, that was not enough, because he did not know how to *actively* love her; to show her *care* and *respect*; and to take *responsibility* for his side of the relationship. He took life very seriously – grimly, depressively - especially politics, and he did not have any sense of humour.

So he lost her anyway! She got involved with a man who did know how to love her, actively; to bring sunshine into her life, with music and laughter! And she left Daniel!

Years later, looking back on this episode of his life, Daniel realized that, at that time, he actually knew very little about *how to love a woman*, even though he knew how to bring her to orgasm; but he did not know what to do about that.

And some years after that, he came to understand that, the reason he did not know how to love Ramira was that *he had come from a family in which his father and mother did **not** love him*; and did not know how to love each other!

They had no sense of humour, in the main, especially his father (on whom he, non-consciously, modelled himself).

(See Byrne, 2017a, *Metal Dog*; a semi-autobiographical story of Daniel's early years)[116].

G3 Learning how to love

Next, the story of Juliet, who met Daniel in Bangladesh. They formed a quick and close friendship, and, at one point, she declared to their friends and associates that she was going to "teach Daniel how to love!" Daniel had no idea what that meant, because he had no idea what 'love' could be about!

Soon afterwards, they became lovers.

Daniel enjoyed intercourse with Juliet, and gave her regular orgasms by digitally stimulating her clitoris (with his ring-finger, held absolutely straight, so it could not hook under her clitoris and cause her pain!) This was completely new for her. She knew how to love, it seems, but she had never been treated to a clitoral orgasm by any of her previous lovers!

She later told Daniel that she took this experience – of his approach to physical lovemaking - back into her marriage, and tried to persuade her husband, Bart, to stimulate her clitoris. But Bart *could not be bothered!* He just wanted to engage in quick bouts of intercourse, which was all about his pleasure. *(Wham, bam! Thank you, Ma'am!)*

Not surprisingly, Julia left Bart within a couple of years of that time; but not to be with Daniel, who had been posted back to the UK.

What does this tell us?

1. Some women have husbands or partners who don't *know* how to pleasure them; to give bring them to orgasm.

2. Some men do *know* – or are *informed by their partner* - how to do this; but they can't be bothered to do it; because, for them, sex is about self-indulgence, and not about mutual satisfaction.

3. Some women have husbands or partners who do know how to bring them to orgasm; but who do not know how to tenderly and gently love them; to show care, respect and responsibility; and to create fun and laughter in their lives.

4. The law of karma dictates that those selfish men, described in point 2 above, end up being rejected by their partners. (Part of the reason for this is that the woman's *dissatisfaction* makes it impossible for her to *fantasise* about her unloving husband or partner; and *fantasy* is a huge part of what arouses the woman to the point of wanting to engage in sexual intercourse).

~~~

The two stories above, taken together, help us to understand that:

1. Knowing *how to love* another person does not guarantee that we will understand how to give them sexual pleasure, right up to earth-shaking

orgasm.

2. Knowing how to bring another person to earth-shaking orgasm does not guarantee that we will know how to actively love them, such that they feel cared for, respected, and enlivened by our intimate verbal and non-sexual contact. And:

3. To be a good marital partner we need to know how to do *both* – to be a good *sex partner*, and a good *love partner*! One of those, on its own, no matter how good, is *not enough!*

G4 Postscript

The clitoris is very important, if we are to be able to achieve equality in sexual relationships between men and women.

There are few if any serious barriers to men achieving orgasm in the form of sex which is most commonly practiced in our modern British, European and American cultures: penetration of the vagina by the penis. But for women who are involved in relationships with men who do not know the importance of the clitoris, as the seat of female sexual excitement and release (for most if not all women), there is a very serious problem indeed. And that problem is that it can be an uphill struggle to get men to take the clitoris seriously.

Even Alex Comfort (the author of *The Joy of Sex*), in 1970, failed to take the clitoris seriously enough. As Susan Quilliam said, when interviewed by Sarah Lyall: "He mentions the clitoris, he honours the clitoris, he says it's important. ... That was a lot more than most people did in those days. But he only mentions it *in passing a few times* and has no specific section on it. ... Not because he was anti-clitoris, but because he just didn't know". (Lyall, 2008).

~~~

Let's look at some statistics regarding the female orgasm, from a comprehensive review by David Spiegelhalter (2015):

"...in the 1970s (Ms) Shere Hite, like Kinsey, focused on orgasm as the defining aspect of sexual expression and fulfilment. She had no gradual lead in: her second question was 'Do you have orgasms? If not, what do you think would contribute to your having them?' Her much-quoted (1*) statistic is that 30% (of women) have orgasms through penetrative sex alone, which means that 70% don't. ..." (Pages 228-229).

If that statistic was irrefutably accurate, then more than two-thirds of men should expect that their female partner would *never* climax during sexual intercourse, and would *always* need digital or lingual stimulation to achieve an orgasm. However, Spiegelhalter (2015) – with the simple code, (1*), is telling his readers that Shere Hite's statistics are "numbers that are unreliable". (Page 8).

The quotation above, from Spiegelhalter, continues like this: "But in the 1992 US NHSLS, 29% of women reported that they always had an orgasm during sex, 41% usually, 21% sometimes, 8% rarely or never". (Page 229).

The source given for this US NHSLS study is this: Michael et al., (1994)[117].

If you look up Michael et al (1994) on Amazon, you find this description of the study: "Based on interviews with 3,432 adults, a group of social scientists offers a detailed, accurate report on Americans' sexual habits, including how frequently they have sexual intercourse, what they do in bed, and how many people are homosexual".

However, this sample is *far too small* to generalize to the whole American population. The Law of Large Numbers demands that any study should take the square root of the target population, and add 1; which for the US would be a minimum of 15,492 – so this study is too small by a factor of almost 5:1. This makes it surprising that David Spiegelhalter did not notice this fact, which would have led him to classify this study also as (1*). However, as argued by Daniel Kahneman (2012), even professors of statistics misinform their graduate students regarding which statistical tests are most suitable for their research studies. Statistics are often abused and misunderstood!

My own view, trying to be as cautious as possible, and to stand on the most solid ground possible, is to go along with Spiegelhalter's argument that Shere Hite's research results are not representative – Pages 9 and 10, Spiegelhalter (2015) – but to accept his judgement that Hite was right (and reasonable) in her claim that *"...many women* did not find their men communicative and loving, and thought they were too focused on the mechanics of sex". And while Spiegelhalter sees Hite's statistics as inaccurate, he reckons her "messages seem plausible".

~~~

Let us now take a look at a book which takes Michael et al., (1994) fully into account, and still makes a strong case for attending to the clitoris!

According to Kerner (2011):

> It takes much longer for a female to reach orgasm, because the female orgasm is more complicated than the male. He cites Michael et al., (1994) as saying that "men reach orgasm during intercourse far more consistently than do women, and that three fourths of mean, but less than a third of women, always have orgasms. Less than a third! That means more than two out of three women on average are consistently denied their climax – good reason to start hiding the cutlery". (Page 18 of Kerner, 2011).

Kerner comes up with a 'magic number' for the minutes of foreplay required to get a woman to boiling point: 21 minutes or more. This leads him to ask this question of men: "...is twenty minutes of focused attention, applied appropriately, really too much to ask, especially if it can save your sex life?" (Page 19).

Kerner (2011) recommends that men postpone their own pleasure, until the woman has climaxed. (This principle is called 'Ladies before Gents'!) This requires patience and skill on the man's part. But imagine how grateful your partner will be when you show this much love through attention to her sexual needs!

If you want to get some training in how to manipulate the clitoris and vagina of your partner with your fingers, then the appendices at the end of Kerner (2011) could help; or try Reiss (2017), which is an online blog.

There is also a 1.5 minute video introduction to the female genitals, including the clitoris and its hood, on a blog by Matt Bean (2009).

You might also benefit from reading *The Joy of Sex*, the latest (2011) edition. And, remembering the need for twenty minutes of warming up, you might want to take a look at the illustrated guide to foreplay by Richard Craze (1999).

And, if cunnilingus (or tongue to vagina stimulation) appeals to you, then Kerner's (2011) book could be a suitable education in how to do it.

The people who know about the clitoris are the women. So, if you are a man, and you have a female sexual partner, you should *ask her* about her clitoris; where it is; how *she* manipulates it if she wants to masturbate; and how *you* could *massage it* for her, without *hurting* her, to show your *love* for her, and your *desire* to give her the kind of pleasure you can get from ejaculating in her vagina! (Fair's fair!)

But don't obsess about it. Foreplay involves the lips, neck, breasts, nipples, stomach, thighs, hips, labias (or vaginal lips), vaginal opening and clitoris.

The best time to stroke the clitoris is when it has been warmed up by more general foreplay, because by then there will already be some vaginal lubrication. *But ask her.*

Ask her.

Ask her.

Consult her.

Let her influence you.

Ask how well you are doing. What it feels like. What might be better?

Never stop consulting!

And always remember:

Good sex depends upon good communication, and good relations out of bed, and a sense of equality, and of loving and being loved.

No part of sex can be separated for long from a feeling of loving and being loved.

~~~

Appendix H: Daniel's piecemeal sex education

H1 Introduction

Writing about human sexuality, as an *academic subject*, might seem achievable to a British academic, but writing for couples about sexuality – as in the case of my writing in this book - seems a stretch too far, for a practicing counsellor! Perhaps especially for a *British* counsellor!

I (Jim Byrne) would not feel comfortable conducting a public sex education class, through text, or face to face; so I decided - since the readers of this book do deserve some coaching in good and bad approaches to sex in their sex-love relationships - that I would sub-contract the task to Daniel O'Beeve.

What follows is a statement written by Daniel – and sent to me in the form of a letter - to suit the audience of this first volume.

H2 Irish, British and American social views of sex, by Daniel O'Beeve

I (Daniel) was born into a culture which denied the existence of sex, and was quite neurotic about sex. This was the culture of Catholic Ireland, post-1945. But this culture was perhaps not much different from the Victorian era in Britain, which has influenced the British people right up to the late 1950's, and, in some cases, beyond that point. In Ireland, when I was growing up, some people were most likely pious and ignorant, while others were hypocritical in pretending to go along with the suppression of sex, while covertly exploiting others. (This was especially true of some priests and some Christian brothers).

In the UK at that time, according to Julian Barnes (2018: page 17), the sex education of young people in the early 1960's was "...a mixture of sentimentality, pornography and misrepresentation"[118]. Both societies experienced inadequate sex education of one kind or another.

Even though Barnes (2018) describes his character, Paul, as having an affair with a woman in her forties, (when he was just nineteen?), she is prudish, and is in no position to teach him 'the arts of love'. (Page 29). And he did not understand the female orgasm, and assumed that "...if you manage to keep going long enough, (with sexual intercourse) it will at some point be automatically triggered in the woman". (Page 30).

The main message that I want to communicate in this letter is that this view is totally wrong; delusional; and the root of much relationship misery, mainly for women, but also, in the longer run, for the men.

When Barnes' character, Paul, gets into later life – perhaps in his seventies – he looks back at his youthful relationship with the older Susan (who later became an alcoholic and was committed to a mental hospital when Paul was about forty years old) – and he wonders about their sex life:

"He remembered when she had told him, just like that, how many times they had made love. A hundred and fifty-three, or some such number. Back then, it had thrown him into all sorts of pondering. Should he have been counting too? Was it a lapse in love that he wasn't, or hadn't? And so on. Now" – when he was in his seventies, and Susan was long gone out of his daily life – "he thought: a hundred and fifty-three, the number of times he had *come* up to that point. But what about her? How many orgasms had she had? Indeed, did she ever have one? There was pleasure and intimacy, surely; but orgasm? At the time he couldn't tell, nor did he ask; nor know how to ask. To put it more truthfully, he had never thought of asking. And now it was too late". (Page 200).

Some of the best social psychology I have found has been in the pages of really good quality literature, and Barnes is up there with the stars. He has surfaced a hugely important question.

My way of expressing, or repackaging his questions, would be as follows: "Do you (male readers) know *whether or not* your female partner has an orgasm; or has ever had an orgasm? And do you *care enough* to find out? And do you care enough *to learn how to make sure* you know what she needs you to do to ensure that she *will* have an orgasm?"

Don't leave it (as Paul did) until it's too late!

~~~

The situation of ignorance about sex was no better in the USA, as described by Bernard Zilbergeld (1995) – originally published in 1978:

Zilbergeld begins by writing about the sources of information that a young boy will use when learning a professional role, like a doctor.

Some of the information is reliable, and some unreliable.

> "Learning about sex is similar in many ways but also much more difficult. We all want to learn about sex since it seems like such an important part of being masculine and adult, but, because of all the double messages we get from our parents and other sources, it is a subject loaded with anxiety. Such anxiety is not conducive to clear thinking, viewing things in perspective, or calmly assessing how what we hear or read fits with our own values and experience. And sex is one of the few areas of life where it is almost impossible to observe accurately how others are doing it.

> "It is of course possible to obtain sexual information – we are deluged with it – but much of this information is absurdly exaggerated and inaccurate and the growing boy has no way of knowing this". (Pages 23-24)[119].

Earlier Zilbergeld (1995) had written about the great disservice that American literature of a particular type has done in creating false images of what it means to be a 'successful, sexual male'!

(Remember the fantasy of 'The Big Steel Cock!')

Anyway, I agree with Eric Berne (1973/1981), where he writes that sex education is like any other area of education, such as geography or history; in the sense that it cannot be packaged into a single conversation[120] – but takes a whole lifetime to master; and many people never master geography or history. And perhaps it is also true that most people never master sexuality!

H3a My own personal experience

The earliest reference to 'sex' that I (Daniel) can recall is this: Whist being washed in a zinc bath, at the age of two or three years, being told by my mother not to touch my 'teapot'. And noticing that my older sister, who was less than five years old, did not seem to have a 'teapot'.

I did not realize what a handicap my mother was setting up for me [and my sister], with this coy, shame-loaded injunction. (And, of course, I could not see my sister's little 'action button' [clitoris]; which was never mentioned!) And, of course, I never learned that my mother had a clitoris – and I am assuming today, when I am in my early seventies, that my father also had never heard mention of the idea that his wife had a clitoris!.

And, horror of horrors, in some parts of the world today, men (and their female supporters), try to eliminate the clitoris from the real world through a barbaric, painful, damaging form of surgery: Female Genital Mutilation (FGM).

Why is it *wrong* for a young child to touch their genitals? Surely there must be gentle ways of educating children to understand that their genitals have *no socially permitted use until marriage has been completed* (if that is the rule in the society under review- or until they reach the age of eighteen years – or whatever)?

Surely, it should be possible for a society to teach young children that their genitals have a wonderful, creative, and enjoyable function, within the socially prescribed sphere of marriage (or cohabiting, as is the case in modern Britain and other modern, urban cultures)?

In his book, *The Way of Zen*, Alan Watts wrote that it was a total mystery to him as to why Christianity did not make sex-love a sacrament![121] But Christians in general, and Catholics in particular, made sex a sin! A sin by nature! Even *thinking about sex* was said to be a sin.

My first formal sex education class was also my last. It was given by Brother Herbert, when I was about twelve years old, in a Christian brother's school, in Dublin[122]. And it was basically a calumniation of womanhood – a vile distortion of the nature of femininity, delivered by a sex-guilty pederast who should never have had anything to do with the education of children! Fortunately this slur on female sexuality failed to affect me negatively – in the way intended – because I had accidentally collected some empirical data which contradicted his 'teaching'. I knew that female genitals smelled wonderful! (See 'Metal Dog – Long Road Home'; in which Jim Byrne (2017a) tells my story as I told it to him).

About one year later, I overheard my mother – who was alienated from my father – describing to my older sister the details of her first sexual encounter with my father. The point of the story was to highlight my father's ignorance, insensitivity, and lack of competence. It was a serious wound to my growing masculinity. I felt ashamed of being male; of being my father's son!

I do not recall any further 'sex-education' until I was about sixteen years old, and in a bar with some fellow members of the Dublin Judo Club. Those fellows were passing around a little booklet and chuckling. Eventually it fell into my hands, and I was shocked to see a series of images of a milkman being invited into a female customer's home, resulting in what was, for me, a strangely exciting coupling on a sofa; only to be followed by the arrival of the milkman's horse, which wanted to get in on the act. My Catholic conditioning pulled the shutters down on that pornographic image, and I passed the booklet back to the person who had handed it to me. (I was confused! I had no prior 'education' into which to fit this image! [Thank 'God'!])

Then I struck lucky: When I was eighteen years of age, and living in a new urban area, in England, I met a man of about my own age, from Galway. Despite being from Galway, which I (having grown up in Dublin City) might have thought would be a kind of 'backwater' – this man (Dolan) told me he had read *The Encyclopaedia of Sex* – (possibly an early edition of Westheimer, 2000). This seemed very surprising. It did not seem necessary to have *a whole encyclopaedia* for the subject of sex, given that it only comprised the following elements: a 'teapot'; the absence of 'a teapot'; female genitals which smell exciting; an incompetent male introducing his penis, briefly, into his wife's vagina; a milkman; a housewife and a horse! (Oh, yes: also kissing, dancing closely; breasts; and 'wet dreams'!)

H3b My learning from an accidental meeting

So what did I learn from *the learned Dolan?*

Firstly, it takes a lot longer for a woman to become sexually excited than it does for a man. And because of this, the man has to be patient, and skilful.

Secondly, there are essentially two positive ways, and two negative ways, for a man to stroke the body of a woman: The two positive ways are these:

(1a) *Dragging* (but never *pushing*) the balls of the fingers, slowly and lightly; or

(1b) Curling the fingers into a loose fist, and *pushing* (but never *dragging*) the flat nails slowly and gently along the woman's skin.

The two negative ways are the opposites of those approaches:

(2a) pushing the balls of the fingers along the skin; or

(2b) dragging the fingernails abrasively along the skin. (These *negative approaches* are likely to get you kicked out of the bed!)

Thirdly, the procedures described in (1a) and (1b) above result in sexual excitement, when administered with *the approval* of the woman, when she is *actively and obviously* in the mood for love!

Fourth, penetration of the vagina by the penis is a hit and miss affair, as far as many, if not most women are concerned. This is not a reliable way of causing her to experience sexual excitement. Instead, at the top of the vagina, near the pubic bone, is a small organ, called the clitoris, which is the seat of sexual excitement and orgasm. (When a woman feels sexual excitement inside the vagina, there is a strong case for seeing this as stimulation of the clitoris from the inside, or underside). See Appendix G, on the importance of the clitoris.

Fifth. At this point, Dolan showed me a full colour picture of an open vagina: that is to say with the labia separated, so the urethra and vaginal opening were visible. For some reason that I did not understand then, and do not understand now, my mind closed down; and that was the end of the 'tutorial'.

H4 First love, and first sexual experience

Fast forward to the later 1960's in Blackpool, when I was twenty-three years old, and involved in a short-lived sexual relationship with a twenty-eight year old woman[123]. This relationship lasted about eight or ten weeks (roughly) and ended with her being unfaithful to me; and my leaving and moving to Bristol.

On the way out of Blackpool, while waiting on the platform for my train, I found a book on sale at a kiosk. It was entitled, *The Myth of the Vaginal Orgasm* – Koedt (1968/1970); and it reminded me of my conversation with Dolan.

I bought the book, and read it on the train. Now I knew why my relationship with Belinda had failed; and why she was unfaithful to me. I had been indulging my appetite for stimulation of my penis, and ignoring her need for stimulation of her clitoris! (Simple!)

So I learned that lesson the hard way, but I have never forgotten it since! Women do not get the same kind of intensity of enjoyment from sexual intercourse that men do - (although the underside of their clitoral complex, which is inside the vaginal opening, [mistakenly called 'The G Spot'], can receive some limited degree of stimulation, through the upper wall of the inside of the vagina, some but not all of the time, during intercourse. But this is not enough, under normal circumstances, [and certainly not routinely!], to bring her to orgasm – hence the need for digital or lingual stimulation of the clitoris).

The safest assumption for a man to make is this:

"My female partner will need clitoral stimulation; of a type to be defined and described by her; and administered by me (with a straight finger, or my tongue), with her guidance and support".

H5 Second love and more setbacks

My next lesson was even harder. I met Ramira in London; lived with her; gave her good, digitally induced, clitoral orgasms; married her; and moved to Oxford with her; where she got involved with another man, because he was fun, and he knew how to *actively love her*; whereas I was relatively cold and incapable of loving anybody (at that time). That was the contradiction. I looked relatively attractive to women; nice/ presentable/ handsome. I could deliver good orgasms. *But I did **not** know how to love.*

That's what had been missing from Dolan's summation of the *Encyclopaedia of Sex*. Humans do not normally *separate* sex from love, and when they do, it does not fare well for them! Humans function best when they learn how to integrate sex with love. (See *Metal Dog – Long Road*

Home; by my colleague, Dr Jim Byrne, 2017a).

And that was my next lesson.

H6 Learning how to love

In Bangladesh, when I was thirty years old, I met Juliet; and she and I clicked, like two pieces of a jigsaw puzzle. We enjoyed talking to each other; drinking tea; and making love. We were instant friends. And she told some of our acquaintances that she was going to teach me 'how to love'. I had no idea what that meant – given my family background. But she did somehow unfreeze my heart, and I learned to integrate feelings of *sexual passion* with *affection* and *longing* and *attachment*; somehow.

So I now had love and sex integrated (to some degree)! But this time the lesson to be learned was different. This time the lesson was that *there is no good way to be involved in somebody else's marriage*. Juliet was married to Bart, and Bart was pained by her infidelity with me!

Eventually, I realized the nature of the lesson, and left, broken hearted, and returned to Oxford. (*Metal Dog – Long Road Home*; by my colleague, Dr Jim Byrne, 2017a)

H7 Finding my soul-mate, at last

But I could not stay in Oxford, and moved north, where I met Tee, who became my life partner; and who opened me up to all kinds of psychological and spiritual experiences, and a whole new level of love – in the broadest and deepest sense - plus friendship; and fun! By working our way through couples therapy together; and also pursuing various forms of personal development (including Zen meditation; Gestalt therapy; Transactional Analysis; Erhard Seminar Training (est); Positive Mental Attitude (PMA), etc.; we eventually leaned to 'stand in love', instead of 'falling in love'.

Tee learned to be more assertive, and less in Adapted Child ego state; and I learned to be less pushy, more Adult, and less in Controlling/Critical

Parent ego state. (See Appendix B).

We learned to have an adult, mature, mutual relationship of intimacy; in which we both felt securely attached to each other. (She had been more secure than me from the start, and my avoidant attachment style was healed by her constancy and ability to remain calm when I became avoidant! [See Chapter 6, sections 6.10 – 6.12(b)])

We learned to regulate each other's central nervous systems for health and happiness!

At that point, my 'sex education' was complete – or rather, *my sex-love apprenticeship was over*, and I entered into the era of being a loving *journeyman*!

H8(a) The problem of sexual coercion and rape

This is a horrible subject for a man to have to write about; but it is essential information for any younger men reading this book; and for some women to see the situation from a particular perspective.

My first insight into the problem of sexual coercion occurred when I was about fifteen years old, and I got home one day to find there was a family crisis. My older sister, Caitlin, who was approaching sixteen years of age, had gone for a walk in the Phoenix Park with a boyfriend, and he had tried to force her to have sex with him. She ran away, and was rescued and brought home by another, gentler kind of young man.

When I was leaving home at the age of eighteen years, my mother told me how her boss's son had forced her to have sex with him, when he drove her home from work one evening. She told the story in such a muddled way, that I had difficulty understanding what had happened; but years later she explained that it had been rape.

So, some men do force themselves on women, in what is obviously *illegal* rape; coercion by the man, and lack of consent by the woman.

According to Germaine Greer (2018): "...a certain very dangerous kind of man uses his sexuality as a weapon to degrade and destroy women. The vast majority of men have no desire to do that, but that doesn't mean they are truly concerned by whether or not their female partners welcome their attention".

Greer goes on to object to 'perfunctory sex' – which is not about love-making, but rather about the man assuming the right to have indifferent sex with his partner when the mood seizes him, regardless of her wishes. This is a form of rape, which, by indicating *indifference* and *neglect*, and *absence of love*, is perhaps often **more destructive** of the woman's self-esteem than a straight-out vicious rape might be.

This is a horrible indictment of certain forms of 'modern masculinity', of a kind which still insists, in the twenty-first century, that every wife "...has a duty to satisfy her husband, whether she like(s) it or not"! (Greer, 2018).

No such duty exists, and to assume such a duty is to engage in banal rape!

I am so very glad that, somewhere in my thirties, I stumbled across a copy of *The Kama Sutra* (Burton, 1883/1991). I do not recall the year. I do not recall what was on the cover. I do not recall very much at all of the overall shape or content of the book, apart from these details.

1. It was not primarily about sex, even though there are a lot of images of sexual positions.

2. It seemed to be primarily about love, and the manners of love, including a lot of love poems.

3. But the most important point for me was right at the beginning. Sir Richard Burton, who published the work (which was translated in his name by three other individuals), writes about *a chivalry tradition* which arose in ancient India, perhaps two thousand years before Christ. This movement arose in the context of conventional marriage arrangements, whereby young girls were married off to older boys, and 'delivered to them' before they had reached sexual maturity. Some of those young men decided that they would not indulge the common practice of forcing themselves upon their child-brides. Instead, they would say to their bride:

"These are our sleeping quarters. But I want you to take the bed. I will sleep on this mat on the other side of the room. I will never visit you in your bed. But if you ever decide that you wish to visit me on this mat, then I would be delighted to greet you there!"

Needless to say, these sensitive, caring, loving and patient young men were eventually rewarded by totally voluntary visits to the mat by their young bride, and between them they explored perhaps the widest range of sexual positions, and forms of sexual love, ever recorded by any society on Earth.

This chivalry movement impressed me so much, that I 'joined it'. I practice this approach to sex, whereby sex is initiated and consented to by the female. That does not mean that the male cannot touch her, or kiss her, in passing; in ways that she finds congenial and enjoyable. But the final decision regarding when to make love, or how to make love, is left to the female 'regulatory clock'. And it is always 'making love' – and never about the male 'getting his rocks off'!

The *animal side* of human nature gives us our sex urges; but the *cultural side* of humanity gives us *the agreed on forms of sex-love encounter* – making love! And the agreed on forms of lovemaking do not include the male forcing himself on the female.

Men who go out drinking alcohol in the evening should be particularly careful when they get home. Alcohol has the tendency to knock out your conscience (your **Good Controlling Parent** ego state). Be very careful not to engage in non-consensual sex with your partner. Make a commitment to keep love-making to a time when you are both totally sober. To a time and place which has been agreed in advance by you and your partner. Remember those morally-mind Indian youths who put macho males in the West to shame!

H8(b) Final notes of guidance: Key learning points

1(a). Do not try to separate sex from love. And, as Richard Templar (2016: page 112-113) suggests: "Make sure your lovemaking is making love".

1(b). Although making love will relieve your sense of sexual frustration, aim to use that as a fuel to provide the energy *to express your love* for your partner.

1(c). Always make love at a time and place which is agreeable to both of you. Do not subject your partner to any kind of pressure, physical or emotional, to do anything that that they would not choose to do, and/or that they would prefer not to do.

1(d). If you are a male, making love to your female partner: make sure you understand the importance of foreplay. Start at the lips, move to the neck and breasts; nipples, stomach, hips, then – eventually – her vagina, labias, and the clitoris, when your partner is warmed up and moist.

1(e)(i). If, when you have progressed to her genitals, she goes 'off the boil': pause; accept the frustration or set-back; and go back to the lips and neck, and start all over again, pleasuring her; warming her up. (It could take twenty minutes or more to complete the lovemaking process; so be patient, loving and kind).

1(e)(ii). Follow this principle: The lady *comes* first! If you rush to orgasm, she will be left behind, and it is very hard for you to continue with foreplay when you have already climaxed! So, *Ladies before Gents*. (Here is one general exception to this rule: If following the 'Ladies Before Gents' rule leads to you [the male partner] missing out on your orgasm completely, then fairness and equality dictates that you should move to an alternating system: *Whoever came first last time, comes second this time!* [Fairness is important!])

1(f). The size of your penis is less important than what you do with it; and what you do with your fingers, lips; and, if it is to your taste, your tongue. You can take care of your female partner's sexual needs with a combination of foreplay, clitoral stimulation, and penetration – regardless of size or firmness of your penis.

1(g). If you are prone to premature ejaculation, *think cool thoughts* to calm down your sexual excitement; and try to keep your penis out of contact with your partner while you are engaging in foreplay. If that does not solve the problem, see a sex therapist for advice and guidance.

1(h). If you (the male partner) find it hard to generate enough friction to reach orgasm yourself, after helping your partner to reach climax, then keep a towel in the bed, and dry your penis and the outer areas of her vagina to ensure there is not too much lubrication.

2. If you come from a family in which your mother and father did not know how to love each other, go into therapy, and work on your 'Inner Couple' programming (which is your inner template for your own adult relationship. [See Chapter 11]).

3. Make sure to work on your sex education! If necessary, consult a sex therapist. And/or read some of the books or blogs mentioned above.

4. Do not try to exploit your sexuality for *entertainment*. It is much more *significant* than that.

5. Seek out a partner who is also a very good friend - (Shackleton et al 2018) - who is on a journey towards learning and growing; and commit to an equal relationship.

6. Make sure you are compatible in the area of *agreed on goals* for the future of your relationship. (Shackleton et al, 2018)

7. Seek to become a mature, sex-love partner to a good friend. Make sure that you and your partner develop your senses of humour; and keep your expectations in line with reality!

8. Make sure you talk to your partner; find out how they feel; what they think; and clear up problems as they arise. Strive to maintain a 5:1 ratio of positive to negative moments in your relationship.

9. Find out what your partner enjoys: in and out of bed. What kind of social life do they want? What kind of home life? How often do they like to make love? How would they like to make love? Do they enjoy the way you touch them? Is there anything they want you to change about the way you approach them; touch them; stimulate them; etcetera?

10. Make sure you continue to 'date' your partner after you get married or settle down. Go out for enjoyable, relaxing times together, and remember to laugh and have fun.

11. If (and when) you run into problems in your relationship, use them as learning opportunities. Seek answers in books. And use good counsellors, coaches and psychotherapists, to help you to find answers to your developmental challenges.

12. Do not expect your sex education to be complete before you are in the middle to later years of your life, or even later!

~~~

Daniel O'Beeve, Paris, France, July 2018

~~~

Appendix J: Brief introduction to One-Conditional Self-Acceptance

By Jim Byrne, November 2018

This is a brief extract from my book which critiques Rational Emotive Behaviour Therapy: See Byrne (2017b)[124]. The purpose of this appendix is to teach the importance of moral emotions, among couples as much as elsewhere.

J1 The need for *appropriate guilt* as a moral emotion

It is my contention that appropriate guilt and shame are important 'moral emotions'. Without guilt and shame, we could do whatever harm we wished to others, with a clear conscience. Therefore, I reject completely the idea of unconditional self-acceptance; and I advocate instead a form of 'radical acceptance' of our inefficiencies and poor general judgements; while insisting that we must take responsibility for not harming others – which means we must take responsibility for being moral beings. We cannot accept ourselves *unconditionally*; but we can accept ourselves 'radically', regardless of our *inefficiencies* and *ineffectiveness*, so long as we conform to one condition – that one condition is that we must act as moral beings, as dictated by the Golden Rule.

In Chapter 11 of Byrne (2017b), I explored the concept of *unconditional self-acceptance* (USA), developed by Dr Albert Ellis (1962, 1994). In order to understand the background to the development of this idea, I investigated the concept of *unconditional positive regard* (UPR), which had previously been developed by Dr Carl Rogers.

I then related the idea of unconditional self-acceptance (USA) to some of the most important concepts in moral philosophy, including the ideas of *praise* and *blame*.

Then I related all of these ideas to the newly emerging field of study of 'moral emotions', and showed that Albert Ellis was (at least theoretically, notionally) in the 'ethical rationalist' tradition created by Jean Piaget (1952, 1954), which holds that moral judgements are driven by *linguistic reasoning*, rather than by emotional intuitions (as argued by Haidt, 2001, 2003, 2006).

I say that Ellis was 'theoretically' an ethical rationalist because, in practice, he was not actually a moralist of any description, being mainly a *pragmatic promoter of prudence* rather than *moral codes* and *rules*. (Wiener, 1988: pages xi-xii). He expressly forbade all forms of the moral imperatives: *should, must, have to, got to, need to, ought*. And he insisted that nobody should ever be *blamed* for anything. Furthermore, he insisted that life does not have to be *fair*! For these reasons, he cannot be said to have any kind of *discernible* moral philosophy.

In examining the views of Carl Rogers and Barry Stevens (1967/1998), I came to the following conclusions: <u>Unconditional</u> positive regard, for ourselves and/or others, does not make good sense. We need to relate to people on the basis of *how they <u>behave</u>*. We would **not** unconditionally accept having a son or daughter who behaved viciously, or maliciously, with others. We would see it as our *duty* to change that aspect of their functioning, and we would not be very happy with them while we were working for that change.

Professor Jonathan Haidt (2006) argues that we seem to have an innate neurological predisposition to respond with *gratitude* to people who treat us fairly; and to respond with *vengeance* towards those who treat us unfairly. Clearly we would be vulnerable to exploitation and abuse to the extent that we responded to unfairness with *unconditional regard* for the perpetrator.

This is a very important point. Just because Carl Rogers can find – at an advanced stage in his life – a sense of 'inner guide' that he can trust to be good and wholesome – and just because Barry Stevens can find in her mind an *enlightened* state in which there is only 'one being', and that that being is Barry, and you, and me, and everybody else, all connected up together – *it does not <u>follow</u>* that we should *promulgate* this (*inner* directedness – without considering outside [social] influences) as a <u>universal</u> *philosophy of life* to be followed by everybody.

Why not?

Because many people will pull those elevated insights down to the level of the gutter, and use them to justify all kinds of nefarious actions. I have demonstrated this principle using the experience of Hindu enlightenment insights and India's problems with moral corruption.

Furthermore, Rogers is here *discounting* the impact which his early socialization - (with Christian parents, and attendance at a Christian seminary for part of his undergraduate study!) - must have had in producing his 'inner (moral) guide' - and he was certainly wrong to imply that this inner guide is invincible. (Indeed, he has been accused of at least one seriously unethical action in his life: See Cohen, 1997: page 206)[125].

I reject the idea that we are all *innately enlightened*, or that we could use our *personal* enlightenment to *escape from* social morality. We (as a society) need to teach people at the level at which they currently exist, which is mainly the level of the pavement, not the level of the clouds. That is why, in Buddhism, the individual is trained to be a moral person; a moral person; a moral person. Over, and over, and over again.

Alongside this process, the individual is encouraged to meditate; to meditate; to meditate. Over, and over, and over again. Through those two processes, a solid, *admirable kind of social being is shaped*: a *moral* being.

The meditation process might eventually bring about a sense of *personal liberation*, but not a sense that, since we are all one, *I can take your stuff*. Neither could it result in the view that, since there is only *one* being, I can kill you, and no harm will have been done. (Of course, some elements of Buddhism are just as extreme as extreme Stoicism!)

Some Buddhist philosophy may also be taught and studied (in *moderate* Buddhist circles), but not of a kind that will cause the individual to discount the value of other peoples' lives; nor their right to be respected, honoured, and left to get on with their own journeys.

Ethical functioning must always *take precedence* over enlightenment.

Furthermore, to use 'enlightenment' as an excuse for immoral behaviour has to be one of the lowest forms of *self-serving rationalization*.

J2 Defining 'unconditional self-acceptance'

I then looked at Albert Ellis's principle of 'Unconditional Acceptance' of self and others. Unfortunately for Albert Ellis, there are two aspects of the definition of the word "accept" which could be relevant to his argument. The first is: "...(to) regard favourably". And the second is: "... (to) put up with".

I have ruled out the second of these definitions, on the grounds that Albert Ellis was not simply asking us to 'put up with' ourselves and others. (Of course, I could be wrong about that; and perhaps Albert Ellis was saying we should "put up with the bad behaviour of others" and "accept the bad behaviour of our own creation").

If we go for the first of these definitions, then it would seem that "self-acceptance" and "self-regard" mean the same thing; so that Ellis was not moving as far from Rogers as he thought. (And again, it seems to be self-evidently unjustified [in moral terms] to 'regard favourably' somebody who is behaving unethically or immorally).

Ellis was interested in how to avoid his *identified problem* which was, in his view, that sometimes counselling clients were upset because they could not accept themselves when they'd behaved badly or inadequately.

More generally, he saw that problem as one of *rating yourself* highly when you succeed, or when you get love and respect from others; and then, on the other hand, *rating yourself* lowly when you fail in work, or fail to get love and respect from others.

This is a common problem, but as I showed earlier, Ellis's approach is not the only way to go about solving it. Ellis's solution was this: "Never rate your 'self' as a whole human being at all. Only rate your *acts* and *deeds*. And accept yourself *unconditionally*, whether or not you do well, and whether or not anybody loves you".

What is missing from Ellis's presentation is *a serious consideration of morality*. He omits to distinguish between "personal effectiveness issues" and "personal morality".

In E-CENT, we teach that *it is okay to let ourselves and other people off the hook when we or they behave ineffectively or inefficiently* in relation to our personal effectiveness issues, or practical goals and actions in the world. However, it is quite another matter to say, as Albert Ellis said: "Even if you *kill* a few people, that (action) will not make you *bad*". (But, of course, it will! It will make you a dangerous murderer; and a criminal!)

And Ellis explicitly said that *we should offer unconditional acceptance to Adolf Hitler*. Erwin (1997) argues against this position, using the illustration of how to evaluate Himmler (one of Hitler's right-hand men). Edward Erwin insisted that Himmler *should __not__ be told he can accept himself unconditionally.*

Instead, Erwin argues, "Even if it would make Himmler extremely happy and neurosis-free, he still should not have engaged in self-acceptance *if doing so encouraged him to continue as before* (in terms of his crimes – JB).

"There are *other things* to consider besides Himmler's happiness and freedom from neurosis." (Erwin, 1997: page 108). And those 'other things' include *moral* and *legal* issues, which are ignored by Ellis (and Rogers and Stevens).

J3 We reject __un__-conditional self-acceptance and unconditional positive regard, and substitute __one__-conditional acceptance

We do not accept Albert Ellis's (or Carl Rogers') amoral (and indeed, immoral) positions. On the contrary, if you kill just one person, that will make you __necessarily__ *persona non grata* with the rest of society, because you are a __threat__ to the peace and viability of society. It will make you __a law breaker__.

You will be arrested and deemed culpable (or blameworthy) – unless you can present extenuating circumstances – such as temporary insanity, or reasonable self-defence – which will *exculpate* you (or *nullify* your blameworthiness).

You will be treated – quite appropriately – as *a bad person,* (a person who does not act *morally!*) - unless and until you have paid your debt to society, and have shown *remorse* and *made amends.*

When Albert Ellis invented his system of unconditional self- and other-acceptance, (USA/UOA), he was obviously operating at the 'transcendental' level of the *Upanishads*: the Hindu texts which caused so much *moral confusion* in India. These amoral transcendental positions make no connection with practical, everyday reality. They are quite inhuman and immoral. And that is why in E-CENT counselling, *we only __accept__ our clients, and each other, on the basis of being __committed to moral action__ in the world.*

We call this '*one-conditional* acceptance' of self and others. As long as we are committed to behaving morally, and working hard at that commitment, then it does not matter if we fail in terms of our *practical effectiveness goals and targets* (such as being efficient or successful in material matters), or in our *general judgements* (such as backing the wrong business option and losing some money).

~~~

Appendix K: How to study this book in order to change your relationship behaviours and skills

By Dr Jim Byrne

Introduction

Although my doctoral degree is in counselling – and I have practiced counselling and psychotherapy for more than twenty years, including with lots of couples – my master's degree was in education, and I spent many years studying how people learn; and especially the frailty of human memory. So, I know in my bones that, if you read this book just once, you will forget 99% of what you have read here in just a few days!

If you want to change the way you function in your romantic relationship, then you need to follow the guidelines that I have produced below.

The importance of review

Tony Buzan (1973), in his book on how to learn, reviewed the Ebbinghause 'curve of forgetting', and demonstrated that the likelihood of being able to recall studied material is *proportional to the number of times the information is reviewed.*

There are three main ways of reviewing the material.

(a) You can read the whole text all over again, twice or three times; or even several times;

(b) You can take notes and review your notes over and over again, several times; or:

(b) You can convert your notes into 'mind maps', and review the mind maps over and over again many times. (Mind maps are described in Buzan, 1973; but they are essentially ways of producing diagrams from linear notes – like spider diagrams – but with key words and phrases only;

in different colours; with added images (like little sketches and symbols); to make the notes more memorable and more easily recalled when needed).

My recommendations

With regard to your studying of this book: if you want to become a better lover, a more successful relationship partner, then you have got to review the content of this book over and over again.

The simplest strategy is that taught by Dale Carnegie in his (1983) book on *'How to win friends and influence people'*; which was this:

You must begin with: "...a deep, driving desire to learn, a vigorous determination to increase your ability to deal with people". (Page 67). Or, in the current case, a deep and driving desire to learn how to be a better, more loving, more successful relationship partner.

The second requirement is this: "Read each chapter rapidly at first to get a bird's-eye view of it. You will probably be tempted then to rush on to the next one. But don't. Unless you are reading merely for entertainment. But if you are reading because want to increase your skill in human relations, then go back and *re-read each chapter thoroughly*. In the long run, this will mean saving time and getting results". (Page 67, Carnegie 1983).

As you read, mark anything that stands out for you, with a pen, or with a coloured highlighter.

"3. *Stop frequently in your reading to think over what you are reading*. Ask yourself just how and when you can apply each suggestion. That kind of reading will aid you far more than racing ahead like a whippet chasing a rabbit". (Page 67).

Write some notes about key points as you go along. (See the section on 'constructing your own index', below).

"4. *Read with a red crayon, pencil, or fountain pen, in your hand; and when you come across a suggestion that you feel you can use, draw a line beside it. If it is a* four-star suggestion, then underscore every sentence, or mark it with 'XXXX'. Marking and underscoring a book (will) make it more interesting and far easier to review rapidly".

Once you have marked key areas of the book, you can go back frequently and re-read the bits that you underlined or made a margin-mark against.

At the end of point 5, Dale Carnegie writes:

"...if you want to get real, lasting benefit out of this book, don't imagine that skimming through it once will suffice. After reading it thoroughly, you ought to spend a few hours reviewing it every month. Keep it on your desk in front of you every day. Glance through it often. Keep constantly impressing yourself with the rich possibilities for improvement that still lie in the offing. Remember that the use of these principles can be made habitual and unconscious only by a constant and rigorous campaign of review and application. *There is no other way*".

Construct your own personal Index of this book

If you want to maximize the benefit of this book to you, you must *'make it your own'!*

That involves not only following the guidelines above, but also constructing your own index of this book. I have been doing this for years with those books that matter the most to me. I use the blank pages (or backs of pages) in the front and back of important books that I am reading, to note two things:

1. *The page number* of a piece of information that I want to make sure I never lose. Anything I want to come back to again and again.

2. *A label* which will remind me of the basic content of the piece I want to be able to find again.

To make this process easier for you, I have created Appendix L, which is allocated space within which you can hopefully construct your own index.

~~~

If you read this book once you will quickly forget it.

If you read it once, and do not apply it, it will be as if you have never read it.

If you read it once or twice, and apply some of the content once or twice, you may make some little gains, but you will soon lose them again.

To keep it alive and functioning as a part of your relationship life, you have to read it over and over again, take notes, read the notes over and over again, and go back to the book whenever you spot that you have slipped back to some earlier habit you thought you had broken!

The more you apply the principles you learn from this book, the more you will change and grow as a lover and a good, successful relationship partner.

Also, the more you reflect (in writing) upon your relationship skills and experiences, the more you will grow in emotional intelligence and relationship skill.

Set up a diary to reflect upon your learning from this book.

Sit down at the end of each week and write out these questions:

1. Did I make any mistakes, or errors of judgement, in the way I related to my partner this week?

2. If so, what did I do wrong, or unskilfully?

3. What did I do in my relationship communication or behaviour (this week) that was particularly successful, and/or that went down well?

4. Could I have done even better?

5. Reflecting upon my answers to points 1-4 above, what lessons can I learn that I could apply in the week ahead?

This process of reflective learning will make you more and more skilful in your relationship behaviours, and more and more emotionally intelligent.

Summary

1. Make a strong commitment to master the principles taught in this book.

2. Read each chapter (and appendix) twice before moving on to the next chapter (or appendix).

3. Stop often and reflect upon what you are reading and what you are learning from that reading. Think about how you could apply particular insights or principles in your current relationship.

4. Mark the text, with margin notes, underlining, coloured highlights (and turn down page corners if that appeals to you, as a way of marking particularly important pages!); and also note page numbers, and concept labels, and write them into the spaces provided in your personalized index, in Appendix L.

5. Sit down at the end of each week, with your diary, and review your progress. What did you do well? What could have been done better? In what ways did you slip up or slip back? And what could you learn from the week that would help you and your relationship in the future?

6. Sit down at the end of each month, and review this book from beginning to end. Look at your personal index, and check particular entries to remind yourself of what you had noted, and why.

~~~

Appendix L: Construct your own index of this book

As explained in Appendix K, the purpose of Appendix L is to provide you with some space in which to construct your own index of the key ideas in this book which you want to be able to find again and again, to review them and apply them in your life.

Page No.	Content label

Appendix M: How to change your relationship habits

M1 Introduction

By Jim Byrne and Renata Taylor-Byrne

In Chapter 11, we set out to teach you how you were originally wired up by your family of origin to have a particular *model* for relationship. We call that model 'The Inner Couple'. And, in that chapter, also, we endeavoured to teach you how to reprogram yourself to have 'A Revised Inner Couple'. Your revised inner couple will guide you to enter into, and only stay in, happy and emotionally healthy relationships.

Quite clearly, Chapter 11 is about how to change your relationship habits by changing your Inner Couple. However, there may still be some areas of your functioning where you have developed bad habits that are not automatically changed by the Inner Couple work. And for that reason, and because habit-change is fundamentally important to personal change in every area of life, including in your relationships, we have included a general guide to habit-change in this appendix.

M2 Some extracts on habit change from our book on diet and exercise

In this section I will present some extracts from Part 6 of Taylor-Byrne and Byrne (2017) on how to change your habits. This text originally referred to how to change habits in the areas of diet and exercise, but these ideas can be used in any area of your life:

Our approach to behaviour change

We believe in *gradual* change!

We do not want to encourage you to *overload yourself* with self-change action lists! Or, to put it better: We do not want you to believe that you *have to change* **everything** on your self-change list *today, right now,* **immediately** and totally!

You cannot do it anyway. Because we are creatures of habit, if we try to change too much too quickly, the deeply emotional, habit-based part of us will panic, and rebel; and not allow it to happen. It's too scary.

So, therefore, change takes time.

Change take effort.

Change takes commitment.

And the best way to proceed is *slowly*, in *small* steps. And always plan change in ways that are *self-supporting*, and not self-undermining!

A personal example

To make this point well, I (Jim) would like to present an example from my own life:

About fifteen years ago, I found I had lost all my self-discipline in relation to daily physical exercise. I had gone from being a regular exerciser to a regular procrastinator! I could not bring myself to do any exercise whatsoever. So, for a long time I was stuck in this 'pre-contemplation' stage. I was not planning to change anything!

Then, as the weeks and months drifted past, I became more and more annoyed with myself, because I knew I was risking serious damage to my physical health and my emotional wellbeing. At this point I became a 'contemplator'. I was *contemplating*, or *thinking about*, change, but I could not quite bring myself to *do* anything about it. I kept 'planning' to change; or 'trying' to change; but I did not change!

Then one morning I felt so bad about my procrastination, that I became 'determined' to do something about it. This is, obviously, called the 'Determination Stage' of behaviour change. (Prochaska, Norcross and DiClemente, 1998)[126]. That was when I remembered the **Kaizen** method of 'gradual improvement'[127]. This system, introduced to Japan by some American teachers, including W. Edwards Deming, at the end of the Second World War, teaches a process of gradual refinement and progress, instead of huge jumps and big goals.

So I decided on the smallest goal I could come up with, which would be acceptable to me.

I felt I could run on the spot, right by my armchair, for thirty seconds, and then sit down. I stood up – (this is the Action step) - feeling hopeless, and I did it.

I ran on the spot to the count of thirty. That is to say, when my left foot hit the floor, I counted '1'. Then, when my right foot hit the floor, I counted 'And'. When my left foot fell again, I counted '2'. And so on, up to thirty foot falls; like gentle jogging, but on the same spot.

Then I sat down. *I felt great!*

I felt such a sense of *self-efficacy* – and *self-esteem* – that I was amazed. Such a small step forward, and such a big reward in terms of how good I felt about myself.

So, the next day, I decided to run on the spot for the count of sixty (foot lifts and falls). When I sat down, I felt even better.

The third morning, I could not stop when I reached 60, or 120, or 240. I was hooked.

I had persuaded the resistant, emotional, non-conscious part of myself that I would not die, or fall apart, if I did my physical exercises; so I went back to doing my old Judo club calisthenics, my Chi Kung, and my press-ups and sit-backs.

And this is the key point: *This is how we want you to tackle whatever personal-change goals you come up with, as a result of reading ... this book.*

We do not want you to demoralize yourself, by *aiming too high*, too soon, only to fail; and then to abandon all attempt at personal change.

We want you to be *realistic*, and we want you to give yourself the best chance of *succeeding* in making those changes you choose for yourself!

(You could apply this approach to setting up a system to review this book on couple relationships. See Appendix K, and include some gradual change goals based on that appendix).

~~~

A second example: Using rewards and penalties

The second story I want to tell you follows on from the first.

So, I did my exercises four or five mornings each week, for quite some time, but then I began to skip them, if I was 'too busy'; or if I was 'running late'.

So, I remembered another very important principle of behaviour change: rewards and penalties!

So I made this commitment to myself:

"Every morning that I do my exercises, I will give myself permission to read six pages of a novel that I like, as a reward. And if I fail to do my exercises, I will immediately take *two £1 coins* (which totals close to $3 US) from my bookcase shelf, and go out into the street, and drop them both down the nearest drain, so they become irretrievably lost!"

Needless to say, I did not skip any exercise sessions from that point onwards!

(You can use this system of rewards and penalties to the challenge of studying this book on couple relationships. Take a look at Appendix K, and ask yourself:

"What kinds of rewards and penalties could I have in place to keep me on track in studying this book using the suggestions in Appendix K?")

~~~

In Section 2 ... below, Renata Taylor-Byrne presents an even more powerful system of behaviour change, which you can use to make those changes you want to make to your relationships.

~~~

M3 - Section 2: How to change your negative habits

By Renata Taylor Byrne - Copyright © Renata Taylor-Byrne 2016-17/2018

~~~

The nature of habits

What are habits?

Here are two definitions from the Merriam-Webster dictionary:

(1) Habit is "... (a) *behaviour pattern acquired by frequent repetition or physiologic exposure that shows itself in regularity or increased facility of performance"* and/or:

(2) It's *"...An acquired mode of behaviour that has become nearly or completely involuntary."*

~~~

And here is the viewpoint of one of the fathers of American psychology:

"All our life, so far as it has definite form, is a mass of habits".

William James, 1892

~~~

We are habit-based creatures, and the more we know about how we form habits, the *easier* it will be for us to change old ones that aren't working for us, and to create new ones.

A researcher at Duke University in 2006 discovered that more than 40% of the activities people engaged in every day were habits, and not decisions they had made. And some theorists would say that our habit-based functioning is as high as 95% (Bargh and Chartrand, 1999)[128].

Throughout the animal world, habit-based behaviour is the norm. This has served animal survival well, which is why it is ubiquitous.

Humans have the greatest capacity of all animals to change our habits, but we will never become habit-less.

Our brains have developed the ability to create habits because they allow our brains to save effort, and to function more efficiently without having our minds cluttered with the mechanics of the many basic behaviours we have to follow each day.

The structure of a habit

In his book, *The Power of Habit,* Charles Duhigg[129] looked very closely at the specific features of what makes up a habit. In his view, a habit is like a loop that has three parts: the cue; the routine; and the reward. Here is a picture of that loop:

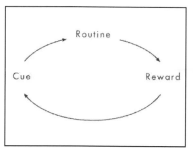

Firstly, there is a *cue* (a trigger that starts off a *routine*: e.g. the sound of the alarm clock in the morning is a cue, which triggers the routine of getting up).

Here's *an example of a cue* that I recently found in the *Sunday Times Magazine*, in an article authored by Viv Groscop (who performed her one-woman show at Edinburgh in August [last] year [2017]). Viv stated that, to make her exercise routine strong, she started keeping her workout clothes and trainers next to her bed, so they were *the first things she saw- the cue! – in the early morning*, as soon as she woke up. (She lost 3 stone [or 42 pounds in weight] in one year through changes in her exercise and nutrition habits).

Secondly, this cue is followed by *a routine.*

A routine is here defined as *any* pattern of behaviour. Examples include: eating, going to the pub, watching a TV programme, going to the gym, doing homework, buying clothes, smoking, placing a bet, etc.

Third and finally, there is a *reward* – the most important part of the loop.

All habits have a *reward* at the end of them. Here are some examples of rewards:

(1) The feeling of comradeship when drinking at the pub;

(2) The rush of pleasure after you have just done a bout of exercise;

(3) Giving yourself a cup of (decaffeinated!) coffee when you've done your

daily exercise. And:

(4) Seeing the *good, pleasurable results* of any difficult task.

~~~

The importance of craving!

*For habit change to work you have to **crave** the reward.*

This is an important alert: You have to *really crave* the reward, or you *won't* have the incentive to change your behaviour. Charles Duhigg describes a research project undertaken by the National Weight Control Agency. The agency examined the *cues/routines/rewards* for eating food that had been created by people who were successful dieters. They investigated more than 6,000 people's routines.

What was discovered was that *all* the successful dieters eat a breakfast (which was cued by the *time* of day). But they also had very real, *very desirable **rewards*** in place for themselves if they stuck to their diet plans – and it was the reward that they craved. (For example, being able to fit into new clothes in a smaller size; or having a flatter belly, etc.)

And if they felt they were *weakening* in their commitment to weight control, they **changed** *their focus onto the rewards* that they would get if they *kept* to their plans. This visualisation, of the very real rewards they would get, kept them strong in the face of temptation.

Apparently people who started new exercise routines showed that they were more likely to follow an exercise routine if they chose a *specific cue* (first thing in the morning, or as soon as they get in from work, or before bedtime).

*So having a cue in place is **crucial** to initiating the new behaviour (or routine).*

The new behaviour (or **routine**) follows from the cue.

Let me give you a personal example: Jim and I get up in the morning, and the first thing we do is to have breakfast, because we **crave** the pleasure of raw salad with seeds and nuts, and minor embellishments.

The *end of breakfast* **cues** us to meditate, and we crave the rewards of meditation, (a lot of which have to do with stress management, health and happiness, plus creativity).

Then, *the end of meditation* **cues** us to begin our physical exercise (Chi Kung [or Qigong], the Plank, some press-ups and sit-backs, and so on]) which we do because we **crave** the physical and mental health benefits that we gain.

So, the **reward** is what people crave at the end of their routines. Some of the *rewards* mentioned in Duhigg's research were having a (small amount of) beer, or an evening of watching the TV without guilt.

As my own experiment, I (Renata) wanted to establish a daily habit of exercising my arm muscles, to firm them up. Therefore, I set up a **cue** which is the start of the BBC TV quiz program, **'Pointless'**, at 5.15pm every day.

When I hear the theme music for *Pointless*, I get out our "Powerspin" device – which simulates weight training - and I do a pre-planned (recommended) set of exercises. This exercise **routine** is designed to strengthen my arms and back muscles, and my core (or stomach muscles); and it is very simple, but involves some physical exertion.

And the **reward** for me (which I *crave* strongly – otherwise it won't work) is the knowledge that my arms and back and core muscles are getting stronger and fitter, and that this will keep me fit and able to carry heavy objects into old age! And so far, so good – I've only skipped my exercises a few times!

Duhigg's own experiment

Charles Duhigg did a really interesting personal experiment to see if he could change one of his own habits. He was eating too many cookies (or biscuits) and he was starting to put on weight. He videoed an explanatory description of his experiment, which you can see on YouTube. He broke the habit, by working out what the reward was (and it had nothing to do with cookies/biscuits).

Once he knew what the reward was, he found it very easy to substitute a new routine which did not involve eating junk foods, but which gave him the same desirable reward!

Here is the address of his video clip at YouTube:
https://youtu.be/W1eYrhGeffc

~~~

The importance of substitution

What if we have a habit that we want to change? Can we get rid of it?

The temptation is to say 'yes'! But Charles Duhigg states that we **can't** get rid of old habits, as such, and in full – but what we can do is *substitute* new routines for the old ones, and get the same rewards. So this involves 'changing' part of the habit; and not 'getting rid of the habit'.

He explains that a golden rule of habit change, which has been validated by repeated studies for a long time, is as follows:

"To change a habit, we must keep the old <u>cue</u>, which delivers the old <u>reward</u>, but change <u>the routine</u>.

"That's the rule: if you use the same cue, and provide the same reward, you can shift the routine and change the habit. Almost any behaviour can be transformed if the cue and reward stay the same". (Page 62)

He gives the example of someone who wants to give up cigarettes.

If the person wanting to quit smoking fails to find something else to do (a new routine), when they start to crave what they get from nicotine, then they will be unable to stop!

It will be *too hard* for them.

...

Stopping addictions

Charles Duhigg states that *'Alcoholics Anonymous'* (**AA**) is an effective organization in helping people reduce their alcohol drinking habits because it examines and shines a very clear light on the **cues** which trigger drinking in people; and the **AA** program deliberately encourages people to **identify** the **cues** and **rewards** that encourages their alcoholic habits, and then *assists them* as they try to find new behaviours (or routines).

So the implied question that **AA** asks an alcoholic is: *"What rewards do you get from alcohol?"* Duhigg writes: *"In order for alcoholics to get the same rewards that they get in a bar, AA has built a system of meetings and* **companionship** *– (the individual 'Sponsor' that each person works with) – that strives to offer as much escape, distraction and catharsis as a Friday night bender."* (Page 71)

If someone wants to get support from another person, they can receive this by talking to their *sponsor* or by going to a *group meeting*, rather than "toasting a drinking buddy".

A researcher called J. Scott Tonigan has been looking at the work of *AA* for more than ten years, and he states that if you look at Step 4 of the 12 step program, (which is to make a *'searching and fearless inventory of ourselves and to admit to God, to ourselves* and *another human being the exact nature of our wrongs'*), you will see that something crucial is taking place, which he sums up like this:

"It's not obvious from the way they are written, but to complete those steps,

*someone has to create a list of **triggers** for all their alcoholic urges. When you make a self-inventory, you're figuring out all the **things** that make you drink..."* The **cues!**

The rewards of drinking

The *AA* organisation then asks alcoholics (or people who are alcohol dependent) to look really hard for the **rewards** they get from alcohol, and the **cravings** that are behind the behaviour. And what is discovered?

*"Alcoholics crave a drink because it offers escape, relaxation, companionship, the blunting of anxieties and an opportunity for emotional release....the **physical effects** of alcohol are one of the least rewarding parts of drinking for addicts."* (Page 71)

So what *AA* does is to get individuals to create *new routines* for their spare time, *instead of going out drinking*. Instead, they can relax and talk through any worries or concerns they might have at the AA meetings.

*"The triggers (cues) are the same, and the payoffs (rewards) are the same, it's just the **behaviour** that changes,"* states Tonigan.

The result of one experiment

To summarise the value of one particular experiment, Duhigg showed that the former alcoholics in the study only succeeded in eliminating their drinking behaviour because they developed new routines which followed the old *triggers* (or *cues*), and gave them their comforting *rewards*.

Apparently the techniques that were developed by the *AA* for changing habits have also been successfully applied to children's temper tantrums, sex addictions and other types of behaviour.

The **AA** is described in Duhigg's book as an organisation which creates techniques to change the habits associated with the use of alcohol:

"AA is in essence a giant machine for changing habit loops and though the habits associated with alcohol consumption are extreme, the lessons AA provides demonstrates how almost any habit – even the most obstinate – can be changed." Charles Duhigg

He makes it clear in his book that overeating, alcoholism, or smoking, are ingrained habits that take real commitment to change.

They cannot be changed quickly or easily!

But if you know how your habits are working, that makes it easier to experiment with new behaviours (or routines).

~~~

Analysing your own habits

If you look very carefully at the **cues** that cause you to engage in relationship conflict, or relationship indifference, and you work out the rewards that you currently get your conflict-creating, or avoidance, routines, then you may be able to identify a new healthy routine to substitute for your old unhealthy or unhelpful routine.

However, before you move to the practice of trying to change relationship habits using this habit change process, you should definitely complete the Inner Couple process, discussed in Chapter 11, since patterns of behaviour that are based on early childhood trauma are unlikely to easily yield to such a behavioural approach. They need deep emotional excavation and reformulation of feelings and images, which can more easily be gained from the Inner Couple process.

However, once you have completed the Inner Couple process, you might well find you have habits that reduce the quality of your relationship, and then you can certainly use this 'cue-routine-reward' approach to behaviour change.

And two of the key areas of habit that probably need change for most people today are physical activity patterns, and dietary/nutritional patterns.

Creating 'keystone habits'

Exercise seems to be a 'keystone habit' that has a beneficial, 'knock-on' effect on other habits. When people begin exercising, and it can be as little as once a week, they begin to change other, unconnected habits in their lives. It has been discovered that they reduce their smoking, spend money less, and have more understanding for their family and the people they work with.

"Exercise spills over", stated James Prochaska (a University of Rhode Island researcher). *"There's something about it that makes good habits easier."*

Other studies have revealed that families who are in the habit of having their meals together regularly – which is another 'keystone habit' - raise children with higher school grades, more emotional control, better homework skills and increased confidence.

Apparently making your bed every morning is also a keystone habit, which has a spill over effect. It is correlated with a higher level of happiness, stronger skills at sticking to a budget and a higher level of productivity.

So, by beginning to use the kaizen approach (described in Jim's section above), to get in the habit of doing a few minutes exercise each day, you will be starting a cascade of potential change. Over time, you can learn how to exclude all of the toxic foods; to get on to an exciting, healthy and enlivening diet; and to be happier, healthier and more creative. (But do it slowly, gradually, incrementally. And reward yourself at every step)

Habit reversal

Here is a quote by Nathan Azrin, who was one of the people who developed habit reversal training:

*"It seems ridiculously simple, but once you are aware of how your habit works, once you recognise the **cues** and the **rewards**, you're half-way to changing it."*

Today, habit reversal is used to treat gambling, depression, smoking, anxiety, procrastination, and sex and alcohol addiction etc. And you can now use it to change your exercise and dietary habits too.

Charles Duhigg makes the point that although the habit process can be simply described, it doesn't mean that it's *easily* changed.

As Mark Twain argued, a habit cannot be flung out of the window by any person, but has to be coaxed downstairs a step at a time!

You cannot eliminate habits that no longer serve you. You can only *replace them* with new habits that support your goals.

You have to be aware of what you want (the implicit reward – the thing that you crave), and work to create new habits (or routines) that will get you what you want.

Charles Duhigg states:

"It's facile to imply that smoking, alcoholism, over-eating or other ingrained patterns can be upended without real effort. Genuine change requires real work and self-understanding of the cravings driving the behaviours. No one will quit smoking because they can sketch a habit loop.

"However, by understanding habits' mechanisms, we gain insights that make new behaviours easier to grasp. Anyone struggling with addiction or destructive behaviours can benefit from help from many quarters, including trained therapists, physicians, social workers and clergy.

"Much of those changes are accomplished because people examine the cues,

*cravings and rewards that drive their behaviours and then find ways to **replace** their self-destructive **routines** with healthier alternatives, even if they aren't aware of what they are doing at the time. Understanding the cues and cravings driving your habits won't make them suddenly disappear – but it will give you a way to change the pattern."* (Page 77)

It may also help to get you from the 'contemplation stage' of behaviour change to the 'determination stage'.

Once you are determined, you are halfway there. And if you know what the reward will be – and you put secondary rewards and penalties in place – then you are on the home run!

~~~

~~~

Endnotes

[1] Haidt, J. (2006) *The Happiness Hypothesis: Putting ancient wisdom and philosophy to the test of modern science.* London: Arrow Books.

[2] Diener et al, 1999; Mastekaasa, 1994; Waite and Gallagher, 2000. However it is not clear that married people are, on average, happier than those who never married, because unhappily married people are the least happy group of all and they pull down the average; see DePaulo and Morris, 2005, for a critique of research on the benefits of marriage. &

Diener, E., Suh, E.M., Lucas, R.E. & Smith, H.L. (1999) Subjective wellbeing. Three decades of progress. *Psychological Bulletin, 125:* 120-129. &

Mastekaasa, A. (1994) Marital status, distress, and well-being. An international comparison. *Journal of Comparative Family Studies, 25:* 183-205. &

Waite. L.J. and Gallagher, M. (2000) *The case for marriage: Why married people are happier, healthier, and better off financially.* New York: Doubleday. &

DePaulo, B.M. and Morris, W.L. (2005) Singles in society and science. *Psychological Inquiry, 16:* 57-83.

[3] Harker and Keltner, 2001; Lyubomirsky, King and Diener, in press. &

Harker, L. and Keltner, D. (2001) Expressions of positive emotion in women's college yearbook pictures and their relationship to personality and life outcomes across adulthood. *Journal of Personality and Social Psychology, 80:* 112-124. &

Lyubomirsky, S., King, L., and Diener, E. (in press) The benefits of frequent positive affect: Does happiness lead to success? *Psychological Bulletin.*

[4] Baumeister and Leary, 1995. However, it is not certain that marriage itself is more beneficial than other kinds of companionship. Much evidence says yes, particularly for health, wealth, and longevity (reviewed in Waite and Gallagher 2000); but a large longitudinal study failed to find a long-lasting benefit of marriage on reports of well-being (Lucas et al., 2003). &

Baumeister, R.F. and Leary, M.R. (1995) The need to belong: Desire for interpersonal attachment as a fundamental human emotion. *Psychological Bulletin, 117:* 497-529. &

Waite and Gallagher (2000) see earlier footnote, above. &

Lucas, R.E., Clark, A.E., Georgellis, Y. and Diener, E. (2003) Re-examining adaptation and the set point model of happiness: Reactions to changes in marital status. *Journal of Personality and Social Psychology, 84:* 527-539. &

[5] What does it mean, to choose a partner non-consciously? It means that humans are 'creatures of habit'. Think about this: How did you decide to get out of bed this morning? Which muscle did you decide to move first, and how did you tell it to move? The truth is you took no conscious thought at all. You got out of bed, and put some clothes on, without any need to take any conscious thought. You travelled to the bathroom, without the need to consciously decide where you were going, or how to get there. You are a creature of

habit. And you also choose your sex-love partners in the same way: non-consciously. And the criteria you use to choose them are non-consciously available, as habit patterns, from your family of original – outside of your conscious awareness! This is no different from driving (or cycling) to work without taking any conscious thought of where you are going, or which gear you are in, or how to steer the wheels!

[6] Armstrong, J. (2003) *Conditions of Love: The philosophy of intimacy*. London: Penguin Books.

[7] Durbanville (2015) In Romeo and Juliet, Juliet is 13, but how old is Romeo? eNotes, 30 July 2015. Available online: https://www.enotes.com/homework-help/know-that-juliet-13-half-but-how-old-romeo-51141. Accessed 7 July 2018.

[8] "According to the British Social Attitudes Survey, only 2 per cent of couples would approach a marriage guidance counsellor when they first ran into problems. By the time most of us get around to saving our marriage, it's too late". Agnew (1996).

[9] Steinbeck, E. and Wallsten, R. (eds) (1989) *Steinbeck: A Life in Letters*. London: Penguin Books. (Reproduced in Popova, M. (2018) John Steinbeck on Falling in Love: A 1958 Letter of Advice to His Lovesick Teenage Son. In the BrainPickings blog: https://www.brainpickings.org/?mc_cid=40c48c0405&mc_eid =204f4a8f33. Accessed: 28th June 2018.)

[10] Zilbergeld, B. (1995) *Men and Sex: A guide to sexual fulfilment*. London: HarperCollins Publishers.

[11] Teachworth, A. (1999) *Why we Pick the Mates we do: A step-by-step program to select a better partner or improve the relationship you're already in.* Metairie, Louisiana: The Gestalt Press. (Plus Lewis, Amini and Lannon, 2001, below).

[12] Waite, M. (ed) (2012) *Paperback Oxford English Dictionary. Seventh Edition*. Oxford: Oxford University Press.

[13] Lewis, T., Amini, F. and Lannon, R. (2001) *A General Theory of Love*. New York: Vintage Books.

[14] Coleman, A.N. (2002) *A Dictionary of Psychology*. Oxford: Oxford University Press.

[15] Whitbourne, S. K. (2012) What is the passion in passionate love? Does – and should – passion matter for long-term relationships? Psychology Today Online blog. Available here: https://www.psychologytoday.com/us/blog/fulfillment-any-age/201212/what-is-the-passion-in-passionate-love. Accessed: 21st June 2018.

[16] Hatfield, E., & Sprecher, S. (1986). Measuring passionate love in intimate relationships. *Journal Of Adolescence, 9(4),* Pages 383-410. doi:10.1016/S0140-1971(86)80043-4. Accessed: 21st June 2018.

[17] ISSM (2012) What is the normal frequency of sex? International Society for Sexual Medicine. Online blog: http://www.issm.info/sexual-health-qa/what-is-the-normal-frequency-of-sex/. Accessed: 23rd June 2018.

[18] Lyall, S. (2008) Revising 'Sex' for the 21st century. *Fashion and Style: New York Times*

online. ('The Joy of Sex', revised for today). https://www.nytimes .com/ 2008/12/18joy.html. Accessed: 22nd June 2018.

[19] Wallin, D.A. (2007) *Attachment in Psychotherapy.* New York: Guildford Press.

[20] Gordon, L.H. (1969/2016) Intimacy: The art of relationships. How relationships are sabotaged by hidden expectations. *Psychology Today* blog. Available online: https://www.psychologytoday.com/us/articles/196912/intimacy-the-art-relationships. Accessed: 21st June 2018.

[21] Garapick, J. (2014) Committed Relationship - What Does That Really Mean? A blog post. Online here: https://gettingtotruelove.com/2014/06/20/ committed –relationship-mean/. Accessed: 15th August 2018/

[22] Armstrong, J. (2002) *Conditions of Love: The philosophy of intimacy*. London: Penguin Books.

[23] Fromm, E. (1995) *The Art of Loving*. London. Thorsons.

[24] Peck, M. S. (1998) *The Road Less Travelled: A new psychology of love, traditional values and spiritual growth.* London: Arrow Books.

[25] Fisher, R. and Ury, W. (1997) *Getting to Yes: Negotiating an agreement without giving in*. London: Random House.

[26] Gottman, J. (1999) *The Seven Principles for Making Marriage Work.* London: Weidenfeld and Nicolson.

[27] Bolton, R. (1979/1986). *People Skills: How to assert yourself, listen to others, and resolve conflicts.* Englewood Cliffs, NJ: Prentice-Hall Inc.

[28] Triggle, N. (2016) Alcohol limits cut to reduce health risks. BBC News. Online: https://www.bbc.co.uk/news/uk-35255384. Accessed: 11th August 2018.

[29] Shealey, G. (2018) Can exercise improve your sex life? Online blog: HowStuffWorks. Available here: https://health.howstuffworks.com/wellness/ diet-fitness/exercise/can-exercise-improve-your-sex-life.htm. Accessed: 31st May 2018.

[30] Haas, E.M. (2018) Nutritional Programs: Nutritional Program For Sexual Vitality. An online blog at Healthy.net. Available here: Article/ Nutritional _Program _for_Sexual_Vitality/1273/2. Accessed: 31st May 2018.

[31] Natural Partners (2018) Eating for sexual vitality. An online blog. Available here: https://blog.naturalpartners.com/eating-for-sexual-vitality/. Accessed: 31st May 2018.

[32] WikiHow (2018) How to improve sexual health through diet. An online blog. Available here: https://www.wikihow.com/Improve-Sexual-Health-Through-Diet. Accessed: 31st May 2018.

[33] Taylor-Byrne, R.E., and Byrne, J.W. (2017) How to Control Your Anger, Anxiety and Depression, Using nutrition and physical activity. Hebden Bridge: The Institute for E-CENT Publications.

[34] Breus, M.J. (2010) A good night's sleep for good sex: Links between healthy sex life and a

healthy sleep life. *Psychology Today Blog*. Available here: https://www.psychologytoday .com/gb/blog/sleep-newzzz/201004/good-night-s-sleep-good-sex. Accessed: 31st May 2018.

35 Zilbergeld, B. (1995) *Men and Sex: A guide to sexual fulfilment. London: HarperCollins Publishers.*

36 Here is the abstract of a scientific study from 2003, which supports my argument:

...

"**Abstract** - A neuroimaging study examined the neural correlates of social exclusion and tested the hypothesis that the brain bases of social pain are similar to those of physical pain. Participants were scanned while playing a virtual ball-tossing game in which they were ultimately excluded. Paralleling results from physical pain studies, the anterior cingulate cortex (ACC) was more active during exclusion than during inclusion and correlated positively with self-reported distress. Right ventral prefrontal cortex (RVPFC) was active during exclusion and correlated negatively with self-reported distress. ACC changes mediated the RVPFC-distress correlation, suggesting that RVPFC regulates the distress of social exclusion by disrupting ACC activity". (Eisenberger, Lieberman and Williams (2003)).

Eisenberger, N.I., Lieberman, M.D., and Williams K.D. (2003) Does rejection hurt? A fMRI study of social exclusion. *Science, Vol. 302, Issue 5643*, pp 290-292. Available online: http://science.sciencemag.org/content/302/5643/290

~~~

37 E-CENT stands for Emotive-Cognitive Embodied Narrative Therapy. E-CENT counselling was created by Dr Jim Byrne. See the web page: What is E-CENT? here: https://abc-counselling.org/what-is-e-cent-counselling/

38 Firstein, I. (2010) Barriers to effective communication. Online blog, here: https://www.goodtherapy.org/blog/barriers-to-effective-communication/. Accessed: 11th June 2018.

39 Gottman, J. (1997) *Why Marriages Succeed or Fail: and how you can make yours last.* London: Bloomsbury Publishing.

40 Liverpool, L. (2018) A bad marriage can seriously damage your health, say scientists. The Guardian, Online: https://www.theguardian. com/lifeandstyle/ 2018/jul/16/a-bad-marriage-is-as-unhealthy-as-smoking-or-drinking-say-scientists?CMP=share_btn_fb. Accessed: 28th July 2018.

41 Haidt, J. (2006) *The Happiness Hypothesis: Putting ancient wisdom and philosophy to the test of modern science.* London: Arrow Books.

42 Diener et al, 1999; Mastekaasa, 1994; Waite and Gallagher, 2000. However it is not clear that married people are, on average, happier than those who never married, because unhappily married people are the least happy group of all and they pull down the average; see DePaulo and Morris, 2005, for a critique of research on the benefits of marriage. &

Diener, E., Suh, E.M., Lucas, R.E. & Smith, H.L. (1999) Subjective wellbeing. Three decades of progress. *Psychological Bulletin, 125:* 120-129. &

Mastekaasa, A. (1994) Marital status, distress, and well-being. An international comparison. *Journal of Comparative Family Studies, 25:* 183-205. &

Waite. L.J. and Gallagher, M. (2000) *The case for marriage: Why married people are happier, healthier, and better off financially.* New York: Doubleday. &

DePaulo, B.M. and Morris, W.L. (2005) Singles in society and science. *Psychological Inquiry, 16:* 57-83.

[43] Harker and Keltner, 2001; Lyubomirsky, King and Diener, in press. &

Harker, L. and Keltner, D. (2001) Expressions of positive emotion in women's college yearbook pictures and their relationship to personality and life outcomes across adulthood. *Journal of Personality and Social Psychology, 80:* 112-124. &

Lyubomirsky, S., King, L., and Diener, E. (in press) The benefits of frequent positive affect: Does happiness lead to success? *Psychological Bulletin.*

[44] Baumeister and Leary, 1995. However, it is not certain that marriage itself is more beneficial than other kinds of companionship. Much evidence says yes, particularly for health, wealth, and longevity (reviewed in Waite and Gallagher 2000); but a large longitudinal study failed to find a long-lasting benefit of marriage on reports of well-being (Lucas et al., 2003). &

Baumeister, R.F. and Leary, M.R. (1995) The need to belong: Desire for interpersonal attachment as a fundamental human emotion. *Psychological Bulletin, 117:* 497-529. &

Waite and Gallagher (2000) see earlier footnote, above. &

Lucas, R.E., Clark, A.E., Georgellis, Y. and Diener, E. (2003) Re-examining adaptation and the set point model of happiness: Reactions to changes in marital status. *Journal of Personality and Social Psychology, 84:* 527-539. &

[45] According to a Stanford University blog, social ties are good for your health: "In our crazy society, social ties are pretty far down on our "to do" lists, but connection to others is turning out to be more important than we thought. Studies indicate that "social capital" is one of the biggest predictors for health, happiness, and longevity. The problem: we often do not recognize the importance of social connection. Our culture values hard work, success, and wealth, so it's no surprise some of us do not set aside enough time for social ties when we think security lies in material things rather than other people.

"Olds and Schwartz (Associate Clinical Professors of Psychiatry at Harvard Medical School) argue in The Lonely American that loneliness is often mistaken for depression. Instead of connecting with others, we consume a pill. Being lonely is outside of our individualistic world view so we don't even see it as a problem.

"Harvard's Robert Putnam writes about social capital in his book, Bowling Alone, and shows how social ties are not only important for personal well-being, but also for our democracy." Source: BeWell blog, Stanford. Available here: https://bewell.stanford.edu/social-ties-are-good-for-your-health/. Accessed: 1st June 2018.

~~~

[46] Gottman, J. (1997) *Why Marriages Succeed or Fail: and how to make yours last.* London: Bloomsbury.

[47] Levine, A. and Heller, R. (2011) *Attached: Identify your attachment style and find your perfect match.* London: Rodale/Pan Macmillan.

[48] This may be the percentage for the UK. However, Dr John Gottman gives a higher figure (which presumably reflects the US situation) of 67% divorcing over a forty year period, for first marriages; and ten percent higher for second marriages. (See: Gottman, J. [1999] *The Seven Principles for Making Marriage Work.* London: Weidenfeld and Nicolson).

[49] Available online at Coryro's Blog: http://mblog.lib.umich.edu/~coryro/archives/2007/11/social_ exchange.html. Accessed 9th April 2012

[50] Teachworth, A. (1999/2005) *Why We Pick the Mates We Do: As step-by-step program to select a better partner or improve the relationship you're already in.* New Orleans/New York: Gestalt Institute Press. There is also an audio program on the approach.

[51] Fisher, R. and Ury, W. (1997) *Getting to Yes: Negotiating an agreement without giving in.* London: Random House.

[52] From his second book: Gottman, J. (1999) *The Seven principles for Making Marriage Work.* London: Weidenfeld and Nicolson

[53] Carnegie, D. (1983) *How to Win Friends and Influence People.* Surrey: World's Work Ltd.

[54] Byrne, J. (2010/18) The Story of Relationship: Or coming to terms with my mother (and father). E-CENT Paper No.10. Hebden Bridge: The Institute for E-CENT. Available online: https://abc-counselling.org/my-story-of-relationship-with-mother/

[55] E-CENT stands for Emotive-Cognitive Embodied Narrative Therapy. E-CENT counselling was created by Dr Jim Byrne. See the web page: What is E-CENT? here: https://abc-counselling.org/what-is-e-cent-counselling/

[56] Levine, A. and Heller, R. (2011) *Attached: Identify your attachment style and find your perfect match.* London: Rodale/Pan Macmillan.

[57] Bowlby, J. (1979/2005) *The Making and Breaking of Affectional Bonds.* London: Routledge Classics.

[58] Hart, S. (2011) *The Impact of Attachment: Development neuroaffective psychology.* London: W.W. Norton and Company.

[59] Wallin, D.J. (2007) *Attachment in Psychotherapy.* London: The Guilford Press.

[60] Levine, A. and Heller, R. (2011) *Attached: Identify your attachment style and find your perfect match.* London: Rodale/Pan Macmillan.

[61] For more insights into couple relationships, please see my Couples Therapy page, at ???.

[62] Fromm, E. (1995) *The Art of Loving.* London: Thorsons.

[63] ".... Women are more likely to complain, criticize, or demand change during marital conflict, whereas men are more likely to avoid or withdraw; this gender disparity is one of the most reliable behavioural differences in the marital literature, particularly among distressed couples (Weiss & Heyman, 1990). Called the "wife demand-husband withdraw" or the "negative-withdraw" interaction sequence, it appears to be particularly destructive, linked both cross-sectionally and prospectively to marital discord (Christensen, 1987; Heavey, Lane, & Christensen, 1993). The gender differences in the negative-withdraw pattern have been explained in several ways. Christensen (1987) has argued that differences in the need for intimacy reflect, in part, divergent socialization experiences; in general, women want more closeness, whereas men seek more autonomy. Thus, wives demand and complain as a way of seeking intimacy, and husbands withdraw to maintain greater autonomy. Several studies have supported this conceptualization (Christensen, 1987; Christensen & Shenk, 1991). The conflict structure hypothesis relates gender differences in the negative-withdraw pattern to power differences in the structure of conflict (Heavey et al., 1993). For example, Jacobson (1983) has argued that traditional marital relationships provide greater benefits to men than women. Because men have less interest in changing the status quo, they are more likely to withdraw when confronted with their wives' requests for change. Data from two recent studies (Christensen & Heavey, 1990; Heavey et al., 1993) support this hypothesis." (Kiercolt-Glaser, 1996, page 325).

[64] For the Ohio State University research, "(the) researchers recruited 43 married couples, recording hostile behaviour and taking blood samples. Those who demonstrated more hostile behaviours had higher levels of one biomarker for leaky gut, and high levels of inflammation throughout the body". (Knapton, 2018).

[65] Bolton, R. (1979/1986). *People Skills: How to assert yourself, listen to others, and resolve conflicts.* Englewood Cliffs, NJ: Prentice-Hall Inc.

[66] Clinard, H.H. (1985) *Winning Ways to Succeed with People.* Houston: Gulf Publishing Company.

[67] Klein, M. (1940) Mourning and its relation to manic-depressive states, in *The Selected Melanie Klein.* Edited by Mitchell, J. (1986). London: Penguin Books.

[68] Skynner, R. and Cleese, J. (1987) *Families and How to Survive Them.* London: Methuen.

[69] E-CENT stands for Emotive-Cognitive Embodied Narrative Therapy. E-CENT counselling was created by Dr Jim Byrne. See the web page: What is E-CENT? here: https://abc-counselling.org/what-is-e-cent-counselling/

[70] The one condition that you should apply to your partner's behaviour, and your own, is that *it should be moral (and legal).* Apart from that one condition, you should otherwise accept them and yourself relatively unconditionally. I call this approach 'one-conditional acceptance'. Or 'radical acceptance'.

[71] Shealey, G. (2018) Can exercise improve your sex life? Online blog: HowStuffWorks. Available here: https://health.howstuffworks.com/wellness/ diet-fitness/exercise/can-exercise-improve-your-sex-life.htm. Accessed: 31st May 2018.

[72] Byrne, J. (2018) *Lifestyle Counselling and Coaching for the Whole Person: Or how to integrate nutritional insights, exercise and sleep coaching into talk therapy*. Hebden Bridge: The Institute for E-CENT Publications.

[73] Fromm, E. (1995) *The Art of Loving*. London. Thorsons.

[74] Steiner, C. (1999) *Achieving Emotional Literacy*. London: Bloomsbury.

[75] Gottman, J. (1997) *Why Marriages Succeed or Fail: and how you can make yours last*. London: Bloomsbury Publishing.

[76] E-CENT stands for Emotive-Cognitive Embodied Narrative Therapy. E-CENT counselling was created by Dr Jim Byrne. See the web page: What is E-CENT? here: https://abc-counselling.org/what-is-e-cent-counselling/

[77] An 'affective state' is a state of the body-brain-mind of an individual, in which there is physiological arousal and a felt sense of emotional attraction ('positive affect') or aversion ('negative affect'). For most practical purposes, among counsellors, the word affect may be used interchangeably with 'feelings' and 'emotions'.

[78] Bruner, J. (1986) Actual Minds, Possible Worlds. Cambridge, MA: Harvard University Press.

[79] (For example: John Money's failure to 'reassign' the sexual identity of David Reimer. Source: https://samanthakatepsychology.wordpress.com/ 2012/ 04/ 28/david-reimer-possibly-the-most-unethical-study-in-psychological-history/. Accessed: 30th December 2015.)

[80] Spector, T. (2013) *Identically Different: Why you can change your genes*. London: Phoenix.

[81] Bargh, J.A. and Chartrand, T.L. (1999) The unbearable automaticity of being. *American Psychologist, 54(7): 462-479.*

[82] Gray, J. (2003) *Straw Dogs: thoughts on humans and other animals*. London: Granta Books.

[83] Gladwell, M. (2006) *BLINK: The power of thinking without thinking*. London: Penguin Books.

[84] Stewart, I. and Joines, V. (1987) *TA Today: A New Introduction to Transactional Analysis*. Nottingham: Lifespace Publishing.

[85] Stewart, I. (1989) *Transactional Analysis Counselling in Action*. London: Sage.

[86] Berne, E. (1947/1986) *A Layman's Guide to Psychiatry and Psycho-analysis*. Harmondsworth: Penguin Books. Page 328 (Chapter Nine, Transactional Analysis, by John M. Dusay, MD).

[87] Verma, D. (2018) 3 Types of Ego States and Transactional Interactions between Each... Available online: http://www.shareyouressays.com/knowledge/3-types-of-ego-states-and-transactional-interactions-between-each-personalities/100117. Accessed: 5th November 2018.

[88] Stewart and Joines (1991) define 'switch' like this: "... a moment when the (game) players experience that something unexpected and uncomfortable has happened". ((Page 6). Stewart, I. and Joines, V. (1001)*TA Today: A new introduction to transactional analysis*. Nottingham: Lifespace Publishing.

[89] Satir, V. (1972/1983) *Peoplemaking*. London: Souvenir Press. Chapter 5.

[90] Byrne, J. (2018) *Lifestyle Counselling and Coaching for the Whole Person: Or how to integrate nutritional insights, exercise and sleep coaching into talk therapy*. Hebden Bridge: The Institute for E-CENT Publications.

[91] Panksepp, J. (1998) *Affective Neuroscience: The foundations of human and animal emotions*. Oxford University Press.

[92] Schore, A.N. (2015) *Affect Regulation and the Origin of the Self: The Neurobiology of Emotional Development*. London: Routledge.

[93] Smith, P.K., Cowie, H., and Blades, M. (2011) *Understanding Children's Development. Fifth edition*. Chichester, West Sussex: Wiley.

[94] Siegel, D.J. (2015) *The Developing Mind: How relationships and the brain interact to shape who we are*. London: The Guilford Press. Pages 152-153.

[95] E-CENT stands for Emotive-Cognitive Embodied Narrative Therapy. E-CENT counselling was created by Dr Jim Byrne. See the web page: What is E-CENT? here: https://abc-counselling.org/what-is-e-cent-counselling/

[96] Wallin, D.A. (2007) *Attachment in Psychotherapy*. New York: Guildford Press.

[97] Kashdan, T. and Biswas-Diener, R. (2015) *The Power of Negative Emotion: How anger, guilt and self-doubt are essential to success and fulfilment*. London: Oneworld Publications.

[98] Teychenne M, Costigan S, Parker K. (2015) The association between sedentary behaviour and risk of anxiety: A Systematic Review. *BMC Public Health, 2015*. Cited in *Medical Daily*, here: http://www.medicaldaily.com/constantly-sitting-down-being-sedentary-could-worsen-anxiety-and-mental-health-338952

[99] Borchard, T. (2015) 10 Ways to Cultivate Good Gut Bacteria and Reduce Depression. Everyday Health Blog. Available online: http://www.everydayhealth.com/columns/therese-borchard-sanity-break/ways-cultivate-good-gut-bacteria-reduce-depression/

[100] NHS Choices (2016) Moodzone: Exercise for depression. https://www.nhs.uk/conditions/stress-anxiety-depression/exercise-for-depression/. Accessed: 1st August 2018.

[101] Taylor-Byrne, R.E. and Byrne, J.W. (2017) *How to control your anger, anxiety and depression, using nutrition and physical activity*. Hebden Bridge: The Institute for E-CENT Publications.

[102] Byrne, J. (2018) *Lifestyle Counselling and Coaching for the Whole Person: Or how to integrate nutritional insights, exercise and sleep coaching into talk therapy*. Hebden Bridge: The Institute for E-CENT Publications.

[103] Vitale, J. (2006) Life's Missing Instruction Manual: the guidebook you should have been given at birth. Hoboken, NJ: John Wiley and Sons Inc.

[104] Freud, S. (1995) Beyond the pleasure principle. In: Gay, P. (ed) *The Freud Reader.* London: Vintage Books. Pages 594-595; 618-621.

[105] Storr, Anthony (1989) *Freud: a very short introduction,* Oxford, Oxford University Press. (Pages 60-61). And:

Kitzinger, C. (1997) Born to be good? – What motivates us to be good, bad or indifferent towards others? *New Internationalist, No.289, April 1997.*

[106] James, O. (2002). *They F*** You Up: how to survive family life.* London. Bloomsbury.

[107] Zimbardo, P. (2007) *The Lucifer Effect: how good people turn evil.* London: Rider. Page 3.

[108] Milgram, S. (1974) *Obedience to Authority.* New York: Harper and Row.

[109] Dovidio, J.F. (1984) Helping behaviour and altruism: An empirical and conceptual overview. In L. Berkowitz (ed), Advances in experimental social psychology. Vol. 17, pages 361-427. New York: Academic Press.

[110] Dawkins, R. (1989) *The Selfish Gene,* Second edition, Oxford University Press.

[111] McLeod, S. (2015) Piaget's Theory of Moral Development. Online blog. Available here: http://www.simplypsychology. org/piaget-moral.html. Reviewed on 12th June 2018.

[112] Nelson-Jones, R. (2001) *Theory and Practice of Counselling and Therapy.* Third edition. London: Continuum.

[113] Haidt, J. (2006) *The Happiness Hypothesis: Putting ancient wisdom and philosophy to the test of modern science.* London: William Heinemann. Pages 158-160.

[114] The clitoris is visible as a small blob of fleshy material at the external top of the vagina, just below the pubic bone. "The visible part of the clitoris looks like a small, pink 'blob'. It's actually the 'glans' (or head) of the clitoris, which in structure is very like a miniature version of the glans (head) of the penis. --- Behind it is the clitoral body, which contains two small cylinders of erectile tissue, similar to those found in the penis. --- Covering the body is a little fold of pink tissue called 'the clitoral hood'. During sexual excitement, the hood swells slightly, so that the clitoris is less visible. --- At the back of the clitoral body, the clitoris divides into two, like an upside down letter 'V'. The two legs (or 'crura') of this V extend downwards into the labia, and also into the front wall of the vagina. --- It is widely stated by anatomical authorities that there are 'up to 8,000' erotic nerve endings in the clitoris. This is by far the highest number in any part of the female body." Source: Delvin (2016).

[115] Lynch, B. (2018) 'I can't get no satisfaction: Are you on the wrong side of the "orgasm gap"?' *Metro Newspaper, UK. Thursday 22nd November 2018.* Pages 39-41.

[116] Byrne, J. (2017a) *Metal Dog – Long Road Home: A mythical journey through the eye of a needle.* The fictionalized memoir of an improbable being. Hebden Bridge: The Institute for E-CENT Publications.

[117] Michael, R.T., John H. Gagnon, Edward O. Laumann, Gina Kolata (1994) *Sex in America: A Definitive Survey.* Little Brown and Co.

[118] Barnes, J. (2018) *The Only Story.* London: Jonathan Cape. Page 17.

[119] Zilbergeld, B. (1995) *Men and Sex: A guide to sexual fulfilment.* London: HarperCollins Publishers.

[120] Berne, E. (1973/1981) *Sex in Human Loving.* Harmondsworth, Middlesex, UK. Penguin Books.

[121] Watts, A. (1962/1990) *The Way of Zen.* London: Arkana/Penguin. Pages 125-127, and 179-192.

[122] Byrne, J. (2017a) *Metal Dog – Long Road Home: A mythical journey through the eye of a needle.* Hebden Bridge: The Institute for E-CENT Publications.

[123] See Byrne (2017a).

[124] Byrne, J. (2017b) *Unfit for Therapeutic Purposes: The case against Rational Emotive and Cognitive Behavioural Therapy (RE&CBT).* The Institute for E-CENT, with the CreateSpace platform.

[125] Cohen, D. (1997) *Carl Rogers: A critical biography.* London: Constable.

[126] Prochaska, J.O., Norcross, J.C. & DiClemente, C.C. (1998). *Changing for Good.* Reprint edition. New York: Morrow.

[127] Kaizen: A philosophy of continuous improvement, often in very small steps. In E-CENT we emphasize the importance of *gradual* change through *small* steps in personal habit change, because attempts at big steps often backfire, because the habit-based part of us rebels against the challenge of dramatic change.

[128] Bargh, J.A. and Chartrand, T.L. (1999) 'The unbearable automaticity of being'. *American Psychologist, 54(7):* 462-479.

[129] Duhigg, C. (2013) *The Power of Habit: Why we do what we do and how to change.* London: Random House.

~~~

21537090R00262

Printed in Great Britain
by Amazon